About the Authors

Prof. S.S.Chahar began his teaching work in the Department of Political Science, Kurukshetra University in 1986. Presently he is working as the Chairman of Department of Public Administration as well as, Director, Centre for Haryana Studies, M.D. University, Rohtak. He has evinced keen interest in the study of state politics since the beginning of his academic career. He has 20 books and 66 well researched papers published to his credit. The books— 'Ombudsman in India and other Countries: A Comparative Study,' 'Indian Government and Politics', 'State Administration in India', 'Water Problem in India' etc. are in the process of publication. He has attended more than 120 seminars, conferences and workshops and delivered inaugtural address in many of them. He is a resource person of HIPA, HIRD and several educational institutes on important topics like RTI, consumer protection, democratic decentralization, district planning, budgetary system etc. He has been chosen for awards like Best Citizen of India, 2012 and Shiksha Rattan Puraskar, 2013.

Dr. Neera started her teaching career in 2006 as a consultant to teach the M.A. classes, Political Science in Directorate of Distance Education, M.D. University, Rohtak. At the same time she has been teaching the degree classes in AIJHM College, at Rohtak since 2009. She has obtained her M.A. (Political Science) degree with first division. She also did her masters in Public Administration with first division and a gold medal in M.Phil. She topped the University Research Scholarship Entrance Examination of Political Science and secured Ph.D. degree in 2009. She has qualified NET in June 2013. She has 4 books and 18 well researched papers to her credit. She has attended more than two dozen seminars and has contributed several papers.

Dr. Anju Rani has an outstanding academic career with first division throughout. She won distinction in M.Phil in Political Science. She has obtained her Ph.D. degree in 2012. She has authored 2 books and 8 research papers. She has been teaching in CRA Girls College, Sonepat.

Parliamentary Elections in India

S.S. Chahar
Neera and Anju

CONCEPT PUBLISHING COMPANY PVT. LTD.
NEW DELHI-110059

ISBN-13: 978-93-5125-067-8

First Published 2015

Published and Printed by

Concept Since 1974

Concept Publishing Company Pvt. Ltd.
A/15-16, Commercial Block, Mohan Garden
New Delhi-110059 (India)
T: 25351460, 25351794, *F*: 091-11-25357109
E: publishing@conceptpub.com, W: www.conceptpub.com
Editorial Office: H-13, Bali Nagar, New Delhi-110 015, India.

Cataloging in Publication Data--Courtesy: D.K. Agencies (P) Ltd. <docinfo@dkagencies.com>

Chahar, S. S., author.
Parliamentary elections in India / S.S. Chahar, Neera and Anju.
pages cm
Includes bibliographical references (pages) and index.
ISBN 9789351250678

1. India. Parliament. Lok Sabha--Elections.2. Elections--India--Haryana. 3.Haryana (India)-Politics and government. I. Neera (Neera Rani), author. II. Anju Rani, author. III. Title.

DDC 324.954558 23

VICE-CHANCELLOR

MAHARSHI DAYANAND UNIVERSITY
ROHTAK-124 001, (HARYANA) INDIA

Off. : 01262-274327, 292431
Res. : 01262-274710
Fax: 01262-274133, 274640

Foreword

Election studies in India have engaged public attention more than ever before in the recent past. In-depth studies have been carried out on various aspects of Lok Sabha and Vidhan Sabha elections, in institutions of higher education and research. In common man's perspective, elections are a means of socio-economic and political change in a participative democracy like ours. Political education and mass participation are prerequisites for success of the electoral process. A transparent and efficacious system of periodical elections provides an opportunity to every segment of society to capture the levers of power and participate in the process of decision-making.

The constitutional scheme in India makes it clear that the Legislature and the executive authority of the Centre as well as the states has been placed in the hands of the representatives of the people chosen at regular intervals. The introduction of universal adult suffrage and the abolition of communal electorate are the most progressive and radical features of the Indian Constitution. The principle of universal adult suffrage makes our Constitution the world's largest democracy. It provides for a separate chapter on elections unlike most other constitutions which leave out election to be dealt with by the Legislature.

Despite the growing importance of the parliamentary elections, only a few studies in the field have been conducted in Haryana so far. Prof. Chahar and his associates have made a good attempt to examine the electoral process of the Lok Sabha elections in Haryana since 1967 which would help better appreciation of electoral process at the state level.

I congratulate Prof. Chahar and his team for their initiative.

Er. H.S. Chahal

Preface

Election studies in India have gained prime importance during the last two decades or so. In Indian universities, a lot of work has been done on different Vidhan Sabha and Lok Sabha elections from different perspectives. In common man's view, elections are a means of socio-economic and political change in the country. Political education, mass mobilization and mass participation also take place through the electoral process. The political awakening among the masses is raised to the climax by the electoral environment. In democracies elections are an important method to test the legitimacy of a political system. They provide an opportunity to various segments of society to capture the levers of power and thereby influence the process of decision-making. General elections thus are a trial to strength among various social forces competing with one another for capturing the position of power. Elections are particularly conspicuous and revealing aspects of most contemporary political systems. In democratic, secular, socialist India, the administrative set up at the Centre and State levels is based on adult franchise, direct elections, individual freedom, and competitive parties.

In view of the above facts, it is felt that parliamentary elections in Haryana should be studied.

We have been helped by a number of persons in numerous ways in brining out this work which involves the classification and tabulation of vast data and information on Lok Sabha elections. First of all, we have an enduring obligation to our parents who encouraged and inspired us at all stages of this work.

Our special thanks are due to Prof. S.S. Tiwana, Prof. Suresh Mishra, Prof. Sanjeev Sharma, Dr. R.S. Gulia besides many others. Discussion with them were important for our formulations.

Our thanks are also due to all members of departments of Political Science and Public Administration for their constructive suggestions from time to time. Mentions may be made of Prof. Shashi Mehra, Prof S.S. Dahiya, Prof. Anjana Garg, Dr. R.K.Kundu, Dr. Jagbir Narwal, Dr. Anil, Dr. Vinay, Dr. Kuldeep Nara, Dr. Ashok Khasa besides many others.

Above all we are thankful to Prof. K.C.Yadav for extending all sorts of help in the completion of the first chapter.

We express our gratitude to several members of Parliament, Library staff of the Parliament, Punjab and Haryana Vidhan Sabha for extending all sorts of help in getting relevant matter for the work.

We will be failing in out duty if we do not express our deep sense of affection to our brothers and sisters who have provided emotional succor when we needed it the most.

Rohtak **S.S. Chahar, Neera and Anju**

Contents

Introduction

Election studies in India have become quite popular during the last two decades. In India, a lot of studies been conducted on parliament and state assembly elections from different perspectives. In common man's view elections are an instrument of transforming the socio-economic conditions in the country. Political education, mass mobilization and mass participation also take place through the elecatoral process. The public is educated politically by getting its maximum participation in electoral process. In democracies elections are an important method to test the legitimacy of a political system. They provide an opportunity to various segments of society to capture the levers of power and thereby influence the process of decision-making. General elections thus are a trial to strength among various social forces competing with one another for capturing the position of power. Elections are particularly conspicuous and revealing aspects of most contemporary political systems. In democratic, secular, socialist India, the democratic set up at the centre and state levels is based on adult franchise, direct elections, individual freedom, and competitive parties.

Taking note of the above cited facts, it may be said that the study of elections in India is of particular importance because the elections are not treated here merely as a ritualistic or symbolic exercise but they are an effective means for the recruitment of political elite and for political socialization of the masses. The elections at the Central level have a connotation for the people totally different from what the State level elections have for the electorate, the reason being that at the Central level elections, the electorate thinks more of nationhood and party politics. On the other hand, at the State level elections, both the party and the individual are important for the electorate. However, State level elections are quite significant because states have been assigned an important role in the Indian political system.

The constitutional scheme in India makes it clear that the Legislative and the executive authority of the Centre as well as the states has been placed in the hands of the representatives of the people chosen at regular intervals by means of free and fair elections. The introduction of universal adult suffrage and the abolition of communal electorate are the most progressive and radical features of the Indian Constitution. By introducing the universal suffrage, the Constitution has made India the world's biggest democracy. It has to be made clear that when the question for the adoption of universal suffrage was considered in the Constituent Assembly, it removed the apprehensions and made it clear to the members that adoption of the universal suffrage would not be a dangerous experiment in India. It clarified:

"Some people have doubted the wisdom of adult franchise. Personally, although I look upon it as an experiment the result of which no one will be able to forecast today, I am not dismayed by it. I know the village people who will constitute the bulk of this vast electorate. In my opinion, our people possess intelligence and common-sense. They also have a culture which the sophisticated people of today may not appreciate but which is solid. They are able to take measure of their own interest and also of the interests of the country at large as things are explained to them."

Thus, election is the very heart of the representative democracy and it is an essential and inseparable part of the modern democratic process. Winston Churchill, the Prime Minister of Great Britain explained the merit of electoral process in the following words:

> "At the bottom of all tributes paid to democracy is the little man, walking into a little booth, with a little pencil making a little cross on a title bit of paper, no amount of rhetoric or voluminous discussion can possibly diminish the overwhelming importance of the point."

With a view to appreciate the fuller role of the elections in a democratic system it has to be considered from different angles—

(i) From the point of view of the individual voter, elections are the means by which he takes his share in political power by voting for the representative of his choice.

(ii) From the point of view of the voters collectively, elections are the means by which they bring the decision-makers under popular control, a control that is ever present in the minds of representatives because any part of their behaviour in office (or in the case of aspiring candidates out of office) may affect their chances at the next election.

(iii) From the point of view of the representatives, the election result is an authorization to make decisions to govern within the broad drift of a policy platform, if there is one, subject to the sanction of the next election. Thus, the election result invests representatives and their decisions with legitimacy. In short, the government which is produced almost as a by-product and invested with legitimacy is the chief social purpose of the whole electoral process.

In addition to the above multi-dimensional ramification of elections, there are following main purposes for which elections have been instituted:

(i) An electoral office reflecting the main trends of opinion within the electorate.

(ii) Governing according to the wishes of the majority of the electorate.

(iii) The election of representatives whose personal qualities best fit them for the function of government.

(iv) Strong and stable government.

Article 325 of the Constitution of India reads: "There shall be one general electoral roll for every territorial constituency for election to either House of Parliament or to the House or either House of the Legislature of a state and no person shall be intelligible for inclusion in any such roll or claim to be included in any special electoral roll for any such constituency on grounds only of religion, race, caste, sex or any of them."

This provision ensures that in independent India a citizen votes as an individual and not as a member of this or that religious community or of a particular class or interest. In other words, the provision underscores the fact that all Indians, despite their different religions, castes and interests constitute a single political community. The two provisions, universal adult franchise and a common electoral roll taken together have, therefore, laid the foundation of a full scale democracy in India.

It may be pointed out that the Constitution of India has provided a separate chapter on elections. In this respect, it has made a departure from the usual practice of constitutions to leave elections as a comparatively unimportant subject to be dealt with by the Legislature. The fact that detailed provisions in this regard have been made in the Constitution show how anxious the constitution-makers had been to safeguard the democratic system and electoral process in India and ultimately the political right of the citizens of India as an integral part of the Constitution itself. At the state level also, elections for the popular chamber, Vidhan Sabha, are more important than for the Vidhan Parishad.

Despite the importance of the parliamentary elections, studies in the field have remained almost neglected until the 1957 elections due to the lack of behavioural orientation among the Indian political scientists and their apathy towards the study of national politics in India.

Before we start to discuss the Lok Sabha elections in Haryana, it would be appropriate to have a glance on the Central Legislative Assembly elections of Punjab from 1920 to 1947.

Central Legislative Assembly Elections in Punjab

Punjab, the land of five rivers, was occupied by the British in March 1849. Because of its strategic location and fertile land, it was an asset of prime importance to the Raj. The Indian Councils Act of 1861 provided Legislative Councils to Bombay and Madras and as well as in other provinces. In pursuance of the latter provision, Bengal and the United Provinces got Councils in 1863 and 1866 respectively. But Punjab got a Legislative Council comprising nine members in 1897. Its members were nominated by the Lt. Governor.

Punjab was given only one out of the 27 elected seats in the newly-created 60-member Central Legislature as per Government of India Act,1909. The situation at the provincial level was also equally bad; the strength of the Punjab legislature was restricted to 24, whereas Assam, far more backward, and much less populated got 30 seats.

Some substantial changes in the structure and functioning of the Central and provincial legislatures were made in the Government of India Act, 1919 like bicameral Legislature at the Centre, Council of State and Legislative Assembly : (i) the Council of State (or the Upper House); and (ii) Legislative Assembly comprising 60 (27 nominated and 33 elected) and 145 (42 nominated and 103 elected) members respectively. There were 4 directly elected members to the former, and 12 to the latter. The community-wise and special distribution membership is depicted in Table 1.1.

Table 1.1 : Distribution of Punjab seats in the Central Legislature, 1920-47

House	*Community/Special Class*	*No. of seats*
Council of State	Muhammadans	2
	Sikhs	1
	Non-Muhammadans	1
Total		4
Legislative Assembly	Muhammadans	6
	Sikhs	2
	Non-Muhammadans	3
	Landholders	1
TOTAL		12

Source : Page 7 August 1920; NAI, Home Public, File No. 120/1920.

The position in Punjab was still better than other provinces in the case of franchise. But the electorate was divided on caste and creed lines as well as on urban-rural basis weakening the forces of nationalism.

No person was eligible to be a voter who was not a British subject, female was not eligible, should not be a member of any other legislative body, should not be a dismissed/suspended legal practitioner, unsound mind, not under the age of 25 years, a bankrupt or undischarged insolvent, and a convict of 6 months imprisonment, default of filing returns. Ordinarily, one could cast one vote in a Muhammadan or a Sikh or a general constituency, but an extra vote in the landholders' constituency.

The qualifications of a voter for the Central Legislature are given in Table 1.2.

Table 1.2 : Property/Status Qualifications for the Central Legislature Voters, 1920-47

Council of State	*Legislative Assembly*
(i) Ownership/tenancy/assignment of land/crown land having the revenue value of not less than Rs. 750 p.a.	(i) Ownership/tenancy/assignment of land/crown land having the revenue value of Rs. 100 p.a.
(ii) Payment of income-tax on Rs. 15,000 p.a.	(ii) Ownership/tenancy of immovable property not being land assessed to land revenue, but including a building on such land of not less than Rs. 15,000 in value or giving annual rent of not less than Rs. 336 p.a.
(iii) Non-official membership of the either house of the Central legislature of the Punjab legislature.	(iii) Payment of income-tax on Rs. 5,000 p.a.
(iv) Provincial darbariship.	For Landholders' Const. (iv) Ownership/assignment of land having revenues value of not less than Rs. 1,000 p.a.
(v) Non-official presidentship or vice-presidentship (past or present) of the municipalities; or chairmanship/vice-presidentship of the district boards.	
(vi) Fellowhip (honorary or otherwise (past or present) or any university	
(vii) Non-official presidentship/vice-presidentship of central cooperative bank or registered Cooperative unions.	
(viii) Titles mahamahopadhaya, shams-ul-ulma, etc.	

Source: Page. 7 August 1920; 30 July 1923; 28 August 1923, NAI, Home Public File No. 134, 1924.

The candidates used to file their nominations in a specific form called 'Form 1' along with a security of Rs. 500 to the Returning Officer appointed by the provincial government for conducting the elections. If the number of candidates exceeded the vacancies in existence for a constituency, elections were held. Each voter was required to cast his vote in person under his signature and marking the ballot paper with cross mark. After the declaration of results both the successful and unsuccessful candidates were required to submit their expenses returns within a month of election. An unsuccessful candidate could challenge the election of the successful candidate by filing a petition within 14 days. After preliminary investigations, if the Governor-General was convinced that the allegations levelled were worth looking into the election could be cancelled.

The successful candidate was required to take an oath or affirmation of loyalty to the Crown.

The tenure of the member was 5 years for the Council of State and 3 years for the Legislative Assembly.

This election system continued till the independence of India. Though the Government of India Act, 1935 proposed fundamental changes in it giving a federal legislature at the Centre, but nothing was implemented. In August 1947, the Central legislature was replaced by the Constituent Assembly.

As per Montagu-Chelmsford Reforms, 1919, the strength of the Punjab Legislative Council was raised to 94 members – 23 nominated and 71 elected. The former were nominated by the Governor, including all the members of the Executive Council of the Governor, not more than 14 as official members; and 5 as representatives of the Europeans, Anglo-Indians - 2, Indian Christians - 1, labour - 1 and the Punjabi officers and soldiers of HM's Indian Forces - 1.

The 71 members of the latter category were directly elected by the people from different types of constituencies, as shown in Table 1.3.

Table 1.3 : Types of Constituencies in the PLC, 1920-35

Designation of the Constituencies	*Urban*	*Rural*	*Total*
Muhammadans	5	27	32
Non-Muhammadans	7	13	20
Sikhs	1	11	12
Special	–	–	7
Tolal			**71**

Source : NAI, Home Public, File No. 145, 10 June 1920

The communal representation divided the society, i.e. the Muslims of Punjab - 55.2 per cent were given 40.4 per cent seats whereas those of Bengal - 54.6 per cent were given 30.8 per cent seats. The Hindus of Punjab - 32 per cent were given 25.5 per cent seats whereas Muslims of U.P. - 14.3 per cent were given 26 per cent seats. The things were further spoiled by urban-rural divide. However, the Unionist Party made strenuous efforts to cut across the communal lines in the legislature.

Position of Different Political Parties in the PLA, 1923-1947

1923	
Swarajya Party	12
Unionist Party (including Moderates)	33
Gurdwara Prabhandak Committee	9 (5 Extremists)
Independents	17 (Hindu-11, Muslim-5, European-1)
Total	**71**
1926	
Unionist Party (Rural)	31
Hindu Maha Sabha	12
Central Sikh League (inc. 1 Moderate Sikh)	11
Khilafatists	3
Congress	2
Independents	12
Total	**71**
1930	
Unionist Party	37
National Progressive Party	20
Others (?)	14
Total	**71**
1937	
Unionist Party	98
Congress	18
Khalsa National Party	13
Hindu Maha Sabha	12
Akalis	11
Ahrar	2
Muslim League	2
Itihad-i-Millat	2
Congress Nationalist Party	1
Independents	16
Total	**175**

1946 (After the death of Sir Chhotu Ram in 1945)

Muslim League	73
Congress	51
Unionist Party	19
Akalis	21
Independents	11
Total	**175**

Source : 1923 : NAI, Home Public B, File No. 952/1924.
1926 : NAI Home Public, File No. 542/2/1926.
1930 : Azim Husain, *Op. cit.*, p. 163.
1937 : K.C. Yadav, *Haryana Ka Itihas* (Delhi: 1981), Vol. III, P. 201.
1946 : NAI, Home Political, File No. 79/46; 94/4/45 Reforms.

Note: For details see Annexture I

Thus it is concluded that the Unionist Party dominated the political scene in Punjab from 1926 to 1945. The Congress was not allowed to hold even party meetings or public meetings in Haryana region. However, the Congress came to limelight after the death of Sir Chhotu Ram in 1945 as well as withdrawal of the Muslim League from the political process of the state.

2

Parliamentary Elections, 1952-1967

After independence the first Parliamentry elections in Punjab were held in 1952 when a total of 172 nominations were received for 15 seats. After scrutiny of papers there were 101 contestants in the field. The Congress swept the election by fetching 14 seats leaving one to SAD. It is very intresting that all the seats falling in Haryana region, namely Ambala-Shimla, Karnal, Rohtak, Jhajjar-Rewari, Gurgaon, Hissar and Fizalka-Sirsa were captured by the Congress.

The 2nd Lok Sabha elections in composite Punjab were held in 1957 when 135 nominations were filed for 17 seats. After withdrawals and rejections as many as 85 candidates were left in the fray. Again the Congress won 16 seats leaving one to CPI (Jhajjar). Thus, out of 7 seats comprising the Haryana region, i.e. Rohtak, Ambala, Jhajjar, Gurgaon, Hissar, Kaithal and Mahendergarh, the Congress won 6 seats.

The 3rd Lok Sabha elections were held in 1962 for 22 seats in Punjab when 173 nominations were registered. After the scrutiny 107 candidates contested the election. This time, the Congress lost 8 of the 22 seats. The Jana Sangh and Akali Dal won 3 each whereas Socialist and HLS captured one each. Thus, the seats of Karnal, Rohtak and Mahendergarh were fetched by Jana Sangh whereas Jhajjar went in the account of HLS and Hissar in the Socialist.(For details see Annexture 2)

The parliamentary elections in Haryana were held for the first time in 1967 after its formation in 1966.

A total of 86 candidates filed their nominations for the Lok Sabha elections. However, 16 withdrew from the field and 3 were rejected leaving 67 (77.90%) as contestants.

The Congress nominated its candidates on all the seats whereas the BJS on 7, Swatantra-2, SSP-5, RPI-2, CPI-3, CPM-2, PSP-1, apart from 36 Independents in the field.

Nominations and withdrawals of different categories of candidates are given in Table 2.1.

Table 2.1 : Nominations, withdrawals etc. : 1967 Lok Sabha Elections

Category	*No. of Candidates*	*Nominations*	*Rejected*	*Withdra-wals*	*Contestants*
General	7	67	3	14	50
Reserved	2	19	–	2	17
Total	9	86	3	16	67

Note : 12 Candidates each in Mahendergarh and Sirsa Constituencies.

No. of Contestants in Different Constituencies

Contestants =	2	4	5	7	8	9	12
Constituencies =	1	1	1	1	2	1	2*

**There were 12 contestants in Mahendergarh and Sirsa each.*

There were 2 contestants in one, 4 in one, 5 in one, 7 in one, 8 in two, 9 in one and 12 candidates in two, i.e. each in Mahendergarh and Sirsa.

Campaigning

The Congress Party promised in its manifesto an independent and democratic society, effective implementation of five year plans, modern science and technology, cooperative movement to minimize the urban-rural disparity and increasing migration to cities, better education, more employment, land reforms, more wages for agricultural labour, modernizing agriculture, fair prices for agricultural produce, more credit for rural areas, more forest area, encouraging the animal stock, betterment of backward classes and minorities, prohibition, population control, effective foreign policy etc.

The Swatantra Party included in its manifesto the issues like fundamental rights, industrialisation, agricultural development and more loan facilities, national unity, curbing corruption, more ethical values, to reduce government expenditure and taxes, to abolish the licence and *permit raj*, compulsory elementary education, more help to farmers, agricultural industries, more cooperative societies etc.

The Praja Socialist Party emphasized on more vital internal security, remaining economic disparities, to regulate the Mizo and Naga rebels, remunerative market prices for agricultural produce, to reduce unemployment, welfare of SCs and BCs, more education, strong defence policy, to solve the Kashmir problem, electoral reforms, to solve the boundary disputes with neighbouring countries etc.

The Samyukta Socialist Party (SSP) called for agricultural reforms, enhancement in prices of agricultural produce, to enhance the production of foodgrains, primary education, Hindi as mother tongue, reform in sales tax, reduction in non-plan expenditure, to improve the irrigation system, strong defence policy, strong economy etc.

Bharatiya Jana Sangh announced for strong foreign policy, national unity, decentralization, independent judiciary, social security, economic reform, food policy, loan to artisans and farmers, better irrigational, fertilizer and seeds facilities, swadeshi, self-employment, tax reform, transport improvement etc.

The CPI stood for more economic freedom, ban on monopoly, welfare schemes for common masses, concession in estate tax, promotion of agriculture production, social welfare of depressed, minorities and neglected sections of society; secularism, more education for women etc., whereas the CPM called for land reform, equality, language policy, preservation of social and cultural values, bank nationalization, good relations with China, Pakistan etc.

On the whole cow protection and inflation were the main issues having more impact on electoral campaign of different political parties.

Voting and Results

About 72.6 per cent electors exercised their franchise. However, it was highest 76.94 per cent in Kaithal and the lowest 67.65 per cent in Mahendergarh as shown in Table 2.2.

Table 2.2 : Electors and Voters: A Constituency-wise view in 1967 Lok Sabha Elections

Constituencies	*Electors*	*Voters*	*%age*
Ambala (SC)	459451	329601	71.74
Karnal	463594	358681	75.51
Kaithal	484420	372708	76.94
Rohtak	477706	362943	75.98
Jhajjar	501785	367852	73.30
Gurgaon	527625	369196	69.97
Mahendergarh	491115	332233	67.65
Hissar	473354	335463	70.87
Sirsa (SC)	507661	365218	71.84

Source: Report, Lok Sabha Elections, 1967.

The above table reveals that the highest number of voters (76.94%) excercised their franchise in Kaithal Lok Sabha constituency followed by Rohtak (75.98%), Karnal (75.51%), Sirsa (71.84%) and lowest (67.65%) in Mahendergarh.

The men-women ratio of electors is given in Table 2.3.

Table 2.3 : No. of Electors and Voters : A Men-Women Ratio

	Electors		*Voters*		
Category	*Men*	*Women*	*Men*	*Women*	*Total*
General	1803547	1616052	1358570	1131906	2490476
SC	525982	441130	398187	296652	694819
Total	2329529	20571812	1756757	1428538	3185295

Source : Report, Lok Sabha Elections, 1967.

The votes polled, valid and rejected are given in Table 2.4.

Table 2.4 : No. of Valid votes polled, rejected ballot papers, 1967

Category	*No. of valid votes polled*	*No. of rejected ballot papers*	*% of electors voting*	*% of rejected ballot papers*
General	2385555	104921	72.83	4.21
SCs	666664	28155	71.84	4.05
Total	3052219	133076	72.01	4.18

Source : Report, Lok Sabha Elections, 1967.

The figures pertaining to Lok Sabha results are given in Table 2.5.

Table 2.5 : Results of 1967 Lok Sabha Elections in Haryana

Parties	*Contestants*	*Valid votes polled*	*%*	*Deposit forfeited*	*Seats won*
INC	9	1344830	44.1	–	7
BJS	7	605838	19.9	2	1
Swatantra	2	170951	5.6	1	–
SSP	5	167973	5.5	4	–
RPI	2	70920	2.3	2	–
CPI	3	51758	1.7	3	–
CPM	2	25479	0.8	2	–
Praja SP	1	10905	0.4	1	–
Independents	36	603565	19.8	34	1
Total	67	3052219			9

Total Electors	=	4386311
Voters	=	3185295 (73.6%)
Valid Votes	=	3052219 (95.82%)
Invalid Votes	=	133076 (4.35%)
Voting Percentage	=	72.6%

As cited in Table 2.5, 72.6 per cent people exercised their franchise including 55.15 per cent men and 44.84 per cent women. More than 95 per cent votes were found valid.

The Congress secured 44 per cent votes with 7 seats, namely Karnal, Kaithal, Rohtak, Jhajjar, Mahendergarh, Hissar and Sirsa.

The BJS got 19.9 per cent votes with one seat and the Independents got one seat with 19.8 per cent votes.

About 94.44 per cent Independents lost their deposits whereas 73.13 per cent of the total contestants could not save their deposits.

A constituency-wise view of Lok Sabha election results is given in Table 2.6.

Table 2.6 : Some Facts of Lok Sabha Elections, 1967: A Constituency-wise view

Name of Constituency	*Electors Voters & %age*	*Valid & Rejected Votes %age*	*Name of winning candidate/ Total Contestants*	*Party*	*Votes Polled*	*%age*
Ambala (SC)	459451 329601 71.74	316269 13332 4.04	S. Bhan 5	BJS	128003	40.47
Karnal	463594 350081 75.51	336205 13876 3.96	M. Ram 2	INC	168204	50.03
Kaithal	484420 372708 76.94	357691 4.03	G.L. Nanda 9	INC	180770	50.54
Rohtak	477706 362943 75.98	350700 12243 3.37	R.Singh 8	INC	176258	50.26
Jhajjar	501785 367852 73.31	356887 11565 3.14	S.Singh 8	INC	209492	58.80
Gurgaon	527625 369196 69.97	349394 19802 5.36	A. Gani 9	INC	88326	25.28
Mahendergarh	491115 332233 67.65	313998 18235 5.49	G. Singh 12	INC	93903	29.91
Hissar	473354 335463 70.87	321280 14183 4.23	R. Kishan 7	INC	115963	36.04
Sirsa (SC)	507661 365218 71.84	350395 14823 4.06	D. Singh 12	INC	193919	55.34

Source: Report, Lok Sabha Elections, 1967.

The RPI got 11.80 per cent votes in Gurgaon and 9.50 per cent in Mahendergarh only.

Similarly, the vote percentage of Independents was very poor in almost all the constituencies.

The CPI and CPM could get 7.70 per cent and 2.50 per cent votes respectively in Jhajjar constituency. The CPI got 3.50 per cent votes in Gurgaon and 3.40 per cent in Sirsa constituencies only.

Performance of Different Political Parties

Congress : The performance of the Congress in different constituencies is given in Table 2.7.

Table 2.7 : Performance of the Congress : A Constituency-wise view in 1967 Elections

Constituencies	*Votes Polled*	*%age*
Ambala (SC)	119303	37.70
Karnal	168204	50.00
Kaithal	180770	50.50
Rohtak	176258	50.30
Jhajjar	209492	58.80
Gurgaon	87018	24.90
Mahendergarh	93903	29.90
Hissar	115963	36.10
Sirsa (SC)	193919	55.30

Source: Report, Lok Sabha Elections, 1967.

The Congress captured 7 seats. However, it secured maximum votes 58.8 per cent in Jhajjar followed by 55.50 per cent in Kaithal, 50.30 per cent in Sirsa and Rohtak and lowest 29.90 per cent in Mahendergarh.

Table 2.8 explains the performance of BJS.

Table 2.8 : Performance of the BJS : A Constituency-wise view in 1967 Election

Constituencies	*Votes Polled*	*%age*
Ambala (Res.)	128003	40.5
Karnal	168001	50.0
Kaithal	–	–
Rohtak	120662	34.4
Jhajjar	17206	4.8
Gurgaon	70166	20.1
Mahendergarh	47165	15.0
Hissar	54635	17.0
Sirsa (Res.)	–	–

Source: Report, Lok Sabha Elections, 1967.

Since the BJS contested 7 seats while leaving Kaithal and Sirsa, it could capture one only. Its performance was better in Karnal constituency with 50 per cent votes followed by Ambala – 40.5 per cent , Rohtak–34.4 per cent and the lowest 4.8 per cent in Jhajjar. Its position in Mahendergarh and Hissar was below average.

How did the SSP perform in the election is pointed out in Table 2.9.

Table 2.9 : Performance of the SSP : A Constituency-wise view in 1967 Elections

Constituencies	*Votes Polled*	*%age*
Ambala (Res.)	–	–
Karnal	–	–
Kaithal	–	–
Rohtak	6803	1.9
Jhajjar	9038	2.5
Gurgaon	–	–
Mahendergarh	19695	6.3
Hissar	108784	33.9
Sirsa (Res.)	23653	6.8

The performance of the Swatantra Party is given in Table 2.10.

Table 2.10 : Performance of the Swatantra Party : A Constituency-wise view in 1967 Elections

Constituencies	*Votes Polled*	*%age*
Ambala (Res.)	–	–
Karnal	–	–
Kaithal	153760	43.00
Rohtak	–	–
Jhajjar	–	–
Gurgaon	–	–
Mahendergarh	–	–
Hissar	–	–
Sirsa (Res.)	17191	4.90

Source: Report, Lok Sabha Elections, 1967.

Despite its good performance in Kaithal, it could not fetch any seat. The Communist's performance is given in Tables 2.11 & 2.12.

Table 2.11 : Performance of the CPM : A Constituency-wise view in 1967 Election

Constituencies	*Votes Polled*	*%age*
Ambala (Res.)	–	–
Karnal	–	–
Kaithal	–	–
Rohtak	–	–
Jhajjar	8899	2.5
Gurgaon	16580	4.8
Mahendergarh	–	–
Hissar	–	–
Sirsa (Res.)	–	–

Source: Report, Lok Sabha Elections, 1967

The CPM also could not open its account in the Lok Sabha and lost its deposits in both the constituences.

Table 2.12 : Performance of the CPI : A Constituency-wise view in 1967 Elections

Constituencies	*Votes Polled*	*%age*
Ambala (Res.)	–	–
Karnal	–	–
Kaithal	–	–
Rohtak	–	–
Jhajjar	27464	7.7
Gurgaon	12276	3.5
Mahendergarh	–	–
Hissar	–	–
Sirsa (Res.)	12015	3.4

Source: Report, Lok Sabha Elections, 1967.

In all the three constituencies as cited above, the CPI lost its deposits.

In the whole, the Congress performed well in Jhajjar and other three constituencies whereas the BJS could fetch only one seat out of 7 contested by it. Its performance was very bad in southern Haryana. The SSP fared very poor except Hissar, the Swatantra except Karnal. The communists could not get even 8 per cent votes in any constituency.

3

Parliamentary Elections, 1971

The Lok Sabha elections, 1971 were preponed by one year. In 1969, the Congress split into two groups – Congress (I) and Congress (O). This time, more attention was given to caste factor while nominating the candidates, e.g. Jat candidates from Rohtak and Jhajjar and a Muslim from Gurgaon having 22.41 per cent votes.

A total of 109 candidates filed their nominations when 42 withdrew, 4 were rejected leaving 63 in the field.

The BJS won the seat of Ambala. However, the Independent captured the Gurgaon seat by securing 25.28 per cent votes.

More than 94 per cent Independents lost their deposits, whereas on the whole the percentange was about 73 per cent.

The Congress contested all the 9 seats, Congress (O) = 4, BJS-3, VHP-3, SUC-2, PSP-2, RPK-5, CPM, SSP, SAD, FAL, CPI one each and 29 Independents.

Nominations: The details of nominations are given in Table 3.1.

Table 3.1 : Nominations, withdrawals, contestants etc. 1971 Elections

Category	*Nominated*		*Rejected*		*Withdrawals*		*Contestants*	
	M	*W*	*M*	*W*	*M*	*W*	*M*	*W*
General	94	1	4	–	36	1	54	–
Res.(SC)	14	–	–	–	5	–	9	–
Total	108	1	4	–	41	1	63	–

Source : Report, Lok Sabha Elections, 1971.

A category-wise view of nominations, contestants etc. is given in Table 3.2.

Table 3.2 : Nominations, withdrawals, contestants etc. 1971 Elections

		Electors			*Voters*		
		Total	*Men*	*Women*	*Total*	*Men*	*Women*
General Category	U	580662	312524	268138	367394	197863	169531
	R	3136131	165016	1486115	2081299	1158905	922394
	T	37106793	1962540	1754253	2448613	1356768	1091925
		63.25	33.40	29.85	65.88	36.50	29.38
General Category	U	201015	109709	91306	120884	65535	55349
	R	850932	456962	393970	499122	291973	207149
	T	105947	566671	485276	620006	357508	262498
		61.37	33.06	28.31	58.94	33.99	24.95
General Category	U	781677	422233	359444	488278	263398	224880
	R	3987063	2106978	1880085	2580421	1450878	1129543
	T	4768740	2529211	2239529	2580421	1714276	1354423
		62.82	33.32	29.50	64.85	35.95	28.40

Source : Report, Lok Sabha Elections, 1971.

The SAD fielded its candidate only in Ambala, a reserved constituency for Scheduled Castes, who got merely 3.30 per cent votes. The BKD also nominated its only candidate from Kaithal segment who received 3.20 per cent votes. The RPK contested from five constituencies, namely Karnal, Jhajjar, Gurgaon, Hissar and Sirsa while getting 2 per cent, 3.70 per cent, 1.8 per cent, 0.50 per cent and 1.50 per cent votes respectively. The VHP put up its only candidate from Mahendergarh who won the seat with 46.80 votes.

SAD contested from Ambala only and got 3.3 per cent votes, NCO from Karnal – 7.1 per cent and Hissar 13.9 per cent, CPM from Kaithal-1.1 per cent , apart from other several groups and Independents whose performance is listed in Table 3.4.

The constituency-wise figures are given in Table 3.3.

Table 3.3 : Constituency-wise Nominations, 1971 Elections

Name of Constituency	Number of Candidates														
	Nominated			Nominations Rejected			Withdrawn			Contestants			Forfeited Deposite		
(A) General	M	W	T	M	W	T	M	W	T	M	W	T	M	W	T
Karnal	13	-	13	-	-	-	6	-	6	7	-	7	5	-	5
Kaithal	16	-	16	1	-	1	6	-	6	9	-	9	7	-	7
Rohtak	9	-	9	-	-	-	1	-	1	8	-	8	6	-	6
Jhajjar	7	-	7	-	-	-	1	-	1	4	-	4	2	-	2
Gurgaon	25	1	26	2	-	2	12	1	13	12	-	12	10	-	10
Mahendergarh	9	-	9	1	-	1	3	-	3	6	-	6	4	-	4
Hissar	15	-	15	-	-	-	7	-	7	8	-	8	6	-	6
Ambala (SC)	8	-	8	-	-	-	4	-	4	4	-	4	2	-	2
Sirsa (SC)	6	-	6	-	-	-	1	-	1	5	-	5	3	-	3
Total (Gen)	94	1	95	4	-	4	36	1	37	54	-	54	8	-	8
SC	14	-	14				5	-	5	9	-	9	5	-	5
State Total	108	1	109	4	-	4	41	1	42	63	-	63	45	-	45

Source : Report, Lok Sabha Elections, 1971.

As ponted out in Table 3.3, the maximum nominations were received in Gurgaon-26 followed by Kaithal-16, Karnal 13 and the minimum 6 in Sirsa constituency.

Table 3.4 : Parties in Fray : 1971 Elections

	National Parties								*State Party*	*Unrecognized Parties*	*Independents*	*Total*
	INC	NCO	SWA	BJS	SSP	PSP	CPI	CPM				
Contestants	9	4	-	3	1	2	1	1	6	8	29	63
Elected	7	-	-	1	-	-	-	-	1	-	1	9
Deposit Forfeited	-	2	-	-	-	2	-	1	4	8	28	45

Source : Report, Lok Sabha Election, 1971

The maximum contestants belonged to the Congress Party followed by the NCO, Swatantra and state parties. As many as 29 Independents also fought the elections. However more than 71 per cent candidates could not save their deposits including 28 of the 29 Independents and all splinter groups.

Compaigning and Issues

Haryana was carved out of Punjab soon before the 1967 general election. The whole state of erstwhile Punjab, therefore, was torn into two communal wings. While the Sikhs dominated the politics of Punjab, Haryana was a Hindu majority area with a strong Congress base. Yet the first major defections occurred from within the Congress here toppling the Congress ministry after elections in 1967. This necessitated another election in 1968.

B.D. Sharma, Chief Minister, who decried defections, for his colleagues had betrayed him, himself had to defect one day to make this state the most important hotbed of defectors' politics which overtook the whole country later. That is how Haryana was famous, politically speaking.

The Congress promised for a strong Central Government, removal of poverty and inequality, self-reliance in food production, labour participation in management, better Centre-State relations, education for more people, improvement in supply of electricity, irrigational facilities, better health services, welfare of SCs and BCs, more employment, land reform, whereas the Congress (O) called for unified leadership, more production and employment, better rural economy, scheme of irrigation and power supply to small and marginal farmers, land reform, price stability, more industries, work to all, combating corruption, more funds for weaker sections etc.

The BJS declared to remove unemployment, price stability, abolition of inspector *raj*, compliance of directive principles of state policy, power to farmers at subsidized rates, help to agriculture labour, potable water to every village, welfare of disabled and SCs and BCs, equal pay for equal work, hostels for working women etc.

The CPI called for control over prices, unemployment, land reform, free education to children up to age of 14 years, voting right to those attained the 18 years of age, more health services, control over bureaucracy etc., whereas the CPM promised to control corruption, protection to Muslims and weaker sections, more employment etc.

On the whole, 'Garibi Hatao' was the main slogan given by the Congress. With this slogan, Indira Gandhi addressed the election meetings in the state whereas the BJS promised to provide power at cheap rates to small farmers.

At the time of the general election in 1967 cow protection was a major issue. Cow slaughter had been outlawed in the state but a large section of the people swayed by religious sentiments was agitated over the action of the Union government to introduce legislation at the Central level. The soaring price was another issue. Though government employees were in a belligerent mood, yet the Congress won a majority of the Lok Sabha seats because of the pressure exerted by castes and sub-castes.

In the 1967 Lok Sabha elections, the undivided Congress profited a great deal by the multiplicity of opposition candidates. The number of contestants, which was 67 in 1967, had gone down to 62 in 1971. Despite the fact that the multiplicity of candidates was working against the new Congress in most constituencies, the Congress won.

Caste and creed played a big role in the election strategy. At Kaithal the Old Congress had set up a Jat because about 25 per cent of the votes in the constitutncy were Jats. The new Congress candidates at Rohtak and Jhajjar were also Jats. So, were those of its major rivals, the Jana Sangh and the Old Congress. The Rohtak constituency had about 30 per cent Jat votes and Jhajjar over 40 per cent.

The largest single community was in the Gurgaon constituency of Meo Muslims – about 1,30,000 in a total electorate of 5,80,000. The new Congress and the Vishal Haryana Party had Muslim candidates. The percentage of Brahmins varied from six to nine from constituency to constituency. The alliance banked on the former chief minister and old Congress leader, Bhagwat Dayal Sharma, to swing the Brahmins into the opposition camp. The new Congress sought to counter Sharma's influence by telling the Brahmin voters that Mrs. Gandhi was a Brahmin. The big handicap of the New Congress was that it had more Jats, Brahmin and Ahir leaders against it in 1971 than the undivided Congress had in 1967.

The opposition acted on the assumption that the New Congress might gather more votes of the Haryana and backward classes than the Old Congress did in 1967. It was, therefore, seeking to neutralize the likely New Congress gains by working on the desire for owning property among the non-Harijans who constituted 80 per cent of the voters. But this did not work. It also tried to take advantage of the factional pulls among them in the same manner in which the New Congress was exploiting factionalism among the Jats, Ahirs, Banias and Brahmins.

There was indeed no question of the poll bringing about any

ideological polarizations. No one was working for it. The New Congress was sustained by the rural elite and the well-to-do urbanites. Parties like the PSP, the SSP, the CPI and the CPM hardly existed in Haryana. None of them held a seat either in the Vidhan Sabha or the Lok Sabha elections.

The differences among the New Congress, the Old Congress, the Vishal Haryana Party and the Jana Sangh in Haryana were based more on the clash of personalities and postures than on distinctions in their economic beliefs and objectives.

Politics of defection therefore remained an issue with the Congress particulary in elections in Haryana since the advent of the state. Stability was also the cry of the hour.

In 1971 another factor which worked to the advantage of the Congress was the absence of any opposition party with sufficient resources of ideological clarity to pose a challenge to it. The manifestos released by the various parties offered the voter little choice. Most of them had waxed eloquent on democracy, socialism and secularism. While the Congress had pledged itself to the eradication of poverty and unemployment, the Jana Sangh had promised cheap irrigation and power and ceiling on land holdings. The Socialists offered revenue remission on holdings up to 4 hectares and a minimum holding of 2 hectares for each agricultural family. It had also held out promise of full employment and, failing that, unemployment doles.

Election Day and Results

3068699 – 64.35 per cent of the 4768740 electorate—exercised their voting right including 55.86 per cent males and 44.13 per cent females. About 97 per cent votes were found valid and the Congress secured 51.25 per cent with 7 seats namely Ambala, Karnal, Kaithal, Jhajjar, Gurgaon, Hissar and Sirsa.

The SSP contested from Hissar while getting 27.40 per cent votes. The Forward Bloc and CPM, both fought from Kaithal constituency and got 1.90 and 1.10 per cent votes respectively. The Social Unity Centre (SUC) nominated its candidates in Rohtak and Jhajjar while getting 0.50 per cent and 4.40 per cent votes respectively. The Independents could not get even one per cent votes in majority of the constituencies.

A view of voters in different constituencies is given in Table 3.5.

Table 3.5 : Population, Electors, Voters and Valid Votes Polled, 1971 Elections

Name of Constituency	Population (1961)	Number of				Percentage			
		Electors 1970	Votes 1971	Valid Votes	Rejected	Electors Votes	Votes	Rejected Votes	Valid Votes
Ambala (SC)	885785	490572	295410	287719	7691	55.38	60.22	2.60	58.65
Karnal	827167	504480	327638	316780	10858	60.99	64.95	3.31	62.79
Kaithal	846886	519031	351635	342698	8957	61.28	67.75	2.54	66.03
Rohtak	843728	514278	329327	322537	6790	60.95	64.04	2.06	62.72
Jhajjar	857913	551818	370363	362654	7709	64.32	67.12	2.08	65.72
Gurgaon	872819	584957	398638	387206	11430	67.02	68.15	2.87	66.19
Mahendergarh	820170	527551	349098	340031	9087	64.32	66.17	2.60	64.45
Hissar	807878	514878	321994	315311	6683	63.71	62.56	2.08	61.26
Sirsa (SC)	828197	561375	324596	317602	6994	67.78	57.82	2.15	56.58
General	5876561	3716793	2448693	2387217	61476	63.25	65.88	2.51	64.23
SC	1713982	1051947	620006	605321	14685	61.37	58.94	2.37	57.54
State Total	7590543	4768740	3068699	2992538	76161	62.82	64.35	2.48	62.75

Source : Report, Lok Sabha Elections, 1971.

The BJS secured 10.91 per cent votes with one seat, namely Rohtak. Similarly, VHP got 8.93 per cent votes with one seat, namely Mahendergarh.

A total of 45 candidates, 71.42 per cent could not save their deposits.

The Congress encashed the slogan 'Garibi Hatao' when the poor people cast their votes in its favour.

Table 3.6 : Election Results : Lok Sabha, 1971

Party	*Seats contested*	*Seats won*	*Valid Votes polled*	*Deposit forfeited*
Congress (I)	9	7	1572929	–
BJS	3	1	334830	–
VHP	3	1	274091	–
Congress (O)	4	–	339213	2
BKD	1	–	10895	1
RPK	5	–	18108	5
SUC	2	–	17577	2
BKD	1	–	10895	–
SAD	1	–	9413	1
FAL	1	–	6604	1
SSP	1	–	86510	1
CPM	1	–	3917	1
PSP	2	–	5942	2
CPI	–	–	–	–
Independents	29	–	163512	28
Total	63	10	2992538	45

Seats : 9; Electorate: 4768035; Total votes polled : 3068699; Total valid votes: 2992538; Invalid votes: 76161 and Percentage of voting : 3.5 per cent .

Performance of Different Political Parties

Congress: its performance is given in Table 3.7

Table 3.7 : Performance of the Congress : A Constituency-wise View.

Constituencies	*Votes Polled*	*%age*
Ambala (Res.)	196709	68.4
Karnal	152249	48.1
Kaithal	155000	45.2
Rohtak	138738	43.0
Jhajjar	189860	52.4
Gurgaon	199333	51.5
Mahendergarh	157226	46.2
Hissar	170204	54.0
Sirsa (Res.)	213610	67.3

Source : Report, Lok Sabha Election, 1971.

The performance of the Congress improved in 1971 when it secured more votes almost in every constituency. However, it got maximum 68.4 per cent in Ambala followed by 67.3 per cent in Sirsa – both reserved ones, Hissar – 54 per cent, Jhajjar – 52.4 per cent and the lowest 46.2 per cent in Mahendergarh.

Performance of BJS is highlighted in Table 3.8.

Table 3.8 : Performance of the BJS : A Constituency-wise View

Constituencies	*Votes Polled*	*%age*
Ambala (Res.)	74433	25.9
Karnal	116988	36.9
Kaithal	–	–
Rohtak	143409	44.5
Jhajjar	–	–
Gurgaon	–	–
Mahendergarh	–	–
Hissar	–	–
Sirsa (Res.)	–	–

Source : Report, Lok Sabha Election, 1971.

The performance of the BJS was worse in 1971 Lok Sabha election. However, it secured more than 44 per cent votes in Rohtak and it was taken as a setback to the Cogress getting 43 per cent votes. Moreover, it could nominate its candidate only in three constituencies against 7 in 1967. Its vote percentage decreased in Karnal and Ambala.

How did the Congress perform is given in Table 3.9.

Table 3.9 : Performance of the Congress (O) : A Constituency-wise View

Constituencies	*Votes Polled*	*%age*
Ambala (SC)	–	–
Karnal	22558	7.10
Kaithal	129462	37.08
Rohtak	–	–
Jhajjar	143245	39.50
Gurgaon	–	–
Mahendergarh	–	–
Hissar	43948	13.90
Sirsa (SC)	–	–

Source : Report, Lok Sabha Election, 1971.

As the Congress split into two groups in 1969 at the stance of Indira Gandhi – Congress (I) and Congress (O). The latter performed well in Jhajjar and Kaithal but very poor in Karnal and Hissar. It could not contest the remaining 5 seats. However, it failed to enter the Lok Sabha.

Data pertaining to RPK is given in Table 3.10.

Table 3.10 : Performance of the RPK : A Constituency-wise View

Constituencies	*Votes Polled*	*%age*
Ambala (Res.)	–	–
Karnal	6449	2.0
Kaithal	–	–
Rohtak	–	–
Jhajjar	13564	3.7
Gurgaon	6781	1.8
Mahendergarh	–	–
Hissar	1436	0.5
Sirsa (Res.)	4878	1.5

Source : Report, Lok Sabha Election, 1971.

The RPK contested five seats and fared very poor in all of them securing less than 4 per cent votes leading to forfeiture of deposits of all its candidates.

4

Parliamentary Elections, 1977

The Lok Sabha poll in March 1977 in Haryana was different in several respects from the one held six year earlier. This time Haryana elected 10 MPs, one more than in 1971. The strength of the electorate had gone up to more than 5.7 million, an increase of about one million.

The constituencies were demarcated afresh because of the creation of three new districts. There were now ten districts as against seven in 1971.

The delimitation of constituencies notified in December 1974, on the basis of which elections were to be held had materially altered the boundaries of at least four Lok Sabha constituencies – Kaithal, Hissar, Sirsa and Gurgaon. A fourth constituency had emerged. It was named after the newly created district of Bhiwani, the home-town of the chief minister, B.D. Gupta, and his predecessor, Bansi Lal, who was the Union Defence Minister.

A category-wise view of constituencies is give in Table 4.1.

Table 4.1 : Number of Constituencies

Parliamentary Constituencies				*Assembly Constituencies*			
Gen	*SC*	*ST*	*Total*	*Gen*	*SC*	*ST*	*Total*
8	2	–	10	73	17	–	90

Source: Report, Lok Sabha Elections, 1977.

The figures pertaining to nominations, rejections belonging to different categories are shown in Table 4.2.

Table 4.2 : Candidates nominated, nominations rejected, withdrawn and contested

		Nominated			*Nominations Rejected*			*Withdrawn*			*Contesting*		
Catagory	*Seats*	*M*	*W*	*T*	*M*	*W*	*T*	*M*	*W*	*T*	*M*	*W*	*T*
GEN	8	90	2	92	2	–	2	48	–	48	40	2	42
SC	2	14	–	14	–	–	–	6	–	6	8	–	8
ST	–	–	–	–	–	–	–	–	–	–	–	–	–
Total	10	104	2	106	2	–	2	54	–	54	48	2	50

Source: Report, Lok Sabha Elections, 1977.

As per Table 4.2 only two females filed nominations out of 106 candidates. However, 54 of them withdrew leaving 50 in the field.

A district-wise break up of candidates nominated, rejected, contested is given in Table. 4.3.

Table 4.3 : Candidates Nominated, Nominations Rejected, Withdrawn and Contested

Name of Constituency	*Nominated*			*Nominations Rejected*			*Withdrawn*			*Contestants*		
	M	*W*	*T*	*M*	*W*	*T*	*M*	*W*	*T*	*M*	*W*	*T*
Ambala(SC)	8	–	8	–	–	–	4	–	4	4	–	4
Kurukshetra	14	–	14	–	–	–	6	–	6	8	–	8
Karnal	14	–	14	–	–	–	9	–	9	5	–	5
Sonepat	10	1	11	1	–	1	5	–	5	4	1	5
Rohtak	8	–	8	–	–	–	3	–	3	5	–	5
Faridabad	13	–	13	–	–	–	6	–	6	7	–	7
Mahendergarh	20	–	20	–	–	–	13	–	13	7	–	7
Bhiwani	6	1	7	1	–	1	3	–	3	2	1	3
Hissar	5	–	5	–	–	–	3	–	3	2	–	2
Sirsa (SC)	6	–	6	–	–	–	2	–	2	4	–	4
TOTAL	104	2	106	2	–	2	54	–	54	48	2	50

Source : Report, Lok Sabha Elections, 1977.

Campaign

The resignation of Jagjivan Ram from the Union Government and the Congress, the formation of the Janata Party and the Congress for Democracy and large-scale resignations of former Congress ministers, MPs, MLAs and thousands of active workers had made a great impact on the people in the state who had suffered under the strong-arm rule of Bansi Lal for seven years.

The myth that Haryana was a solid Congress-dominated state had been exploded by the resignations from the Congress legislature party and various district Congress committees. The defections from and in-fighting in the Congress legislature party and Pradesh Congress at this critical juncture was bound to and of course, did affect the poll prospects of the party candidates.

The resignation of Jagjivan Ram had given a jolt to the entire Harijan community in the state, which constituted 25 per cent of electorate. In the 1971 poll they had voted *en bloc* for the Congress, swayed by the "*garibi hatao*", slogan of the then Prime Minister, Indira Gandhi.

The Congress campaigners had been putting up a spirited defence of the declaration of the emergency but for which, they asserted, the country would have been in the grip of chaos and political instability. They stressed that the Janata Party would never succeed in ensuring political stability which was necessary for economic development.

Crowds were brought to the meetings in trucks and buses. They shouted "*jai*" for Indira Gandhi while converging on the venue but on the return journey their "*jai*" was for the Janata Party.

At every election meeting, the focus of the Congress leaders' speeches was the progress in Haryana – its terrific growth rate, its canals and its power stations. But this listing of achievements was too late to win over the people unhappy over forced sterilization and loss of freedom and liberty.

Because of the fear that had gripped them, the people could not open their mouths during the 20 months of emergency but when the chance came their way, they recorded their protest.

Women shut the doors of their dwellings and those who feared they would be picked up for sterilization fled in panic to nearby fields.

State roadways buses were diverted to health centres and male passengers, irrespective of their age or infirmities, were herded to the operation room and sterilized. Those going out for morning walks were herded together by policemen and rushed to health centres in vans. A high official of the State Bank of Hissar was one of such people taken to a health centre. Luckily for him some people there recognized the old man and he thus escaped.

People were picked up from courts, colleges and offices for sterilization. District and village level government officials, school teachers and other such functionaries were allotted sterilization quotas. Failure to achieve the target meant all kinds of punishment. To add to all this was the active participation of the police and youth Congress leaders in the atrocities.

In the Rewasa case, a young man was beaten up, his grandmother "killed" and his mother and maternal uncle were stripped off and thrown in a lock-up. It was this case that roused the electorate of Bhiwani and it became a matter of honour and self-respect for them to bring about Bansi Lal's defeat.

The deputy commissioner, as an opposition member pointed out in the Assembly, had become more powerful than the ministers. Some of the top district officials had turned active campaigners for the Congress candidates.

The Congress election campaign was feeble and fussy compared to the sharp, clear, simple and hard-hitting campaign of the Janata Party. The Congress campaigners everywhere were caught on the wrong footing. They had to answer to the questions agitating the minds of the people. All they could do in the desperation was to tender apologies for the wrongs done by them or their party but it was now too late. The people had decided to punish the Congress and they did it in no uncertain manner.

Haryana is traditionally a caste-ridden state and even though the people were more politically conscious now than they were in 1971; caste and clan considerations did also influence their judgement. They had been kept in view by all the parties in selecting candidates.

The main point made by the Janata Party was that in 1971 the "Indira wave" had split the opposition vote and disorganized its poll campaign.

Rural voters, who earlier formed the hard core of the Congress, were in a different mood. They were sore over the way the family planning programme was implemented in the state, particularly in the rural areas after the imposition of the emergency. The excesses committed during the sterilization drive on the Harijans, Muslims and other weaker sections had left a deep scar and they were not in a mood to forgive those responsible for it. They were not happy over the state government's attitude towards their economic problems. Most of them continued to live below the poverty level.

The section of the rural population which had been benefited under the 20-point programme of the government, however, voted for the Congress candidates, but their percentage was too small to make a big dent. The rural youth, most of them educated and unemployed were more politically conscious than their elders. They complained that there was no sign of the promises made by the Congress leaders in the 1971 Lok Sabha elections been fulfilled.

Coming as it did between an excellent *kharif* harvest and a promising *rabi* crop, the poll was expected in the normal course to bring a wind fall of votes to the ruling party. But farmers were sore over the "un-remunerative" prices fixed for food-grains. They were also concerned at the mounting rate of unemployment.

Then, the attitude of employees of the state government and corporations to the Congress had become unfavourable following the enforcement of the massive sterilization programme covering couples having two or more children. The "goodness" in the programme is evident from the fact that with the approach of the election, the "incentives" had been withdrawn.

Private college teachers were also unhappy with the Congress in view of the non-implementation of pay-scales recommended by the University Grants Commission.

Congress leaders tried to impress upon Harijans that after becoming Defence Minister, Bansi Lal, former Chief Minister, would fix a quota for their community in recruitment to the army – a step which was not taken by Jagjivan Ram when he was minister in-charge of defence. They also claimed that retirement benefits for ex-servicemen, like pension and gratuity were increased recently at the instance of Bansi Lal. All this was meant for consumption of a large number of ex-servicemen on the electoral rolls, especially in Rohtak, Gurgaon and Mahendergarh districts.

It had become a food surplus state from a traditionally deficit state. They were also exploiting the demand made by the Akali Dal for scrapping the decision on the division of the Ravi-Bias waters which benefited Haryana more than Punjab. This issue was used against the Janata Party candidates because of the Janata alliance with the Akali Dal.

The 42nd Amendment of the Constitution had also emerged as an election issue.

They stressed their commitment of democracy and freedom of the press as opposed to the "dictatorial" trends at the Centre and pre-censorship of newspapers introduced in the wake of the Declaration of Emergency.

The shops and houses in the towns and cities through which these VIPs used to pass were painted pink. The ugly sewer lines and drains were covered with flower-pots. The lawns were made to look greener. The electric and telephone poles were painted silver and buntings and flags decorated the whole route.

The Congress contested nine out of ten seats, leaving one to the Vishal Haryana Party candidate, Rao Birendra Singh, who contested from Mahendergarh. Much interest was focused on Bhiwani where Bansi Lal was pitted against his old ministerial colleague, Mrs. Chandrawati.

Voting Day and Results

In Haryana, 57 lakh voters went to the polls in the one-day poll on March 16 to elect 10 members to the Lok Sabha.

The number of males in 1977 was 30 lakhs more than the women voters.

The population, number of electors and voters are shown in Table 4.4.

A constituency-wise views of electors and voters is given in Table 4.5.

Table 4.4 : Population, Electors, Voters, 1977

Population (1971 Census)			*Electors*			*Voters*		
Gen	*SC*	*Total*	*M*	*W*	*T*	*M*	*W*	*T*
8140875	1895933	10036808	3047804	2718850	5766654	2310566	1913839	4224405
81.11	18.84		52.85	47.15	57.46	75.81	70.39	73.26

Source : Report, Lok Sabha Elections, 1977.

Table 4.4 shows that 18.84 per cent of the total 10036808 of population are Scheduled Castes. The ratio of men-women electorate is 52.85 : 47.15 per cent whereas the voters ratio is 75.81:70.39 per cent meaning thereby that the rate of voting is higher among women than men.

Table 4.5 : Population, Electors, Voters etc.

Name of Constituency	*Population*				*Electors*			*Voters*		
	Gen	*SC*	*ST*	*Total*	*M*	*W*	*T*	*M*	*W*	*T*
Ambala(SC)	755186	230833	–	986019	277520	243527	521047	217539	178730	396269
Kurukshetra	788595	186690	–	975285	287710	251142	538852	234535	191410	425945
Karnal	814943	173494	–	988437	295156	261047	556203	230733	192012	422745
Sonepat	845440	175275	–	1020715	313869	283799	597668	237617	197026	434643
Rohtak	812713	178551	–	991264	300497	277493	577990	211569	187058	398627
Faridabad	873421	150414	–	1023835	321819	279405	601224	238625	187075	425700
Mahendergarh	899185	183320	–	1082505	334381	318132	652913	244686	227773	472459
Bhiwani	808081	180863	–	988944	312539	278350	590889	237922	197580	435502
Hissar	790884	199110	–	989994	294140	259616	553758	226847	182553	409400
Sirsa (SC)	752427	237383	–	989810	309773	266339	576112	230493	172622	403115
TOTAL	8140875	1895933	–	10036803	3047804	2718850	5766654	2310566	1913839	4234405

Source : Report, Lok Sabha Elections, 1977.

A constituencywise picture presented in Table 4.5 proves that we have the maximum population in Mahendergarh constituency-10,82,505 followed by Faridabad-10,23,835 and Sonepat-10,20,715 and the minimum is Kurukshetra–9,75,285. Similarly we have the maximum electors in Mahendergarh followed by Faridabad and Sonepat. But in the case of voters, Bhiwani followed Mahendergarh.

A record average polling percentage of 73.26 was registered. Out of the total electorate of 57,64,601 this time, 42,24,405 exercised their franchise. Invalid votes were 78,861.

The maximum polling percentage of 79.05 was recorded in the Kurukshetra constituency where 4,25,945 voters out of the total electorate of 5,38,825 cast their preference. Ambala followed with 76.05 per cent, Karnal 76 per cent, Hissar 73.93 per cent, Bhiwani 73.70 per cent, Sonepat 72.72 per cent, Mahendergarh 72.36 per cent, Faridabad 71.07 per cent, Sirsa 69.97 per cent and Rohtak 68.97 per cent.

The number of valid, rejected votes is given in Table 4.6.

Table 4.6 : Valid votes polled, Rejected, No. of Poling Stations and Average of Electors Polling Station

Votes Polled	*Votes Rejected*	*No. of Polling Stations*	*Average No. of Electors Polling Station*
4148544 71.94	75861 1.80	6299	915

A constituency-wise narration is given in Table 4.7.

Table 4.7 : Valid Vote Polled, Rejected Votes and No. of Polling Stations.

Name of Constituency	*Valid Votes Polled*	*Rejected Votes*	*No. of Polling Stations*
Ambala(SC)	387189	9080	547
Kurukshetra	418857	7088	596
Karnal	415837	6908	573
Sonepat	428524	6119	659
Rohtak	392871	5756	600
Faridabad	417485	8215	666
Mahendergarh	462881	9578	734
Bhiwani	427584	7918	663
Hissar	401528	7872	624
Sirsa (SC)	395788	7327	637
TOTAL	4148544	75861	6299

Source : Report, Lok Sabha Elections, 1977.

The CPI contested from Ambala and Krurukshetra and got 3.60 per cent and 2.70 per cent votes respectively, whereas the CPM could get only 0.30 per cent in Faridabad. The VHP contested from the Ahir dominated seat, Mahendergarh and lost to the BLD by getting 41.70 per cent votes. Almost all Independents lost their security deposits.

The data relating to election results is given in Table 4.8.

Table 4.8 : Election Results, 1977

Party	*Contested*	*Valid votes*	*%*	*Forfeited*	*%*	*Seat won*
BLD	10	2918446	70.35	–	–	10
Congress	9	744862	17.62	4	–	–
CPI	2	25289	0.61	2	–	–
Forward	1	2444	0.05	1	–	–
VHP	1	192867	4.64	–	–	–
CPM	1	1118	0.03	1	–	–
CUS	2	4850	0.12	2	–	–
Ind.	24	258668	6.23	23	–	–
Total	50	4148544	100.00	33		10

Source : Election Report on the Sixth General Elections, 1977.

In 1977 Lok Sabha election, 73 per cent people exercised their voting right including 54.69 per cent males and 45.30 per cent females. The number of valid votes was higher to 98.2 per cent . The BLD got 70 per cent of the valid votes while winning all the 10 seats. The Congress could get about 17 per cent of the valid votes getting no seat. The impact of excesses of the emergency was clear.

The Janata Party with an overall polling percentage of 70.34 was followed by the Congress 17.95 per cent, Independents 6.32 per cent, Vishal Haryana Party 4.64 per cent and CPI 0.60 per cent.

Among the 50 contestants, the winning Janata Party candidate, B.D. Sharma, a former chief minister, registered the highest polling percentage of 81.99 securing 3,40,961 votes in the Karnal constituency. His four opponents, including the Congress candidate, lost their deposites.

The maximum percentage registered by a Congress candidate was by Bansi Lal, former Defence Minister, in the Bhiwani constituency who was defeated by the Janata Party nominee, Mrs. Chandrawati, by a margin of 1,61,242 votes. He was polled 1,27,839 votes returning a polling percentage of 29.92 per cent. This was in sharp contrast to the minimum polled (1,84,848) by the winning Janata Party candidate, Dharam Vir Vashist, in the Faridabad constituency registering 44.30 polling percentage.

Among the Congress candidates Tayyab Hussain recorded minimum polling percentage of 13.91 in the Faridabad constituency. He lost his deposit.

In comparison to this, even the defeated Congress supported Vishal Haryana Party's Rao Birendra Singh and an Independent, Khurshid Ahmed, who polled 41.67 and 41.53 per cent votes in their respective constituencies of Mahendergarh and Faridabad.

Out of the total 90 Assembly segments in the state Congress led only in one in Tosham in the Bhiwani constituency with Bansi Lal securing 27,519 against Mrs. Chandravati's 21,744. However, Mrs. Chandravati led impressively in all the other eight segments and also in postal ballots obtaining 1,604 against Bansi Lal's 1,441.

Janata Party candidates also led in all the segments except in Tosham in Bhiwani and four segments in Faridabad constituency (Hathin, Ferozepore Jhirka, Nuh and Taoru) where the defeated Independent Khurshid Ahmed led and in three segments in Mahendergarh constituency (Jatusana, Mahendergarh and Ateli) where the defeated Congress-supported Vishal Haryana Party's Rao Birendra Singh led.

Of the 50 contestants, 33 including four Congress candidates, lost their deposits.

The maximum victory margin of 2,80,223 votes was recorded in Sonepat constituency from where Mukhtiar Singh (Janata Party) routed his nearest Congress rival Mrs. Subhashini who along with the other four opponents lost deposits. The lowest victory margin 27,333 votes was registered in the Faridabad constituency.

One of the two women candidates in the fray, Mrs. Chandravati of the Janata Party emerged victorious while Mrs. Subhashini of the Congress was defeated.

The party-wise performance is given in Table 4.9.

Table 4.9 : Votes Polled and Percentage According to Parties

No.of Seats		*Total No. of Valid Votes*	*No. and Percentage of valid Votes polled by National Parties*							
			National Parties					*State Parties*	*Regd. Parties*	*IND*
Uncont-ested	*Contested*		*INC*	*BLD*	*CPI*	*CPM*	*NCO*			
—	10	4148544	744862 17.62	2918446 70.35	25289 0.61	1118 0.08	—	195311 4.70	4850 0.12	258668 6.24

Source : Report, Lok Sabha Elections, 1967.

The BLD secured all 10 Lok Sabha seats with 70.35 per cent votes whereas the Congress could not open its account in the Lok Sabha even with 17.62 per cent votes. Thus, it was a landside victory for the BLD.

Performance of Major Political Parties

Congress: its performance is depicted in Table 4.10.

Table 4.10 : Performance of the Congress: A Constituency-wise view in 1977 elections

Constituencies	*Votes Polled*	*%age*
Ambala (SC)	99096	25.6
Kurukshetra	71322	17.0
Karnal	64125	15.40
Sonepat	66677	15.60
Rohtak	60905	15.50
Faridabad	157615	37.80
Mahendergarh	—	—
Bhiwani	127893	29.90
Hissar	79072	19.70
Sirsa (SC)	117693	29.70

Source : Report, Lok Sabha Elections, 1977

The congress secured the highest–37.60 per cent votes in Faridabad constituency followed by Bhiwani-29.90 per cent, Sirsa, a reserved constituency-29.70 per cent and the lowest 17 per cent in Kurukshetra. Its support base declined in every constituency sharply in comparison to the 1971 Lok Sabha polls.

The performance of BLD is pointed out in table 4.11.

Table 4.11 : Performance of the BLD : A Constituency-wise view in 1977 Elections

Constituencies	*Votes Polled*	*%age*
Ambala (SC)	264590	68.30
Kurukshetra	322164	76.90
Karnal	340961	82.00
Sonepat	346900	81.00

(Contd...)

Table 4.11 : *(Contd...)*

Rohtak	320550	81.60
Faridabad	184948	44.30
Mahendergarh	255881	55.30
Bhiwani	289135	67.60
Hissar	322456	80.30
Sirsa (SC)	270861	68.40

Source : Report, Lok Sabha Elections, 1977.

The BLD performed well in almost all the constituencies. However, it secured 82 per cent votes in Karnal, followed by 81.60 per cent in Rohtak, 81 per cent in Sonepat, 80.30 per cent in Hissar, 76.90 per cent in Kurukshetra and the lowest 44.30 per cent in Faridabad. However, it bagged all the 10 Lok Sabha seats.

5

Parliamentary Elections, 1980

As the Janata Party cracked under its own weight just after 30 months when the Lok Sabha was dissolved and mid-term polls were declared in 1980.

As there were three-cornered contests in all the 10 constituencies in 1980, the CPI and CPM were no force to reckon with since they had never found representation even in the State Assembly. They had small pockets of influence among industrial workers but these were of no consequence to the outcome of the poll.

Faridabad had the highest concentration of Meo Muslims—as many as 1.89 lakh. The Muslims had fielded Tayyab Hussain and the Janata Party Khurshid Ahmed. In Mahendergarh there were over 2.4 lakh Ahirs and their undisputed leader was the Congress-I candidate, Rao Birendra Singh, though he too lost in the 1977 elections. The Congress-I also claimed Sirsa, where its candidate, Dalbir Singh, was elected in 1967 and 1971.

With large areas of Haryana in the grip of drought, voters of this predominantly agricultural state were more concerned about prospects of their crops than those of political parties in the Lok Sabha poll in 1980. The general attitude of apathy towards the elections had, if anything been, aggravated by the spate of defections which had confused and dismayed them.

Figures pertaining to nominations is given in Table 5.1.

A Constituency-wise number of contestants is given in Table 5.2.

Table 5.1 : Candidates Nominated, Nominations Rejected, Withdrawn and Contested

		Nominated			*Nominations Rejected*			*Withdrawn*			*Contestants*			*Forfeited Deposits*		
Cat.	Seats	M	*W*	*T*	*M*	*W*	*T*	*M*	*W*	*T*	*M*	*W*	*T*	*M*	*W*	*T*
GEN	8	188	6	194	3	–	3	70	3	73	115	3	118	94	1	95
SC	2	28	2	30	3	–	3	8	–	8	17	2	19	11	2	13
ST	–	–	–	–	–	–	–	–	–	–	–	–	–	–	–	–
Total	10	216	8	224	6	–	6	78	3	81	132	5	137	105	3	108

Source: Report, Lok Sabha Elections, 1980.

As per Table 5.1, a total 224 nomination, were filed including of women, whereas 5 women finally contested the election against the big number 132 of men.

Table 5.2 : Contests According to No. of Candidates

No.of Seats	*Uncon-tested*	*Number of Seats Contested by Candidates*											*Details of above*	*No. of candidates*
10	–	–	–	–	–	–	2	–	–	1	1	6	1(12),2(15), 1(17), 1(19) and 1(24)	137

Source: Report, Lok Sabha Elections, 1980.

A total of 137 candidates contested the Lok Sabha polls in 1980. The number of contestants varied from 12 to

Caste in Electoral Politics

The caste factor and other social considerations undoubtedly played a key role in determining the pattern of voting in rural areas. This vital aspect had been kept in mind by each of the three contenders – the Janata Party, the Lok Dal and the Congress-I – while selecting candidates in 1980.

All of them wooed the landowning community, comprising mainly Jats. The Lok Dal, which professed to be a rural oriented party drawing inspiration from the then Haryana caretaker prime minister, Charan Singh, had sought to give political expression to the peasantry's economic and other demands. Sonepat had 2.7 lakh Jat votes and Rohtak 2.66 lakh.

A large section of landowners in Haryana had social ties across the Yamuna in U.P., thought that the main seats of their culture were Rohtak and Hissar. They had also been under Arya Samaj influence. The task of securing their support was thus obviously easier for a party which assured them of higher prices for their produce and adequate supply of water, power and other inputs, especially from a socio-religious platform.

The caste factor has dominated the election scene in Haryana and the contestants had no reluctance about basing their electoral arithmetic mainly on it. They did talk about economic issues, the evils of emergency, the law and order situation, high prices and shortages, but in their hearts they were convinced that it was caste which would determine their electoral fortunes.

Slogans against the emergency and its perpetrator, the charge against Charan Singh of being the destroyer of Janata unity or the Lok Dal's countercharge of the Janata having been captured by communal forces, did not appeal to the voters, and hence, could not influence the election results.

The contestants were mobilizing support on the basis of their castes, "*gotras*", "sub-castes" and "*khaps*" (endogamous groups) and even emphasizing the differences among the various castes and sub-castes to further their interests.

The Congress (I) camp appeared to presume that emergency excesses had become a non-issue in 1980 elections.

One of the promises being held out by the Congress (I), along with those contained in its manifestos, was that it would get the Sutlej-Yamuna link completed in both Haryana and Punjab. Its leaders asserted that the development efforts had come to a standstill in Haryana since the Janata Party came to power.

On the other hand, Janata campaigners emphasized that as much as 80 per cent of the budget was being spent on the rural areas now, while the Congress had "hardly done anything" to eradicate poverty during its 30-years rule, the Janata government had, for the first time, given earnest attention to the promotion of rural development.

The Lok Dal hoped to cash in on the esteem in which Charan Singh and Devi Lal were held by farmers. Its campaign underscored the large-scale relief operations undertaken by the Devi Lal ministry after the devastating floods in 1977.

Devi Lal, they pointed out, had offered matching grants to panchayats for rural development work and initiated a big programme for construction of harijan "*chaupals*". This, according to them, could be adequate to reassure the weaker sections that the landowning community had no animosity against the Scheduled Castes.

The land-owning community by itself did have some decisive say since the Jats constituted a sizable electors in many of the Lok Sabha constituencies. To be specific, they were a force to reckon with in at least five constituencies. Two constituencies, Sirsa and Ambala, were reserved for the Scheduled Castes.

In 1977, Jat candidates who contested the poll on the Janata ticket were returned from Sonepat, Rohtak, Bhiwani and Hissar. Another representative of this community was added to the Janata list after the Karnal Lok Sabha by-election.

Following the split in the Janata Party in 1979, MPs from Faridabad, Mahendergarh, Bhiwani, Kurukshetra and Karnal joined the Lok Dal which compelled to seek alternative candidates for at least six of the seats won by those who had chosen to remain loyal to the Janata Party.

Thanks to the caste appeal, every political party faced a scramble for its ticket from Jat aspirants. But the selectors of every party faced two problems. First, Jat voters by themselves could ensure the victory of candidates belonging to their caste. Secondly, Jats were divided into two groups. This had naturally impelled even fielding Jat candidates to forge political alignments with locally influencial non-Jat groups like Rajputs, Brahmins, Ahirs, Gujjars, Aroras and Punjabis.

The state Lok Dal President and former Chief Minister, Devi Lal, in 1980, decided to challenge Mukhtiar Singh, his Janata counterpart, in Sonepat, which had returned him in 1977. He had shifted Mani Ram Bagri from Mathura in U.P. to another Jat bastion, Hissar, leaving Mrs. Chandravati to fend for herself in Bhiwani where she faced a formidable rival, Bansi Lal once again.

Swami Indervesh had been shifted to Rohtak to challenge Sher Singh of the Janata Party.

Two of the Congress (U) Nihal Singh in Mahendergarh and Ranbir Singh in Rohtak, had filed nomination papers on the Lok Dal ticket. Apparently, the Lok Dal was unable to find anyone more suitable than Nihal Singh to oppose Birendra Singh, Congress (I) MLA, in the Ahir-dominated Mahendergarh constituency which was considered the latter's pocket-borough.

The Janata Party had selected six new candidates, including the local government minister, Khurshid Ahmed (Meo-dominated Fridabad), Ram Bilas Sharma (Mahendergarh), the Finance Minister, Balwant Rai Tayal (Bhiwani), Kersa Ram (Sirsa-reserved), Bhisan Singh (Kurukshetra) and Mrs. Sushma Swaraj, former Labour Minister (Karnal).

The Lok Dal had shifted Raghbir Singh from Kurukshetra to Karnal in place of M.S. Lathar, who had been dropped. Manohar Lal Saini had been shifted from his former constituency of Mahendergarh to Kurukshetra, while Swami Indervesh had been fielded in Rohtak.

The caste composition of the electorate could not have been overlooked by the Congress (I) when it selected Birendra Singh for Mahendergarh, Bansi Lal for Bhiwani and Tayyab Hussain for Faridabad.

In the 1977 elections, the Janata Party made a clean sweep of all the 10 seats, whereas in 1971 the Congress had won seven and the Vishal Haryana Party and the Jana Sangh 3 seats at that time. In the previous Assembly elections, the Janata had won 74 seats and the Congress three. But the latter's strength went up to eight with the joining of five Vishal Haryana Party legislators. In a house of 90, the Janata now had a strength of 47 and the Lok Dal 33.

Before the 1980 elections the general picture of electors in individual constituencies was as under:

Rohtak

This was often described as the heart of Haryana and hub of Jat politics, with over 2,50,000 Jat votes. Sher Singh, a former Congress man, won on the Janata ticket from here in 1977, trouncing his Congress rival by about 2,60,000 votes. He had been elected as a Congress candidate from Jhajjar in 1971 while Mukhtiar Singh (Jana Sangh) had won from Rohtak which consisted of the Sonepat area at that time. Both happened to belong to the Jat community. The erstwhile Jana Sangh had a pocket of influence in the city but the winning margin came from the villages.

Sonepat

Mukhtiar Singh Malik of the Janata had been winning from here not because of the Jana Sangh influence but due to support of his caste group. He won in 1977 as the Janata candidate and in 1971 as the Jana Sangh candidate.

Faridabad

The constituency, earlier known as Gurgaon, had seen big battles between two families of Meo Muslims who formed the largest single community here. Khurshid Ahmed of the Janata and Tayyab Hussain of the Congress (I) clashed again. The Janata wave in 1977 helped Dharamvir Vashisht win against both the Meo veterans but his margin of victory was rather small as compared to other contestants in Haryana. Together the two Meo leaders had polled more votes than Vashisht but the advantage of split in the Meo votes apparently went to him. Tayyab Hussain had won in 1971 but at that time, Khurshid Ahmed was not in the contest. A new factor in 1980 was the labour trouble in Faridabad which went as it was bound to go, against the Janata, it being the ruling party in the state.

Mahendergarh

The largest single community here was of Ahirs, a community to which

Rao Birendra Singh belonged. The Gujjars, more or less a parallel community, also were in a large number in the constituency. Almost totally rural, the constituency elected Manohar Lal Saini, a lightweight member of a minority community, in 1977, because of the Janata wave. Rao Birendra Singh was defeated though he got about 2,00,000 votes against Saini's 2,50,000. In 1971, the Rao had won on the Vishal Haryana Party ticket with a small margin of about 2,000 votes over his Congress rival. However, the VHP was a part of Congress (I) while the Janata had split into Janata and Lok Dal.

Bhiwani

The constituency, most of which was in Hissar earlier, was formed only before the 1977 general election, possibly for Bansi Lal. It saw him humbled in the very first election he contested to the Lok Sabha. He was defeated by Mrs. Chandrawati of the Janata in 1977 in virtually a straight contest, by over 1,70,000 votes.

Hissar

Two Mani Rams – Mani Ram Bagri and Mani Ram Godara – had clashed in the constituency earlier too. They did so in 1980 on hebalf of the Lok Dal and the Congress (I) with Inder Singh Sheokand of the Janata who was elected in 1977 being the third main candidate. Godara had won in 1971 defeating Bagri, who represented SSP at that time, by about 86,000 votes. Bagri had moved to Mathura in 1977 and so Sheokand trounced Jaswant Singh (Congress) by a big margin. The Jind area of the constituency was a strong pocket of the Lok Dal. Chief Minister Bhajan Lal belonged to this area and exerted his influence for the Janata candidate, though became a Congress (I) member later.

Sirsa

The reserved constituency had elected Chand Ram, of the Janata Party in 1977. Before him, it used to be a Congress seat having elected Dalbir Singh, President of the Haryana Congress (I). In 1971, Chand Ram was vanquished and, rendered to this position by the Lok Dal which he had joined two months earlier but had left later to become a Congress (I) man.

Karnal

It was traditionally a Congress seat where the Jana Sangh had got some foothold. Karnal and Panipat were taken from the Congress by the Janata in 1977 and retained by it in a by-election in 1978 though with a very reduced margin. In fact, it was the first by election after the Congress defeat in the north. Bhagwat Dayal Sharma had won it in 1977 and M.S. Lather in 1978. Madho Ram of the Congress had defeated Rameshwaranand (Jana Sangh) in 1971, the latter having won the seat earlier. Somehow, it had come to known as a seat for a Brahmin candidate and most parties looked for Brahmin candidates. It also had a good number of Punjabi settlers who mattered in the elections.

Kurukshetra

Parts of this constituency were earlier known as Kaithal from where Gulzari Lal Nanda of the Congress had won in 1971 defeating his nearest rival who belonged to Congress-O. Together, they polled almost three-fourths of the total votes and it was virtually a Congress stronghold. Most of it was rural with a Jana Sangh pocket in the twin towns of Yamunanagar and Jagadhri. Like in Karnal, there was a good number of Sikhs and other Punjabi settlers. In 1971, Raghbir Singh won against the Congress candidate, D.D. Puri, with a big margin.

Ambala

This was the second reserved constituency in Haryana which had the twin-towns of Ambala city and Ambala cantonment with the erstwhile Jana Sangh and Congress (O) sharing influence among the urban population. The Congress used to monopolize the rural vote until it got a setback in 1977 when an erstwhile Jana Sangh leader, Suraj Bhan, won on the Janata ticket defeating Ram Prakash of the Congress, with massive margin who had defeated Suraj Bhan in 1971. Earlier too, it had returned the Congress candidates.

Voting and Results

The number of electors and voters is given in Tables 5.3 and 5.4.

Table 5.3 : Electors and Voters, 1980

Type of Const.	*No. of Seat*	*Total Electors*			*Electors who Voted*		
		M	*W*	*T*	*M*	*W*	*T*
Gen	8	2973101	2631433	5604534	2079855	1552598	3632453
SC	2	702709	605722	1308431	466934	377139	844073
ST	–	–	–	–	–	–	–
Total	10	3675810	3237155	6912965	2546789	1929737	4476526

Source: Report, Lok Sabha Elections, 1980.

Table 5.4 : Electors, Voters etc.

Name of Constituency	*Electors*			*Electors who Voted*		
	M	*W*	*T*	*M*	*W*	*T*
Ambala(SC)	329264	266211	615475	234427	186507	420934
Kurukshetra	346391	303822	650213	253325	181653	434978
Karnal	356103	310945	667048	251105	188365	439470
Sonepat	376450	332523	708973	272455	202958	475413
Rohtak	363552	326463	690015	244142	186747	430889
Faridabad	401762	339072	740832	268784	181143	449927
Mahendergarh	403089	376133	779222	270307	228442	498745
Bhiwani	375795	333270	709065	265861	208242	474103
Hissar	349961	309205	659166	253876	175052	428928
Sirsa (SC)	373445	319511	692956	232507	190632	423139
Total	3675810	3237155	6912965	2546789	1929737	4476526

Source: Report, Lok Sabha Elections, 1980.

The number of valid votes, rejected votes is given in Table 5.5.

Table 5.5: Valid Votes Polled, Rejected Votes and No. of Polling Stations

Type of Cont.	*Valid Votes Polled*	*Rejected Votes*	*No. of Polling Stations*	*Percentage of Electors who voted*
Gen	3555164	77289	6183	64.81
SC	826121	17952	1469	64.51
ST	–	–	–	–
Total	4381285	95241	7852	64.76

Source: Report, Lok Sabha Elections, 1980.

A party-wise break-up of votes polled is given in Table 5.6.

Table 5.6 : Votes Polled and Percentage According to Parties, 1980

No.of Seats		*No. & Percentage cf valid Votes polled by National Parties*									
Uncont-ested	*Cont-ested*	*INC(I)*	*INC(U)*	*JNP*	*JNP(S)*	*CPI*	*CPM*		*State Parties*	*Regd. Parties*	*IND*
	10	4381285	1426261 32.55	3162 0.07	1232914 28.14	1468713 33.52	–	–	1650 0.04	12927 0.30	235638 5.38

Source: Report, Lok Sabha Elections, 1980.

As per Table 5.3, we have men-women electors ratio of 53.17:46.83 per cent whereas as it is 56.89:43.11 per cent in votes polled in 1980 Lok Sabha elections. The Scheduled Caste as electors were 18.92 per cent and 18.85 per cent as voters.

From constituency-wise perspective, Mahendergarh had the highest number of electors as well as voters whereas the Ambala has the lowest numbers in this regard as shown in Table 5.4.

The final picture of percentage of votes polled by various parties was: Total electorate 69,12,210; votes polled 44,76,526; the Congress(I) 14,26,261 (32.55 per cent), the Janata Party 12,32,914 (28.14 per cent), the Lok Dal 14,68,713 (33.52 per cent), the Congress (U) 3,182 (0.07 per cent), the SUCI 1,982 (0.04 per cent), the Ram Rajya Parishad RPI(K) 10,479 (0.24 per cent), RPI 2,850 (0.07 per cent) and Independents 2,28,478 (5.22 per cent).

A constituency-wise view of valid and rejected votes is given in Table 5.7.

Table 5.7 : Valid Votes Polled, Rejected Votes & No. of Polling Stations

Name of Constituency	*Valid Votes Polled*	*Rejected Votes*	*No. of Polling Stations*	*Percentage of Electors who voted*
Ambala(SC)	412408	8526	682	68.39
Kurukshetra	425976	9002	710	66.90
Karnal	430635	8835	707	65.88
Sonepat	465269	10144	793	67.06
Rohtak	420140	10749	752	62.45
Faridabad	440853	9074	807	60.73
Mahendergarh	487566	11179	896	64.00
Bhiwani	465020	9083	790	66.86
Hissar	419705	9223	728	65.07
Sirsa (SC)	413713	9426	787	61.06
Total	4381285	95241	7652	64.76

Source : Report, Lok Sabha Elections, 1980.

The Lok Dal candidates led in 44 of the 90 Assembly segments of the 10 Lok Sabha constituencies in Haryana, according to analysis of the election results. The Congress (I) led in 29 segments and the Janata Party only in 17.

The analysis showed that though the Lok Dal had polled the maximum votes, its performance in the city and town segments was very poor.

Figures pertaining to election results are shown in Table 5.8.

The Janata Party and the Congress (I) fared badly in the rural segments. The Janata Party polled less than 10,000 votes in 26 segments and the Congress (I) in 19 segments.

Table 5.8 : Election Results, 1980

Party	*Contested*	*Total Electorals*						
		Valid votes	*%*	*Invalid votes*	*%*	*Forfeited*	*%*	*Seat won*
Janata(S)	10	1468713				1		4
Congress(I)	10	1426261				–		5
Janata	10	1232914				–		1
RPK	3	6194				3		–
Ramrajya	3	4776				3		–
Cong.(A)	2	3182				2		–
SOC	1	1952				1		–
Forward	1	1650				1		–
Ind.	97	235638				97		–
Total	137	4387285			2.12	108	78.83	10

Source : Election Report on the Sixth General Election, 1980.

Rao Birendra Singh (Congress-I), Devi Lal and Swami Indervesh (both Lok Dal) secured more than 50 per cent of the total votes polled in their respective constituencies.

The election results had exploded the myth of the caste factor being decisive in Haryana. It seems true that only Jats had been elected from the Jat-dominated constituencies (Rohtak, Sonepat, Hissar and Bhiwani) and that a strong non-Jat contender (Balwant Rai Tayal) was rejected by the Jats in Bhiwani. But then it belied the earlier assumption that only a Jat follower of Charan Singh could be successful, because Bansi Lal of the Congress-I had won despite the fact that he was opposed, among others by Mrs. Chandrawati of the Lok Dal. The idea that the Lok Dal could win only on the basis of the Jat votes had been disproved in Kurukshetra, too, where Manohar Lal Saini had won on the Lok Dal ticket. This suggested that the Lok Dal appeal had been carried to non-Jat farmers too, particularly the Rors.

In Faridabad, the Janata Party failed to gauge public resentment over the October incidents in which eight workers were killed and did not take effective steps to heal the wounds. Bhajan Lal admitted that the party lost in Faridabad mainly because the workers did not vote for it. Again the party relied too much on the emotional appeal of Jagjivan Ram and took it for granted that the bulk of the Harijans (*Chamars*) would support its candidates. The expectation had not come true in all constituencies.

The voting trend also belied the idea of a Jana Sanghs hold in urban areas. Mrs. Sushma Swaraj did not get the desired lead in Karnal and Panipat against her Congress-I rival, Chiranji Lal Sharma.

The Congress-I, however, managed to keep its traditional pockets safe in 1980. Dalbir Singh had been winning the Sirsa seat since 1967 (with an exception in 1977) and the Karnal seat had also remained with the party.

The poll figures were also interesting. The Congress-I got five seats when it got 24 lakh votes. The Lok Dal won four seats with 13.68 lakh votes and the Janata which polled 12.23 lakh votes got only one seat. This showed that the popularity was not proportionately reflected in the election results. In 1971, the Congress had won seven seats with 15.72 lakh votes.

The Congress-Lok Dal alliance had been thrashed in Mahendergarh where Rao Nihal Singh forfeited his security deposit as against Rao Birendra Singh (Congress-I) who secured 51 per cent of the votes polled. Of the four members of the dissolved Lok Sabha fielded again by the Janata, only one (Suraj Bhan) had won in 1980.

The groups like RRP, RPII, SUC remained confined to Karnal, Faridabad, Bhiwani and Sirsa while getting less than one per cent votes.

Performance of Parties

Congress: a constituency-wise performance of the party is given in Table 5.9.

Table 5.9 : Performance of the Congress : A Constituency-wise View

Constituencies	*Votes Polled*	*%age*
Ambala (Res.)	142998	34.7
Kurukshetra	109573	25.7
Karnal	151786	35.3
Sonepat	97572	21.0
Rohtak	78396	18.7
Faridabad	151665	34.4
Mahendergarh	247238	50.7
Bhiwani	194437	41.8
Hissar	99363	23.7
Sirsa	153233	37.0

Source: Report, Lok Sabha Elections, 1980.

The performance of the Janata Party in different constituencies is highlighted in Table 5.10.

Table 5.10 : Performance of the Janta Party (S) : A Constituency-wise View

Constituencies	*Votes Polled*	*%age*
Ambala (Res.)	100931	24.5
Kurukshetra	159196	33.4
Karnal	117861	22.4
Sonepat	255363	54.7
Rohtak	219004	52.1
Faridabad	119043	27.0
Mahendergarh	73931	15.2
Bhiwani	99578	21.4
Hissar	192074	45.8
Sirsa	131732	31.8

Source: Report, Lok Sabha Elections, 1980.

The show of Janata Party is pointed out in Table 5.11.

Table 5.11 : Performance of the Janata Party : A Constituency-wise View

Constituencies	*Votes Polled*	*%age*
Ambala (Res.)	145293	35.2
Kurukshetra	131267	30.8
Karnal	129458	30.1
Sonepat	87344	18.8
Rohtak	97564	23.7
Faridabad	159507	34.4
Mahendergarh	155891	32.0
Bhiwani	144366	31.0
Hissar	93228	22.2
Sirsa (Res.)	98996	23.5

Source : Report, Lok Sabha Elections, 1980.

As per Table 5.10, the Janata Party (S) electoral base declined sharply in all constituencies in comparison to 1977 Lok Sabha elections whereas the base of the Congress rose and it captured 5 of the 10 seats geting more than 35 per cent votes there. However, the Janata Party could get one seat despite having more than 30 per cent votes in 6 constituencies as shown in Table 5.11.

6

Parliamentary Elections, 1984

This time, Haryana like other neighbouring states, has surprised by returning all the 10 Congress candidates, never before this party had secured such a grand victory either in bagging seats or in polling votes (54.95%). The highest swing to Congress (I) vote percentage as compared to 1980 elections has been in Haryana (22.6%). Earlier in 1967, and 1971, the Congress won 7 out of 9 seats had polled 44.1 per cent and 52 per cent votes respectively.

In 1977, the Congress with 17.95 per cent of votes could not get a single seat as the anti-Congress wave swept the state and all the 10 seats went to Janata Party with 70.35 per cent – highest since 1966 – of votes. In 1980, despite the Indira wave, the Congress (I) could win only 5 out of the 10 seats and got 32.29 per cent of the votes polled. The Lok Dal with 33.75 per cent of the votes, higher than the Congress (I) could get 4 seats and 1 seat was secured by Janata Party with 28.11 per cent of the votes.

Nomination Politics

A category-wise narration of nomination etc. is given in Table 6.1.

Nomination is an important phase of election. With the selection of a candidate, the battle is said to be half won. During this phase, factionalism within political parties swings to the surface and the party leaders have to accommodate various interests for the final victory. In Haryana, both Congress as well as opposition parties had to face this tussle. In Congress (I) besides Bansi Lal's and Chief Minister Bhajan Lal's rival camps, there were several other factions and a temporary

Table 6.1 : Candidates Nominated, Withdrawn, Contested etc

Name of State: Haryana		Nominated			Nominations Rejected			Withdrawn			Contestants			Forfeited Deposite		
Cat.	*Seats*	*M*	*W*	*T*	*M*	*W*	*T*	*M*	*W*	*T*	*M*	*W*	*T*	*M*	*W*	*T*
GEN	8	302	16	318	7	–	7	143	6	149	152	10	162	136	10	146
SC	2	65	–	65	2	–	2	25	–	25	38	–	38	34	–	34
ST	–	–	–	–	–	–	–	–	–	–	–	–	–	–	–	–
Total	10	367	16	383	9	–	9	168	6	174	190	10	200	170	10	180

Source: Report, Lok Sabha Elections, 1984.

The nominations increased from 244 in 1980 to 383 in 1984 Lok Sabha elections and so those of women. Similarly, there was an increase in number of contestants from 137 in 1980 to 200 in 1984 as depicted in Table 6.1.

Table 6.2 : Contest According to No. of Candidates

No.of Seats	*Uncon-tested*	*Number of Seats Contested by Candidates & above Candidates*											*Details of 13 candidates & above*	*No. of candidates*
10	–	–	–	–	–	–	–	–	–	–	–	10	1(16),3(17), 1(19),1(20), 1(21),1(22) and 1(33)	200

The number of contest tents varied from 16 to 33 in different constituencies as pointed out in Table 6.2.

accommodation was brought about by the Central High Command. It was reported that three ministers of Bhajan Lal's ministry were fielded Harpal Singh, Kurukshetra, Birender Singh Hissar, and Rahim Khan Faridabad, were reluctant to fight the elections and their names were recommended to ease them out of the state politics by the Chief Minister.

The name of one more, S.S. Surjewala was dropped only when this fact was brought to the notice of the High Command, by his supporters. One dominant personality of Haryana, Chand Ram then one of the General Secretaries of AICC, could not get the party nomination from Ambala (Reserved Seat) as he was considered a sworn enemy of Jagjivan Ram who was being wooed by Congress (I) for alliance during the nomination stage. It was reported from reliable sources that only two persons nominated from Ambala, Ram Parkash and from Sonepat, Dharampal Malik had their allegiance to Bhajan Lal.

The opposition parties too suffered from intra-party factionalism and their dissensions. The Lok Dal-BJP Janata alliance which emerged afterwards also could not keep itself intact because of differences between the top leaders, Charan Singh and Chander Shekhar. A new front of convenience and necessity, although the antipathy between Charan Singh and Jagjivan Ram is a well known fact, was forged upon by DMKP-Congress (J) after the announcement of the elections which represented opposite interests. This alliance was felt unavoidable by Devi Lal on the ground that merely his and Charan Singh's traditional support in the state would not ensure victory of their candidates in view of new caste-alignment (non-Jat) in Haryana brought about by Bhajan Lal during the 1983 Lok Sabha bye-elections in which he himself was defeated. The seat distribution between the two alliance partners also sowed seeds of discontention among the rank and file of the parties and resulted into rebel Lok Dal candidates, Swami Indra Vesh-Faridabad, Mani Ram Bagri-Rohtak and Gurdial Singh Saini-Kurukshetra, Sumitra Devi-Hissar in the field and the defection of some others to the Congress fold.

In all, 383 candidates filed their nominations, 8 were rejected, and 175 withdrew their nominations, 200 candidates including 10 women were left in the field. Congress (I) contested all the 10 seats, BJP-6, Janata-6, DMKP (Lok Dal)-6, Congress (J)-4, CPI-1, 167 were

Independents. There was an alliance of DMKP-Congress (J) for elections. Thus, the contests were mainly triangular or 4 cornered and in two constituencies, it was a straight one. 9577 polling stations were established out of which 769 were for Harijans and weaker-sections of society for the first time to avoid intimidation by the dominant castes. No special polling stations were made for women.

Campaign and Issues

The current elections, after the expiry of the normal term of 5 years were preceded by certain unusual political upheavals in the country – the tension in Punjab culminating to 'Blue Star Operation' and consequent thereof assassination of Prime Minister Indira Gandhi and the occurrence of riots and violence. Although there were apprehensions about the postponement of elections by Mrs. Gandhi after the Punjab events, her physical elimination rather made Rajiv Gandhi to pre-pone the same to cash on the sympathy factor. The election was fought by the Congress Party on the issue of 'danger to the country' from within and without aiming at its disintegration and that only the Congress (I) could and would save the country by keeping it together. The assassination was considered as a part of a vicious and unholy plan to divide India. On the economic front, it promised to implement the policy to give substance to the slogan 'food, work and productivity'. The opposition parties blamed Congress (I) for the present unfortunate conditions in Punjab, deteriorating law and order, rising prices, and inflation. They also raised the issue for more state autonomy.

In Haryana also these national issues were raised and top ranking central party leaders like Rajiv Gandhi, Chandra Shekhar, Charan Singh, Jagjivan Ram and L.K. Advani toured the various constituencies of Haryana and campaigned for their respective parties. But in Haryana the parochial and local loyalties were also an important issue. Every political party planned its strategy on caste and community alignments. The developmental issues were also raised to make state politics as result oriented. DMKP tried to raise the cause of peasantry and impressed upon the rural people that if returned to power it will strive for better terms of trade between the country side and cities and for a greater share of government benefits for farmers.

The Congress (I) stressed on the need to reform educational system. The opposition also raised the issues of shortage of electricity, water, mal-administration, corruption and defections but these did not have much impact on the masses. The Congress (I) with massive men, money and mass-media organized election campaign which reached the remotest corner of the country. The TV, Radio coverage of Mrs. Gandhi's last rites, advertisements in almost all newspapers, and periodicals with catchy slogans, use of video films, playing of pre-recorded cassettes, young Prime Minister's clean image and pleasant personality helped the ruling party to a great extent. The opposition and Independent candidates could not afford such a luxury, for want of financial resources. Although the campaign and the polling was peaceful in the state, yet a few instances of poll violence were reported in Hissar constituency. In Mahendergarh, the Election Commission had to order re-poll in three polling stations on account of booth-capturing. At places, a few fake voters were also discovered.

Ambala, a reserved constituency, has an electorate of 694840 inhabiting the 9 segments of State Assembly, Ambala, Ambala Cantt., Kalka, Naraingarh, Sadhaura, Naggal, Mulana, Jagadhri and Chachrauli. 69.85 per cent of the electorate, 485364 exercised their voting right. Ram Parkash of Congress (I) secured 283062 votes and won the seat from his known political opponent Suraj Bhan of BJP, sitting MP with a very good margin of 177352 votes in almost a straight contest in 1980 elections.

This time 6 per cent Sikh votes were crucial in this constituency. As a result of this factor, the electioneering, at times, took a communal character, although the position of the rival parties seemed equal. Harijans, 23.92 per cent and backward class, 15.4 per cent votes were likely to be divided. Congress (I) wooed Brahmin and Harijan votes while the DMKP harped on 10 per cent Jat and 4 per cent Muslim electorate.

Kurukshetra witnessed a bitterly contested political battle by four stalwarts nominated by different parties and 15 Independents. The Congress (I) put up State Agriculture Minister Harpal Singh, a Punjabi Hindu, former Party President of the state unit. The sitting MP Manoharlal Saini was nominated by the DMKP Kamla Verma, belonging to backward class and President of Haryana BJP who had been a State Minister for Health, was the third candidate while the fourth was the Janata Party nominee, Bishen Singh. The constituency had an electorate of 727716. The votes polled were 516555 (70.9 per cent). The segments of Kurukshetra parliamentary constituency are Thanesar, Pehowa, Gulha (Res.), Kaithal, Pundri, Pai, Shahbad, Yamunanagar and Radaur (Res.).

Karnal, having an electorate of 746675, had the largest number of candidates-33 in the state and of these only 4 were party nominees and the rest Independents. Since Haryana's creation, it has been considered a Brahmin constituency although they number only 7.5 per cent . The biggest vote-bank here is that of Harijans who comprise about 19 per cent followed by backward class 16 per cent, Punjabi Hindus 14 per cent, Jats 13 per cent, Muslims 12.5 per cent and Sikhs 7.5 per cent settled in the assembly segments of Karnal, Nilokhery, Indri, Jundla (Res.), Gharaunda, Asandh (Res.), Panipat, Samalkha and Naulatha.

Chiranji Lal Sharma, the sitting MP of the Congress, won the seat by polling 247063 votes, out of 516886 votes polled (69.2 per cent), Devi Singh of Congress (J) supported by DMKP, got 14811 votes. Ajit Singh of Janata Party received 2279 and Mrs. Sushma Swaraj of BJP, also a Brahmin, polled 77870 votes. The margin between the two top contestants was 78952. Earlier in 1980 General Elections, Mrs. Swaraj was defeated by Mr. Sharma by a margin of 22300 votes.

Sonepat constituency was carved out in 1971 and the contest here was the toughest one in Haryana parliamentary elections in 1984, six assembly segments fell in Sonepat, Kailana, Rai, Rohat, Baroda (Res.) and Gohana whereas Julana (Res.) and Safidon in Jind district and Bahadurgarh.

Jats account for nearly 30 per cent of the total electorate in this constituency. There were some other communities strong-holds such as Punjabi Hindus – about 15 per cent and Sikhs – nearly 10,000. While traditionally, the Punjabi Hindus had been the back-bone of BJP, supporters of Congress (I) were Sikhs and the votes of Brahmin, Harijans and backward classes have generally been divided. The BJP neither nominated anyone for this seat nor issued any directive in favour of any other candidate, although Sonepat segment returned the BJP candidate Devi Das in 1982 election. In the bye-election, the BJP had deserted Lok Dal, their NDA partner, but supported Congress (I) candidate Rizk Ram to see the fall of DMKP leader Devi Lal, who was helped by Sikhs owing to his alignment with Akalis as well as Nihang Sikhs. The same trend seemed to have prevailed this time also.

Rohtak parliamentary constituency fell in the Jat heartland of the state. The Assembly segments are Rohtak, Hassangarh, Kiloi, Meham, Kalanaur (Res.), Beri, Sahlawas, Jhajjar (Res.) and Badli. It had an electorate of 742031. The total votes polled were 446881 (60.22 per cent). In addition to 16 Independents, only 3 main political parties put up their candidates, i.e. Congress (I) – Hardwari Lal, DMKP – Dr. Sarup Singh and BJP – Hukam Chand Goel.

The community-wise electorate were — Jats-2.8 lakhs, Brahmins-60,000, Punjabi Hindus-72,000, Harijans-1.40 lakhs, Mahajans-28,000, Sainis-10,000, Ahirs-45,000, Rajputs-16,000 and Gujjars-5,000.

Mahendergarh, the southern constituency of Haryana, bordering Rajasthan, U.P., and Delhi consisted of Assembly segments of Mahendergarh, Sohna, Gurgaon, Pataudi (Res.), Bawal (Res.), Rewari, Jatusana, Ateli and Narnaul. It had an electorate of 855878 and dominated by Ahirs. There were 4 party candidates and 14 Independents including 2 women.

Besides his personal image, caste factor was also in favour of the Congress candidate as he got the support of all agricultural castes which comprise about 50 per cent of the electorate. The influence of Congress (I) MLA Dharam Bir Gauba in Gurgaon helped him get many of the Punjabi Hindu votes (about 44,000). State Industries Minister Smt. Shakuntala Bhagwaria had active support from all sections of society. The voting strength of other communities was Brahmins, 62,000, Harijan Chamars-95,000, Harijan non-Chamars-37,000 and Backward classes-76,000. The Congress (I) got a big chunk of the Harijan and backward caste votes.

Faridabad had the largest electorate of 869828 including 394141 women in the state and has been dominated by the politics of Meo-Muslims (12.15 lakhs) generally, who inhabit the Mewat belt in the eastern districts of Faridabad and Gurgaon. The community-wise break-up of voters was 1.25 lakh-Jats, 77,000-Punjabi Hindus, 60,000-

Brahmins, 35,000-Mahajans, 33,000-Rajputs, 30,000-Balmikis, 11,000-Gujjars and Ahirs, 21,000-Sikhs, 92,000-Chamar Harijans. There were about 2 lakh people who worked in industrial units in the constituency including some 50,000 from other states of India. The constituency, contagious to Delhi, has a large number of industries. It has Assembly segments of Faridabad, Nuh, Hathin, Hassanpur (Res.), Mewla Maharajpur, Palwal, Ferozepur-Jhirka, Taoru and Ballabgarh.

There was a straight contest in this constituency between the Congress (I) nominee Rahim Khan, State Minister for Irrigation and Power belonging to 'Chharaklot' sub-caste of Meos and Tayyab Hussain of 'Dhengal' sub-caste of the same community put up by Congress (J) and supported by DMKP, CPI and CPI(M). Among the 19 Independent candidates in the field, 2 were prominent – Swami Indervesh sitting MP, Rohtak, a Jat, rebel from DMKP on the denial of ticket, banking upon the help of BJP and Arya Samaj and Chheti Lal Verma, multi-millionaire contractor, supported by Jats.

Bhiwani had an electorate of 782290 of the 9 Assembly segments, Adampur and Hansi fell in Hissar District and Bhiwani, Bawani-Khera, Tosham Mundhal-khurd, Dadri, Badhra and Loharu in Bhiwani district itself. There were 2.53 lakh Jats, 66330-Brahmins, 45265-Rajputs, 38050-Mahajans, 33562-Ahirs, 12669-Sainis, 29552-Aroras, 7977-Gujjars, 4758-Bishnois, 37479-Dhanaks, 18220-Balmikis, 79917 Chamars and 14914 others.

Hissar parliamentary constituency is spread over two districts – Narwana, Kalyat, Uchhana-kalan, Rajaund and Jind in Jind district and Barwala, Narnaul, Ghirai and Hissar in Hissar destrict itself. It had an electorate of 737667. There were 3 party candidates and 14 Independents including 2 women.

Hissar is considered as the bastion of Jats, who have 2.6 lakh votes. The strength of other major communities was Rajputs-10,000, Mahajans-50,000, Brahmins-60,000, Khatri-Aroras-42,000, Chamar Harijans-68,000, Balmiki and Dhanak Harijans-57,000, Sikhs-15,000 and backward castes 32,000, Jat and Harijans votes were divided; other Hindu votes except those of Sikhs, were captured by Congress (I). Of the 9 Assembly segments, it had the support of 8. Although it had won

4 segments in 1982 elections, and 3 Lok Dal MLAs and one Independent later defected to Congress (I).

Sirsa (Res.) is the biggest constituency spread over more than 6000 sq. kms. Having an electorate of 785461 situated in the western side of the state, bordering Punjab and Rajasthan. Out of the 9 Assembly segments—Sirsa, Dabwali, Rori, Ellanabad, Darba-kalan, Ratia, Fatehabad, Tohana and Bhatu-kalan, 6 returned Congress (I) candidates in 1982 elections, two seats went to Independents, one later defected to Congress (I) to become Minister and the other joined Janata Party and then again defected to DMKP. The 9th segment was bagged by Lok Dal.

Sikhs were considered as the decisive factor in Sirsa as they numbered about 1.15 lakhs (15 per cent of the electorate). The number of Jats the back-bone of DMKP was almost equal to those Sikhs. The strength of other sections of society was Harijans-1.45 lakhs, Punjabis-65,000, Brahmins-32,000, Mahajans-35,000, Bishnois-30,000 and BCs-55,000.

During the 1984 Lok Sabha elections, there was an electorate of 77,25,698 in Haryana with an increase of 8 lakh voters in comparison to 1980. As many as 51,63,799 voters (66.85%) exercised their franchise and the total number of invalid votes was 90,392 (1.75%).

Number of electors, voters etc. is shown in Table 6.3.

Table 6.3 : Electors, Voters, 1984

Name of State: Haryana	*Type of Const.*	*No. of Seat*	*Total Electors*			*Electors who Voted*		
			M	*W*	*T*	*M*	*W*	*T*
	Gen	8	3337306	2907083	6244389	2354339	1807152	4161491
	SC	2	804992	676565	1481557	563741	438567	1002308
	ST	–	–	–	–	–	–	–
	Total	10	4142298	3583648	7725946	2918080	2245719	5163799

Source: Report, Lok Sabha Elections, 1984.

The details of election results are given in Table 6.4.

The valid and rejected votes as per different political parties as well as constituency-wise break up are highlighted in Tables 6.5 and 6.6.

Table 6.4 : Election Results, 1984

Total Electorals = 7725946

Party	*Contested*	*Voting*	*%*	*Valid votes*	*%*	*Invalid votes*	*%*	*Forfeited*	*%*	*Seat won*
Congress	10			2787655	53.98			–		10
Congress(o)	–			–	–			–		–
Lok Dal	6			969203	19.10			1		–
Congress (J)	4			532326	10.49			1		–
BJP	6			382447	7.54			4		–
CPI(M)	–			–	–			–		–
Janata(S)	7			73108	1.44			7		–
CPI	1			44475	0.88			1		–
Ind.	166			284193	5.60			166		–
Total	200			5073407	100.00	90392	1075	180	78.83	10

Source : Report on the Eighth General Election of the House of the People in India, 1984, Vol.II, Election Commission of India, New Delhi, 1984, pp. 12-13.

As indicated in Table 6.4, the Congress won all the 10 seats with 53.98 per cent votes. The Lok Dal and the Congress (J) got 19.10 and 10.49 per cent votes receptively with no seat. The other parties and splinter groups could not save deposits of their candidates as depicted in Table 6.4.

Table 6.5 : Valid Votes Polled, Rejected Votes and No. of Polling Stations

Type of Cont.	*Valid Votes Polled*	*Rejected Votes*	*No. of Polling Stations*	*% of Votes Polled*	*% of Rejected Votes*
Gen.	4089555	71936	7894	66.64	1.73
SC	983852	18456	1683	67.65	1.84
ST	–	–	–	–	–
Total	5073407	90392	9577	66.84	1.75

Source: Report, Lok Sabha Elections, 1984.

Table 6.6 : Lok Sabha Elections, 1984 : Voters, Valid and Rejected Votes

Constituencies	*Electors*		
	Men	*Women*	*Total*
Ambala (SC)	377839	317001	694840
Kurukshetra	392477	335239	727716
Karnal	398356	348319	746675
Sonepat	418346	364159	782505
Rohtak	391872	350158	742030
Faridabad	475668	394160	869828
Mahendergarh	445644	410234	855878
Bhiwani	417918	364372	782290
Hissar	397025	340442	737467
Sirsa (SC)	427153	359564	786717
Total	4142298	3583648	7725946

Source: Report, Lok Sabha Elections, 1984.

The highest number of electors were in Faridabad-869828 leaving behind Mahendergarh to 855878, Sonepat-782505 and lowest-694840 in Ambala constituency as shown in Table 6.6.

A party-wise break up of valid votes is given in Table 6.7.

Table 6.7 : Votes Polled and Percentage According to Parties, 1984

Name of State	*No.of Seats*		*Total No.of*	*No. & Percentage of valid Votes polled by National Parties*										
	Uncont-ested	*Cont-ested*	*Valid Votes*	*INC*	*ICS*	*JNP*	*BJP*	*LKD*	*CPI*	*CPM*	*State*	*Regd Parties*	*IND Parties*	
Haryana 284112	–	10			5073407	2787655	–	73189	382447	96920344475		–	532326	–
		54.95			1.44	7.54		19.10	0.88	10.49			5.60	

Source: Report, Lok Sabha Elections, 1984.

Of the total valid votes 5073407, the Congress secured 54.95 per cent, a gain of 20.28 per cent in comparison to 1980 Lok Sabha elections whereas the Lok Dal suffered a loss of 14.64 per cent in these elections. Thus, it was all gains for the Congress fetching all 10 seats for the first time in its electoral history of the state.

A comparative picture of party-wise percentage of votes in various contituencies is given in Table 6.8.

Table 6.8 : Constituency-wise Relative Voting Strength of Parties – 1980 and 1984 Lok Sabha Elections in Haryana – Votes in Percentage

Parties Constituencies	*Year*	*Cong.(I)*	*BJP*	*Janata*	*DMKP Lok Dal*	*Cong(J) Cong(U)*	*CPI*	*Indepen-dents*
Ambala	1984	59.52	22.23	–	3.24	–	9.35	5.66
	1980	34.67	–	35.23	24.27	–	–	5.63
Kurukshetra	1984	54.08	7.35	7.95	25.92	–	–	4.70
	1980	25.72	–	30.82	35.37	–	–	6.09
Karnal	1984	48.67	15.34	0.45	–	29.18	–	6.36
	1980	35.25	–	30.06	27.37	0.24	–	6.41
Sonepat	1984	48.54	–	0.78	47.95	–	–	2.73
	1980	20.97	–	10.77	54.89	0.46	–	4.91
Rohtak	1984	49.26	5.06	–	42.22	–	–	3.46
	1980	18.60	–	23.20	52.09	–	–	6.06
Faridabad	1984	54.01	–	–	–	28.57	–	7.42
	1980	34.40	–	34.35	27.00	–	–	4.23
Mahendergarh	1984	60.68	21.98	0.92	–	12.30	–	4.12
	1980	50.70	–	31.97	15.17	–	–	2.15
Bhiwani	1984	66.00	–	–	–	30.44	–	3.56
	1980	41.81	–	31.05	21.41	–	–	5.73
Hissar	1984	51.98	–	2.32	41.39	–	–	4.31
	1980	23.67	–	22.21	45.91	–	–	8.35
Sirsa	1984	54.66	1.66	1.21	38.54	–	–	3.93
	1980	37.04	–	23.44	31.84	–	–	7.67
Total	1984	54.95	7.54	1.44	19.10	10.49	0.88	5.60
	1980	32.29	–	28.11	33.74	0.07	–	5.73

Source: 1984 Election Results as per Haryana Government Election Office, Chandigarh.
1980 Election figures—The Indian Political Science Review – Election Issue – July 1980, p. 201.

The study of constituency-wise electoral contests and the comparative voting strength of political parties, as indicated in Table 6.8 brings forth that except the Congress-I, all parties had a steep decline. All the 167 Independents and 13 party candidates lost their security deposits. Besides the winning Congress candidates, one in each constituency could secure the minimum 6 per cent of votes to avoid forfeiture of security deposit.

The Congress (I)'s highest percentage was in Bhiwani-66 per cent and the lowest in Sonepat-48.54 per cent while it secured the highest lead of 230215 votes over BJP in Mahendergarh and won the Sonepat seat by a thinnest margin of 2941 from DMKP Vice-President Ch. Devi Lal. The main opposition group, i.e. DMKP gained the highest percentage in Sonepat-47.95 per cent while in Ambala it had the lowest percentage of 3.24. Janata Party candidates had very poor show in all the 6 constituencies and all of them forfeited their security deposits. The BJP's performance had comparatively been better than that of Janata, but of the 6 candidates, two in Ambala-22.23 per cent and Mahendergarh-21.98 per cent could attain a face-saving performance. Congress (J) proved to be more effective in comparison to both the BJP and the Janata. Its only candidate out of four lost the security deposit. Its highest percentage was in Bhiwani-30.44 per cent. The DMKP-Congress (J) alliance secured 29.59 per cent of the total votes.

As compared to 1980 elections, Congress (I) gained a vote swing of 22.6 per cent. The DMKP, earlier Lok Dal came down from 33.74 per cent with 4 seats in 1980 to 19.10 per cent and drew a blank, Janata Party's fall was still steeper. It could just capture 1.44 per cent of the valid votes in 1984 elections, while in 1980, its tally was 28.11 per cent and won one seat. The BJP and the Congress (J) were not in the election field in 1980 as separate entities. The lone CPI candidate in Ambala who secured 9.35 per cent votes in his constituency works out to 0.88 per cent of the total votes in the state. The leftist parties have obviously no following in Haryana and even in the state assembly, they have not been able to send a single member since the creation of state. In 1980 Lok Sabha elections, the CPI and CPM did not nominate any candidate. However, in 1977, both the parties had put up their candidates, who obtained 0.61 and 0.03 per cent votes, respectively. With this picture, the CPI has gained marginally in the electoral politics.

As far as the 167 Independents are concerned, although their number had increased in comparison to 1980 elections, but they have not been able to improve their voting strength. It has rather marginally gone down from 5.73 per cent to 5.60 per cent. Only in Faridabad, Swami Indervesh, a rebel Lok Dal, and an industrialist could get a sizable number of votes-32228 otherwise the votes of Independent candidates ranged from the lowest figure of 187 to 6311 only.

The performance of 10 women candidates had not been creditable. Even two party nominee of the BJP, Sushma Swaraj in Karnal and Kamla Verma in Kurukshetra could not save their security deposits in spite of the fact that both had legislative experience and had worked as state ministers.

The election results show that the state leadership, by and large, remained with the agricultural castes, mainly the Jats as already stated. Out of the 8 (2 being reserved) constituencies, 6 returned agricultural caste candidates (Jats-4, Ahir-1 and Meo-1). Only Brahmin and Punjabi were elected from Karnal and Kurukshetra respectively.

The performance of women candidates in different constituencies is given in Table 6.9.

Table 6.9 : Lok Sabha Elections 1984, Women Candidates

Constituencies	*Name of Woman Candidate*	*Party*	*Votes Polled*	*%*	*Margin from elected candidates*
2- Kurukshetra	Kamla	BJP	37432	7.36	46.72
2-Kurukshetra	Kala	IND	1941	0.38	57.70
3-Karnal	Sushma Swaraj	BJP	77870	15.34	33.33
3-Karnal	Kalawati	IND	718	0.14	48.53
3-Karnal	Jasbir Kaur	IND	477	0.09	48.58
3-Karnal	Parbati	IND	384	0.08	48.59
7-Mahendergarh	Bimla Devi	IND	4967	0.83	95.85
7-Mahendergarh	Om Wati	IND	3280	0.55	60.13
9-Hissar	Sumitra Devi	IND	3248	0.67	51.31
9-Hissar	Harbans Kaur	IND	775	0.16	51.82

Source: Report, Lok Sabha Elections, 1984.

Preformance of Different Political Parties

Janata Party: its performance is given in Table 6.10.

Table 6.10 : Performance of Parties: Janata Party, 1984 Elections

Constituencies	*Votes Polled*	*%age*
Ambala	–	–
Kurukshetra	40410	7.94
Karnal	–	–
Sonepat	3920	0.78
Rohtak	–	–
Faridabad	–	–
Mahendergarh	5458	0.92
Bhiwani	–	–
Hissar	11217	2.32
Sirsa (Res.)	6115	1.20

Source: Report, Lok Sabha Elections, 1984.

The Janata Party contested in Kurukshetra, Sonepat, Mahendergarh, Hissar and Sirsa and got less than 2.5 per cent votes in 4 of them whereas it secured 7.94 per cent votes in Kurukshetra. Thus, the performance was very poor is given in Table 6.10.

The performance of Lok Dal is pointed out in Table 6.11.

Table 6.11 : Performance of the Lok Dal : 1984 Elections

Constituencies	*Votes Polled*	*%age*
Ambala (Res.)	15370	3.23
Kurukshetra	131836	25.92
Karnal	–	–
Sonepat	240550	47.95
Rohtak	185363	42.22
Faridabad	–	–
Mahendergarh	–	–
Bhiwani	–	–
Hissar	200161	41.39
Sirsa (Res.)	195923	38.54

Source: Report, Lok Sabha Elections, 1984.

The achievements of the BJP are given in Table 6.12.

Table 6.12 : Performance of the BJP : 1984 Elections

Constituencies	*Votes Polled*	*%age*
Ambala (Res.)	105710	22.23
Kurukshetra	37432	7.36
Karnal	77870	15.34
Sonepat	–	–
Rohtak	22207	5.06
Faridabad	–	–
Mahendergarh	130757	21.98
Bhiwani	–	–
Hissar	–	–
Sirsa (Res.)	8471	1.66

Source: Report, Lok Sabha Elections, 1984.

However, the performance of the Lok Dal and the BJP was some what better than the Janata Party. The Lok Dal got more than 40 per cent votes in Sonepat, Rohtak and Hissar but no seat. It secured 38.54 per cent in Sirsa and the lowest 3.23 per cent in Ambala as pointed out in Table 6.11. On the other hand the support base of the BJP declined sharply in urban areas like Ambala, Kurukshetra, Karnal, Sirsa etc. where it could get about 1.66 to 22.23 per cent votes as given in Table 6.12 However, the Congress support base improved tremendously when it got more than 48 per cent votes in all constituencies.

The performance of the Congress is shown in Table 6.13.

Table 6.13 : Performance of the Congress : 1984 Elections

Constituencies	*Votes Polled*	*%age*
Ambala (Res.)	283062	59.52
Kurukshetra	275112	54.08
Karnal	247063	48.93
Sonepat	243491	48.93
Rohtak	216294	49.27
Faridabad	285214	54.01
Mahendergarh	360971	60.68
Bhiwani	347226	66.00
Hissar	251367	51.98
Sirsa (Res.)	277855	54.66

Source: Report, Lok Sabha Elections, 1984.

7

Parliamentary Elections, 1989

The 8th Lok Sabha was dissolved about one month earlier than its term of five years and the Election Commission declared its elections in November 1989. At the moment, Devi Lal was the Deputy Prime Minister of India. During this period, the Chief Minister of Haryana was changed four times on the direction of Party High Command.

Three Lals of Haryana–Devi Lal, Bhajan Lal and Bansi Lal participated in the elections.

A view of nominational politics is given in Tables 7.1 and 7.2.

The Congress and the Doordarshi Party contested all the 10 seats, whereas the Janata Dal contested 8, SP(B) -9, Janata Party and Lok Dal-5 each, BJP-2, CPI & CPM and SPP-one each apart from 271 Independents. Thus, a total of 480 nominations were filed but after withdrawal as many as 324 candidates were in the fray.

Campaigning

The Congress promised for welfare of the Scheduled Castes to extend their reservation for another 10 years, developmental programmes for women and children and technical education for minorities, to lower the age of voting from 21 to 18 years, programmes for farmers and agricultural labour, free education for poor and girls, structural charges in the economy, rapid industrialization, more employment, reforms in public distribution systems, potable water to all, new education policy, family welfare schemes, justice for all etc.

It also announced for a strong foreign policy, more voluntary organizations, responsible administration and good governance.

The National Front declared to eliminate corruption, reforms in

Table 7.1 : Nominations, Rejections, Contestants etc.

Cat.	Seats	Nominated			Nominations Rejected			Withdrawn			Contestants		
		M	*W*	*T*	*M*	*W*	*T*	*M*	*W*	*T*	*M*	*W*	*T*
GEN	8	426	8	434	6	–	6	124	5	129	296	3	299
SC	2	44	2	46	2	–	–	17	2	19	25	–	25
ST	–	–	–	–	–	–	–	–	–	–	–	–	–
Total	10	470	10	480	8	–	8	141	7	148	321	3	324

Source : Report, Lok Sabha Elections, 1989.

Table 7.2 : Contests According to No. of Candidates

No.of Seats	*Uncontested*	*Number of Seats Contested by Candidates*											*13 & above candidates*	*Detail of 13 & above Candidates*	*No. of candidates*
10	–	–	–	–	–	–	–	–	–	1	–	–	9	1(16), 2(18), 2(24),1(28), 1(32),1(33) & 1(122)	324

Source : Report, Lok Sabha Elections, 1989.

The number of nominations increased from 383 in 1984 to 480 in 1989 Lok Sabha elections whereas the number of contestants enhanced from 200 in 1984 to 321 in 1989. Out of 10 nominated women, only 3 contested the elections as depicted in Table 7.1. The number of contestants varied from 16 to 33 in various constituencies as given in Table 7.2

electoral system to strengthen the parliamentary democracy and federalism, national unity and integrity. It promised to provide employment to minorities, more participation of women in political process, employment to youth, to strengthen the rural economy, labour welfare, freedom of press, cordial Centre-state relations, to prevent the misuse of Article 356, democratic decentralization, right to information, to accept the court's judgement on Babri Masjid, more importance to agriculture etc. It also raised the issues of land reforms, price control, crop insurance, to identify the sources of black money, to go for de-licencing, export-import policy, labour policy, programmes for senior citizen, women and handicapped and to formulate an atomic policy.

The BJP stood for national unity and integrity, Commission for minorities and human rights, impartial election system, reforms in justice system, democratic decentralization, protection to agriculture, to improve the cow race, national industry policy, tax policy, consumer protection, labour welfare and right to work etc. It also announced for more infrastructure in urban areas, more education, sports, family welfare and population control etc.

The Communist Party of India declared for economic reform, Navodaya schools, land reforms, more help to labour, Scheduled Castes and other poor sections of the society, social security, to reduce the crime against women, cordial Centre-state relations, to control corruption, more small and cottage industries, more employment, compulsory primary education, old age pension to senior citizens etc.

The Janata Party called for right to work, corruption free society, judicial protection, freedom of press, electoral reforms, democratic decentralization, reduction in non-plan expenditure of government, agricultural reforms to bridge up the urban-rural gaps, to formulate national water and electricity policy, environmental protection, new educational policy, drinking water for all, programmes for women and youths, social insurance, secular society etc.

The CPM declared the Congress Party as a danger for the nation, more employment, to control the rising prices, to protect the labour, more economic help to farmers, reforms in education system, more powers to states, new national jute and cotton policy, land reforms, national unity and integrity, to protect the rights of poor and minorities, promotion of culture and language, to support the non-align movement, peace and co-operation with neighbouring countries etc.

Voting and Results

There were a total of 9636688 electorate in comparison to 7725946 in the 1984 Lok Sabha elections, with an increase of 19.82 per cent. About 7760889 (80.53 per cent) belonged to general categories including 53.74 per cent males and 46.25 per cent females. Of the 1875799 (19.46 per cent) Scheduled Caste electorate 54.75 per cent were males and 45.24 were females.

About 64.41 per cent people cast their votes in this election. However, 80.63 per cent electorate belonging to general category exercised their franchise including 75.78 per cent males and 42.21 per cent females, whereas the voting percentage in Scheduled Castes was 19.36 per cent including 57.07 per cent males and 42.92 per cent females.

The number of electors and voters is given in Table 7.3.

Table 7.3 : Electors, Voters etc.

Type of Contestants	*No. of Seats*	*Total Electors*			*Electors who Voted*		
		M	*W*	*T*	*M*	*W*	*T*
Gen	8	4171901	3589988	7760889	289072	2112909	5004981
SC	2	1027062	848737	1875799	686109	516035	1202144
ST	–	–	–	–	–	–	–
Total	10	5197963	4438725	9636688	3578181	2628944	6207125

Source : Report, Lok Sabha Elections, 1989.

Out of 9636688 electors, 19.46 per cent were Scheduled Castes whereas their percentage as voters was 19.36. The male-female ratio in electors was 53.94:46.06 per cent and 47.65:42.35 per cent in voters as given in Table 7.3.

The number of valid and rejected votes is highlighted in Table 7.4.

Table 7.4 : Valid Votes Polled, Rejected Votes and No. of Polling Stations

Type of Contestants	*Valid Votes Polled*	*Rejected Votes*	*No. of Polling Stations*	*% of Votes Polled*	*% of Rejected Votes*
General	4920634	84347	10272	64.49	1.71
SC	1183152	18992	2461	64.09	1.61
ST	–	–	–	–	–
Total	6103786	103339	12733	64.41	1.66

Source : Report, Lok Sabha Elections, 1989.

About 98.33 per cent votes were found valid and only 1.67 per cent were rejected as shown in Table 7.4. The Congress and the Janata Dal got 46.15 and 38.90 per cent of the valid votes as pointed out in Table 7.5.

A party-wise break up of votes polled is given in Table 7.5.

Table 7.5 : Votes Polled and Percentage According to Parties, 1989

No.of Seats		*Total No.of Valid Votes*	*No. & Percentage of valid Votes polled by National Parties*							*State Parties*	*Regd. Parties*	*IND*
Uncontested	*Contested*		*INC*	*JD*	*BJP*	*CPI*	*ICS (SCS)*	*JNP (JP)*	*LKD (B)*			
–	10	6103786	2816831 46.15	2374534 38.90	507217 9.31	15161 0.25	–	40979 0.67	4931 0.08	–	124669 2.04	219434 3.60

Source : Report, Lok Sabha Elections, 1989.

Table 7.6 contains men-women break-up of electors in different constituencies.

Table 7.6 : Lok Sabha Elections : Constituency-wise Valid and Rejected Votes

Constituencies	*Men*	*Women*	*Total*
Ambala (SC)	489263	410036	899299
Kurukshetra	495451	420429	915880
Karnal	506834	439786	946620
Sonepat	510037	433151	943188
Rohtak	488925	419869	908794
Faridabad	615430	515827	1131257
Mahendergarh	552329	505207	1057536
Bhiwani	507908	436721	944629
Hissar	493987	418998	912985
Sirsa (SC)	537799	438701	976500
Total	5197963	4438725	9636688

Source : Report, Lok Sabha Elections, 1989.

The maximum electors are in Faridabad-1131257 followed by Mahendergarh-1057536 and Sirsa-976500 and minimum is in Ambala-899299 as highlghted in Table 7.6.

A broad view of election results is given in Table 7.7.

Table 7.7 : Election Results, 1989

Party	*Contested*	*Voting*	*Valid votes*	*%*	*Invalid votes*	*%*	*Forfeited*	*Seat won*
Congress	10		2816831	46.15			–	4
JD	8		2374534	38.90			–	6
BJP	2		507217	8.31			–	–
SP(B)	9		99164	1.62			9	–
Janta(JP)	5		40979	0.67			5	–
Doordarsi	10		21003	0.34			10	–
CPI	1		15161	0.25			1	–
Lok Dal	5		4931	0.08			5	–
SOC(S)	1		2232	0.03			1	–
Riya	1		1382	0.02			1	–
Padap	1		918	0.01			1	–
Ind.	271		219434	3.60			271	–
Total	324	6207126	6103786	100.0	103339	1.66	304	10

Source : Report on the Ninth General Election of the House of the People in India 1989, Vol.II, Election Commission of India, New Delhi, 1984, pp. 20-21.

Doordarshi Party contested from Ambala (Res.) – 0.89 per cent, Kurukshetra-0.20 per cent , Karnal – 0.85 per cent, Faridabad – 0.15 per cent , Mahendergarh – 0.61 per cent, Bhiwani – 0.02 per cent, Hisar – 0.14 per cent, Rohtak – 0.11 per cent, Sonepat – 0.24 per cent, CPI from Karnal – 2.55 per cent only.

More than 98 per cent votes were found valid. The Congress got 46.15 per cent and secured 4 seats, namely Bhiwani, Faridabad, Ambala and Karnal.

The Janata Dal obtained 38.90 per cent votes with 6 seats, namely Rohtak, Sonepat, Hissar, Sirsa, Kurukshetra and Mahendergarh.

Sushma Swaraj of the BJP got 44.65 per cent votes but could not win, other two Independent women could not get even one per cent of votes.

Performance of Parties

Congress: the performance of the party is discussed in Table 7.8.

Table 7.8 : Performance of the Congress : 1989 Elections

Constituencies	*Votes Polled*	*%age*
Ambala (Res.)	264074	46.24
Kurukshetra	263452	43.43
Karnal	274465	46.11
Sonepat	237287	39.22
Rohtak	201238	33.11
Faridabad	404646	57.81
Mahendergarh	301295	47.28
Bhiwani	357625	60.12
Hissar	246394	42.94
Sirsa (Res.)	266355	43.52

Source : Report, Lok Sabha Elections, 1989.

The show of DP is given in Table 7.9.

Table 7.9 : Performance of the Doordarshi Party : 1989 Elections

Constituencies	*Votes Polled*	*%age*
Ambala (Res.)	5056	0.84
Kurukshetra	1233	0.20
Karnal	5064	0.85
Sonepat	1446	0.24
Rohtak	692	0.11
Faridabad	1045	0.15
Mahendergarh	–	–
Bhiwani	143	0.02
Hissar	830	0.14
Sirsa (Res.)	1619	0.26

Source : Report, Lok Sabha Elections, 1989.

The base of the BSP is given in Table 7.10.

Table 7.10 : Performance of the BSP : 1989 Elections

Constituencies	*Votes Polled*	*%age*
Ambala (Res.)	45389	7.94
Kurukshetra	8912	1.47
Karnal	7631	1.28
Sonepat	2190	0.36
Rohtak	1998	0.33
Faridabad	6723	0.96
Mahendergarh	–	–
Bhiwani	14609	2.46
Hissar	3074	0.54
Sirsa (Res.)	8638	1.41

Source : Report, Lok Sabha Elections, 1989.

How did the BJP perform in different constituencies is given in Table 7.11.

Table 7.11 : Performance of the BJP : 1989 Elections

Constituencies	*Votes Polled*	*%age*
Ambala (Res.)	241425	42.27
Kurukshetra	–	–
Karnal	265792	44.65
Sonepat	–	–
Rohtak	–	–
Faridabad	–	–
Mahendergarh	–	–
Bhiwani	–	–
Hissar	–	–
Sirsa (Res.)	–	–

Source : Report, Lok Sabha Elections, 1989.

The position of Janata Dal in different Lok Sabha segments is pointed out in Table 7.12.

Table 7.12 : Performance of the Janata Dal : 1989 Elections

Constituencies	*Votes Polled*	*%age*
Ambala (Res.)	–	–
Kurukshetra	301640	49.72
Karnal	–	–
Sonepat	308291	50.95
Rohtak	390243	64.21
Faridabad	273419	39.04
Mahendergarh	304805	47.83
Bhiwani	200295	33.67
Hissar	291073	50.72
Sirsa (Res.)	304768	49.80

Source : Report, Lok Sabha Elections, 1989.

The Congress got the higest votes-60.12 per cent in Bhiwani followed by Faridabad-57.81 per cent of and lowest-39.22 per cent in Sonepat, as given in Table 7.8. The Doordarshi Party could not get even one per cent votes in any constituency as shown in Table 7.9. At the same time the BSP remained below one per cent in 4 constituencies and below two per cent in 3 and below eight per cent in the remaining areas as given in Table 7.10. The performance of Janata Dal was better than the Congress as well as the BJP as pointed out in Table 7.11 and Table 7.12.

8

Parliamentary Elections, 1991

On the issue of parliamentary elections, the Haryana Governor, Dhanik Lal Mandal said, on May 18, 1991, that he did not want to get into a confrontation with anyone on the recent unprecedented outburst of the Prime Minister, Chandra Shekhar, against him and his administration.

While addressing a news conference convened to give information on the poll arrangements at the Raj Bhavan, Mandal, however, said "all the steps he had taken were intended to ensure peaceful, free and fair election, the like of which the state has never seen before.

Mandal, when pressed for details, said Chandra Shekhar was his associate of the socialist movement days. As Prime Minister he had made his observations, which he had taken note of. On whatever points he had to reply, he had replied, the Governor said.

When a reporter specifically referred to the elections, Mandal said, that "step has also been taken towards the end of holding free and fair elections." He pointed out that there was no untoward incident anywhere in the state since May 3, 1991.

The Governor said the transfers in the police set-up had been ordered with the concurrence of the Election Commission. If the Election Commission wants some changes, they would do accordingly Mandal said, when asked whether, there was any move towards restoring the *status quo ante*, in view of the PM's criticism.

A reporter wanted to know whether Mandal was considering resigning from office in view of the PM's criticism, as is done in public life, Mandal merely said: "that may be your view...."

The Governor said in reply to a question, that the administration had sent the list of allottees of discretionary quota plots, to the Election Commission. He refused to give further details on the subject.

Mandal said on its part the government had made satisfactory arrangements for the May 20 poll, and its feedback from all sources was that the atmosphere was conducive to the holding of peaceful, free and fair poll. He emphasized that there was no question of counter-manding elections anywhere in the state on account of the law and order situation. He assured the public and the Election Commission, that the polling would be peaceful.

Mandal said 700 villages falling in 14 constituencies had been identified as sensitive, and para-military forces would be deployed in them. In all, 12,742 polling stations would be set up in the state. Of this 1246 would be for the weaker sections in their *bastis.*

Elaborate law and order arrangements had been made, and the sale of liquor has been banned with effect from Saturday, the Governor said. Restrictions on the movement of fast vehicles would come into force well before the election and be effective till the evening of May 30, 1991 and four-wheelers and goods carriers would not be allowed to transport people.

Nomination Politics

A category-wise data of nominational politics is highlighted in Tables 8.1 and 8.2.

The Congress, the Janata Party, the BJP and Doordarshi Party nominated their condidates in all the 10 constituencies whereas the Janata Dal contested 7, HVP-4, CPM-3, Lok Dal-2, BSP, SJP, RKD, Hindu Mahasabha, Forward Bloc-I each.

A total 34 nominations were filed including 10 women and 43 scheduled castes. However, as many as 198 of them contested including 6 women and 26 scheduled castes as pointed out in Table 8.1

The number of contestants varied from 11 to 40 in different constituencies, as given in Table 8.2.

The number of nominations came down from 480 in 1989 to 344 in 1991 and so the contestants from 324 to 198. The women

Table 8.1 : Nominations, Rejections, Contestants etc.

Cat.	Seats	*Nominated*			*Nominations Rejected*			*Withdrawn*			*Contestants*		
		M	*w*	*T*	*M*	*w*	*T*	*M*	*w*	*T*	*M*	*w*	*T*
GEN	8	294	7	301	5	–	5	121	3	124	168	4	172
SC	2	40	3	43	–	–	–	16	1	17	24	2	26
ST	–	–	–	–	–	–	–	–	–	–	–	–	–
Total	10	334	10	344	5	-	5	137	4	141	192	6	198

Source : Report, Lok Sabha Elections, 1991.

Table 8.2 : Contests According to No. of Candidates, 1991

No.of Seats	*Uncon-tested*	*Number of Seats Contested by Candidates*								*10 or more candidates*	*Detail of Candidates*	*No. of candidates*
10	–	–	–	–	–	–	–	–	–	10	1(11),1(14), 1(15),1(17), 1(19),1(22) 1(23),1(26),& 1(40)	198

participation in nomination remained the same but the number of contestants rose from 3 in 1986 to 6 in 1991 as shown in Table 8.1. The number of contestants in different constituencies ranged between 11 to 40 as given in Table 8.2.

Compaigning

The Congress released its election manifesto with an emphasis on economic reforms, to reduce tax burden of poor, disclosure of black money, to reduce the price of diesel, kerosene, salt, bicycle, cotton etc, more employment avenues to rural youth, policies of agricultural sector, reservation of backward classes, Social Justice, health and family welfare, new education policy, houses for slum dwellers, electoral reforms, potable water in rural areas, responsive administration, National water policy, science and technology in vallage, good foreign relations etc.

The BJP stood for free and fair elections, law and order, construction of Ram Mandir, special provisions for J & K, Punjab, Ladakh, Telengana, Ulfa movement. It talked of more rural development, good industrial policy, cow protection, employment policy, power policy, transport policy, education for all, housing facilities to poor, good foreign relations and strong defence policy etc.

The National Front promised for agriculture reforms, more irrigation facilities, drinking water for all, rural development, good economic policy, women development, loan at cheaper rate of interest, ban on child labour and women traffic, housing facilities for all, educational reforms, more generation of power, better industrial policy, population control etc.

The CMP declared for good centre-state relations, national unity, erasing Article 356, resolution of J & K, Assam problem, economic independence, nationalisation of industries, more workers participation in management, compulsory education, non-aligned foreign policy etc, whereas the CPI talked of national security, decentralization, economic development, right to work, free education, free health facilities etc.

The Janata Dal declared for agriculture development, eradication of rural poverty, educational reforms, no to inspector *raj*, to increase the foreign currency, decentralization, women empowerment, protection to dalit and backwards, economic equality etc.

Thus, every political party declared several programmers to secure more votes for their candidates.

The BSP contested from Ambala (Res.) only and got 17.59 per cent votes. Doordarshi Party contested almost constituencies but got less than one per cent votes like that of 1989. The RPK contested from Kurukshetra and secured 0.21 per cent votes. Lok Dal contested from Karnal and obtainted 0.73 per cent votes. Ram Parkash, sitting Congress MP and Suraj Bhan of BJP who captured the seat thrice were in the contest from Ambala Lok Sabha seat. Chand Ram contested on the symbol of Smajwadi Janata Party whereas Shyam Chand on Janata Dal ticket.

But the rebels and Independents created problem for both the Congress and the BJP. Moreover, the emergence of the BSP who fielded Aman Kumar Nagra, who was in jail for resisting the forceful occupation of land for Sugar Mill rendering the Harijans homeless.

Almost all political parties faced a dearth of suitable candidates and tried to field their old horses. The exit of Rao Birendra Singh and Bansi Lal from the Congress created crisis in Mahendergarh and Bhiwani seats. Bhajan Lal was also not willing to contest the Lok Sabha election. The Congress fielded Chiranji Lal Sharma from Karnal and the BJP Fateh Chand Vij.

Similarly, the JD-HVP faced a candidate crisis in Karnal.

In Sonepat, there was the tough contest between the Congress (I) candidate Dharampal Malik and the SJP-Kapil Dev Shastri. Out of 10 lakh votes 3.45 lakh were Jats, 2.95 lakh SCs & BCs, 1 lakh Punjabis, 11000 Rajputs. Kitab Singh Malik was made to withdraw from the field as the JP-HVP candidate.

Hissar : As many as 17 candidates were in the fray. Of the 9.09 lakh votes, 3.38 lakhs were Jats, 75000 Brahmins, 52000 Banias, 50,000 Punjabis, 1.24 lakh BCs, 1.90 lakh SCs etc.

The main contest in Hissar was among the Jai Prakash of the SJP, Narain Singh of the Congress, Parmanand of the JP-HVP alliance and Sriniwas Goel of the BJP. However, Parmanand and Goel were far behind in the campaign. In total there were 17 candidates in the fray.

Ambala : The contest was between the Congress (I), the BJP and the JD. The Congress fielded its sitting MP Ram Prakash whereas the

BJP Suraj Bhan, the BSP fielded Aman Kumar and the J.D. – Ram Prasad.

Rohtak : The main contest was between the Congress and the SJP. The Prime Minister Chander Shekhar and Dy. Prime Minister Devi Lal visited the constituency but got a poor response from the electorate. Devi Lal faced a tough contest from Bhupender Singh Hooda of the Congress (I). The HVP fielded Inder Singh Dhull, the BJP, Raj Kumar Sharma. A total 26 candidates were in the field.

Of the 9 lakh voters 3.5 lakh were Jats and half of the Jats had soft corner for Hooda.

Sirsa : It includes 9 Assembly segments and 2.25 lakh of the total 9.75 lakh voters were Harijans, 1.90 lakh Backwards, 1.78 lakh Jats, 1.79 lakh Sikhs, 74000 Punjabis, 52000 Banias, and 42000 Brahmins.

Selja had won four elections from there since 1967 as the Congress candidate. Het Ram, Sakhi Ram Bhatt were the JP and the HVP alliance candidates, Pyare Lal Ranga as the BJP and Jagmit from Akali Dal were in the fray. The Congress expected the support of 2.25 lakh SC votes and a section of Punjabis whereas Bhatt pinned hopes on Backward and Sikhs.

Karnal : The JP-HVP put up a Sikh candidate C.P.S. Nain, as Sikhs have 1.10 lakh votes. He was also expected to get votes from 50000 Rajputs and 1.20 lakh Jats. The SJP fielded Ranjit Singh to woo 80000 Rors votes. The BJP put up Fateh Chand Vij replacing I.D. Swami as there were 2.36 lakh Punjabi voters.

Mahendergarh: A total of 19 candidates were in the fray having triangular contest among the SJP, the Congress (I) and the HVP. The Congress fielded Col. Ram Singh, the SJP-Rao Birendera Singh and the HVP – Naresh Yadav, the BJP – M.L. Yadav, whereas Raghu Yadav contested as an Independent.

Voting and Results

Out of 9725297 electors 6403796 (65.84 per cent) exercised their franchise including the females and S.C voters. A detail in this regard is given in Table 8.3 and 8.4.

Table 8.3 : Electors, Voters, 1991

Type of Const.	*No. of Seat*	*Total Electors*			*Electors who Voted*		
10	–	*M*	*W*	*T*	*M*	*W*	*T*
Gen	8	4205352	3617060	7822412	2865724	2194271	5059995
SC	2	1036932	866553	1903485	743145	600656	1343801
ST	–	–	–	–	–	–	–
Total	10	5242284	4483613	9725297	3608869	279427	6403796

Source : Report, Lok Sabha Elections, 1991.

The number of electors increased from 9636688 in 1989 to 9725297 in 1991 Lok Sabha elections, thus 9.17 per cent more than earlier. The men-women ratio was 205352:3617060 (53.76:46.23 per cent). The percentage of Scheduled Caste electors was 19.57 per cent (1903485) having men-women ratio of 54.47: 45.53 per cent.

The voting took place on May 20,1991. For this purpose 12736 polling stations were set up including 65 for the scheduled castes.

The total electors were 9725297 having male-female ratio of 53.90:46.10 per cent whereas it was 56.36:43.6 per cent among voters. The precentage of Scheduled Caste electors was 1957 and those of voters 20.98 per cent as given in Table 8.3.

The no. of valid and rejected votes is pointed out in Table 8.4.

Table 8.4 : Valid, Rejected Votes etc.

Type of Cont.	*Valid Votes Polled*	*Rejected Votes*	*Missing Votes*	*Ballot Papers Set apart*	*No. of Polling Stations*	*% of Votes Polled*	*% of Rejected Votes*
Gen	4902940	154291	1364	1400	10273	64.69	3.05
SC	1303853	39890	58	–	2463	70.60	2.97
ST	–	–		–		–	–
Total	6206793	194181	1402	1400	12736	65.84	3.03

Source : Report, Lok Sabha Elections, 1991.

A view of party-wise election data can be seen in Table 8.7.

Table 8.7 : Votes Polled and Percentage According to Parties, 1991

No.of Seats		*Total No.of Valid Votes*	*No. & Percentage of valid Votes polled by National Parties*							
Uncont-ested	*Cont-ested*		*INC*	*JD*	*BJP*	*HVP*	*JD(S)*	*JP*	*ICS*	*LKD*
	10	6206793	2310003 37.22	775213 12.49	631146 10.17	331794 5.35		1577389 25.41		8824 0.14

The Congress got the maximum votes-37.22 per cent followed by the Janata Party-25.41 per cent, Janata Dal-12.49 per cent. The Lok Dal could not get even one per cent vote as depicted in Table 8.7.

The details of election result can be seen in Table 8.8.

Table 8.8 : Election Results, 1991

Total Electors = 9725297

Party	*Contested*	*%*	*Valid votes*	*%*	*Invalid votes*	*%*	*Forfeited*	*%*	*Seat won*
Congress	10		2310003	37.22			-		9
Janata Party	10		1577389	25.41			1		-
Janata Dal	7		775213	12.49			4		-
BJP	10		631146	10.17			9		-
HVP	4		331794	5.35			3		1
BSP	1		111353	1.79			-		-
SP	1		70368	1.13			1		-
Lok Dal	2		8824	0.41			2		-
Doordarshi	10		24496	0.39			10		-
JKMP	3		19351	0.31			3		-
P. Dal	1		2213	0.04			1		-
RPI(K)	1		1325	0.02			1		-
SKAD	1		1125	0.02			1		-
H. Sabha	1		1053	0.02			1		-
Forward Bloc	1		987	0.02			1		-
Ind.	135		340153	5.48			135		-

Source : Report on the Ninth General Elections of the House of the People in India 1991, Vol.II, Election Commission of India, New Delhi, 1991, pp. 30-31.

The votes secured by different political parties is given in Table 8.5.

Table 8.5 : Votes Polled and Percentage according to Parties, 1991

No. of Seats		Total No. of Valid Votes	State Parties	Registered Parties	IND
Un-contested	Contested				
1	2	3	4	5	6
–	10	6206793	112340 1.81	451725 7.28	340153 5.48

A narration of electors and voters is given in Table 8.6.

Table 8.6 : Voters, Valid and Rejected votes

	Electors			Electors who voted		
Constituencies	Men	Women	Total	Men	Women	Total
Ambala (SC)	497041	415349	912390	361151	292365	653526
Kurukshetra	501777	426199	927970	365012	291681	656693
Karnal	509679	441308	950987	360767	286934	647701
Sonepat	513565	435442	949007	340502	264184	604686
Rohtak	495730	424138	919868	339259	225627	564886
Faridabad	621801	519959	1141760	419683	295919	715602
Mahendergarh	556458	507476	1063934	353920	293101	647021
Bhiwani	508426	441014	949440	332877	263492	596369
Hissar	497916	421524	919440	353704	273333	627037
Sirsa (SC)	539891	451204	991095	381994	308281	690275

Source: Report, Lok Sabha Elections, 1991.

The Congress won 9 of the 10 seats with 37.22 per cent votes. It got the highest number of valid votes in Ambala, Kurukshetra, Karnal, Sonepat, Rohtak, Faridabad, Mahendergarh, Hissar and Sirsa. The HVP fetched the Bhiwani seat with only 331794 (5.35 per cent) votes whereas the Janata Party with 25.41 per cent votes could not enter the Lok Sabha. At the same time the Janata Dal and the BJP secured 12.49 and 10.17 per cent votes respectively but could not get any seat. The BSP and S.P. could not secure even two per cent votes each. Other splinter groups like Doordarshi Party, JKMP, RPJ, Hindu Mahasabha, Forward Bloc could not secure even a half per cent votes and all their candidates lost the deposits. Moreover, the Independents got 5.48 her cent and all 135 lost their deposits.

Selja won from Sirsa while obtaining 42.92 per cent votes. She was the lone woman to win the election.

Performance of Parties

Janata Party: the position of the party in different constituencies is highlighted in Table 8.9.

Table 8.9 : Performance of the Janata Party : 1991 Elections

Constituencies	*Votes Polled*	*%age*
Ambala (Res.)	56138	8.87
Kurukshetra	135117	21.24
Karnal	145598	23.33
Sonepat	74011	12.58
Rohtak	–	–
Faridabad	217443	37.40
Mahendergarh	–	–
Bhiwani	–	–
Hissar	85241	14.04
Sirsa (Res.)	61665	9.19

Source : Report, Lok Sabha Election, 1991.

The performance of the Janata Party was poor in Ambala, Sirsa—both reserved constituencies where it could get 8.87 and 9.19 per cent votes respectively. Similarly, it secured 12.58 per cent votes in Sonepat and 14.04 per cent in Hissar. However, the percentage was a bit higher in Kurukshetra-21.24 and Karnal-23.33 per cent. The maximum votes were secured by the party in Faridabad-37.40 per cent but could not win any seat as given in Table 8.9.

The performance of the Janata Dal is given in Table 8.10.

Table 8.10 : Performance of the Janata Dal : 1991 Elections

Constituencies	*Votes Polled*	*%age*
Ambala (Res.)	112028	17.70
Kurukshetra	182758	28.72
Karnal	132444	21.22
Sonepat	202770	34.46
Rohtak	210662	38.43
Faridabad	70972	10.25
Mahendergarh	169820	27.09
Bhiwani	100288	17.31
Hissar	206818	34.06
Sirsa (Res.)	188829	28.15

Source : Report, Lok Sabha Election, 1991.

The Janata Dal obtained higher per cent of votes in most of the constituencies in comparison to the Janata Party. It got 38.3 per cent votes in Rohtak constituency followed by Sonepat-34.46 per cent, Hissar-34.06 per cent, Kurukshetra-28.72 per cent and the lowest in Ambala-17.70 per cent (See Table 8.10).

The loss of the BJP is depicted in Table 8.11.

Table 8.11 : Performance of the BJP : 1991 Elections

Constituencies	*Votes Polled*	*%age*
Ambala (Res.)	124464	19.66
Kurukshetra	79653	12.52
Karnal	81780	13.10
Sonepat	29773	5.06
Rohtak	23802	4.34
Faridabad	103403	14.93
Mahendergarh	60342	9.63
Bhiwani	48570	8.38
Hissar	35486	5.84
Sirsa (Res.)	43873	6.54

Source : Report, Lok Sabha Election, 1991

The performance of the BJP was poorer than those of the Janata Party and Janata Dal in most of the constituencies. It got the highest percentage of votes in Ambala-19.66 followed by Faridabad-14.93 per cent, Karnal-13.10 per cent and the lowest in Rohtak-4.34 per cent (See Table 8.11).

The show of the Congress is pointed out in Table 8.12.

Table 8.12 : Performance of the Congress : 1991 Elections

Constituencies	*Votes Polled*	*%age*
Ambala (Res.)	196406	31.03
Kurukshetra	212783	33.44
Karnal	200770	32.17
Sonepat	247572	42.08
Rohtak	241235	38.43
Faridabad	268965	38.84
Mahendergarh	241808	38.58
Bhiwani	179525	30.98
Hissar	233012	38.37
Sirsa (Res.)	287927	42.92

Source : Report, Lok Sabha Elections, 1991.

The performance of the HVP is given in Table 8.13.

Table 8.13 : Performance of the HVP : 1991 Elections

Constituencies	*Votes Polled*	*%age*
Ambala (Res.)	–	–
Kurukshetra	–	–
Karnal	–	–
Sonepat	–	–
Rohtak	43804	7.99
Faridabad	–	–
Mahendergarh	46134	7.36
Bhiwani	–	–
Hissar	–	–
Sirsa (Res.)	31766	4.74

Source : Report, Lok Sabha Election, 1991

The Congress secured more than 30 per cent votes in all constituencies, the highest in Sirsa-42.92 per cent. The HVP could not get more than 8 per cent votes in all the three constituencies, it contested but even then won one seat (see Tables 8.12 & 8.13)

9

Parliamentary Elections, 1996

The Congress and the Samata Party contested all the 10 seats in the state, followed by 8 seats each by the Congress (T) and the Janata Party. The HVP and its electoral ally the BJP had fielded 4 and 6 candidates respectively. As many as 26 candidates were contesting these elections on the symbol of other parties in the state and a record 209 Independents were also in the fray for the 10 Lok Sabha seats. Also in the fray were five women candidates. They were: Congress candidate Selja (Sirsa-SC), Samata Party nominee Kailasho Devi (Kurukshetra) and Congress (T) candidate Bimla Mour (Sonepat), Mrs. Vidhya Devi and Mrs. Vinod Kumari were contesting as Independents from the Hissar and Ambala (SC) constituencies respectively.

Haryana had record 209 Independents

A record of 209 Independents were trying their electoral fortunes in Haryana where a total of 294 candidates were in the fray for the April 27, 1996 polls.

The Bhiwani Lok Sabha constituency had the maximum number of 32 Independent contestants, followed by 31 in the Faridabad constituency. Lowest number of 12 Independents were in the Ambala (SC) constituency while there were 13 in the Karnal constituency.

Nominational Politics

A view of constituencies, electors and category-wise nominations is given in the Tables 9.1 to 9.3.

Table 9.1 : Number and Type of Constituencies

	Type of Constituency		
General	*SC*	*ST*	*Total*
8	2	–	10

Source: ECI Report ID-GE96 LS17.

Table 9.2 : Male-Female Electors

No. of Electors		
Men	*Women*	*Total*
6005913	5146943	11152856

Source : ECI Report ID-GE96 LS18.

Table 9.3 : No. of candidates and nature of party

No. of Seats	*No. of parties*					*No. of candidates*				
	N	*S*	*U*	*Z*	*T*	*N*	*S*	*U*	*Z*	*T*
10	49	4	31	210	294	29	–	29	209	267

N-National Parties, S-State Parties, U-Regd. (Unrecognized) Parties, Z-Independent, T-Total
Source : ECI Report ID-GE96 LS20.

A view of male-female ratio of nominations and contestants including the Scheduled Caste is pointed out in Table 9.4.

Table 9.4 : Category-wise nomination etc.

	Type of Constituency			
	General	*SC*	*ST*	*Total*
Constituencies	8	2	0	10
Nominations Filed				
Men	384	60	0	444
Women	10	5	0	15
Total	394	65	0	459

(Contd...)

Table 9.4 (contd.)

Nominations Rejected				
Men	27	6	0	33
Women	0	0	0	0
Total	27	6	0	33
Nominations Withdrawn				
Men	109	17	0	126
Women	4	2	0	6
Total	113	19	0	132
Contesting Candidates				
Men	248	37	0	285
Women	6	3	0	9
Total	254	40	0	294
Forfeited Deposits				
Men	229	31	0	260
Women	5	2	0	7
Total	234	33	0	267

Source : Report, Lok Sabha Elections, 1996.

There were three serious contenders for power in Haryana, namely the Congress, the Haryana Vikas Party (HVP) and the Samajwadi Janata Party (SJP).

It was the personality, not the issue that had taken centre-stage in the Lok Sabha and Assembly polls in Haryana. The SJP was projecting Om Prakash Chautala as the future Chief Minister. The HVP was also projecting its supremo, Bansi Lal as an "able administrator" and the best candidate for being Chief Minister. The Congress was sticking to Bhajan Lal as an "able Chief Minister" who provided Haryana with a "stable" government.

The number of voters, votes polled and polling stations is given in Table 9.5.

Table 9.5 : Voter Turn out and Polling Stations

Electors	*Voters*	*Votes Polled %*	*Rejected %*	*No. of Polling Stations*
11152856	7860863	70.48	3.13	15625

Source: ECI Report ID-GE96 LS19.

The men-women ratio of electors was 53.86 per cent as given in Table 9.2.

A total of 459 nominations were filed including 15 those of women. After withdrawals and scruting as many as 294 contested the elections including 9 women as pointed out in Table 9.3.

Alliance: BJP ties up with HVP

Though the BJP was in dilemma whether it should ally with the SJP led by Devi Lal or the Bansi Lal's HVP. Finally, it decided for an alliance with the HVP both for Assembly and Lok Sabha elections. It was a setback to SJP which too was trying to woo the BJP. The alliance of BJP and HVP contested six and four seats respectively. Of the 90 Assembly seats, the HVP contested 65 seats and the BJP 25. This indicated that the HVP concentrated more on the Assembly seats than on the Lok Sabha seats. It was also decided that while the candidates of the two parties contested the election on their party symbol, but the electioneering was undertaken jointly on the basis of a common manifesto.

Om Prakash Chautala criticized the alliance that it was "marriage of convenience". It is interesting to note that both Chautala and Bansi Lal were anxious to go in for an alliance with BJP because both are largely rural based parties and an alliance with BJP could help them get the backing of a significant chunk of the urban vote and this was essential to offset the calculations of the Congress.

The Congress in Haryana did not go in for seat adjustments or a formal election alliance with any party in the state.

In the last general elections, the Congress had succeeded in getting the Jat support after projecting Birender Singh as Chief Minister. The Jats, however, felt cheated when he lost the race of Chief Ministership to Bhajan Lal. So the Rao Birender Singh-Ram Prakash combine left the Congress in protest against such tardy behaviour of the Congress and Chief Minister Bhajan Lal's style of functioning. Former HPCC President Birender Singh had succeeded in forging a common front with the CPM, the CPI, the Janhit Morcha and the Arya Sabha Party.

The electoral battle in Haryana was once again among the three Lals – Bhajan Lal (Congress), Bansi Lal (HVP) and Devi Lal (SJP). However, there was a little difference this time instead of projecting himself as the future Chief Minister, Devi Lal was projecting his son, Om Prakash Chautala for the coveted position.

In the wake of the hawala controversy, Bansi Lal enjoyed an edge over both Devi Lal and Bhajan Lal whose names are being linked to the controversy. An impression had gone around that if he becomes the Chief Minister, he may put an end to corruption and nepotism, which was highlighted by a recent High Court ruling quashing the appointment of over 1700 police constables recruited in 1995.

Campaigning

Local issues rather than national questions dominated the electoral scenes in Haryana.

Giving the state political stability, restoring rule of law, ending criminalization of politics and starting the development process were the Congress's main electoral planks. The Congress was boasting that it had completed 5 years without the Meham like incidents or disturbance.

Prohibtion and water pact were the main poll issues of Bansi Lal's HVP. Bansi Lal wooed the electorate by announcing that he would enforce prohibition within an hour of his coming to power.

The SJP was raising a number of issues like the Yamuna water accord, power and water shortage and delay in completion of the Sutlej-Yamuna link canal. This time the SJP leadership was no longer haunted by the Meham episode which was largely responsible for the downfall of the Devi Lal in the last election. Devi Lal was doing an emotional appeal to the electorate saying that 'only Gods know how many more times I would come to you for support.'

Voting and Results : out of the 11152856 electors 7860863 cast their votes including the women and SC in 15625 polling stations set up in different parts of the state.

A view of electors and voters is set in Table 9.6.

Table 9.6 : Electors, Voters, 1996

Type of Const.	*No. of Seat*	*Electors*			*Voters*		
		M	*W*	*T*	*M*	*W*	*T*
Gen	8	4838438	4143367	8981805	3414633	2774759	6189392
SC	2	1167475	1003576	2171051	907105	764366	1671471
Total	10	6005913	5146943	11152856	4321738	3539125	7860863

Source : Report, Lok Sabha Elections, 1996.

The men-women ratio of electors 53.85:6.15 per cent whereas it is 54.97:45.03 per cent incuding 21.26 per cent Scheduled Caste voters as given in Table 9.6.

The number of valid and rejected votes is given in Table 9.7.

Table 9.7 : Valid, Rejected Votes etc.

Type of Contituencies	*Polling %*	*Valid Votes*	*Rejected Votes*	*Rejected Votes %*	*Missing Votes*	*Polling Stations*
Gen	68.91	5991327	195636	3.16	2429	12559
SC	76.99	1620316	50785	3.04	370	3066
Total	70.48	7611643	246421	3.13	2799	15625

Source : Report, Lok Sabha Elections, 1996.

The participation of women in voting is given in Table 9.8

Table 9.8 : Women's Participation in Polls

State	*Women Electors*	*Women Voters*	*Poll %*	
			Women	*Total*
Haryana	5146943	3539125	68.76	70.48

Source : ECI Report ID-GE-LS22.

The performance of women candidates is given in Table 9.9.

Table 9.9 : Performance of Women Candidates

State	*No. of Seats*	*No. of Women*		
		Candidates	*Elected*	*F.D.s*
Haryana	10	9	1	7

Source : ECI Report ID-GE-LS23.

It was 68.91 per cent voting among the general public whereas 76.99 per cent among the Scheduled Castes. About 96.82 per cent votes were found valid. For smooth voting as many as 15625 polling stations were set up as given in Table 9.7.

Interestingly out of 5146943 women electors, 68.76 per cent cast their votes against 30.48 per cent of the state as a whole as pointed out in Table 9.8.

Out of 9 women contestants one was elected whereas the deposits, of 7 were lost as highlighted in Table 9.9.

The figures of election results are given in Table 9.10.

Table 9.10 : Election Results, 1996

Total Electorals = 11152856

Party	Contested	Voting	%	Valid votes	%	Invalid votes	%	Forfeited	%	Seat won
Congress	10			1723087	22.04			2		2
Samata Party	10			1447340	19.04			4		–
BJP	6			150723	19.74			–		4
HVP	4			1156322	16.19			–		3
Congress(T)	6			501958	6.59			4		–
JD	8			171005	2.25			8		–
SP	8			116845	1.54			8		–
BSP	3			56172	1.13			3		–
JP(S)	6			15960	0.21			6		–
BJS	1			15112	0.20			1		–
CPI	1			14292	0.19			1		–
JHM	1			27573	0.36			2		–
SHS	2			9404	0.12			4		–
JSTP	4			9223	0.12			2		–
AR(S)	2			10134	0.13			1		–
MKP	1			6347	0.08			1		–
ICS	1			3645	0.06			2		–
Forward	2			3418	0.04			2		–
ABDUP	2			2432	0.03			1		–
BLP	1			2332	0.03			1		–
PPNSS	1			1996	0.03			1		–
BKDJ	1			1900	0.02			1		–
SKAD	1			689	0.01			1		–
	1			882	0.01			1		–
	1			520	0.01			1		–
Ind.	210			780122	10.24			209		1
Total	294			7611643	100.00			267		10

Source : Report on the General Election to the House of the People in India 1991, Vol.I, Election Commission of India, New Delhi, 1996, pp. 2-7, 2-8, 8-10, 40.

A category-wise performance of different political parties is given in Table 9.11.

Table 9.11 : Seats Won in State by Parties, 1996

Party	*General*	*SC*	*ST*	*Total*
IND	1	–	–	1
BJP	3	1	–	4
HVP	3	–	–	3
INC	1	1	–	2
Total	8	2	–	10

Source : Report, Lok Sabha Elections, 1996.

The ratio of contestants and winners is given in Table 9.12.

Table 9.12 : Contestants, winners etc.

Party	*Seats Contested*	*Seats Won*	*FD in Seats*	*Votes Polled by Party*	*% of Votes Polled*
Congress(T)	8	0	8	171005	2.25
BJP	6	4	0	1502723	19.74
CPI	1	0	1	27573	0.36
INC	10	0	2	1723087	22.64
JD	8	0	8	116845	1.54
JP	6	0	6	15960	0.21
SAP	10	0	4	1447340	19.01
BSP	6	0	4	501958	6.59
FBI	2	0	2	2432	0.03
HVP	4	3	0	1156322	15.10
ICS	2	0	2	1418	0.04
SHS	4	0	4	9223	0.12
SP	3	0	3	86172	1.13
ABDUP	1	0	1	1996	0.03
ABJS	1	0	1	14292	0.19
ARS	1	0	1	6367	0.08
BKD(U)	1	0	1	882	0.01
BLP	1	0	1	1900	0.02
JHM	2	0	2	9404	0.12
JPS	1	0	1	15112	0.20
JSIP	2	0	1	10134	0.13
PPNMS	1	0	1	889	0.01
RKD	1	0	1	520	0.01
RKP	1	0	1	3635	0.05
RPI	1	0	1	2332	0.03
IND	210	1	209	780122	10.25

Source : Report, Lok Sabha Elections, 1996.

The detail of women candidates and their performance is given in Table 9.13.

Table 9.13 : Women Candidates, 1996

Constituency	*Sr.No.*	*Candidate*	*Cand. Type*	*Party*	*Type*	*Vote Polled*	*%*
1. Ambala (SC)	12	Vinod Kumari	Gen	IND	Z	5127	0.64
1. Ambala (SC)	19	Raj Shree	SC	IND	Z	1276	0.16
2. Kurukshetra	2	Kailasho Devi	Gen	SAP	N	240395	29.99
3. Karnal	18	Santosh	Gen	FBL	U	1548	0.19
4. Sonepat	6	Bimla Mor	Gen	AIIC(T)	N	8638	1.23
5. Rohtak	24	Santosh Singh	Gen	JSTP	U	829	0.13
6. Faridabad	35	Santosh	Gen	IND	Z	645	0.08
9. Hissar	20	Vidya Devi	Gen	IND	Z	1102	0.15
10. Sirsa (SC)	1	Selja	SC	INC	N	275459	33.5

Source : Report, Lok Sabha Elections, 1996.

Total = 1115256
Women = 5146943
Nomination = Total = 459, W = 15, SC = 5
Contestants = T = 294, W = 9, SC = 3
Deposits forfeited = 7, SC = 2

From Kurukshetra, Kailasho Devi of Samata Party got 240395 votes and was defeated by HVP Candidate, Om Parkash Jindal who got 292172.

Selja of the Congress got 275459 votes defeated Sushil Indora of Samata Party who secured 260312 votes.

Similarly, the alliance bagged 7 of the 10 Lok Sabha seats. It helped the HVP in extending its influence beyond Bhiwani to the Jat-dominated areas of Hissar, Sonepat and Kurukshetra, besides parts of Ambala, Karnal, Yamunanagar, Panipat, Faridabad and Rewari.

A political analyst commented that "These polls could mark the beginning of the end of the purely personalized politics of the three Lals in the State. While the two Lals were eclipsed at the hustings, Bansi Lal has emerged in a new role." Adds P.K. Sandhir, a Hissar advocate, who has watched the HVP from close quarters: "Bansi Lal emerged as a force outside the Congress only when he bolstered his old image with the tie-up."

The Congress, which had staged a remarkable recovery in 1991, has been clearly humbled. Against its tally of 9 Lok Sabha and 51 Vidhan Sabha seats last time, it is down to 2 Lok Sabha and 9 Vidhan Sabha seats scattered all, over the state. "Five years ago, the Congress benefited from the swing against the instability wrought by Om Prakash Chautala. Also, the Congress garnered votes from all quarters by keeping the leadership issue open", said a senior Congress leader.

In fact, for the past few years, the people, apparently disillusioned with the party in power in the state, have been seeking a change. They were unhappy with Chautala. The crafty Bhajan Lal, provided stability but projected himself communal and ineffective leader and his influence in the Congress started to wither away. "It is a vote against unchecked erosion of democracy at the grassroots level caused by money and muscle power," explained a political scientist at Chandigarh.

The "old" Bansi Lal is remembered for giving an iron-fisted thrust to development-memories that give credibility to the "new" Bansi Lal's promises of prohibition, water, power and a clean administration that have gone well with the people.

The alliance with the BJP made the seasoned Jat from Bhiwani relevant in the numerous small towns of the state. His image as a firm administrator infused confidence among the small traders who were worried over the deteriorating law-and-order situation.

Jats comprise nearly 39 per cent of Haryana's population. The Congress hoped that the Jat vote would be divided between the HVP and the Samata Party. The HVP made up for this erosion by winning urban votes due to its alliance with the BJP. On the other hand, the Samata Party's calculations went aray with the near-rejection of the Congress in the cities. Said a Chautala supporter: "We expected the Congress to wean away a sizable chunk of the urban vote, which did not happen due to the alliance, which was a masterstroke."

Veteran Rohtak Congressman, Chander Bhan Gupta ascribes the HVP-BJP win to the urban swing on the crucial 20 seats in Haryana cities. These seats, which have traditionally gone to the Congress, swing in favour of the HVP-BJP combine this time as they feel left out and deprived of the spoils of power. With the Samata Party wooing only the rural voter, the HVP-BJP alliance cashed in on this void in small towns.

Undoubtedly, the alliance was helped by the negative vote against the Congress regime's unresponsive governance. However, veteran Haryana politician and academician, Hardwari Lal feels that this time there was a definite tide in favour of Bansi Lal due to his development-oriented image. Others also feel that Bansi Lal is seen by masses as a strong administrator who can get things moving. They are not bothered about his arrogance.

The BJP benefited considerably from the alliance, for the first time in recent years, the party wrested as many as 11 Vidhan Sabha seats. "The party's clout, dwindling since 1987, is beginning return becasue of the swing in its favour at the national level", said a BJP supporter.

However, political analyst D.R. Chaudhary feels the alliance is a marriage of convenience, since religious sentiments or identiy mean little to Bansi Lal while these are fundamental to the BJP. The BJP could make things difficult for him by indulging in arm-twisting. On the other hand, HVP supporters insist that there is no reason for the alliance to falter. "The BJP's Hindu orientation will not come in the way as communal tensions don't exist even in the areas of Mewat with a sizable Muslim population", said a HVP advocate.

The elections have sealed Devi Lal's political fate and he will find it difficult to bounce back. Yet, the Samata Party, which improved its tally to 24 Assembly seats, can't be wished away. Political analysts say that though Bansi Lal got a fair share of the Jat vote, the Jat community by and large has still shown its support for Devi Lal, particularly in the Rohtak and Sirsa areas.

Political observers feel that the Samata Party will have to look beyond family rule. Says Hardwari Lal: "Since Devi Lal's third generation was in politics, there may have been a feeling against dynastic rule." It is also have to widen its support base.

Devi Lal's campaign suffered a set back at the time of party ticket for the Assembly seats. Aspirants for the party ticket lost interest in the party's campaign. Devi Lal's grandson Ajay Singh Chautala was initially supposed to oversee his grandfather's campaign. However, his pre-occupation with his father Om Prakash Chautala's campaign in Narwana forced him to entrust the campaign management to his confident from Sirsa who ignored even loyal locals who sincerely wanted to see the Tau through his last battle.

The party members for the Assembly segments falling in the Rohtak Lok Sabha constituency campaigned only for themselves. Many of them chose to seek votes for themselves alone and even want to the extent of allowing their supporters to vote for them for the Assembly and for the Congress nominee, Bhupender Singh Hooda for the Lok Sabha. This was evident from the fact that in the Kiloi Assembly segment while the party nominee, Sri Kishan Hooda, secured a massive win, the Tau lost in this segment by a big margin. The detailed results are as under :—

A constituency-wise position of different political parties is depicted in Table 9.14.

Table 9.14 : How they finished in Haryana (1996 Lok Sabha Election Results)

Constituency	*Winner/Runner-Up*		
	1st	*2nd*	*3rd*
Ambala	BJP	Congress	BSP
Kurukshetra	HVP	Samata Party	Congress
Karnal	BJP	Congress	Samata Party
Sonepat	IND	Samata Party	HVP
Rohtak	Congress	Samata Party	BJP
Faridabad	BJP	Congress	
Mahendergarh	BJP	Congress	BSP
Bhiwani	HVP	Congress	Samata Party
Hissar	HVP	Samata Party	Congress
Sirsa	Congress	Samata Party	BJP

Source : Report, Lok Sabha Elections, 1996.

Bhajan Lal is left with a handful of MLAs and this leaves him little scope for exercising his notorious, manipulative skills. Devi Lal has lost his "last political battle", which he waged for his son, and Chautala's dream of taking over the reins in Haryana lies shattered.

Bansi Lal's electoral pact with the BJP has brought rich dividends for both the parties, and together with his Rohtak rally turned the anti-establishment tide in his favour to the detriment of Chautala.

The BJP leadership, in turn which was vacillating between Chautala and Bansi Lal before finally setting for an alliance with the latter, has much reason to rejoice for making the right choice. For the first time ever the party has won such a large number of seats in State that has never been its stronghold.

Bansi Lal was hated for his arrogance and administrative excesses especially during the emergency but hailed as the "architect of modern Haryana". Now that he has mellowed with age and adversity, and given the corruption in the Congress, the masses have once again turned to the "builder" in him in order to revive the economic development of the State.

Bansi Lal has also promised to introduce total prohibition in the state which is expected to increase the welfare of the family and check the abuse of women. However, at the same time it could well deliver a crippling blow to Bhajan Lal's family as his son-in-law owns the largest distillery chain in the State.

Bansi Lal first became the Chief Minister of the state in 1968 and continued till 1975. It was during this sting that he laid the foundation for the development of the State.

Arrogance was his only drawback. As the Defence Minister, he was abrasive and often insulted even senior officers. He once briskly asked the Defence Secretary and the Chief of Air Staff to leave a meeting as they had advised him that he should not have invited Rajiv Gandhi for the high-level confidential meeting merely because he was the son of a Prime Minister.

Bansi Lal's name was held in mortal dead during the dark days of the emergency. His ruthless implementation of the forced sterilisation drive to promote Sanjay Gandhi's family planning programme and the crackdown on political opponents brought about his downfall. Prosecuted for his excesses during the emergency with the setting up of the Shah Commission, he had to face the ignominy of being handcuffed during the Morarji Desai regime.

With the collapse of the Janata Party, and the Congress returning to power in 1980, the cases against him were withdrawn. However, he could not regain his political importance as he had fallen from grace with the Gandhi family due to his dubious role in the emergency.

The death of Sanjay Gandhi, to whom he was considered particularly close and the rise of Rajiv Gandhi, struck a further blow to Bansi Lal's political fortunes as he did not enjoy the same rapport with the elder Gandhi who preferred to promote Bhajan Lal.

But he got a ministerial berth at the Centre again and continued till 1986. He returned to take over the reins in Haryana in June 1986, a year before the Assembly elections were due. However, the subsequent anti-Congress wave that swept the state saw him going into oblivion.

Bansi Lal then floated his own party, and as Bhajan Lal and Devi Lal dominated the political scene, his Haryana Vikas Party (HVP) was reduced to playing a retatively minor role until now when a major electoral success came his way.

Strangely enough, the Congress lost its hold on the Muslims of Haryana. Out of the four Muslim dominated Assembly constituencies in the state, the HVP-BJP combine has bagged two seats while one seat each has gone to the Congress (Tiwari) and the Samata Party. The Congress candidates were nowhere in the reckoning in these constituencies and were relegated to the fourth or firth places. In the constituencies of Hathin, Tauru, Nuh and Ferozepur Jhirka.

Interpretation of Results

As much as 70.48 per cent voting took place. However, the voters belonging to general category ranked highest in voting with 79 per cent followed by 20.98 per cent by Scheduled Caste votes.

However, the voters from the general category were higher with 78.73 per cent including 55.16 per cent males and 44.83 per cent females. Whereas 27 per cent Scheduled Caste voters exercised their voting right including 54.26 per cent males and 45.73 per cent females.

It won 2 Lok Sabha seats, namely Sirsa and Rohtak whereas the BJP got 19.74 per cent valid votes while winning 4 Lok Sabha seats namely Ambala, Karnal, Faridabad and Mahendergarh. The HVP obtained 15.19 per cent votes with 3 seats namely Kurukshetra, Bhiwani and Hissar. Thus the BJP-HVP alliance got 7 Lok Sabha seats.

A total of 6206793 (96.92%) votes were found valid and the Congress secured 22.04 per cent while 9 Assembly seats, namely Ambala, Kurukshetra, Karnal, Sonepat, Rohtak, Faridabad, Mahendergarh, Hissar, Sirsa.

Selja again won the seat from Sirsa with 33.50 per cent votes. As many as 267 (87.37 per cent) candidates lost their deposits.

Return of Bansi Lal

Ab Ki Bari, Bansi aur Behari. This time Bansi Lal and Atal Behari has clicked in Haryana and Bansi Lal returned to power after a long gap of nine years.

The mandate proves the relevance of the politics of accommodation even in a caste-ridden state. The HVP-BJP combine managed to win nearly half (44) of the 90 assembly seats and succeeded in wresting power from the wily Bhajan Lal contesting alone five years ago, the HVP had only 12 seats. Similarly, the alliance has bagged seven of the 10 Lok Sabha seats (against just one in 1991).

The Congress, against its tally of 9 Lok Sabha and 51 Vidhan Sabha seats last time, now got only 2 Lok Sabha and nine Vidhan Sabha seats scattered all-over the state.

The Samata Party improved its tally to 24 Assembly seats. These polls would mark the beginning of the end of the purely personalized politics of the three Lals in the state. While the two Lals were eclipsed at the hustings, Bansi Lal has emerged in a new role. The elections have sealed the politial life of Devi Lal for ever.

The HVP's victory has been particularly satisfying for the party in several constituencies. Though Bhajan Lal held on to Adampur against Bansi Lal's son Surinder Singh. Surinder Singh, who also contested from the Bhiwani Lok Sabha constituency defeated Congress candidate Jangbir Singh, who had joined the Congress after winning the 1991 election on the HVP ticket. Other important HVP-BJP candidate also recorded convincing victories were, industrialist, O.P. Jindal (Kurukshetra), Jai Prakash (Hissar), Suraj Bhan (Ambala), Ram Singh (Mahendergarh), I.D. Swami (Karnal).

The HVP-BJP triumphs in the Assembly elections mirrored some broad trends: One, the HVP victory came from Narnaul, where Jaswant Singh defeated the Samata Party's Ram Dhan, leaving Power Minister Virender Singh on third place. Broadly, the party did well in Haryana. The BJP too played a significant role in several important defeats.

Paradoxical Performance of the SJP

Perhaps the most curious factor in the election was the paradoxical performance of the Samajwadi Janata Party (SJP), now incorporated into the Samata Party. The principal opposition party in Haryana since Devi Lal took over as Chief Minister in June 1987 after a spectacular triumph, it managed to increase its share of Assembly representation from 16 in 1991 to 23 in 1996. For a party that had expected to come to power, however, the defeats were more spectacular than the triumphs. Devi Lal fought the battle from the Rohtak Lok Sabha seat principally around the sentimental appeal of sending the patriarch to Parliament for a last time. He, however, suffered a humiliating defeat, his son Om Prakash Chautala also lost the Narwana seat, but managed to hang on the Rori constituency.

The defeat of the Congress was humiliating for it as 14 of the 15 State Cabinet Ministers, 11 Ministers of State and the Chief Parliamentary Secretary had all lost, with just four Ministers, including Bhajan Lal, managed to save their electoral honour.

Owning moral responsibility of the defeat of the Congress, Haryana Chief Minister Bhajan Lal submitted his resignation to Governor Mahavir Prasad on May 10, 1996. The Haryana Vikas Party (HVP), led by Bansi Lal, which had emerged as the single largest party with 34 seats invited to form the government along with its allies, the BJP, which had secured 10 seats.

Performance of Different Political Parties

The peroformance of the Congress is given in Table 9.15

Table 9.15 : The performance of the Congress

Constituencies	*Vote Polled*	*Percentage*
Ambala (SC)	166408	20.85
Kurukshetra	142302	17.76
Karnal	146148	18.25
Sonepat	57615	8.23
Rohtak	198154	31.71
Faridabad	230778	28.23
Mahendergarh	216999	27.39
Bhiwani	181271	24.82
Hissar	107953	14.91
Sirsa (SC)	275459	33.50

The Congress got maximum votes in Sirsa-33.50 per cent followed by Rohtak-31.71 per cent, Faridabad-28.23 per cent and minimum in Karnal-8.23 per cent as given in Table 9.15.

The performance of the BJP, Samata and HVP is shown in Tables. 9.17, 9.18 and 1.19.

Table 9.16 :The performance of the BJP

Constituencies	*Vote Polled*	*Percentage*
Ambala (SC)	253555	31.77
Kurukshetra	–	–
Karnal	338013	42.20
Sonepat	–	–
Rohtak	158376	25.34
Faridabad	292294	35.76
Mahendergarh	265034	33.45
Bhiwani	–	–
Hissar	–	–
Sirsa (SC)	195451	23.77

On the other hand, the BJP performed well in Karnal getting 42.20 per cent votes followed by Faridabad-35.76 per cent, Mahendergarh-33.45 per cent and remained poor in Sirsa-23.77 per cent as evident from Table 9.16.

Table 9.17 : The performance of the Samata Party

Constituencies	*Vote Polled*	*Percentage*
Ambala (SC)	135702	17.00
Kurukshetra	240395	29.99
Karnal	126604	15.81
Sonepat	182012	26.00
Rohtak	195490	31.28
Faridabad	35372	4.33
Mahendergarh	66049	8.34
Bhiwani	73654	10.09
Hissar	131750	18.20
Sirsa (SC)	260312	31.66

However, the Samata Party got highest votes in Sirsa-31.66 per cent followed by Rohtak-31.28 per cent and the lowest in Faridabad-4.33 per cent as revealed in Table 9.17.

Table 9.18 : The performance of the HVP

Constituencies	*Vote Polled*	*Percentage*
Ambala (SC)	–	–
Kurukshetra	292172	36.45
Karnal	–	–
Sonepat	151294	21.61
Rohtak	–	–
Faridabad	–	–
Mahendergarh	–	–
Bhiwani	406454	55.66
Hissar	306402	42.32
Sirsa (SC)	–	–

The HVP contested in four constituencies and performed well in Hissar-55.66 per cent followed by Sirsa-42.32 per cent as seen in Table 9.18.

10

Parliamentary Elections, 1998

Caste is the dominant factor in the state politics of Haryana. The Jats who have greater political ambitions, are more or less anti-Congress, the Ahirs and the Brahmins, by and large, act according to the directions of their respective leaders. The refugees, who migrated to India after partition, and settled in Haryana, are, by and large, supporters of the BJP. However, these refugees prefer to vote for a refugee candidate as against the local Haryana candidate irrespective of the party he represents. Similarly, the agriculturist and non-agriculturist classes are opposed to each other, which is a hangover from the days of Sir Chhotu Ram, the leader who tried to free the agriculturists from the exploitation by the non-agriculturist classes.

Nomination View

A narration of constituencies, nominations and contestants is given in Tables. 10.1 and 10.2.

Table 10.1 : Number and Types of Constituencies

Type of Constituency				*Election*
Gen	*SC*	*ST*	*Total*	*Completed*
8	2	–	10	10

Table 10.2 : No. of Candidates per Constituency, 1998

Seats	*Constituencies with Candidates Numbering*								*Total Candi-dates*	*Candidates in a Constituency*		
	1	2	3	4	5	6-8	9-10	>10		Avg.	Min.	Max.
10	–	–	–	–	–	–	2	8	10	14	9	21

A category-wise data pertaining to nomination politics is given in Table 10.3.

Table 10.3 : Men-women ratio in nominations

	Type of Constituency			
	General	*SC*	*ST*	*Total*
Constituencies	8	2	0	10
Nominations Filed				
Men	156	30	0	186
Women	8	3	0	11
Total	164	33	0	197
Nominations Rejected				
Men	23	7	0	30
Women	3	2	0	5
Total	26	9	0	35
Nominations Withdrawn				
Men	19	3	0	22
Women	0	0	0	0
Total	19	3	0	22
Contesting Candidates				
Men	114	3	0	134
Women	5	0	0	6
Total	119	3	0	140
Forfeited Deposited				
Men	92	15	0	107
Women	4	0	0	4
Total	96	15	0	111

Source: Report, Lok Sabha Elections, 1998.

The number of contestants varied from 2 to 21. Out of 197 nominations, 11 were those of women. However, 6 women contested the election against 134 men.

Campaigning

'Tau purania galtee maaf karo, thailee sarkar saaf karo'. One could find such a slogan during the 12th general elections on numerous banners with others hanging either on electric poles or in the middle of the roads and streets all through the state of Haryana. The former Deputy Prime Minister Devi Lal's rechristened Haryana Lok Dal-Rashtriya (HLDR), which in alliance with Kashi Ram's Bahujana Samaj Party, resorted to its old unique selling point. The politicians set their foot at every nook and corner of the state – whether it was the Ram Lila maidan of a district headquarter or the chowk of a tehsil or a sequestered hamlet, the politicians could be witnessed everywhere addressing the people, exhorting them to vote for either themselves or a particular candidate or a party.

The state sends 10 representatives in the Lok Sabha. While Rohtak, Sonepat, Sirsa, Jind, Bhiwani and Hissar are Jat dominated constituencies. Faridabad has 4,50,000 Muslim Meos and Ambala has Punjabi and Sikh voters in commanding position. Of the five major political parties only the Congress contested all the ten seats, while Bansi Lal's Haryana Vikas Party fought on four seats, it left five seats for the BJP, which was a partner in the government. For the Sonepat seat, the party didn't field any candidate and, instead, supported an Independent. Similarly, the HLD-R fielded its candidates in seven constituencies and in the remaining three its poll ally BSP's candidate were in fray.

Interesting battle could be witnessed in Rohtak constituency, which had the highest concentration of Jat electorate, where Devi Lal himself contested. People did not seem to be happy with the attitude and autocratic style of functioning of Bansi Lal. Here "*Tau*", as the octogenarian Devi Lal is known, and Bhupinder Singh Hooda fought. "*Tau*", was there with his "last appeal", Devi Lal was bogged down by ill-health and had to be virtually carried around. He was also unable to speak much, but the rural folk mostly came to the show only to have a last glimpse of "*Tau*". Ultimately, *Tau's* "last appeal" was not accepted by the electorates of Rohtak and Bhupinder Singh Hooda won by a thin margin of 383 votes.

Voting and Results

The voting took place on February 16, 1998 and about 68.99 per cent voters exercised their franchise. 80.51 per cent voters from the general category cast their votes including 56.76 per cent males and 43.23 per cent females. 19.48 per cent Scheduled Caste voters participated in voting including 55.97 per cent males and 44.02 per cent females. The size of electors is given in Table 10.5.

Table 10.4 : Size of Electorate

No. of Electors		
Men	*Women*	Total
5978903	5107992	11086895

Table 10.5 : Voter Turnout

Electors	*Voters*	*Poll %*	*Rejected %*	*No. of Polling Stations*
11086895	7649117	68.99	1.24	15449

A category-wise of votes polled is given in Table 10.6.

Table 10.6 : Category-wise valid votes etc.

Name of State	*Type of Contituencies*	*Polling %*	*Valid Votes*	*Rejected Votes*	*Rejected Votes %*	*Missing Votes*	*Polling Stations*
Haryana	Gen	69.04	6081131	76687	1.25	949	12383
	SC	68.81	1491673	18064	1.21	613	3066
	Total	68.99	7552804	94751	1.24	1562	15449

Table 10.7 : Electors and Voters

Name of State	Type of Const.	No. of Seat	Electors			Voters		
Haryana	10	–	M	W	T	M	W	T
	Gen	8	4814344	4106779	8921123	3495901	2662868	6158767
	SC	2	1164559	1001213	216772	234174	656176	1490350
	Total	10	5978903	5107992	11086895	4330075	3319042	7649117

Source : Report, Lok Sabha Elections, 1998.

Of the total 11086895 electorate, 53.92 per cent were men. About 68.99 per cent of electorate cast their votes. The Scheduled Castes also participated in the poll-68.81 per cent as given in Table 10.7.

The election results are shown in Table 10.8.

Table 10.8 : Total Contestants, Seats Won. FD in Valid Votes.

Party	*Seats Contested*	*Seats Won*	*FD in Seats*	*Votes Polled by Party*	*% of Votes Polled*
BJP	6	1	0	1427086	18.89
BSP	3	1	1	580152	7.68
CPI	1	0	1	11270	0.15
CPM	1	0	1	25366	0.14
INC	10	3	3	1965397	26.02
JD	4	0	4	28513	0.38
AIIC(S)	1	0	1	6559	0.09
HVP	4	1	0	875803	11.60
JP	2	0	2	2936	0.04
SHS	3	0	2	145452	0.93
SP	5	0	5	15783	0.21
ABHM	1	0	1	426	0.01
ABHS	1	0	1	441	0.01
ABJS	1	0	1	1677	0.02
AJBP	2	0	2	1669	0.02
BKKUP	1	0	1	1819	0.02
BSP(A)	1	0	1	5819	0.08
HLD(R)	7	4	0	1956087	25.90
LS	1	0	1	2992	0.04
MSP	1	0	1	968	0.01
NPAP	1	0	1	919	0.01
SJP(R)	5	0	3	402382	5.33
IND	78	0	78	93288	0.24
	140	10	111	7552804	

Source : Report Lok Sabha Elections, 1998.

About 98.74 per cent votes were declared valid and Haryana Lok Dal (R) got 25.90 per cent with 4 seats, namely Kurukshetra, Sonepat, Hissar and Sirsa. The Congress secured 26.02 per cent votes and captured 3 seats, namely Karnal, Rohtak and Mahendergarh whereas the BJP got 18.89 per cent votes, HVP-11.60 per cent and BSP-7.68 per cent with one seat each, namely Faridabad, Bhiwani respectively.

As many as 111 (79.28 per cent) candidates lost their deposits. 6 women contested the election and Kailasho Devi won from Kurukshetra.

The defeat of HVP-BJP in the elections was the result of its highly unpopular policies. The HVP could manage only one seat. Bansi Lal's son, Surinder Singh, defeated the HLD(R)'s Ajay Chautala, son of Om Prakash Chautala, by a margin of 9711 votes. The BJP won only the

Faridabad seat where its candidate Ramchander Bainda defeated the Congress (I)'s Khurshid Ahmed. Simmering communal tension, coupled with an industrial recession, appeared to have aided the BJP.

Among the victims were former Deputy Prime Minister Devi Lal who lost to the Congress(I)'s Bhupinder Singh Hooda in the Rohtak constituency by a thin margin of 383 votes.

The BJP-HVP government had to pay a heavy price for its prohibition policy in Haryana, by retaining only two seats out of seven it held in the 11th Lok Sabha. The Congress, with 3 per cent swing in its favour and with 26 per cent vote share, gained one seat—from two to three. The BSP won the Ambala seat by a margin of 2864 votes while the Haryana Vikas Party could retain only Bhiwani seat with a margin of 9711 votes. Anti-incumbency factor also worked against it. The Congress with three seats and Haryana Lok Dal (Rashtriya) with four seats gained grounds in the state.

The participation and performance of women is given in Table 10.9, 10.10 and 10.11.

Table 10.9 : Women Participation in Polls

		Poll %	
Women Electors	*Women Voters*	*Women*	*Total*
5107992	3319042	64.98	68.99

Table 10.10 : Performance of Women Candidates

State	*No. of Seats*	*No. of Women*		
		Contenstants	*Elected*	*F.D.s*
Haryana	10	6	1	4

Table 10.11 : Women Candidates, 1998

Constituency	*Sr.No.*	*Candidate*	*Party*	*Party's Type*	*Vote Polled*	*%*
2. Kurukshetra	4	Kailasho Devi	HLD(R)	U	333387	43.57
4. Sonepat	8	Kalawati	IND	Z	243	0.04
6. Faridabad	17	Poonam Singh	AJBP	U	673	0.07
6. Faridabad	15	Sumitra	IND	Z	800	0.09
8. Bhiwani	5	Laxmi	ABHM	U	426	0.06
10. Sirsa (SC)	2	Selja	INC	N	215521	29.48

Performance of the different political parties: A constituency-wise view

Congress : The performance of the Congress is given in Table 10.11.

Table 10.12 : Performance of the Congress : A Constituency-wise View

Constituencies	*Votes polled*	*Percentage*
Ambala (SC)	174171	23.52
Kurukshetra	191867	25.07
Karnal	327750	41.14
Sonepat	82292	11.89
Rohtak	254951	38.66
Faridabad	288679	32.10
Mahendergarh	329126	41.50
Bhiwani	27789	3.71
Hissar	37251	10.10
Sirsa (SC)	215521	29.48

Source : Report, Lok Sabha Elections, 1998.

BJP: The performance of the BJP is given in Table 10.13.

Table 10.13 : Performance of the BJP : A Constituency-wise View

Constituencies	*Votes polled*	*Percentage*
Ambala (SC)	270928	36.58
Kurukshetra	—	—
Karnal	275689	34.60
Sonepat	—	—
Rohtak	130895	19.85
Faridabad	304022	33.81
Mahendergarh	260990	32.91
Bhiwani	—	—
Hissar	—	—
Sirsa (SC)	184562	25.24

Source : Report, Lok Sabha Elections, 1998.

HVP: The performance of the HVP is given in Table 10.14.

Table 10.14 : Performance of the HVP : A Constituency-wise View

Constituencies	*Votes polled*	*Percentage*
Ambala (SC)	—	—
Kurukshetra	181791	23.76
Karnal	—	—
Sonepat	152975	22.10
Rohtak	—	—
Faridabad	—	—
Mahendergarh	—	—
Bhiwani	361257	48.17
Hissar	179780	24.79
Sirsa (SC)	—	—

Source : Report, Lok Sabha Elections, 1998.

HLD(R) : The performance of the HLD(R) is given in Table 10.14.

Table 10.15 : Performance of the HLD(R) : A Constituency-wise View

Constituencies	*Votes polled*	*Percentage*
Ambala (SC)	—	—
Kurukshetra	333387	43.57
Karnal	156565	19.65
Sonepat	290299	41.44
Rohtak	254568	38.61
Faridabad	—	—
Mahendergarh	—	—
Bhiwani	351546	46.87
Hissar	260271	35.89
Sirsa (SC)	309451	42.33

Source : Report, Lok Sabha Elections, 1998.

As said earlier 6 women contested the election but only one could win as evident from Table 10.9.

The Congress got the maximum votes in Mahendergarh-41.50 % followed by Rohtak-38.66 %, Faridabad-32.10 % and the minimum in Bhiwani-3.71 % is given in Table 10.11.

The BJP secured highest votes in Ambala-36.58 per cent followed by Kurukshetra-34.60 %, Faridabad-33.81%, Mahendergarh-32.91 % and lowest in Rohtak-19.85 % as pointed out in Table 10.13.

Except Bhiwani, the H.V.P. could not get good response of the voters as seen in Table 10.14.

Out of seven constituencies, the HLD (R) fared well in Bhiwani by getting 46.87 % votes followed by Ambala-43.57 %, Sonepat-41.44 % and the minimum in Kurukshetra-19.65 %, as revealed in Table 10.15.

11

Parliamentary Elections, 1999

Lok Sabha elections in Haryana were fought in a changed political scenario which affected the campaigning and the final outcome as well. Political alignments and new alliances had come up in sharp contrast to the 1998 polls when the state largely witnessed triangular contests between the HVP-BJP, the INLD-BSP and the Congress (I). This time there were direct contests between the INLD-BJP and the Congress (I) as the HVP and BSP were nowhere in the reckoning.

On the eve of the elections, the sudden withdrawal of Congress support to HVP government in the state triggered the downfall of Bansi Lal's government. Before it, the BJP had withdrawn its support to it. The ironical fall-out was that Om Prakash Chautala, INLD supremo, assumed reins of power for the fourth time with the help of the breakaway faction of the H.V.P. He also forged an electoral alliance with the BJP.

Nominations

Data pertaining to nominations is given in Tables 11.1 and 11.2.

Table 11.1 : Number and Types of Constituencies

Type of Constituency				*Election*
Gen	*SC*	*ST*	*Total*	*Completed*
8	2	0	10	10

Table 11.2 : No. of Candidates per Constituency, 1999

Seats	*Constituencies with Candidates Numbering*								*Total Candidates*	*Candidates in a Constituency*		
	1	2	3	4	5	6-8	9-10	>10		*Avg.*	*Min.*	*Max.*
10	–	–	–	–	–	–	2	8	114	11	6	29

The number of contestants differed from 6 to 29 and on an average 11 condidates contested the polls as shown in Table 11.2.

The number of nominations came down from 459 in 1996 to 142 and so the contestants from 294 to 114. Only 4 women filed their nomination and 3 contested the elections as given in Table 11.3.

A category-wise details of nominations is given in Table 11.3.

Table 11.3: Men-women ratio of nominations

	Type of Constituency			
	General	*SC*	*ST*	*Total*
Constituencies	8	2	0	10
Nominations Filed				
Men	121	17	0	138
Women	4	0	0	4
Total	125	17	0	142
Nominations Rejected				
Men	16	2	0	18
Women	0	0	0	0
Total	16	2	0	18
Nominations Withdrawn				
Men	8	1	0	9
Women	1	0	0	1
Total	9	1	0	10
Contesting Candidates				
Men	97	14	0	111
Women	3	0	0	3
Total	100	14	0	114
Forfeited Deposited				
Men	82	82	0	92
Women	1	1	0	1
Total	83	83	0	93

Source : Report, Lok Sabha Elections, 1999.

The men-women ratio of electors was 54.49:45.51 per cent whereas 58.36:41.64 of voters as pointed out in Table 11.4.

Table 11.4 : Category-wise nominations

	Type of Constituency			
	General	*SC*	*ST*	*Total*
1. No. of Constituencies	8	2	0	10
2. Electors				
Men	4826700	1188680	0	6015380
Women	4019970	1003605	0	5023575
Total	8846670	2192285	0	11038955
3. Electors Who Voted				
Men	3332189	770617	0	4102806
Women	2357858	569300	0	2927158
Total	5690047	1339917	0	7029964
4. Poll Percentage	64.32	61.12	0	63.68
5. Valid Votes	5645274	1327765	0	6973039
6. Rejected Votes				
Votes	43833	11744	0	55577
Percentage	0.77	0.88	0	0.79
7. Missing Votes	940	408	0	1348
8. No. of Polling Stations	12382	3067	0	15449
9. Average No. of Electors Per Polling Station	714	715	0	715

Source: Report, Lok Sabha Elections, 1999.

A party-wise F.D is given in Table 11.5.

Table 11.5 : No. of Candidates and Forfeiture of Deposits, 1999

Seats	*Number of Candidates*					*No. of FDs.**				
	N	*S*	*U*	*Z*	*Total*	*N*	*S*	*U*	*Z*	*Total*
10	20	17	3	74	114	5	11	3	74	93

N = National Parties, S = State Parties, U = Registered (Unrecognized) Parties, Z=Independents.

**FDs* = Forfeiture of Diposits.

Poll Alliances

The Congress did not have any alliance this time. The ruling Indian National Lok Dal (INLD) led by Chief Minister Om Prakash Chautala had forged an alliance with the BJP. The Haryana Vikas Party, led by former Chief Minister Bansi Lal, had entered into seat adjustment with the BSP for three constituencies of Ambala, Mahendergarh and Bhiwani.

BJP-INLD Alliance

The Bhartiya Janata Party (BJP) and the ruling Indian National Lok Dal (INLD) entered into an electoral alliance; with both parties deciding to equally share the 10 parliamentary seats of the state. The BJP fielded candidates from Ambala, Karnal, Faridabad, Mahendragarh and Sonepat. The INLD candidates contested from Hissar, Sirsa, Bhiwani, Kurukshetra and Rohtak. The BJP had won only the Faridabad Lok Sabha seat in the 1998 elections in alliance with the Haryana Vikas Party (HVP). The INLD had four members in the Lok Sabha.

Three Women Contested

Of the three women candidates of prominent parties, two won while one even lost her deposit. The INLD successfully fielded Ms. Kailasho Devi a sitting member from Kurukshetra, while Sudha Yadav wife of a Kargil hero contested on the BJP ticket from Mahendergarh. The defeated prominent women candidate belonged to the Samajwadi Party.

Caste plays an important role in electioneering in the country and Haryana was no exception to it. All political parties had wooed the Jat community leaders to support them in the fray. Jat candidates figure prominently in the list of contestants of all parties. The Jats comprise 30 per cent of electorate in the state and they hold the key to five of the 10 Lok Sabha constituencies where they are in 39 per cent of population.

Straight Contests

Electioneering came to an end for the 10 Lok Sabha constituencies in Haryana on September 3, 1999 with the INLD-BJP combine in a virtual straight fight with the Congress on September 5, 1999.

The combine has tried, successfully to a large extent, to make the contest as a matter of choice between Atal Behari Vajpayee and Sonia Gandhi in the absence of local or economic issues.

The prestige of several top leaders on both ends of political spectrum was at stake. Three former Chief Ministers and an incumbent Chief Ministership had personal interest in the outcome of the elections.

Bhajan Lal (Congress) was locked, perhaps, in the toughest political battle of his life in Karnal where he was pitched against the BJP nominee, I.D. Swami, a former IAS officer, who was humbled by his former political master in 1998. The support of the INLD this time had made Swami a formidable candidate.

Ajay Chautala, elder son of INLD supremo and Chief Minister Om Prakash Chautala took on Surinder Singh, son of former Chief Minister and HVP President, Bansi Lal in Bhiwani in a triangular contest with Dharamveer (Congress) forming the third end.

Another two top Congress leaders of the state, Bhupinder Singh Hooda, Party President and Birender Singh, former Party President, were sweating it out in Rohtak and Hissar, respectively, against relatively lightweight INLD nominees, Capt. Inder Singh and Surinder Singh Barwala.

A former Chief Minister, Rao Birender Singh, had to enter electioneering in support of his son, Inderjit Singh (Congress) to protect his fiefdom, Mahendergarh, which is under a strong attack by a war widow, Santosh Yadav. By fielding Yadav, the BJP hoped to topple the Rao clan by playing upon the sentiments of the voters.

In Sonepat, a veteran Congress leader, Chiranji Lal Sharma, was finding the going tough against the BJP nominee, Kishan Singh Sangwan, who was an INLD member of the dissolved House. Chautala gifted the Sonepat seat as well as the candidate to the BJP on an appeal made by Vajpayee.

An industrialist, Om Prakash Jindal, contesting from Kurukshetra on the Congress ticket seemed to give the run to the sitting INLD M.P, Kailasho Saini. Congress strategists considered, Kurukshetra as one of the possible seats the party could win, thanks to vigorous campaigning by the self-made industrialist.

The All-India Secretary of the BJP Scheduled Caste Morcha, Rattan Lal Kataria, and the Haryana BSP President, Aman Kumar Nagra, faced a strong challenge from Phool Chand Mullana of the Congress in Ambala. The INLD was leaving no stone unturned to wrest the seat from the BSP, which, ironically won this seat with its help last year.

Meanwhile, the state government claimed to have made adequate arrangements for a fair, free and smooth poll.

As many as 114 candidates were contesting the elections with the maximum number of 29 candidates in the Bhiwani constituency and a minimum of six each from Sonepat and Sirsa (SC).

In 1998 Lok Sabha polls there was triangular contest between the HVP-BJP the INLD-BSP and the Congress (I). But in 1999 there was direct contest between the INLD-BJP and the Congress (I) and the H.V.P. and BSP were nowhere in the reckoning.

On the eve of the elections, sudden withdrawal of the Congress support to the HVP government in the state triggered the downfall of Bansi Lal government and Chautala assumed the reins of power fourth time with the help of the breakway faction of the HVP as well as the BJP.

The caste issue took a back seat in the election as it was overlooked by national issues, popularity of Atal Behari Vajpayee and Kargil war.

There was straight contest in 7 constituencies whereas in Ambala, Bhiwani, and Mahendergarh it was tri-cornered.

As many as 39 party nominees and 75 independents joined the fray for September 5, 1997 elections. The INLD and BJP fielded 5 candidates each.

The INLD entered into alliance with the BJP whereas the HVP with BSP for three constituencies.

The Congress fielded its candidates in all constituencies. However, Selja refrained to contest from Sirsa as she had lost the seat in 1996 and 1998.

Congress

The party fielded its candidates in all constituencies. It suffered a set back when Mrs. Shelja former MP and Union Minister declined to contest Lok Sabha polls from the Sirsa reserved constituency, Ms. Shelja now a Secretary in the All India Congress Committee had won this seat in 1991 but lost it in 1996 and 1998 polls. However, political observers feel that she might have opted out of "fear" that the Congress might meet its Waterloo in the battle of the hustings in the changed political scenario in the state. The ground reality was that all the political stalwarts fielded by the Congress faced an uphill task this time because of the INLD-BJP nexus and the fall-out of the dubious role played by the Congress leadership in first extending support to Bansi Lal and later withdrawing it suddenly with no logic.

Despite drawing a blank in all seats in Haryana, the Congress emerged as the single largest party going by the vote share which increased by nearly 9 per cent compared to last time. The party which had a swing of 8.91 per cent points in its favour polled 34.93 per cent of the total valid votes against the ruling Indian National Lok Dal which mustered 28.72 per cent votes and the Bhartiya Janata Party's 29.21 per cent, were victorious in all the 5 seats contested. In terms of votes, the Congress got 24,35,752 ballots out of 69,73,039 valid votes polled. In 1998, the party polled 19,65,397 votes which was 26.02 per cent of the total valid votes.

Of the 90 Vidhan Sabha segments the party's candidates led in 5. Of these three Nuh, Taoru and Ferozepur Jhirka fell in the Faridabad Lok Sabha constituency, one in Mahendergarh and the fifth in Bhiwani (Tosham). The lead in the remaining 85 Assembly segments was shared between the INLD (44) and the BJP (41).The two stalwarts of the party had to lick dust in the prestigious Rohtak and Karnal constituencies. For Bhajan Lal the deal was more shocking as it was his first defeat in an election in his political career of over three decades. Bhupinder Singh

Hooda had a taste of defeat for the first time in his decade long political life.

Other Parties

Mulayam Singh Yadav's Samajwadi Party performed miserably in Haryana. The party polled only 29,393 votes, which was just 0.42 per cent of the valid votes. The Janata Dal (S), Sharad Pawar's Nationalist Congress Party, the RPI, the Akhil Bharatiya Jana Sangh and the CPI (M) too met the same fate. Their respective tally was merely 0.02, 0.06, 0.07, 0.02 and 0.15 per cent. All lost their security deposits.

The fiercest electoral fight was in Bhiwani where Bansi Lal's son, Surinder Singh faced a major challenge from Chautala's son, Ajay Chautala. Also in the fray was former minister Dharamvir on the Congress ticket and he was no less a threat to both Surinder Singh and Ajay Chautala. Though Bhiwani is considered as a stronghold of Bansi Lal; his hold appeared to have weakened this time largely due to some of his alleged unpopular policies during his three-year rule in the state. Ajay Chautala trounced his main rival Surinder Singh by a hefty margin of 2,03,406 votes. The latter finished third in the race.

Karnal witnessed a battle between former Chief Minister Bhajan Lal (Congress) and I.D. Swami a retired IAS Officer of the BJP. In the last Lok Sabha poll, Bhajan Lal had trounced Swami with a margin of over 50,000 votes, this time he was finding himself on a slippery wicket. Swami's biggest plus point was that he was supported by the ruling INLD which has a large rural base. Swami won the race by a impressive margin of 1,47,854 votes. Bhajan Lal had his first Electoral defeat at the hands of Swami.

In Rohtak, Congress Chief Bhupinder Singh Hooda was once again in the fray and a tough fight from the ruling INLD-BJP combine. To take advantage of the Kargil, the combine has fielded ex-serviceman Capt. Inder Singh, Mr. Hooda has been winning since 1991 and in the last three Lok Sabha Elections he trounced no less a person than Deputy Prime Minister Devi Lal. This time he did not smile on him. He also joined the nine of his party who were handed out the hustings.

Caste had always played a key role in feudalistic Haryanvi politics, with Jats calling the shots. This time caste politics played a secondary role as the poll scenario was dominated by national issues, the main one being the popularity and performance of Atal Behari Vajpayee, and the Kargil war. The controversy over Sonia Gandhi's origin did not figure in election campaigning. Haryana was all set to witness virtually staignt fights in 7 out of a total of 10 constituencies. The remaining 3 of Ambala, Bhiwani and Mahendergarh had tri-cornered contest.

The Prime Minister, A.B. Vajpayee addressed a rally at Fatehabad on August 20, 1999 in Hissar and Sonia on August 25, 1999. Hissar has a total of 1025245 votes including 563191 males and 462054 females.

As per Vidhan Sabha constituency-wise the electors were Kalayat 102319, Narwana– 109654, Uchana – 112725, Rajaund – 96470, Jind – 131695, Barwala – 118339, Narnaund – 101594, Hissar – 142658, Ghirai – 109481. In 1998, it was triangle contest and S.S. Barwala won by 26030.

In 1984, Birender Singh of the Congress won in 1989, Jai Parkash won in 1977, Inder Singh of the Janata Party won in 1980, Mani Ram Bagri of the Janata Party won in 1990, Master Narain Singh of the Congress won in 1990, Jai Parkash won in 1997, S.S. Barwala of the INLD won in 1998. In Hissar, there were 8 condidates.

The constituency has 10.25 lakh voters. Birender Singh of the Congress was nominated very late whereas, Barwala started his campaign early. The Congress depended on SC and BC voters. A caste-wise analysis of voters revealed 38 per cent Jats, 22 per cent SCs, traders 6 per cent, Sikhs 5 per cent. Jai Prakash won the election in 1998, now supporting the Congress candidate.

In Karnal, a total 14 candidates were in the fray including N.D. Gupta of SSP, I.D. Swami of the BJP, Bhajan Lal of the Congress and Anup Bishnoi – Son-in-law of Bhajan Lal as an Independent.

In 1998, Vidhan Sabha segment-wise votes were :

Indri – 90923, Nelokheri – 78497; Karnal – 93152, Jundla –

71505, Gharaunda – 80060, Asandh – 78960, Panipat – 104742, Smalkha – 82074, Naultha – 72774.

In Mahendergarh, a total 9 candidates were in the fray including Sudha Yadav of the BJP, Rao Inderjit from the Congress and Raghu Yadav of the BSP. There were 2.5 lakh Dalit voters and about 1 lakh Backwards.

The Kurukshetra saw a straight fight between the sitting MP Gurdial Singh Saini of the Janata Dal and former Haryana Speaker, Tara Singh of the Congress (I).

Rajiv Gandhi addressed the Congress rally to boost the election campaign of the party. The BJP candidate Shiv Partap Bajaj raised the issue of Ram and Roti. The Samajwadi Janata Party nominee Shan Singh Rana was fielded at the stance of the former Prime Minister, Chander Sekhar.

In the last election, Gurdial Singh Saini defeated Harpal Singh of the Congress (I). The Kurukshetra had about 927999 votes including 134543 Jats, 59319 Punjabis, 72473 Brahmins, 57123 Sikhs and 48875 Sainis, apart from 180484 backwards and 192782 Scheduled Castes. Saini pinned hopes on Backward votes in the wake of Mandal report whereas the Congress candidate on Sikhs, Brahmins, Jats and Banias.

Chautala as Chief Minister declared Rs. 10 lakh to each Kargil victim, repair of roads, water and electricity supply round the clock and good law and order structure in the state. Moreover, he promised for water and power relief to farmers, abolish the octroi, abolition of the inspector *raj*, dignity of employees be restored and take cases registeved against them be withdrawn, youth employment on merit, cottage industries be promoted, minimum wage of labour be doubled, pension of senior citizen be doubled etc.

The dwindling fortunes of the HVP headed by former Chief Minister Bansi Lal not only made it difficult for the party to find candidates, but even then it fielded some of them.

The party planned to contest only two seats, i.e. Bhiwani and Kurukshetra. But Ved Pal did not file his papers from Kurukshetra.

Several of its district level leader across the state decide to desert the party either to support the Congress or the INLD candidates in the election.

The BJP-led NDA released its manifesto promising to free the triple curses of "*bhookh, bhay and bhrashtachar*" (Hunger, fear and corruption), reconciliation with minorities, administrative reforms, including those for the police and other civil services, bring GDP growth to the 7-8 per cent, '*berozgari hatao*' (Unemployment eradication), poverty eradication, national water policy for prompt settlement of disputes, health and drinking water, education, and housing for all, empowerment of women, population stabilization by 2010, commission to review Constitution of India, Backward Area Commission for each state, ensure fixed term for all elected bodies, replace no-confidence motion with German system, electoral reforms, national judicial commission to be set up, measures to ensure right of franchise for armed forces, Lok Pal Bill to be introduced, increased expenditure on defence, review Prasar Bharati Act etc.

Voting and Results

Out of 11038955 electorate, 7029964(63.68 per cent) exercised their franchise including the women and S.C, in 15449 polling stations set up in different parts of the state. The size of electorate, their trun out, number of contestants, performance of different political parties etc. are given in Tables 11.6 to 11.19.

Table 11.6 :Size of Electorate

No. of Electors		
Men	*Women*	*Total*
6015380	5023575	11038955

Table 11.7 : Voter Turnout

Electors	*Voters*	*Poll %*	*Rejected %*	*No. of Polling Stations*
11038955	7029964	63.68	0.79	15449

Table 11.8 : Contestants, winners etc.

State: Haryana	*Party Type*	*Party*	*Seats Contested*	*Seats Won*	*FD in Seats Votes*	*Polled by Party*	*% of Votes Polled*
	N	BJP	5	5	0	2036797	29.21
	N	BSP	3	0	3	136330	1.96
	N	CPM	1	0	1	10511	0.15
	N	INC	10	0	0	2435752	34.93
	N	JD(S)	1	0	1	1124	0.02
	S	HVP	2	0	1	188731	2.71
	S	INLD	5	5	0	2002700	28.72
	S	NCP	2	0	2	3940	0.06
	S	RPI	1	0	1	5176	0.07
	S	SP	7	0	7	29393	0.42
	U	ABJS	1	0	1	1230	0.02
	U	AJBP	1	0	1	2204	0.03
	U	BSP(A)	1	0	1	6630	0.10
	Z	IND	74	0	74	112521	1.61
	TOTAL		114	10	93	6973039	

Source: Report, Lok Sabha Elections, 1999.

Number of electors and votes polled in Haryana during 1999 general elections to Lok Sabha is given in Table 11.9.

Table 11.9 : Electors and voters: a constituency-wise view

Constituency	*No. of Electors*	*No. of Voles polled*	*%age of votes polled to No. of Electors*
Ambala (SC)	1091846	698854	64.01
Kurukshetra	1073147	730566	68.08
Karnal	1131448	771194	68.16
Sonepat	1057175	659535	62.39
Rohtak	938878	634235	67.55
Faridabad	1330157	755003	56.76
Mahendergarh	1236918	752654	60.85
Bhiwani	1053603	740347	70.27
Hissar	1025344	646513	63.05
Sirsa (SC)	1100439	641063	58.26
Total	11038955	7029964	63.68

Source: Report, Lok Sabha Elections, 1999.

Women in Election

Total electors = 11038955
Women electors = 5023575
Total Nominations = 142
Women = 4 Scheduled Caste women = Nil
Total Contestants = 114
Women= 3
Scheduled Caste women = Nil
Women security fofeited = 1
Women elected = 2

The participation as well as performance of women in electoral politics is given in Table 11.10 and 11.11.

Table 11.10 : Women Participation in Polls

Women Electors	*Wome Voters*	*Poll % Women*	*Total*
5023575	2927158	58.27	63.68

Table 11.11 : Performance of Women Candidates

State	*No. of Seats*	*No. of Women*		
		Contestants	*Elected*	*FDs*
Haryana	10	3	2	1

The men-women ratio of electors was 54.49 : 5.51 per cent as given in Table 11.6. Faridabad had the highest number of electors–1330157 followed by Mahendergarh–1236918, Karnal–11318 and the lowest in Rohtak–938878 as revealed in Table 11.9.

The participation of women in these election was very poor as only 3 contested. despite they constituted 45.51 per cent of the state electors as given in Tables 11.10. and 11.11.

The Congress faltered but its vote share increased to 34.93 per cent (by 8.91%) whereas the INLD mustered 28.72 per cent and the BJP-29.21percent.

The Congress led only in 5 of the 90 Assembly segments – Taoru, Nuh, Ferozpur-Zhirka, Mahendergarh and Tosham, whereas the INLD led in 44 and the BJP in 41.

Table 11.12 : Women Contestants, winners etc.

Sl. No.	*Candidate*	*Party*	*Party Type*	*Vote Polled*	*%*	*Status*	*Margin*	*Winner's Votes*	*Total Valid Votes*
1	Kailasho Devi	INLD	S	438701	60.61	W	0	438701	723757
4	Kanta	SP	S	5295	0.84	W	361631	366926	633733
1	Sudha Yadav	BJP	S	420706	56.49	W	0	420706	744706

The figures pertaining to election results are given in Table 11.13.

Bhajan Lal licked the dust for the first time in his political carrier of 30 years and Bhupinder Singh Hooda was also defeated.

Samajwadi Party of Mulayam Singh Yadav performed miserably by polling the 0.42 per cent votes whereas JD(S), NCP, RPI, CPI (M) too met the same fate.

Table 11.13 : Election Results : Lok Sabha, 1999

Parties	*Votes Polled*	*%*	*Seats won*
BJP	203677	29.21	5
BSP	136330	1.96	–
CPM	350958	0.98	–
Congress	2435722	34.93	–
JD(S)	1124	0.02	–
HVP	188731	2.71	–
NLD	2002700	28.72	5
NCP	3940	0.06	–
RPI	5176	0.07	–
SP	29393	0.42	–
AJBP	2204	0.10	–
BSP(A)	6630	0.10	–
Independent	112521	1.61	–
Total	–	–	10

Source: Report, Lok Sabha Elections, 1999.
Total electors = 11038955
Voters = 7029964

In Bhiwani, Ajay Chautala trounced his main rival Surinder Singh by a margin of 203406 votes. In Karnal I.D. Swami won the election by 147854 votes defeating Bhajan Lal who won the election in 1998. In Rohtak, Bhupinder Singh Hooda lost the seat who had won it since 1991.

Sushil Indora contested from the INLD and Om Prakash Kharwala from the Congress. In 1996, Selja defeated Indora by 15000 votes. In 1998 Indora got 309451 and defeated Selja. The HVP and BJP lost in Haryana getting 14899 votes.

There were 110439 voters including 594365 of males and 505329 of females.

Prakash Kherwala of the Congress got 199545 votes whereas Selja 215521 in 1998. The INLD candidate Indora defeated his Congress rival by 221654, votes whereas in 1998, he got 309451 votes and won by 90000 votes. The SCs and BCs constituted about 50 per cent votes.

In 1998, it was triangular contest whereas in 1999 it was a straight one. The BJP candidate Hans Raj Swan got 184562 votes in 1998.

Selja who won the seat from the Congress in 1991 and 1996 but opted out of the contest, even after AICC had announced her candidate in 1999 and then Om Prakash Keharwala was made the Congress nominee, Selja was not present when Keharwala filed his nomination paper.

Independents had no say in the Lok Sabha polls this time. Eighty of them together polled 1,12,521 votes totalling a percentage of 1.61 and forfeited their securities.

Election 1999 : BJP-INLD Combine Makes A Clean Sweep

The BJP and its new ally Indian National Lok Dal headed by Om Prakash Chautala made a clean sweep of Haryana's 10 seats. Thanks to Congress's flip-flop policy of first backing former Chief Minister Bansi Lal after BJP withdrew support to his government and then ditching him within a month. Thus, instead of gaining from the anti-incumbency factor, Congress even lost 3 seats it had, 2 to the BJP and one to the INLD. This was despite a near 9 per cent swing that raised its vote share from 26.02 to 34.93 per cent, 23 point lower than the BJP-INLD combine's total of 57.93 per cent.

Bansi Lal's Haryana Vikas Party, which had run a coalition with the BJP for over two years before the saffron party switched sides in return for Chautala's backing at the Centre after the HVP lost its clout in the 1998 Lok Sabha poll, yielded its lone seat to the INLD. Its vote share dropped 8.89 points from 11.6 to 2.71 per cent.

The HVP ally BSP too lost its only seat to the BJP as its support fell 5.75 points from 7.68 to 1.93 per cent. Two; candidates of the CPM and the JDS polled a minuscule 0.15 and 0.02 per cent, while 13 'others' and 74 Independents shared 2.33 per cent. Winning 5 seats with 29.21 per cent, over 10 points higher than the 18.89 it got last time, the BJP gained 4 seats, 2 from Congress and one each from the BSP and HVP. and Chautala's party then going under the name of Haryana Lok Dal (Rashtriya). Its ally, the INLD too won 5 seats for 28.72 per cent, one more than what his earlier party won for 25.90 per cent in 1998. It wrested a seat each from the Congress and the HVP, while retaining 3 the HLDR seats. Two SC seats were shared by the BJP and the INLD, with the first snatching Ambala from the BSP, and the second taking the Sirsa seat it had won last time as HLDR.

Former Congress Chief Minister, Bhajan Lal, who went out of power in the simultaneous Assembly poll in 1996, lost Karnal by 147,854 votes to the BJP's I.D. Swami, whom he had defeated by 52,601 votes in 1998. Haryana Congress Chief, Bhupinder Singh Hooda, who had thrice in a row, defeated Chautala's father, '*Tau*' Devi Lal, a former Deputy Prime Minister in his home turf of Rohtak since 1991, lost to little known Inder Singh of the INLD by 1,44,693 votes.

Bansi Lal's son Surender Singh who had defeated Chautala's son Ajay Chautala last time finished a distant third in Bhiwani with the junior Chautala trouncing Dharamvir of the Congress by over two lakh votes.

The BJP's Sudha Yadav, widow of a Kargil martyr, unseated Inderjit Singh of Congress in Mahendergarh and Kailasho Devi retained Kurukshetra for the INLD instead of Chautala's old party. A third woman candidate contesting on the SP ticket lost her deposit in Rohtak.

In the 1967 poll, the first after the formation of the state, the Congress won 7 of the 9 seats with 44.1per cent votes. 2 other seats were shared by the Bharatiya Jan Sangh and an independent. The Sangh and the Independents polled $\frac{1}{5}$ of the votes each.

After the 1969 split in Congress, Indira Gandhi's Congress (I) won 7 seats in 1971 as its votes went zooming up to 52.6 per cent. The Congress (O) faction polled 11.3 per cent, but a seat eluded it.

The Jana Sangh, which re-emerged as the BJP in 1984, kept its seat though its vote share dropped to 11.2 per cent, while a new Vishal Haryana Party won the remaining seat with 9.1 per cent votes.

Congress (I) was completely swept away by the 1977 Janata wave failing to win even a single seat though it polled 18 per cent votes. The Janata claimed all seats, now raised to 10, with a massive 70.4 per cent mandate. The Vishal Haryana Party concerned 4.6 per cent votes.

Congress (I) won back half the seats in 1980 with 32.6 per cent votes. The Janata Party itself could win only one seat for 28.1per cent votes, while the breakaway Janata Party Secular bagged four seats for 33.5 per cent votes. The Congress made a clean sweep in 1984 as its vote share soared to its highest ever of 55 per cent. Jana Sangh now in its BJP incarnation polled 7.5per cent, while Lok Dal polled 19.1per cent. The Congress decline began in 1989 when its tally dropped to 4 MPs with 46.2 per cent votes as the newly formed Janata Dal bagged six for 38.9 per cent. The BJP failed to win a seat though it polled 8.3 per cent votes. Congress staged a comeback in 1991 winning all but Bhiwani, which went to Bansi Lal's HVP.

Key Contests

In Bhiwani, Bansi Lal, Chief Minister during 1968-75 and 1986-87, won thrice from Bhiwani since 1980 as a Congress nominee. In 1996, his son Surender Singh defeated Jangbir Singh, who won on HVP ticket in 1991 but switched over to the Congress before the poll.

In Rohtak, former Deputy Prime Minister Devi Lal was elected from both Rohtak and Sikar in Rajasthan in 1980, but kept Sikar. In 1991 and again in 1996 he was defeated by Bhupendra Singh of the Congress.

In Kurukshetra, Gulzari Lal Nanda, twice interim Prime Minister, won from here in 1967 and 1971, when it was called Kaithal.

In Faridabad, the constituency with most Muslims in Haryana (25 per cent) was represented by Maulana Abul Kalam Azad in 1957 when it formed part of the Gurgaon seat.

The NCP contested from Sonepat and obtained 0.28 per cent votes.

The HVP contested from Faridabad and secured 4.97 per cent votes, Mahendergarh – 0.28 per cent, Bhiwani 20.69 per cent.

The anatomy of electoral politics since 1967 is given in Table 11.15.

Table 11.14 : Lok Sabha Electoral History in Haryana (1967-1999)

Year	*Leading Party*	*Seats won*	*Vote (%)*	*Runner-up*	*Seats won*	*Vote (%)*
1967	Congress	7	44.1	BJS	1	19.9
1971	Congress	7	52.6	BJS	1	11.2
1977	BLD	10	70.4	Congress	00	18.0
1980	Congress	5	32.6	JPS	4	33.5
1984	Congress	10	55.0	LKD	0	19.1
1989	Janata Dal	6	38.9	Congress	4	46.2
1991	Congress	9	37.2	HVP	1	3.4
1996	BLD	4	19.7	HVP	3	15.2
1998	HLD	4	25.9	Congress	3	26.0
1999	BJP	5	29.21	INLD	5	28.72

Performance of Parties

INLD: the position of the party is given in Table 11.15.

Table 11.15 : Performance of the INLD: 1999 Elections

Constituencies	*Votes Polled*	*Percentage*	
Ambala (Res.)	– *	–	
Kurukshetra	438701	60.61	I
Karnal	–	–	
Sonepat	–	–	
Rohtak	366926	57.93	I
Faridabad	–	–	
Mahendergarh	–	–	
Bhiwani	381255	52.01	I
Hissar	396540	62.03	I
Sirsa	419278	65.98	I

* Because of INLD-BJP alliance these seats were given to the BJP.
Source : Report, Lok Sabha Elections, 1999.

BJP: it bagged five seats in alliance with the INLD. Its performance is shown in Table 11.16

Table 11.16 : Performance of the BJP : 1999 Elections

Constituencies	*Votes Polled*	*Percentage*	
Ambala (Res.)	357460	51.61	I
Kurukshetra	*	–	
Karnal	433733	56.25	I
Sonepat	457056	69.83	I
Rohtak	–	–	
Faridabad	367842	49.34	I
Mahendergarh	430706	56.49	I
Bhiwani	–	–	
Hissar	–	–	
Sirsa	–	–	

* Because of INLD-BJP alliance these five seats were contested and won by the INLD.

Source : Report, Lok Sabha Elections, 1999.

Congress: the performance of the Congress is given in Table 11.17.

Table 11.17 : Performance of the Congress : 1999 Elections

Constituencies	*Votes Polled*	*Percentage*	
Ambala (Res.)	232982	33.65	II
Kurukshetra	275091	38.01	II
Karnal	285879	37.07	
Sonepat	190918	29.17	
Rohtak	222233	35.09	II
Faridabad	333594	44.75	II
Mahendergarh	281566	37.81	II
Bhiwani	177849	24.26	II
Hissar	236088	36.93	II
Sirsa	199552	37.40	II

Source : Report, Lok Sabha Elections, 1999.

Samata Party: its performance is highlighted in Table 11.18.

Table 11.18 : Performance of the Samata Party : 1999 Elections

Constituencies	*Votes Polled*	*Percentage*	
Ambala (Res.)	–	–	
Kurukshetra	–	–	
Karnal	3045	0.39	
Sonepat	1999	0.31	
Rohtak	5295	0.84	
Faridabad	1980	0.27	
Mahendergarh	3114	0.42	
Bhiwani	3171	0.43	
Hissar	–	–	
Sirsa	10789	1.70	III

Source : Report, Lok Sabha Elections, 1999.

BSP: The party could not perform well as depicted in Table 11.19.

Table 11.19 : Performance of the BSP : 1999 Elections

Constituencies	*Votes Polled*	*Percentage*	
Ambala (Res.)	23644	12.8	III
Kurukshetra	–	–	
Karnal	26860	3.48	III
Sonepat	–	–	
Rohtak	–	–	
Faridabad	–	–	
Mahendergarh	25826	3.47	III
Bhiwani	–	–	
Hissar	–	–	
Sirsa	–	–	

Source : Report, Lok Sabha Elections, 1999.

The Congress could not perform well in any constituency because its votes percentage fell considerably. It could get 24.26 per cent in Bhiwani, 29.17 per cent in Sonepat, 33.65 per cent in Ambala as given in Table 11.17.

The performance of the Samata Party was bad to worse as it could not get even one per cent votes in six constituencies and less than two per cent in another as pointed out in Table 11.18.

However, the BSP got 12.8 per cent votes in Ambala and less than 4 per cent in Karnal and Mahendergarh as per Table 11.19.

The performance of the INLD and the BJP was wonderful who got more than 60 per cent votes in Kurukshetra, Hissar, Sirsa and Sonepat as shown in Tables 11.15 and 11.16.

Changes in the Support Bases

The INLD

The relatively small swing in favour of the INLD may be explained, in the first instance, by the fact that it contested a lesser number of seats in the 1999 elections, 5 seats to be precise instead of the 6 that it had contested in the 1998 elections. It had to surrender Sonepat parliamentary constituency, which it had won in the 1998 elections by a huge margin, to its alliance partner, the BJP. It also appears that the BJP too could not get its votes fully transferred to the INLD. A segment of the non-agriculturist high castes and the Punjabi supporters of the BJP did not vote for the candidates of the INLD because they continued to perceive it as an anti-urban, anti-trader, anti-non-agriculturist high castes and anti-Punjabi party. The alliance with the BJP, a party which represents these sections, did not change their perception.

Even the all out efforts of O.P. Chautala led INLD government to woo them by making all types of promises to remove the grievances of the BJP supporters could not remove their apprehensions which were based on the wide publicity of the rowdy activities of the Jai Parkash led Green-Brigade, the youth wing of its earlier incarnation, the Lok Dal. The fact that Jai Parkash had left that party in 1995 and joined Bansi Lal's HVP, and then jumped to the Congress (I) in 1998 along with his followers failed to change the image of the INLD in their eyes.

Chautala's organizational skill proved very useful in mobilizing their support. The formation of the INLD government by him before these elections helped in galvanizing the workers of the party. This helped in mobilizing a high turnout of its voters in the elections. The populist promises of free supply of electricity and water to the agriculturists also played some part in increasing the electoral support of the party. The INLD also once again encashed anti-Bansi Lal feelings in the peasantry which it had exploited in the 1998 parliamentary elections. Chautala also made a very careful choice of the candidates and gave priority to their winning capacity over other factors.

The BJP

There was, however, a large scale swing in the percentage of votes polled by the BJP in the 1999 parliamentary elections despite the fact that it contested five seats instead of seven. The projection of Atal Bihari Vajpayee as the National Democratic Alliance (NDA) candidate for the office of the Prime Minister proved useful to the BJP because of the positive appeal of his personality and satisfaction of most of the voters with the overall performance of his administration. The sympathy for Vajpayee due to the overthrow of his government in April 1998 by one vote and with little justification also benefited the party.

The politicization of the Kargil issue by the BJP proved very effective in Haryana because of the martyrdom of a large number of army personnel and parliamentary forces belonging to Haryana.

But the most important factor that accounted for the large scale gain in electoral support for the BJP was its alliance with the INLD. Despite the fact that the BJP could not get its votes fully transferred to the INLD, the later ensured en bloc transfer of its voters to the BJP. It is evident from the fact it secured 29.21 per cent votes in these elections while it had obtained 19.74 and 18.59 per cent votes respectively in the 1996 and the 1998 parliamentary elections that it had contested as an alliance partner of the HVP.

The Congress (I)

Despite intense factionalism in the state unit of the party, the Congress (I) was able to make large gains in mass support in the 1999 elections in comparison with the earlier ones. A primary factor is that the party was more united. In the earlier elections, the Bhupinder Singh Hooda Congress (I) faction is reported to have had a secret understanding with the HVP of Bansi Lal, while the Bhajan Lal Congress (I) faction is alleged to have allied with O.P. Chautala's 'Party'. Moreover, the Congress (I) put up very strong candidates in the 1999 elections in almost all the parliamentary constituencies, whereas it had fielded weaker candidates in the earlier elections. Since leaders of all three Congerss factions, Bhajan Lal, Bhupinder Singh Hooda and Birender Singh, were in the electoral fray this time, they had little time for sabotaging the elections of their competitors.

The Sonia factor also appears to have helped the Congress (I) in Haryana because the issue of her foreign origin was not an issue in rural Haryana where the caste of a woman is determined by the caste of her husband and not by her own caste. This is evident from the popular saying : '*Jat Ke Ghar Aii To Jatani*' (If a woman of any caste is married to a Jat, she becomes a Jat).

However, the party could not take advantage of the anti-Bansi Lal feelings among the voters because its leadership failed to launch any movement against the unpopular decisions of the Bansi Lal government. It could not do so because of the weakness of the party organization owing to factionalism at all levels. The allegation of the existence of a secret understanding between the President of the Haryana Pradesh Congress Committee, Bhupinder Singh Hooda, and Bansi Lal also proved damaging to the party in this context. The decision of the Congress (I) to extend support to Bansi Lal government in the hope that he would merge the HVP with the Congress (I) only gave credence to the collusion charges. The subsequent withdrawal of Congress (I) support to Bansi Lal's HVP government could not counter the damage done by its earlier decision. Instead, the fall of Bansi Lal's government and the formation of Chautala's INLD state government had a demoralizing effect on the workers of the Congress (I). But for these negative steps, the Congress (I) would have been able to further increase its electoral support.

The HVP

The large scale decline in support for the HVP could be attributed in the first instance to the unpopularity of Bansi Lal owing to the persistence of his authoritarian governing style. He could not retain his earlier image of a development oriented leader as he failed to bring about the economic development in the state during his three years as Chief Minister. His obsession with the introduction of total prohibition in Haryana deprived the state of a significant part of its revenue. Besides, he diverted the energy of his administration to imposing and enforcing prohibition instead of development. Moreover, he had to levy heavy taxes on various sections of society for compensating the loss of the excise duty on liquor. These taxes made his government unpopular. Although he scrapped prohibition after the defeat of his party in the 1998 parliamentary elections, he did not change his style of leadership and had failed to take steps for checking the erosion in his support base.

Stubbornly, Bansi Lal refused to learn any lesson from the defeats of his party in the 1998 parliamentary elections. Since he did not share power with his ministers, it remained centralized in his hands as Chief Minister, members of his family and the Chief Minister's Secretariat. This led to frequent revolts by his ministers who made consistent efforts to topple his government. Instead of accommodating the dissident ministers by sharing power with them, he decided to stay in power through manipulation of support from the BJP leadership or the

Congress (I) at the national and state levels. These tactics made an adverse impact upon his support base as his credibility and integrity became questionable.

The BSP

The almost total evaporation of the BSP electoral support in the 1999 elections has to be ascribed to the ineffective and unpopular leadership of the party at the state level on the one hand and the lack of party organization on the other. The breaking of its alliance with the INLD deprived the BSP of support from the agriculturist castes and the Sikhs who constitute its most reliable vote bank. This is evident from the comparison of its performance in the 1998 and the 1999 parliamentary elections. It also failed to get votes from Gujjars this time because it did not field a candidate from the caste in Faridabad constituency which it had left for its alliance partner, the HVP. Its support base among the Ahirs also almost totally eroded due to the decline in the popularity of its candidate from the Mahendergarh parliamentary constituency. Moreover, it fielded a very weak candidate from Karnal constituency in 1999. The alliance with the HVP also proved very costly to the BSP.

Conclusion

From the ongoing discussion, it may be concluded that, first, it is essential to answer the questions why there is a large discrepancy between the votes polled and the seats won by the major political parties that contested the 1999 parliamentary elections. It can be explained partly by the fact that the alliance between the INLD and BJP resulted ineffectively combining the votes of their supporters in many constituencies. Since their combined votes were higher than that of the Congress (I) or the HVP, the INLD-BJP alliance won all the seats. Congress (I) which polled 8.91 per cent more votes in the 1999 elections in comparison to the 1998 parliamentary elections but failed to retain the three seats won by it in 1998. Secondly, the virtual conversion of the electoral contest into a direct one between it and the Congress (I) helped the INLD-BJP alliance in sweeping the elections. This happened due to the almost total failure of the HVP-BSP alliance. Consequently, the anti-Congress (I) votes became polarized in favour of the candidates of the INLD-BJP alliance in all the 10 parliamentary constituencies.

As regards the changes in the support bases of various parties that took place in Haryana in the 1999 parliamentary elections, these have to be understood by taking into account the pattern of social cleavages and political alignments on the one hand and the role of the national and state level factors on the other. While the national level factors included the pattern of the performances, promises and images of the leaders of the BJP and the Congress (I), the state level factors included the nature of the alliances between the political parties and factions as well as the performances, promises and images of their leaders. The political situation at the national and state level has also to be kept in view as it had a significant bearing on the electoral performance of various contenders.

12

Parliamentary Elections, 2004

In this chapter a modest attempt has been made to analyze the Parliamentary elections, 2004 in Haryana. On the dissolusion of the 13th Lok Sabha on February 6, 2004, the Election Commission announced the schedule of elections on February 29, 2004 with polling to be held in four phases. The INLD and the BJP unit in Haryana held 5 seats each at the time of dissolution. The snap general elections to the 14th Lok Sabha in 10 parliamentary constituencies were held on May 10, 2004 which was the last phase of elections in the country. The election notification was issued on April 16, 2004. The last date of filing the nomination was April 23, scrutiny of papers, April 24, withdrawal till April 26 and polling on May 10, 2004. The counting of votes took place on May 13 and all results were declared up to May 25, 2004.

Nominations

It was for the first time that the candidates were required to file criminal antecedents, affidavits declaring their assets and liabilities, educational qualifications and unpaid dues of any public undertaking or of government.

As many as 232 nominations were filed including 198 from general and 33 from reserved category in comparison to 142 in 1999. The last date for filing the nomination was April 23, 2004. A clear picture pertaining to nominations, rejections and withdrawals is given in Table 12.1.

Table 12.1 : Nominations Filed, Withdrawals, Rejection etc. Men-Women Ratio

	General		*Reserved*		*Total Constituencies Reserved for SC=2, Total %*
	Men	*Women*	*Men*	*Women*	
Nomination Filed	183 (79.22)	15 (6.49)	28 (12.12)	5 (2.16)	231 (100.0)
Nomination Rejected	24 (68.57)	4 (11.42)	4 (11.42)	3 (8.57)	35 (15.15)
Nomination Withdrawn	27 (75.0)	4 (11.11)	4 (11.11)	1 (2.77)	36 (15.58)
Contestants	132 (82.50)	7 (4.37)	20 (12.50)	1 (0.62)	160 (69.26)

Source : Report, Lok Sabha Elections, 2004, p. 21.

As specified in Table 12.1 that 85.71per cent nominations are filed by the candidates belonging to general category. However, the percentage of rejection is relatively less in general category candidates in comparison to the Scheduled Caste candidates, but it is *vice versa* in the case of withdrawals. On the other hand, the percentage of contestants belonging to reserved category is much less to the constitutional provision of 20 per cent.

On the whole as many as 35 nominations (15.15%) were rejected in comparison to 18 in 1999 and another 36 (15.58%) are withdrawn (10 in 1999) leaving 160 (69.26%) contestants in the field (114 in 1999).

A constituency-wise picture of nominations, rejections, withdrawals and contestants is presented in Table 12.2.

As indicated in Table 12.2 that the maximum nominations (33) are filed in Bhiwani Constituency followed by Rohtak (27), Karnal (24), Sonepat and Hissar (22 each), Kurukshetra (20), Faridabad and Ambala (19 each) and least in Sirsa (9). However, the rate of rejection and withdrawals varied significantly in different constituencies. It was interesting to note that the rate of rejection was much less among women candidates in comparison to them.

Moreover, the number of contestants was above 10 in 90per cent of the constituencies with a maximum of 24 at Rohtak and minimum of 8 at Sirsa. The average number of contestants per constituency was 16.

Table 12.2 : Nominations, Withdrawals, Contestants etc. : A Constituency-wise Men-Women Ratio

Sl. No.	*Constituency*		*Men*	*Women*	*Total*
(I)	Ambala (SC)	Nominations	19	2	21
		Rejected	4	0	4
		Withdrawn	3	1	4
		Contestants	12	1	13
(II)	Kurukshetra	Nominations	20	1	21
		Rejected	2	0	2
		Withdrawn	33	1	34
		Contestants	15	–	15
(III)	Karnal	Nominations	24	1	25
		Rejected	2	–	2
		Withdrawn	3	–	3
		Contestants	19	1	20
(IV)	Sonepat	Nominations	22	2	24
		Rejected	3	1	4
		Withdrawn	–	–	–
		Contestants	19	1	20
(V)	Rohtak	Nominations	27	3	30
		Rejected	4	–	4
		Withdrawn	2	–	2
		Contestants	21	3	24
(VI)	Faridabad	Nominations	19	2	21
		Rejected	4	1	5
		Withdrawn	1	1	2
		Contestants	14	–	14
(VII)	Mahendergarh	Nominations	16	3	19
		Rejected	2	1	3
		Withdrawn	1	1	2
		Contestants	13	1	14
(VIII)	Bhiwani	Nominations	33	2	35
		Rejected	4	1	5
		Withdrawn	14	–	14
		Contestants	15	1	16
(IX)	Hissar	Nominations	22	1	23
		Rejected	3	1	4
		Withdrawn	3	1	4
		Contestants	16	–	16
(X)	Sirsa (SC)	Nominations	9	3	12
		Rejected	–	3	3
		Withdrawn	1	–	1
		Contestants	8	–	8

Source : Report Lok Sabha Elections, 2004, pp. 133-143.

Contestants

As many as 160 candidates contested the elections in comparison to 114 in 1999. A constituency-wise men-women ratio is shown in Table 12.3.

Table 12.3 : Contestants : A Constituency-wise Men-Women Ratio

Constituencies	*Contestants*		
	Men	*Women*	*Total*
Ambala (SC)	12	1	13
Kurukshetra	15	–	15
Karnal	19	1	20
Sonepat	19	1	20
Rohtak	21	3	24
Faridabad	14	–	14
Mahendergarh	13	1	14
Bhiwani	15	1	16
Hissar	16	–	16
Sirsa (SC)	8	–	8
Total	152 (95.0)	8 (5.00)	160 (100.0)

Source : Report, Lok Sabha Elections, 2004, pp. 133-143.

As many as 160 candidates remained in the fray after the withdrawal by 36 aspirants. The maximum 24 candidates contested from the Rohtak seat followed by 20 each from Karnal and Sonepat, 16 each from Bhiwani and Hissar, 15 from Kurukshetra, 14 each from Faridabad and Manendergarh, 13 from Ambala and 8 from Sirsa.

The maximum men contested from Rohtak, Karnal, Sonepat and Hissar whereas the number of women contestants remained insignificant. Moreover, there were no women contestants in Kurukshetra, Faridabad, Hissar and Sirsa constituencies. On the whole 95 per cent contestants were men making the elections a male-dominated affair.

On the whole, 30 contestants were affiliated to national parties, 22 to state parties, 32 to unrecognized parties and 76 were Independents. Desperation surfaced in the Congress factions in the wake of a conflict over selection of candidates. Loyalists of Bhajan Lal claimed to switch over to the BJP if the five candidates proposed by their leader would be ignored. However, Bhupender Singh Hooda prepared a separate list of aspirants for these seats. So, the Congress Election Committee could not finalize the candidature for these seats and the decision was deferred for another few days.

The Congress Party High Command did not accommodate Bhajan Lal much and candidates like Naveen Jindal, Kurukshetra, Jai Prakash, Hissar and Avatar Singh Bhadana, Faridabad were sponsored from the faction opposed to him.

A state level convention of the Department of Minority Affairs of the HPCC urged the party to allot at least two Lok Sabha seats to candidates belonging to minority communities.

The Haryana unit of the All India Rajput Mahasabha criticized the Congress for not giving adequate representation to Rajputs in the ticket allocation despite their being 14 per cent of the state population. It demanded one Lok Sabha and 10 Vidhan Sabha seats for the community.

The Haryana Pradesh Backward Classes Kalyan Morcha appealed to all political parties to field at least three candidates from the backward classes in the Lok Sabha elections, i.e. from Kurukshetra, Mahendergarh and Bhiwani.

Two sons of the Haryana Chief Minister, Ajay Singh and Abhay Singh Chautala were nominated from Bhiwani and Kurukshetra Lok Sabha constituencies respectively. The Congress, INLD, BJP, BSP and HVP contested all the 10 Lok Sabha seats whereas the Indian Justice Party led by Udit Raj decided to contest five Lok Sabha seats mainly to oppose the communal forces like the BJP. The Samata Party declared to field its candidates in two constituencies, i.e. Ambala and Rohtak.

A new political outfit, the Samajwadi Labour Party led by Rajender Singh Tanwar came into being on March 1, 2004. It decided to contest three Lok Sabha seats in Haryana, i.e. Hissar, Bhiwani and Rohtak. The Haryana Shiromani Akali Dal fielded its candidates in three Lok Sabha constituencies including Karnal, Ambala and Kurukshetra. However, SAD (Badal) decided to support the INLD candidates. The Sarvjan Samaj Party and Rashtriya Brahmin Maha Sabha decided to contest jointly in the ratio of 3 : 3 seats. On the rest of the four seats, the alliance would support candidates from Scheduled Castes and Backward Classes. The BJP decided to field all five sitting MPs in the Lok Sabha elections in Haryana. The BJP wanted to field Jai Prakash from Hissar if he was not nominated by the Congress. But the delay in the finalization of the Congress candidates put the BJP in difficulty. The Indian Youth Congress President, Randeep Singh Surjewala recommended the names from his wing to the Party High Command for ticket. The SUCI decided to contest three Lok Sabha seats, i.e. Rohtak, Sonepat and Mahendergarh.

In Rohtak, the Congress candidate, Bhupender Singh Hooda appeared to be favourite of the masses despite the intensive campaigning by the Chief Minister for the INLD candidate, Major Gen. Bhim Singh Suhag. The latter was considered as a weak candidate and the party workers were disappointed when Balwan Singh Suhag, an old dedicated and popular INLD leader was denied the ticket.

The HVP fielded Usha Ahlawat and the BSP, Geeta Grewal, a Hooda's divorced daughter-in-law. Incidentally, she was not the BSP's first choice but picked up after the original nominee Lokendra was injured in shoot out and opted to be out of contest. The BJP nominee, Abhimanyu, though a late entrant, launched a high profile campaign.

Despite the personal interest of the Chief Minister in the campaign of his party candidate, the anti-incumbency factor was working against the INLD. There were 1042468 voters in the Rohtak Lok Sabha Constituency including 41 per cent women. Interestingly, two women candidates were put up for the first time in 52 years old political history of the constituency. The Jat voters held a pre-dominant position, 400000 followed by the Brahmin, 90000 and migrant Punjabis, 87000, Scheduled Castes and Backward Classes, 150000 and 25000 respectively. Moreover, Major General Suhag was a green born in politics and lacked a personal political base and was much dependent on the party cadres and second-rung leaders.

Geeta Grewal adopted an emotional approach to campaigning by projecting herself as the victimised 'bahu'.

In the 1999 Lok Sabha elections, Captain Inder Singh of the INLD won the seat by polling 366926 votes. He defeated Bhupender Singh Hooda of the Congress by a margin of 144693 votes.

The Chief Minister, Om Prakash Chautala, who was in Rohtak on the occasion of filing the nomination of his party candidate, warned of strict action against party leaders and workers 'sabotaging' the electoral prospects of Major General Suhag. He said such leaders, including an MLA of the INLD were in league with the candidates of opposition parties. Certain INLD leaders and workers had been allured by wealthy BJP candidate using money power. Chautala alleged while issuing a warning that such 'black sheep' would not be tolerated.

Though Bhupender Singh Hooda got a good response in his Chaupal Sabhas in Rohtak constituency but the people were unhappy with him as he had failed to bring the leadership in this region despite being elected many times. Bhupender Singh Hooda campaigned in his Vikalp Rath. The BJP nominee drew enthusiastic gatherings in the street show, organized in the rural areas.

In Faridabad, the contest was essentially among the INLD, the Congress and the BJP. The Congress nominee, Avtar Singh Bhadana had his own problem. The main Muslim leaders of Mewat, Tayyab Hussain and Khurshid Ahmed resigned from the Congress Party after a denial of ticket to them and came in the open to support the BJP candidate. Moreover, the faction led by Bhajan Lal showed little interest in campaigning for him. Bainda of the BJP also faced a difficult time with the electorate asking what he had done for the constituency during his three successive terms. Moreover, a section of the BJP supporters did not take active part in his campaign. However, the INLD candidate, Mohd. Illyas expected to get a big chunk of 4 lakh Muslim votes.

The Faridabad seat was won by Ram Chander Bainda of the BJP in 1999 by polling 367842 votes who defeated his nearest rival, Zakir Hussain of the Congress by a margin of 34248 votes. The Congress secured 44.0 per cent votes whereas the winning BJP-49.03 per cent.

The Faridabad constituency had about 15 lakh voters with 25 per cent Muslims, 13 per cent Jats, 10 per cent Arora Khatri, 6 per cent Gujjar and Bania each and others. The Meo panchayat organized by the supporters of two former Ministers, Khurshid Ahmed and Tayyab Hussain, decided not to vote for the Congress in Faridabad Lok Sabha constituency in protest against denial of ticket to a Muslim.

In Ambala, Rattan Singh Kataria of the BJP was in contest for the second term and Balwant Singh, the sitting MLA, from the Sadhaura

Assembly segment as an INLD candidate, Mrs. Selja as a Congress candidate who had got shifted from Sirsa constituency. Balwant Singh lost the seat both in 1998 and 1999 Lok Sabha elections.

In Bhiwani, the contestants included the sitting MP of the INLD, Ajay Singh Chautala, Kuldeep Bishnoi of the Congress, Surender Singh of the HVP, Ram Bilas Sharma of the BJP besides others. The methods of election being employed there include money, power, family relations and the caste card. The INLD roped in Vasudev Sharma, a former Congress leader in its fold to get the support of Brahmins. The Brahmins constituted the second largest community after the Jats.

In Bhiwani, the voters admitted that the INLD government had done good work, but a majority of them were in favour of a change. In the beginning, Surender Singh of the HVP was clearly the favourite against Ajay Singh Chautala, the sitting MP of the INLD. But the entry of Kuldeep Bishnoi in the fray as the Congress candidate provided the voters another option. They were conscious of the possibility of Bishnoi's father becoming the next Chief Minister. However, the BJP candidate, Ram Bilas Sharma was in a position to damage the prospects of the Congress candidate.

In 1999, Ajay Singh Chautala won the seat by polling 381255 votes while defeating his rival, Dharamvir of the Congress by a margin of 203376 votes. The INLD polled 52 per cent and the Congress 48 per cent votes.

Mahendergarh, one of the most backward constituencies of Haryana, was locked in multi-corner contest including Swami Dharmender of the INLD, Rao Inderjit Singh of the Congress, Sudha Yadav of the BJP, Anil Rao of the HVP and Raghu Yadav of the Samajwadi Party.

In the caste-ridden politics, shortage of water emerged as a major poll-plank in the region plagued by poor health care facilities, road infrastructure and frequent power cuts, besides rural poverty. In Mahendergarh 28 per cent Ahir voters were always considered decisive. However, 14 per cent of Scheduled Castes also stocked their claims and to influence the decision. The remaining were, 12 per cent Jats, 11 per cent Punjabis, 7 per cent Brahmins, 5 per cent Vaish and about 17 per cent others.

The most preferred leader of Yadav community is Rao Birender Singh and the seat had remained with the Rao family since 1957. However, in 1996 Col. Ram Singh of the BJP won the seat but again it was captured by Rao's son in 1998. In 1999 it was snatched by Sudha Yadav of the BJP by a margin of 139140 votes. In Mahendergarh, the District Ex-services League extended its support to Raghu Yadav, a Samajwadi Party candidate.

As many as 15 candidates were in fray in Kurukshetra. The contest assumed importance because of the presence of Abhay Singh Chautala who was challenged by Naveen Jindal of the Congress, Gurdial Singh Saini of the BJP and Jitender Singh Kaka of the HVP. The former two were considered as outsiders. Gurdial Singh Saini was annoyed with the INLD when Abhay Singh Chautala replaced Mrs. Kailasho Saini who defeated Om Prakash Jindal of the Congress in 1999 by a margin of 163610 votes. The number of women voters in Kurukshetra constituency was 45 per cent of a total of 1161679. On caste lines it had majority of 26 per cent Scheduled Caste voters, 9 per cent Jats, 8 per cent Arora Khatri, 6 per cent Brahmins and others. In Kurukshetra, the main demand of the farmers was the construction of the Dadupur Nalwi Canal pending since 1977.

In Hissar, the last-minute entry of the BJP nominee, Raghvanand into the fray made the fight tough for the INLD and the Congress candidates. Earlier the BJP nominated Jaibeer Godara but he had to be replaced on the last day of filing the nomination papers because his name did not figure in the electoral rolls. The Congress candidate, Jai Prakash faced opposition within his own party because the Bhajan's faction preferred to see their vote bank transferred to the BJP. The INLD candidate, Surender Singh Barwala's attempt to score a hat-trick was mainly hindered by the anti-incumbency factor. However, Om Prakash Chautala, Chief Minister campaigned hard for his nominee.

The President of the Indian Youth Congress, Randeep Singh Surjewala resigned in protest against the denial of party ticket from Hissar Lok Sabha constituency. Both Bhupender Singh Hooda and Birender Singh were against his nomination. On caste lines the constituency comprised 38 per cent Jats having majority of Malik gotra, 22 per cent Scheduled Castes, 9 per cent Brahmins, 5 per cent Sikhs, 6 per cent Arora Khatri and others. In the last election, the seat was won by Barwala while defeating his rival, Birender Singh of the Congress by a margin of 160452 votes.

In Sonepat as many as 20 candidates were in the fray including Mrs. Krishana Malik of the INLD, Kishan Singh Sangwan of the BJP, Sugan Chand Gupta of the BSP and Kirpal Singh of the Janata Dal (Secular). Of the total 1139771 electorate spreading over 509 villages and seven towns — 624984 were males and 509778 females.

Kishan Singh Sangwan had a large number of sympathizers who did not want to be identified because of fear of power. His case seemed to be that 'Votes galore; but workers a few'. The Sonepat seat was won by Kishan Singh Sangwan in 1999 having the biggest margin of over 2.66 lakh votes, i.e. 69 per cent.

Sure of his nominations from the Karnal constituency, I.D. Swami of the BJP started his campaigning much earlier than his rivals, Arvind Sharma of the Congress and Ashok Arora of the INLD. He heavily banked on the extension of Panipat refinery and 'feel good' factor of the party. The presence of rebel Congress candidate, Kuldeep Sharma, son of Chiranji Lal Sharma, a four-time MP from the constituency also provided some relief to I.D. Swami. Moreover, Ashok Arora devoted much of his time in Kurukshetra to convass for Abhey Singh Chautala. Of the total 1240268 electorate, 568587 were women. In 1999, I.D. Swami won the seat while defeating his nearest rival, Bhajan Lal of the Congress by a margin of 147854 votes. This time also I.D. Swami expected to get support from particular faction of the Congress and maximum Brahmin votes. Despite the presence of 20 candidates in the fray, the constituency seemed to have a triangular contest among the Congress, the INLD and the BJP.

In Sirsa, Atma Singh Gill of the Congress threw a tough challenge to Sushil Indora, of the INLD. His being a Sikh tilted the balance in his favour. Moreover, the Kamboj community was hostile to the INLD because of its role in Dabwali municipal elections.

In 1999, Sushil Indora won the seat by polling 419278 votes while defeating his rival Om Prakash of the Congress who polled only 199552 votes. Thus, the INLD secured 65.09 per cent votes whereas the Congress 31.04 per cent.

Above all, the personal contact was the mantra during the election campaign of most of the political parties. Almost all national leaders of the Congress and the BJP addressed the election meetings in Haryana.

Electoral Alliances and Adjustments

Although the INLD parted its ways with the NDA at the Centre and snapped its ties with the BJP in Haryana, it was ambivalent on lending support to Atal Bihari Vajpayee for making him Prime Minister once again. However, Chautala said that NDA Government had worked against the interests of farmers. The party President of State Unit welcomed the break-up with INLD and claimed that the party would create a history by winning all the 10 parliamentary seats. He criticized the Chautala government for registering false cases against the BJP workers.

Among those who quit the Congress Party and joined the INLD were Vasudev Sharma, President of Bhiwani DCC, Kuldeep Sharma, a former President of Karnal DCC and son of Chiranji Lal Sharma, former ministers like Chandi Singh, Khurshid Ahmed, Tayyab Hussain, Satbir Singh Malik, Mrs. Shashi Saini, President of Haryana Mahila Sewa Dal, who contested the 2000 Assembly elections on the Congress ticket. Moreover, Mann Singh Barawa, Shyam Chand Rana etc. also quit the Congress Party.

A large number of leaders/workers of Lok Jan Shakti and BSP joined the INLD in the presence of INLD candidate from Kurukshetra constituency on April 11, 2004. On the other hand, one RPI MLA, Karan Singh Dalal and the Nationalist Congress Party MLA, Jagat Singh Sangwan joined the Congress at the stance of Bhajan Lal on March 29, 2004. Earlier two sitting MLAs, Udhey Bhan and Tejveer Singh, lending support to the INLD also joined the Congress. The BJP was also in touch with Karan Singh Dalal and Jagat Singh Sangwan, but it did not accept Dalal's nomination from Faridabad Lok Sabha constituency. Ranjit Singh Chautala, younger brother of the Chief Minister, joined the BJP on March 1, 2004. Two former ministers, Rao Narbir Singh and Jaswant Singh Bawal joined the BJP. Mrs. Shashi Yadav, a member of national executive committee of the All India Women's Conference and a Congress activist also joined the BJP fold.

Many BSP workers led by its former Chief, Aman Kumar Nagra joined the HVP. The Haryana Pradesh Vyapar Mandal decided to oppose the ruling INLD candidates in the Lok Sabha in view of the anti-trader policies of the government. In a major political development, the Co-operation Minister, Kartar Singh Bhadana, resigned from the Chautala Cabinet on March 30, 2004. The Congress received a boost when Independent MLA from Jhajjar, Dariyao Singh Rajora joined the party on April 29, 2004. He announced his decision at an impressive election meeting at Jhajjar where the party candidate, Bhupender Singh Hooda was present. Janmat Party led by Hari Singh, once a follower of Devi Lal announced its merger with the Congress on April 6, 2004 with a purpose to oppose the INLD nominee in Bhiwani Lok Sabha constituency. The Haryana unit of Lok Jana Shakti Party decided to support to the Congress candidates. However, the State President, Cap. Shamsher Singh Malik and his supporters quit the party in protest against its decision. The CPI(M) decided to support the Congress candidates. Shiv Sena extended its support to the HVP in Mahendergarh. The Dalit Samaj and the Gujjar community extended their support to the BSP candidate in Mahendergarh. Shahi Imam of Jama Masjid, Ahmed Bukhari asked the Muslim voters to go for the BJP. However, a number of Ulema criticized the fatwa issued by the Imam.

The Haryana unit of Bhartiya Kisan Union (BKU) (Khokhar group) decided not to extend its support to any of the political parties in the Lok Sabha polls. However, the Ghashi Ram Nain group announced its support to the Congress Party. The Haryana Jat Maha Sabha extended its open support to the Congress. Its leaders came down heavily on the NDA as well as Chautala government for being anti-farmers. The Sabha had 32000 workers and about 6.25 lakh members. At the same time, the All India Brahmin Mahasabha declared to support the Congress candidate in Haryana when Sonia Gandhi assured its delegation to give due regard and representation to the community in the party.

Campaigning

The main issues included image and caste of the candidate, development work, unemployment, corruption, VAT, high diesel, kerosin and urea prices, non-availability of electricity, breakdown of law and order in rural areas of the State. In rural Haryana, the political attitude and outlook of the people are still shaped by family ties, caste loyalties, kinship networks, economic interests and one's life experience. With no political party in a position to dominate the electoral scene, it was for the first time that the focus shifted to candidates themselves. Given the situation, all parties were looking for political heavy-weights who could hope to win the election on their personal popularity alone.

The announcement of candidates was delayed by many parties. The BJP and HVP announced five candidates each, the ruling INLD could announce just two. The Congress was yet to announce its nominees for all 10 seats. All its senior leaders were reluctant to enter the fray.

The prospects of the Congress Party seemed better because of multi-corner contests and sentiments against the ruling INLD. In contrast, the INLD had a slow start sensing the anti-incumbency factor. However, it hoped to get the support of Jat community despite resentment on issues including power dues and cane prices. The open revolt by a number of Congress leaders in Karnal, Kurukshetra, Hissar and Faridabad could help the ruling the INLD and the HVP to some extent.

In contrast, the HVP did not seem to count for much in any constituency other than Bhiwani. The BJP, too, was not the force as it was at the time of alliance with the INLD.

The ruling the INLD declared a number of sops to its employees while celebrating the 90th birth-anniversary of his father and former Deputy Prime Minister, Devi Lal, e.g. a social security scheme, Devi Rakshak which was introduced in collaboration with the National Insurance Company, aiming at giving Rs. one lakh to dependents if the bread-winner of a family dies. Another concession announced by Chautala was the regularization of the services of all 15000 class-III and IV employees who had been serving for the past three years on as *ad hoc* basis. Moreover, the artists of the state who were above 60 be paid a monthly pension of Rs. 500.

In February 2004, the Haryana Cabinet decided to merge 50 per cent dearness allowance with basic pay with effect from April 1, 2004. The step was taken for a substantial hike in the pay of the employees. The Cabinet also decided to reinstate about 60 general category employees dismissed for launching an anti-reservation agitation in the promotion process.

In case no family member of a deceased government employee is eligible for job on compassionate ground, the nearest kin would be given an *ex-gratia* assistance of Rs. 2.5 lakh. The government employees dying in harness at the age of 55 years or thereafter, his family would be paid an *ex-gratia* of Rs. 2.5 lakh. The assured career promotion policy would be made more transparent and practical.

The Haryana government declared to give Rs. 500 as taxi fare to facilitate poor pregnant women in reaching hospitals for delivery in an emergency situation on January 2, 2004. It also decided to construct community latrines for women in all villages and get health check up of senior citizens in the state. It decided to abolish professional tax which had caused great resentment from institutions like hotels, private gas agencies, automobile agencies, private managed colleges, English-medium private schools, financial institutions, property dealers, builders and contractors, jewellery shops etc. in urban areas. The ruling INLD organized its 'Nav-Sankalp' rally at Jhajjar on March 2, 2004 to celebrate the fourth anniversary of its government. Due to a massive turn out at the rally Chautala said that he would have an open mind on any post-election alliances.

Chautala asked the people to vote for his party on three main considerations: '*Vikas, Shanti and Sadbhavana.*' On employment front he declared to fill over 50000 specially created posts like Gram Vikas Purush, Van Rakshakas etc. He said that, "Haryana has made tremendous progress during the INLD regime and still the state's coffers are overflowing." He asked the villagers to go back and decide what projects they want for their villages and all of them would be completed in a year. Chautala, Chief Minister demanded the removal of the Governor for delivering speeches in favour of the BJP. Farooq Abdullah, former Chief Minister of J & K accompanied Om Prakash Chautala in the election campaign mainly at Pahewa, Fatehabad, Yamunanagar and Ambala. The Samajwadi Party entered the poll arena with the paramount objectives of providing a robust alternative to the people of Haryana. Mrs. Kanta Aladia, President of the Haryana unit of the Party said that the common man was completely disillusioned with the three Lals and willing to vote for any other viable alternative.

The HVP launched its "Mission-2004" with renewed zeal in Ahirwal. With the growing disenchantment of the masses with the Chautala regime on the one hand and the dwindling fortunes of the Congress Party after its rout in the three states of M.P., Chhattisgarh and Rajasthan in the Assembly elections as well as factionalism denting the party creditability in Haryana, on the other hand, the pendulum of popularity seemed to be swimming towards the HVP.

The HVP promised to exempt the house-owners from tax, reduce power tariff across the board besides providing round the clock supply. The tariff of tube-wells would be assessed on the basis of slab system and no arrests be made for the recovery of bank loans, jobs for educated youths and unemployment allowance of Rs. 250 for plus two certificate holders and graduates respectively. The *halwai* tax would be scrapped, removing of statues of Tau Devi Lal from all public places, early construction of SYL, better law and order situation in the state.

The Congress promised to bring a National Employment Guarantee Act to provide work for at least 100 days in a year at minimum wages for every rural household. It would spend 6 per cent of the GDP in education and provide governance with *Samajik Sadbhavana, Yuva Rozgar, Grameen Vikas, Aarthic Utthan, Mahila Sashaktikaran and Saman Avsar*, social harmony, welfare of Kisans, economic uplift, women empowerment and equal opportunity to the sections. It would also seek a consensus on *Dalit* and *Adivasis* getting a reasonable share of jobs in the private sector and strengthen the PDS.

Sonia Gandhi visited many Assembly segments in Rohtak, Jhajjar, Mahendergarh, Sirsa, Senior Congress leader, Natwar Singh addressed an election rally at Jat College, Rohtak while assuring the people that Bhupender Singh Hooda would be included into the Congress Ministry at the Centre. He criticized the NDA government for its failures on defence, foreign affairs and agricultural fronts.

The Chief Minister of Himachal Pradesh also campaigned for the Congress candidates at Ambala. Ironically, Sajnay Datt campaigned for the INLD candidate, Abhay Singh Chautala in Kurukshetra whereas his father Sunil Datt for the Congress candidate in Haryana. Sonia Gandhi promised social justice, employment, equal development of villages and cities and women's empowerment. The Haryana Congress

Sewa Dal decided to organize Sankalp Yatras in all the 10 Lok Sabha constituencies from April 1 to 12, 2004 to mobilize support for its candidates.

The Prime Minister, Atal Bihari Vajpayee, Deputy Prime Minister, L.K. Advani and the Party President, Venkaiah Naidu asked the voters to rise above regionalism and to vote on national issues. The BJP central leadership held public rallies at Ambala, Fatehabad, Hissar, Palwal in a bid to woo the farmers also. Lal Krishan Advani said that parties other than NDA and the Congress-led are alliance were irrelevant. "Voting for any third party is like wasting your vote". He said while criticizing Haryana Chief Minister Om Prakash Chautala who recently parted ways with the NDA. The BJP highlighted the issues of temple and ban on cow slaughter during its election. L.K. Advani promised that Ram Temple would be constructed at Ayodhya while addressing a public meeting at Sonepat. He praised his government for bringing political stability and overall development in the country.

The Prime Minister launched an Insurance Scheme for 370 million workers of unorganized sector, electrification of one lakh villages and one crore households, setting up of 500 to 750 residential schools for girls belonging to SCs, STs, BCs and other minority communities apart from economically weaker sections, new insurance scheme for over 12 lakh Anganwadi workers and helpers, merging of 50 per cent dearness allowance with the basic pay of all employees. The National President of the BSP, Mayawati addressed many election meetings in Haryana while asking the people to reject both BJP and the Congress. However, she avoided criticism of the ruling INLD.

The Ekta Shakti promised to enhance old age pension to Rs. 500 per month, simplification of laws and rules, setting up medical and defence universities, introduction of vocational education, formulation of agricultural policy and construction of Dedupur-Nalvi canal.

Holding of Elections

The polling was held on May 10, 2004. In these elections, the identification of electors was made compulsory, 50 per cent polling staff was deployed from outside the district.

Nirmal Singh, former Revenue Minister and Senior Congress leader was arrested for using criminal force to deter public servants from performing election duty in Naggal Assembly segment.

Munish Grover, a former District President of the BJP was manhandled by the Congress workers at Rohtak. The HVP supporters were injured in a firing in Bamla village in Bhiwani Parliamentary constituency. Some BJP workers were arrested in Sirsa for snatching the electronic machine. The INLD office and four vehicles were set on fire in Mandi Adampur by the Congress workers. Nearly 12 workers of the Congress and BJP were injured in a clash at Rohtak when the vehicle of Captain Abhimanyu, BJP candidate was damaged by the Congress workers and it was free for all happened at the gate of SSP's residence despite the presence of a police party headed by a DSP.

The number of total electorate was 12320557 as compared to 11038955 in 1999. The men-women ratio was 6660631: 5659926. However, the poll percentage was 65.67 as compared to 63.68 per cent in 1999. However, it was 68.11 per cent among men and 62.80 per cent women. It was for the first time that voters in all the 10 constituencies exercised their franchise using electronic voting machines.

A constituency-wise poll-percentage is given in Table 12.4.

Table 12.4 : Poll-Percentage : A Constituency-wise View

Constituency	*Men*	*Women*	*Total*
Ambala (SC)	72.94	68.77	70.69
Kurukshetra	75.31	71.11	73.24
Karnal	69.32	62.43	66.04
Sonepat	67.21	62.21	64.75
Rohtak	65.94	60.54	62.96
Faridabad	58.86	49.77	54.62
Mahendergarh	62.61	57.07	59.44
Bhiwani	75.24	72.08	73.09
Hissar	70.18	65.15	67.74
Sirssa (SC)	71.47	66.29	68.99
Average	68.11	62.80	65.67

Source : Report, Lok Sabha Elections, 2004, pp. 134-143.

The highest turn out was reported from Bhiwani followed by Sirsa 63 per cent, Hissar 62 per cent, Ambala and Rohtak, 61 per cent, each, Sonepat 60 per cent, Karnal 59 per cent, Kurukshetra 58 per cent, Faridabad 55 per cent and Mahendergarh the lowest, 54 per cent.

Four villages in Hissar parliamentary constituency boycotted the poll in protest against the failure of the leadership to solve their long-standing problems including the construction of a minor canal. Earlier, no party was allowed even to campaign in these villages. Moreover, two villages of Ellenabad sub-division boycotted the elections due to chronic shortage of water. Likewise, four villages of Uchana Kalan Assembly segments stayed away against the failure of government to provide drinking water.

Repoll was ordered in 11 booths in the five Lok Sabha constituencies of Ambala, Sonepat, Faridabad, Bhiwani and Kurukshetra on May 12, 2004.

The details of electors, voters in terms of men-women ratio is given in Table 12.5.

Table 12.5 : Number of Electors, Voters : A Constituency-wise Men-Women Ratio

Constituency	*Electors*			*Voters*		
	Men	*Women*	*Total*	*Men*	*Women*	*Total*
Ambala(SC)	645266	554072	1193656	467953	379710	847813
	(54.05)	(45.95)	(100.0)	(51.19)	(48.81)	(100.0)
Kurukshetra	629727	532706	1161933	472534	378146	850994
	(54.19)	(45.81)	(100.0)	(55.52)	(44.48)	(100.0)
Karnal	671727	568617	1240344	464244	354361	819068
	(54.15)	(45.85)	(100.0)	(56.67)	(43.33)	(100.0)
Sonepat	627795	510976	1138771	419733	316777	737319
	(55.12)	(44.88)	(100.0)	(56.92)	(43.08)	(100.0)
Rohtak	573080	482530	1055610	372324	289317	664564
	(54.28)	(45.72)	(100.0)	(56.02)	(43.98)	(100.0)
Faridabad	842158	704420	1546578	494586	350061	844770
	(54.45)	(45.55)	(100.0)	(58.54)	(41.46)	(100.0)
Mahendergarh	754390	674625	1429015	466671	382181	849391
	(52.79)	(47.21)	(100.0)	(54.94)	(45.06)	(100.0)
Bhiwani	642108	550163	1192271	477098	393572	871469
	(53.85)	(46.15)	(100.0)	(54.74)	(45.26)	(100.0)
Hissar	620701	516061	1133597	434180	335499	769998
	(54.75)	(45.25)	(100.0)	(56.38)	(43.62)	(100.0)
Sirsa (SC)	654179	565756	1239935	466901	374737	841683
	(52.75)	(47.25)	(100.0)	(55.47)	(44.52)	(100.0)
Total	6660631	5659926	12320557	4536234	3554361	8090595
	(54.06)	(45.94)	(100.0)	(56.06)	(43.94)	(100.0)

Note : The total of Electors as well as Voters also include the servicemen, postal and proxy votes.

Source : Report Lok Sabha Elections, 2004, pp. 133-143.

Election Results

The results were declared on May 13, 2004 when the Congress wrest 9 of the 10 seats leaving one for the BJP. The first result was declared in just five hours. The ruling INLD could not save the security deposits of its 40 per cent candidates and it was 89 per cent in the case of the HVP. All other parties of splinter groups lost their security deposits cent-per-cent as given in Table 12.6.

Table 12.6 : Lok Sabha Election Results: Seats Contested, Won, Votes Polled etc.

Total Seats = 10

Parties	*Seats Contested*	*Seats Won*	*Votes Polled*	*%*	*Security Forfeited*	*%*
Congress	10	9	3409950	42.13	–	–
BJP	10	1	1393106	17.21	4	40.0
INLD	10	–	1815683	22.43	4	40.0
HVP	9	–	506122	6.22	8	88.88
BSP	10	–	403254	4.98	10	100.0
CPI(ML)(L)	11	–	2487	0.03	1	100.0
AIFB	1	–	2637	0.03	1	100.0
JD(S)	1	–	1346	0.02	1	100.0
RLD	1	–	1849	0.02	1	100.0
SHS	2	–	5235	0.06	2	100.0
SP	6	–	137050	1.69	6	100.0
ABHM	1	–	2224	0.03	1	100.0
BRPP	2	–	2268	0.03	2	100.0
ES	3	–	126924	1.57	3	100.0
FCI	1	–	1037	0.01	1	100.0
JCP	1	–	671	0.01	1	100.0
LJNSP	5	–	6510	0.08	5	100.0
LP(S)	1	–	4172	0.05	1	100.0
NSSP	1	–	730	0.01	1	100.0
RGD	1	–	1977	0.02	1	100.0
RSBP	1	–	999	0.01	1	100.0
RSKP	1	–	379	0.00	1	100.0
RVP	3	–	14222	0.18	3	100.0
SAP	2	–	3133	0.04	2	100.0
Independents	76	–	249413	3.08	76	100.0
Total	160	10	8093378	–	137	

Total Votes Polled	=	8093378
Votes Rejected	=	3502
Valid Votes	=	8089876

Source : Report, Lok Sabha Elections, 2004, p.151.

As indicated in Table 12.6, the Congress swept the poll while getting 9 seats with 42.13 per cent votes, whereas the BJP got only one seat with 17.21 per cent votes. The INLD could not open its accounts even with 22.43 per cent votes polled.

All candidates of parties like the BSP, HVP, JD(S), RLD, LTNSP and others lost their security deposits *en-bloc* and so the Independents. In Ambala, the INC candidate Kumari *Selja* won the election by polling 415264 votes and defeated her rival Rattan Lal Kataria of the BJP by a biggest margin of 234935 votes followed by Inderjit Singh, again of the Congress from Mahendergarh who defeated his rival Sudha Yadav of the BJP by a margin of 210341 votes, Jai Prakash of the Congress defeated his rival Surender Singh Barwal of the INLD by a margin of 182768 votes, Arvind Sharma defeated I.D. Swami of the BJP by a margin of 164762 votes, Naveen Jindal won the seat by a margin of 160190 votes while his rival, Abhay Singh Chautala could get 201864 votes, Avtar Singh Bhadana defeated his rival Mohd. Ilyas of the INLD by a margin of 151929 votes, Bhupinder Singh Hooda won by a margin of 150435 votes from Rohtak constituency whereas his rival could get only 173800 votes.

This shows that the maximum Congress candidates won their seats with a huge margin whereas the only BJP candidate Kishan Singh Sangwan could win his seat from Sonepat with a thin margin of 7569 votes only.

Women Candidates

In Haryana as many as 8 women (3 in 1999) contested the election out of 20 who filed their nominations (4 in 1999). The nomination papers of 7 were rejected at the time of scrutiny and other 5 withdrew from the field as given in Table 12.7.

Only three national parties, namely the Congress, BSP and BJP fielded women candidates whereas one State party, the INLD, nominated one. No woman candidate was fielded from Kurukshetra, Faridabad, Hissar and Sirsa constituencies.

Only one woman candidate each contested from 5 constituencies except Rohtak where 3 such candidates were in the fray. Again only one candidate of the Congress could make it to the Lok Sabha with 49 per cent votes polled in comparison to 2 in 1999.

Interestingly, the candidates belonging to the INLD and the BJP got 27 per cent and 18 per cent votes respectively whereas the remaining candidates lost their security deposits.

Thus, the women were not liked much both by the political parties as well as voters.

Table 12.7 : Women Candidates : Contestants, Winners, Votes Polled etc. A Constituency-wise view (only six constituencies)

Total Seats = 10

District	*Party*	*No. of Contestants*	*Seats Won*	*Votes Polled*	*%*	*Margin*	*Total Valid Votes*
Ambala	Congress	1	1	415264	48.99	234935	847725
Karnal	FCI	1	–	1037	0.13	317911	818927
Sonepat	INLD	1	–	198866	26.98	34611	737119
Rohtak	BSP	3	–	24228	3.66	300007	662049
	HVPB			10334	1.56	313901	662049
	RPP			585	0.09	323650	662049
Mahender-Garh	BJP	1	–	148373	17.47	210341	849305
Bhiwani	Independent	1	–	1950	0.22	288986	871144
Total	–	8	–	800637	16.72	–	4786269

Source : Report, Lok Sabha Elections, 2004, p. 190.

A Comparative Analysis of Lok Sabha Elections, 1999 and 2004

A comparative view of Lok Sabha Elections, 1999 and 2004 in terms of number of contestants, seats won and votes polled to different political parties is depicted in Table 12.8.

The number of political parties/splinter groups in the fray was higher (23) in 2004 in comparison to 12 in 1999. Similarly, the number of contestants was also higher than 1999. The Congress captured nine seats in 2004 whereas it could not open its account in 1999 when the INLD and its ally got five seats each. The Congress polled 42.13 per cent votes in comparison to 34.19 per cent in 1999, whereas its main rival, the INLD got 22.43 per cent in comparison to 28.72 per cent in 1999. However, the BJP polled 17.21 per cent in comparison to 29.21

Table 12.8 : Lok Sabha Elections Results : A Comparison of 1999 and 2004 Elections

Parties	*Seat contested*		*Seats won*		*Votes Polled%*		*Seats*		*Votes%*	
	1999	*2004*	*1999*	*2004*	*1999*	*2004*	*1999*	*2004*	*1999*	*2004*
INC	10	10	–	9	34.19	42.13	–	9	–	7.94
BJP	5	10	5	1	29.22	17.21	4	–	12.0	–
INLD	5	10	5	–	28.71	22.43	5	–	6.29	–
HVP	2	9	–	–	2.71	6.22	–	–	–	3.51
BSP	3	10	–	–	1.96	4.98	–	–	–	3.02
CPI(ML)(L)	–	1	–	–	–	0.03	–	–	–	–
CPM	1	–	–	–	0.98	–	–	–	–	–
AIFB	–	1	–	–	–	0.03	–	–	–	–
SHS	–	2	–	–	–	0.06	–	–	–	–
SP	7	6	–	–	0.42	1.69	–	–	–	1.27
ABHM	–	1	–	–	–	0.03	–	–	–	–
BRPP	–	2	–	–	–	0.03	–	–	–	–
ES	–	3	–	–	–	0.57	–	–	–	–
FCI	–	1	–	–	–	0.06	–	–	–	–
JCP	–	1	–	–	–	0.01	–	–	–	–
LJNSP	–	5	–	–	–	0.08	–	–	–	–
LP(S)	–	1	–	–	–	0.05	–	–	–	–
NCP	2	–	–	–	0.06	–	–	–	–	–
NSSP	–	1	–	–	–	0.01	–	–	–	–

(Contd..)

Table 12.8 : (Contd.)

RGD	–	1	–	–	–	0.02	–	–	–	–
RSBP	–	1	–	–	–	0.01	–	–	–	–
RSKP	–	1	–	–	–	0.00	–	–	–	–
RVP	–	3	–	–	–	0.18	–	–	–	–
SAP	–	2	–	–	–	0.04	–	–	–	–
AJBP	1	–	–	–	0.03	–	–	–	–	–
BSP(A)	1	–	–	–	0.10	–	–	–	–	–
RPI	1	–	–	–	34.19	–	–	–	–	–
Independent	74	76	–	–	0.07	3.08	–	–	–	1.47
TOTAL	114	160	10	10	–	–	–	–	–	–

per cent in 1999. The percentage of votes polled to HVP, BSP, SP increased significantly in 2004 and so the case with regard to independents. To be specific, the electors polled maximum votes to the Congress Party to ensure its success in almost all the constituencies.

Performance of different Political Parties

An analysis of performance of major political parties in different constituencies is given in the following pages.

Performance of the Congress Party

The Congress Party polled the highest percentage of votes in Hissar, 52.89 per cent followed by Ambala, 48.99 per cent, a reserved constituency, Rohtak, 48.97 per cent and the lowest in Sonepat, 30.65 per cent, where the seat was retained by the BJP as indicated in Table 12.9.

Except the Sonepat and Bhiwani constituencies, it polled more than 40 per cent votes including the reserved constituencies of Ambala and Sirsa. The trend of polling indicated a wave in favour of the party almost in all the constituencies.

Table 12.9: Performance of the Congress : A Constituency-wise View

Constituencies	*Votes polled*	*Percentage*
Ambala (SC)	415264	48.99
Kurukshetra	362054	42.55
Karnal	318948	38.95
Sonepat	225908	30.65
Rohtak	324235	48.97
Faridabad	357284	42.30
Mahendergarh	358714	42.24
Bhiwani	290936	33.40
Hissar	407210	52.89
Sirsa (SC)	349397	41.51

Source : Report, Lok Sabha Elections, 2004.

INLD

The performance of the INLD in different constituencies is given in Table 12.10.

Table 12.10 : Performance of the INLD : A Constituency-wise View

Constituencies	*Votes polled*	*Percentage*
Ambala (SC)	130972	15.45
Kurukshetra	201864	23.72
Karnal	113510	13.86
Sonepat	198866	26.98
Rohtak	105640	15.96
Faridabad	205355	24.31
Mahendergarh	115154	13.56
Bhiwani	241958	27.77
Hissar	224442	29.15
Sirsa (SC)	277922	33.02

Source : Report, Lok Sabha Elections, 2004.

The Party polled the highest percentage of votes in Sirsa, a reserved constituency, 33.02 per cent and the lowest in Mahendergarh, 13.56 per cent. Interestingly, it polled less than 16 per cent votes in Rohtak constituency, its strong bation. It got less than 20 per cent votes in Ambala, Karnal, Rohtak and Mahendergarh. On the whole, the party got a poor response in majority of constituencies.

BJP

The performance of the BJP is given in Table 12.11.

Table 12.11 : Performance of the BJP : A Constituency-wise View

Constituencies	*Votes polled*	*Percentage*
Ambala (SC)	180329	21.27
Kurukshetra	126910	14.92
Karnal	154186	18.83
Sonepat	233477	31.67
Rohtak	173800	26.25
Faridabad	171714	20.33
Mahendergarh	148373	17.47
Bhiwani	24467	2.81
Hissar	64722	8.41
Sirsa (SC)	115128	13.68

Source : Report, Lok Sabha Elections, 2004.

The BJP got the maximum votes in the Jat heartland, Sonepat, 31.57 per cent, Rohtak, 26.25 per cent, the reason being the very influential Jat candidates of the party. However, it fared very poor in Bhiwani with only 2.81 per cent votes and Hissar with 8.41 per cent.

HVP

The performance of the HVP is depicted in Table 12.12.

Table 12.12 : Performance of the HVP : A Constituency-wise View

Constituencies	*Votes polled*	*Percentage*
Ambala (SC)	22039	2.60
Kurukshetra	77186	9.67
Karnal	21371	2.61
Sonepat	–	–
Rohtak	10334	1.56
Faridabad	13042	1.54
Mahendergarh	30134	3.85
Bhiwani	266532	30.60
Hissar	19475	2.53
Sirsa (SC)	46059	5.47

Source : Report, Lok Sabha Elections, 2004.

Table 12.12 shows that the HVP polled maximum votes in Bhiwani constituency, 30.60 per cent. But in other constituencies its performance was very poor even to one and a half per cent. Perhaps the plan of its Supremo, Bansi Lal to join the Congress Party leaked prematurely to the electorate who mainly voted for the Congress.

BSP

The performance of the BSP is given in Table 12.13.

Table 12.13 : Performance of the BSP : A Constituency-wise View

Constituencies	Votes polled	Percentage
Ambala (SC)	57028	6.73
Kurukshetra	23057	2.71
Karnal	67392	8.23
Sonepat	37185	5.04
Rohtak	24228	3.66
Faridabad	71459	8.46
Mahendergarh	56181	6.61
Bhiwani	17216	1098
Hissar	25060	3.26
Sirsa (SC)	24428	2.90

Source : Report, Lok Sabha Elections, 2004.

The BSP got higher percentage of votes than the HVP in almost all constituencies except Bhiwani and Kurukshetra. However, the electorate rejected its candidates out-rightly and it could not get even 7 per cent votes in Ambala and 3 per cent in Sirsa, both the reserved constituencies.

Result Analysis

Though the Congress nominee Selja won the Ambala seat with the maximum margin of votes in the State, the Hissar candidate, Jai Prakash polled the maximum number of votes in the State and got elected to the Parliament for the third time. The poll percentage of Selja and Rohtak nominee Bhupender Singh Hooda was 48.99 per cent. On the basis of the vote percentage, Kurukshetra nominee Navin Jindal of the Congress got the third position with 42.55 per cent votes followed by Avtar Singh Bhadana 42.3 per cent, Rao Inderjit from Mahendergarh 42.24 per cent, Atama Singh Gill from Sirsa 41.51 per cent, Arvind Sharma from Karnal 38.95 per cent, Kuldeep Bishnoi from Bhiwani 33.4 per cent and Kishan Singh Sangwan of the BJP 31.67 per cent.

Had the ruling INLD and BJP contested the elections together, the combine would have led in at least 29 Assembly segments. On their own, the INLD and BJP were ahead in 9 and 5 segments respectively. Not only would the two former allies have won in another 15 Assembly segments had there been an alliance, there would have been close contests in at least five segments. Thus, the alliance could actually have led in about 34 segments of the total of 90.

In the case of an alliance of the INLD and BJP, it could have retained the Sirsa seat and at least had finished respectable losers in Faridabad, Kurukshetra and Rohtak constituencies from where they lost by over 1.5 lakh votes. It could even have won in a close contest in Bhiwani also. The specific observations can be listed as under —

- The wrath of the electorate cut across the caste lines, proving the calculations of politicians and pollsters wrong and the INLD candidates lost badly even in Jat-dominated segments.

- The INLD's drubbing this time was more severe than that in the past Meham 1991 elections when the party was able to pick up 16 Assembly segments.
- In four Lok Sabha constituencies the INLD candidates forfeited their security deposits.
- To be fair to the Chief Minister, Om Prakash Chautala, he could not be faulted for lack of development including the rural areas. But two factors mainly went against him, first, the people felt terrorized and second the complete centralization of power in the hands of the Chief Minister and his two sons. And the people found the right opportunity to hit back.
- The ruling party felt complacent after its victory in three Assembly by-elections and did not undertake serious efforts to improve its image.
- The animosity of the Bhartiya Kisan Union, also cost the INLD dear.
- A section of the Sikhs also seemed to have voted for the Congress also explain the defeat of the INLD nominees in the Sikh-dominated segments.
- The implementation of Value Added Tax (VAT) by Haryana government in January 2004 against the wishes of the business community could be one of the reasons of its poor performance.
- The termination of alliance between the INLD and BJP just ahead of the Lok Sabha polls on a bitter note with both sides threatening to show each other their rightful place unmindful of the possibility that could harm both sides.
- The unhappiness of voters with the performance of both the INLD and BJP led to the drubbing.
- The only factor worked in favour of the Congress victory, was 'a mood to change'.
- The elections saw the virtual elimination of parties like the Haryana Vikas Party and the Ekta Shakti whose votes probably shifted towards the Congress because of the fear of the INLD candidates winning again.

- The BJP blamed its previous alliance with the INLD for its defeat in the Lok Sabha polls.
- The BJP could pick up one seat of Sonepat and it finished second in four constituencies of Karnal, Mahendergarh, Ambala and Rohtak.
- People saw Bhupinder Singh Hooda as the future Chief Minister of Haryana, swayed a majority of Jat votes towards the Congress.
- The main complaint of the voters was the total neglect of dedicated workers in the allocation of tickets by the INLD.
- Most of the workers preferred to campaign in the constituencies of Ajay Singh and Abhay Singh Chautala to mark their presence felt.

13

Parliamentary Elections, 2009

After the dissolution of the 16th Lok Sabha, a notification was made on March 2, 2009 *vide* which nominations were received up to April 18, 2009, scrutiny of nominations on April 20, 2009, withdrawals up to April 22, 2009, voting on May 7, 2009 and counting of votes on May 16, 2009. This was the first Lok Sabha election in the state after the delimitation of constituencies by the Election Commission of India in 2007. An element of unpredictability was added because of changed composition of several segments. Caste calculations and political permutations and combinations went awry in many constituencies. Several constituiences were abolished forcing those deprived of their pocket boroughs and shifted to their nearby constituencies. This was bound to trigger inter-party as well as intra-party turf wars amongst ticket seekers.

The BJP criticized the delimitation exercise as it is done on the directive of the Congress Party at the Centre. Interestingly, the delimitation panel orders were challenged in the Supreme Court declaring at least four Assembly seats with lesser SCs population in Haryana as reserved. A PIL was moved by an organization, Guhla Halka Bachao Sanghrash Samiti. The seats were – Radaur, Guhla, Sahabad and Narwana.

Tara Singh Virk, Ex-Speaker, of the Haryana Vidhan Sabha alleged that the delimination Commission has ignored the Punjabi community while undertaking the exercise in Haryana. The Sikhs as well as Punjabis said that the constituancy largely populated by them were either reserved or merged with other nearly constituencies. He told that 1/3 population of Jundla and Asandh were Punjabis and 3/4 by Sikhs. But Jundla is merged with four adjacent segments. The Congress government opposed the working paper of Election Commission prepared during the INLD government where abolition of Rohtak Lok Sabha seat was recommended, the Lok Sabha, constituencies of Ambala and Sirsa be dereserved and Kurukshetra be reserved. Another constituency of Jind is to be created for reservation and Assembly segments like Beri, Meham, Narwana, Palwal, Gohana be reserved. However, the Hooda government got these recommendations reversed.

Abolition of Mullana Assembly segment and substituting it with Barara, abolition of Naultha seat and subtitute it with Israna as a reserved constituency. However, the Delimitation Commission turned down the request of Raghubir Singh Kadian for postponing its meeting in view of his foreign visit. Kadian was associate member being an MLA. It is interesting that associate members to the Commission are appointed by the Speaker, Kadian appointed himself as an associate member. How funny?

In Bhiwani-Mahendergarh seat, Jats constitute the majority and the domination of Yadavs is a gone thing. In Gurgaon, the Meos have a strong presence.

In the wake of delimitaion of Lok Sabha and Assembly seats, the number of reserved seats for SCs has been increased from 79 to 85 and Assemblies from 555 to 610 and for STs from 527 to 545. However, in Haryana the number of reserved seats remained unchanged, i.e. 2 in Lok Sabha and 17 in the Assembly. After the delimitation, district Faridabad would have 4 Assembly segments instead of 5, district Gurgaon 7 instead of 3, Rohtak district 4 instead of 5 and Panchkula 2 instead of one.

The Lok Sabha constituency of Mahendergarh, Kurushektra and Bhiwani were reorganized/renamed by the Delimitaion Commission. It has combined the Mahendergarh-Bhiwani constituency under the new name of Bhiwani-Mahendergarh having five Assembly segments of Bhiwani district and four of Mahendergarh district. It was expected to pose difficulty for Rao Inderjit Singh. Adampur Assembly segment was taken out from Bhiwani seat and made a part of Hissar parliamentary seat.

Kurukshetra was also reorganized. Yamunanager was taken out and Kalayat incorporated in place of it. In Bhiwani, three Assembly segments – Adampur, Hansi and Bawani-Khera were incorporated in Hissar seat whereas Narnaul, Mahendergarh, Ateli and Nangal Chaudhary were included in Bhiwani-Mahendergarh seat. It was a mix of Jats and Ahirs, i.e. majority of Jats in Loharu, Badhra and Tosham whereas Ahirs in Narnaul, Mahendergarh and Ateli. Hansi and Bawani-Khera were merged in Hissar seat.

The delimitation was to affect in terms of abolition of some Assembly segments, creation of new one's as well as reservation of some of them. The affected would be Chautala and Surjewala families. Bhiwani and Mahendergarh seats were merged into one, Gurgaon a new seat was created.

Nominations

As many as 285 candidates filed their nomination papers. During scrutiny of the papers on April 20, 2009, 45 of them were rejected. An account of such information is given in Table 13.1.

The Congress Party took long time in selecting its candidates that much of the sheen was lost by the time it finalized its nominees. Reports of hectic lobbying by various factions and the virtual stand-off between Hooda and his Finance Minister, Birender Singh for the Sonepat seat and with Kiran Chaudhary, Tourism Minister for the Bhiwani-Mahendergarh seat were seen.

Information regarding the nominations and withdrawals is given in Table 13.1.

Table 13.1 : Nomination, Withdrawals, Rejections and Contestants

Constituencies	*Nominations*	*Rejections*	*Withdrawals*	*Contestants*
Ambala (Res.)	16	8	1	7
Kurkushetra	27	6	7	14
Karnal	29	3	3	23
Sonepat	27	4	2	21
Rohtak	23	3	4	16
Faridabad	30	2	5	23
Bhiwani-Mahendergarh	34	5	0	29
Hissar	50	7	5	38
Gurgaon	28	4	0	24
Sirsa (Res.)	21	3	3	15
Total	285	45	30	210*

* This includes 196 males and 14 females.

Source: Report, Lok Sabha Elections, 2009.

The Congress held a joint meeting of three-member screening committee and the state election committee in Delhi in first week of March 2009. The party's sitting MPs were first invited for a feedback. However, MLAs were not consulted. The Screening Committee shortlisted the candidates for Lok Sabha electiond. However, it forwarded all applications, instead of making any recommendations. Baring Rohtak and Kurukshetra, the other eight seats attracted a larger number of aspirants and the highest from Hissar seat (150 applications).

The state committee discussed the broad parameters for the selection of candidates like representation to minorities, women, youth and castes as well as the opposing candidates. It was unanimous about the nominations of Selja from Ambala, Bhupender Hooda from Rohtak, Naveen Jindal from Kurukshetra, Avtar Singh Bhadana from Faridabad, Rao Inderjit Singh from Gurgaon, Jai Parkash from Hissar but it left the final decision of the remaining four seats – Karnal, Sonepat, Bhiwani and Sirsa to party Supremo, Sonia Gandhi because Bhiwani was won by Kuldeep Bishnoi who has formed his own party, Karnal by Arvind Sharma, whose loyalty came under scanner at a time of the trust vote in July 2008 and Sonepat was won by the BJP.

Disillusioned with yet another poor performance in the elections, the Haryana unit of the BJP engaged itself in serious discussions. While selecting the candidates the party in charge of Haryana Affairs, Vijay Goel formed a five member committee to provide a blueprint for this purpose. The committee was asked to grade all 90 Assembly seats based on the party's position which would enable the party to finalize seats it wanted to contest. It would also help to identify seats to be offered to its alliance.

A 45 member deputation of the Haryana Rajput Pratinidhi Sabha met the BJP Chief, Rajnath Singh in Delhi on January 13, 2009 to seek tickets for Rajputs in the Lok Sabha elections. The delegation was led by Hukam Singh Rana who pleaded that Rajputs have been supporting the BJP but the party did not have fielded Rajputs in any Lok Sabha seat in Haryana for the last 25 years despite the number of voters over 2 lakh in Bhiwani, Mahendgarh, 1½ lakh in Kurukshetra and Karnal each, 1¼ lakh in Gurgaon and Faridabad each. The delegation urged the BJP Chief to nominate Shayam Singh Rana from Karnal.

The BSP announced its 8 of the 10 candidates much earlier than the ruling Congress and the INLD-BJP alliance except Sirsa and Mahendergarh. The BSP declared that it would not admit any Jat into its fold as it wanted a Non-Jat Chief Minister in Haryana as pointed out by Mayawati while addressing a rally at Karnal.

Maratha Verma, a bureaucrat and leader of Ekta Shakti Party merged it with the BSP on November 4, 2008 and projected himself as Chief Minister of the state.

The Congress fielded the young candidates from Rohtak, Kuruskehtra, Ambala, Karnal whereas the INLD from Sirsa and Bhiwani-Mahendergrah. However, all the five candidates fielded by the BJP were in their late 60s, except Sudha Yadav.

The state election committee of the BJP recorded 16 names for 6 seats in its meeting held in Sonepat on March 2, 2009. It recorded one to three names for each seat, e.g. Rattan Lal for Ambala, I.D Swami and Manchanda from Karnal, Ram Chander Bainda for Faridabad, Sudha Yadav from Gurgaon, Kishan Singh Sangwan from Sonepat, Abhimanyu and O.P. Dhankhar from Rohtak. The Parliamentary Board of the party finalized the candidates in its meeting held on March 9, 2009.

The Left contested two seats, i.e. the CPI from Karnal and the CPM from Sirsa. Compared to the CPI, the CPM was a bigger player with several pockets of influence. It had some following in farm workers and the poor people of these districts.

A men-women ratio of contestants is depicted in Table 13.2.

Table 13.2 : Men-Women Ratio of Contestants: Lok Sabha Elections 2009

Constituencies	*Women*	*Men*	*Total*
Kurukshetra	1	13	14
Ambala	1	6	7
Sirsa	1	14	15
Gurgaon	2	22	24
Bhiwani	3	26	29
Hissar	1	37	38
Karnal	2	21	23
Rohtak	–	16	16
Faridabad	2	21	23
Sonepat	1	20	21
Total	14	196	210

Source : Report, Lok Sabha Elections, 2009.

However, the HJC(BL) contested all the 10 seats including Bhajan Lal from Hissar but Kuldeep kept himself out of the race. Haryana Congress (BL) played a non-Jat card by alloting tickets to non-Jats in 9 constituencies.

The BSP nominated its candidates from various communities. However, it feared strong resentment from SCs (B). Bhajan Lal divided the SCs in two category A & B. It nominated a stong Muslim candidate, Zakir Hussain from Gurgaon. However, the social engineering of the BSP in Haryana failed miserably.

The SAD (Badal) decided to contest 4 seats – Sirsa, Kurukshetra, Karnal and Ambala. Joginder Singh Aherwan, State President of the SAD alleged that the NDA had been taking the state unit for granted and denied its due for long. So they have legitimate right over these seats which were dominated by Punjabis.

Women Candidates

A very few women have participated in 11 Lok Sabha elections held so far since its formation of Haryana state. The state witnessed its first Lok Sabha elections in 1967 when 67 candidates had entered the fray. These included one woman candidate but in the 1971 Lok Sabha elections, not even a single woman candidate contested the poll. However, the 1984 Lok Sabha elections proved the best for women candidates when of the 200 contenders, the highest-ever number of 10 women participated in the elections. In the 1989 Lok Sabha elections, about 324 candidates entered the fray which included only three women. In the 1996 Lok Sabha elections, only nine women entered the race whereas in 2004, eight women and 2009, 14 women candidates entered the fray.

The figures pertaining to women contestants are given in Table 16.3.

Table 13.3 : Women contestants

	Women	*Men*	*Total*
Kurukshetra	1	13	14
Ambala	1	6	7
Sirsa	1	14	15
Gurgaon	2	22	24
Bhiwani	3	26	29

(*Contd.*.)

Tabble 13.3 :(*Contd..*)

Hissar	1	37	38
Karnal	2	21	23
Rohtak	–	16	16
Faridabad	2	21	23
Sonepat	1	20	21
Total	14	196	210

A picture of Men-Women ratio of contestants since 1967 is given in Table 13.4.

Table 13.4 : Men-Women Ratio of Candidates: 1967-2009

Lok Sabha	*Contestants*		*Winners*	
Elections	*Men*	*Women*	*Men*	*Women*
1967	66	1	9	–
1971	–	–	–	–
1977	48	2	9	1
1980	132	5	10	–
1984	190	10	10	–
1989	321	3	10	–
1991	192	6	9	1
1996	285	9	9	1
1998	134	6	9	1
1999	111	3	8	2
2004	152	8	9	1
2009	196	14	8	2

Source : Report, Lok Sabha Elections : 1967-2009.

But the 2009 Lok Sabha elections set a record with the participation of 14 women candidates. Of the 10 Lok Sabha constituencies, the maximum three women candidates were in the race from the Bhiwani-Mahendergarh constitutency while not even a single woman contestant entered the fray from Rohtak. On the last day of withdrawal of nominations, four of the 18 women candidates had withdrawn their names.

A total of 210 candidates, including 196 men, were left in the race for the 2009 Lok Sabha elections from the 10 constituencies of Haryana. Of the 10 Lok Sabha constituencies, the maximum of three women candidates were in the race for the Bhiwani-Mahendergarh constitutency while not even a single woman contestant has entered the fray from Rohtak. On the last day of withdrawal of nominations, four of the 18 women candidates had withdrawn their names.

•10 per cent of the candidates in the fray were facing criminal charges including five booked for serious crimes, e.g. INLD – 3, Congress – 2, HJC (BL) – 2. About 30 per cent of the candidates were *crorepatis*.

K.R. Punia, a former bureaucrate lanched a new party – Rashtriya Janhit Party on January 29, 2009. He said that current political parties lacked the will power to take on the bureaucratic structure and bring about strong fundamental changes. This required the fomation of new political orders.

A new party, namely Vikas Parishad was formed by three time MLA from Ambala cantonment, Anil Vij. Punjabis were up for more tickets as their welfare subha blamed the Congress Party for ignoring the Punjabis in the fair distribution of tickets. A.C. Chaudhary submitted his representation to the Congress President, Sonia Gandhi as a protest against non-allotment of party ticket to Punjabis in the Lok Sabha election. A state level convention was convened at Panipat to decide the future plan for Assembly elections, 2009.

Alliances

Before a few months to go for the Lok Sabha polls, a host of new permutations and combinations started to emerge on the political horizion of the state. The BJP leaders weighed the options available for a pre-poll alliance–the INLD, the HJC. However, both the BJP and the INLD expected to gain much from their alliance as to complement the urban-rural voters but could not succeed to form any alliance.

The secret understanding between the BJP and the HJC as well as BSP and HJC also took place but of no avail.

Similarly, the INLD-BJP alliance faced hiccups to begin with, but their leaders tried to put up a united face with Om Prakash Chautala, who addressed a series of election meetings even for Kishan Singh Sangwan at Sonepat. Actually Chautala had opposed the candidature of Sangwan in the beginning. The two parties focused their campaign on power shortage, corruption, price-rise and law and order situation in the state besides Rohtak-centric development approach of the government.

The INLD-BJP alliance banked on its traditional pockets of supports in Faridabad, Sirsa and Ambala. However, Ajay Chautala was locked in a tough fight with Shruti Chaudhary and Rao Narender Singh.

In view of the political situation in the wake of formation of a new political outfit by the former Chief Minister, Bhajan Lal and his son Kuldeep Bishnoi, increasing influence of the BSP, some sort of alliance became a necessity for all parties, barring the ruling Congress.

The BJP lacked a strong mass support base in the state, particularly in the rural areas. So, it assessed the options available for a pre-poll partnership in the state, the INLD or the HJC (BL). The options before the INLD were limited. Joining hands with the BSP did not seem viable as the staunch BSP voters were unlikely to accept the INLD men as their alliances and *vice versa*.

The alliance was opposed by the SC leaders like the President of the Ambedkar SCs/STs Advocates Association of Punjab and Haryana High Court, President of Social Justice Party, Haryana, President of Haryana Pradesh Chamar Sangharsh Samiti etc. They blamed Bhajan Lal for creating a division among the SCs by bifurcating them into 'A' and 'B' categories.

The HJC (BL) tried to ally with the BSP under 50:40 formula but the BSP declared that it would project a Brahmin as its Chief Minister candidate in Haryana put a stop to all talks of alliance with HJC (BL). Thereafter, it tried to ally with the BJP and Kuldeep Bishnoi decided to cast his confidence vote in favour of NDA in the Lok Sabha. But the celebration proved shortlived as the BJP finally offered its hands to Om Prakash Chautala despite stiff resistance by the state unit of the party.

Since it was clear that the HJC would have to go it alone, many ticket hopefuls quit the party. They included several senior party leaders who were concerned as close confidents of Bhajan Lal. Kuldeep's somewhat authoritarian handling of the party affairs added to the problem and this particularly frustrated seniors who were contemporaries of his father.

Raj Kumar Gautam, MLA from Narnaud, who opposed the BJP-INLD alliance from the very beginning, resigned from the membership of Vidhan Sabha to the Speaker on April 22, 2009. He was removed as the Leader of the BJP legislature party for criticising the tie-up and wrote several letters to L.K. Advani for scraping it.

After the revolt by Ram Kumar Gautam who resigned from State Assembly over the alliance between the INLD and the BJP, P.K. Chaudhary, former MLA and senior BJP leader openly criticised the alliance while talking to news men at Rohtak on April 29, 2009. He reminded the Party High Command that the people of the state and workers of the BJP had still not forgotten the crime committed during Chautala's regime. He said that the BJP workers would not support the INLD candidates in Lok Sabha elections.

The BJP and the INLD contested 2004 Lok Sabha and Assembly polls separately and fared badly and after that these parties tried to find a strong foothold. All along the BJP publicly declared not to have any connection with the INLD. But in the end it chose to enter into an alliance while overlooking the HJC(BL). But its state level leadership was in disarray and grassroots workers appeared to be confused.

Thus, the BJP successfully managed to win back its alliance with INLD despite the still resistance from the state unit while negotiating five seats. This might be due to reminiscent of 1999 Lok Sabha election when INLD-BJP cotrie bagged all 10 seat. However, in 2004 Lok Sabha elections, the INLD lost all the 10 seats but, one seat went to the BJP. Similarly, INLD could get only 9 seats in the Assembly election 2005.

In spite of an alliance between the INLD and the BJP, symphony between them seemed to be lacking this time in comparison to 1999. There were reports that the BJP workers stayed away from the INLD compaign as they were opposed to the alliance.

Campaigning

The Gurgaon parliamentary constituency include Badshahpur, Pataudi (Res.), Sohna from Gurgaon district, Nuh, Ferozpur-Jhirka, Punhana of Mewat district, Bawal (Res.) and Rewari from Rewari district. A total 1230949 votes with 657161 men and 573788 women including 12194 service voters as many as 24 candidates with Inderjit – Congress, Sudha

Yadav – BJP, Naveen Singh-HJC (BL), Jakir Hussain – BSP, Sunil Yadav – SP, Dinesh Chander Yadav, RKP, Yashpal – LJP, Iswar Singh Tomar – Rastriya Dehat Morcha Party and 9 Independents.

The Faridabad Constituency incorporates Hatin-Hodal (Res.), Palwal, Pirthala of Palwal district, Faridabad N.I.T., Badkhal, Ballabgarh, Faridabad, Tigaon of Faridabad district. A total 1101489 electors with 615838 men and 485651 women including 3023 service voters. A total 23 candidates, Avatar Singh Bhadana – Congress, Ramchander Bainda – BJP, Chetan Sharma – BSP, Chander Bhatia – HJC (BL), Babu Lal – Janata Udaya Party, Rekha Singh – Samast Bharatiya Party, Mukesh Kumar – Haryana Raksha Party, Lata Ram – SP, Gajender Singh – All India Forward Bloc (Subhapist), Devender – Jai Jawan, Jai Kisan Mazadoor Congress, Nisar Ahmed – Rashtriya Nau Jawan Dal, Suraj Bhan — Rashtrya Janadhar Party, Subhash – Rastriya Sena and 10 Independents.

The segments like Kalanwali (Res.), Dabwali, Rani, Sirsa and Ellenabad from Sirsa district, Tohana, Fetehabad, Ratia (Res.) from Fatehabad district, Narwana from Jind district constituted the Sirsa parliamentary constituency. A total of 1308567 electors with 705542 men and 603025 women including 1931 service voters. As many as 15 candidates, Ashok Tanwar of the Congress, Sita Ram of the INLD, Rajesh Kumar of the BSP, Rajinder Prashad of the HJC (BL), Swaran Singh of the Rastriya Janhit Party, Ram Kumar of the CPM, Hansraj of the RPI, Raj Kumar of the J&K National Panthers Party and 7 Independents.

The Hissar parliamentry constituency includes Adampur, Uklana (Res.), Narnaud, Hansi, Barwala, Hissar, Malwa of Hissar district, Bawani-Khera (Res.) of Bhiwani district, Uchana Kalan of Jind district. A total 1192630 electors with 652276 men and 540354 women along with 6509 service voters. There were 38 candidates – Jaiparkash of the Congress, Sampat Singh – the INLD, Bhajan Lal – HJC (BL), Ram Dayal – the BSP, Karan Singh – the RPI, Satpal – the Samast Bharatiya Party, Satpal – the LJP, Roshan Lal – the Bhartiya Justice Party, Jang Bahadur – the BSP, Kishan Kumar – the Rashtriya Janhit Party and 27 Independents.

The Bhiwani-Mahendergarh constituency incorporates Loharu, Badhra, Dadri, Bhiwani, Tosham of Bhiwani district, Ateli, Mahendergarh, Narnaul and Nangal Chaudhary of Mahendergarh district. A total 1215630 electors with 648461 men and 567169 women along with the 22258 service voters. 29 candidates including Shruti Chaudhary of Congress, Ajay Singh Chautala of the INLD, Vikram Singh of the BSP, Narender Singh of the HJC (BL), Saroj Yadav – SP, Anil Kaushik – NCP, Jai Singh – Indian Justice Party, Neelam – Samast Bhartiya Party, Mohinder Singh – BSP, Ved Prakash – Nisswarth Sewa Party and 18 Independents.

Karnal Constituency includes Nilokheri (Res.), Indri, Karnal, Gharaunda, Asandh of Karnal district, Panipat, Panipat city, Israna (Res.), Smalkha of Panipat district. A total 1214475 electors with 669050 men and 545425 women along with 4137 service voters. As many as 23 candidates – Arvind Sharma of the Congress, I.D. Swami – BJP, Virender Kumar – BSP, Ramesh Chhabra – HJC (BL), Manchanda – CPI, Rajeev- SJP (R), Hawa Singh – Rastriya Janhit Party, Rampal – Rastriya Sahara Party, Kalpana Singh – RPI (Shivraj), Prem Kumar – Shiv Sena, Manoj Kumar – Wanchhit Janmat Party, Sushil Kumar Arya – Rastriya Arya Sabha and 12 Independents. The electorate has only 15 per cent Brahmins 101508 whereas Jats are 142630, Aroras 130982, Rors 82000, Chamars 99551, Balmikis 74785, Sikhs 64718, Jhimer 63578, Rajputs 52850, Gujjars 41366, Sainis 30738, Muslims 26790 etc. However, the constituency has sent a Brahmin to the Lok Sabha on several times and Jat only once in 1977 (M.S. Lather).

Ambala (Res.) constituency includes Naraingarh, Ambala cantonment, Ambala city, Mullana (Res.), Sadhaura (Res.) from Ambala district, Pachkula and Kalka from Kalka district, Yamunanagar and Jagadhari Assembly segments for Yamunanagar district. It has a total 1259674 electors with 688928 men and 570746 women including 7968 service voters. A total 7 candidates were in contest including Selja of the Congress, Rattan Lal Kataria of the BJP, Chanderpal of the BSP, Dalbir Singh of HJC (BL), Hemraj-LJP and 2 Independents.

Sonepat constituency includes Ganaur, Pai, Kharkhoda (Res.), Sonepat, Gohana, Baroda of Sonepat district, Julana, Safidon and Jind of Jind district. A total 1098320 electors with 607290 men and 491030 women having 7005 service voters and 21 candidates with Jitender Singh Malik – Congress, Kishan Singh Sangwan – BJP, Devraj Diwan – BSP, Umesh – HJC (BL), Sushila – Jan Chetna Party, Om Prakash – Bhartiya Congress Party, Sukhbir Singh – NCP, Gajinder Krantikari–

Jai Hind Sena, Rajpal – CPM (ML), Jyoti Prakash - SP, Krishan Kumar – LJP, Rohtash – Samast Bharatiya Party, Madan Gopal – Rastriya Dalit Morcha Party and 7 Independents were in the contest.

Rohtak includes Meham, Garhi Sampla, Kiloi, Rohtak, Kalanaur (Res.) of Rohtak district and Bahadurgarh, Badli, Jhajjar (Res.), Beri, Koshli of Jhajjar district. A total 1273118 electors with 694323 men and 578795 women having 20291 service votes and 16 candidates – Deepender of the Congress, Nafe Singh – INLD, Kishanmurti Hooda of HJC (BL), Sudesh – RPI and 10 Independents. During the last 12 parliamentary elections, the Rohtak seat was won by the Congress 7 times and the INLD 3 times.

In Kurukshetra, the Assembly sagements of Shahbad, Radaur, Ladwa, Thanesar, Pehwa, Guhla (Res.), Kalayat, Pundri are incorporated. It has a total 1168405 electorate including 639403 men and 529002 women apart from 3916 service voters. As many as 14 candidates were in the fray namely Naveen Jindal of the Congress, Ashok Arora of the INLD, Jaswant Singh of the HCJ (BC), Gurdial Singh Saini of the BSP, apart from 9 independents. The electorate include 191000 Jats, 110000 Chamars, 70000 Balmikis, 30000 Baniyas, 96000 Brahmins, 55000 Punjabis, 65000 Sikhs, 32000 Rajputs, 69000 Sainis, 42000 Kamboj, 33000 Gujjars. Despite a Jat dominated constituency, it has never returned a Jat so far. It has 39 per cent Jats, 20 per cent SCs, 10 per cent Punjabis and 3 per cent Khatis. To be specific there are 472000 Jats, 525000 non-Jats, 125000 Ahirs.

There was direct fight between the Congress and INLD-BJP alliance on seven seats. Smaller players like HJC (BL) and the BSP exhibitied enormous clout in Hissar, Bhiwani-Mahendergarh and Gurgaon constituencies with caste loyalists being an important factor.

The Congress constituted a 49 member Haryana Campaign Committee led by Vinod Sharma to activate the District. Congress Committees to apprise the voters with the achievements of the state government. Despite the meeting of the committee was presided over by Moti Lal Vora, incharge Haryana Affairs on Febuary 15, 2009 several ministers and MPs played truants like Selja, Kiran Chaudhary, Savitri Jindal, Jai Prakash, Avatar Singh Bhadana, Atma Singh Gill etc.

The Congress began its compaign from Kalka Assembly segment

on Febuary 21, 2009. The Chief Minister flagged off 50 Nav Haryana Raths from Chandigrah on Febuary 25, 2009 to undertake visits to the villages to apprise them with the developmental works done by the Congress government. For this purpose video cassettes and CDs were prepared. The Chief Minister announced Rs. 700 crore bonanza of incentives for various sections of society ahead of Lok Sabha election in May 2009 including pensioners, senior citizens, farmers, freedom fighters, unemployed youth, destitutes, widows, handicapped, anganwadi workers, milk producers etc. He made these announcents during his reply to the discussion on the Governor's Address in the Assembly on Febuary 13, 2009.

In the absence of any obvious incumbency disadvantages and any major national poll issue, the Congress made its development activities and welfare schemes as poll agenda. It hoped to gain from the torrent of free bees and populist incentives such as free plots, hike in old age and widow pension, waiving electricity dues, scholarship to school students and unemployment allowances etc.

The Chief Minister, Bhupender Singh Hooda raised his claim over Chandigarh and a separate High Court for Haryana at Hissar while addressing a press conference on April 22, 2009. He talked of equal distribution of water between North and South Haryana.

Prime Minister, Man Mohan Singh, Congress President, Sonia Gandhi, General Secretary, Rahul Gandhi, Prime Minister-in-waiting, L.K. Advani, Gujrat Chief Minister, Nerendra Modi etc. addressed the election meetings in the state.

Sonia Gandhi while addressing a election meeting at Ambala and Hissar on April 30, 2009 said when L.K. Advani was the Dy. Prime Minister and Home Minister, several terrorist attacks took place and terrorists were given safe passage to Kandhar. The Congress could only provide stability and safety to the nation. She mentioned NREGA, waiving of agriculture loans and good prices for agriculture produce as her achivements. She praised Hooda government for doing good work for the development and welfare of people of the state.

Narendra Modi, Chief Minister of Gujarat addressed an election meeting in support of the BJP candidate, Ram Chander Bainda at Faridabad on May 7, 2009. He raised the issue of SEZ, scarcity of electricity, drinking water, better education and health facilities in villages. The inflation had broken the backbone of poor and they were forced to live without food on alternate days. He criticised the Prime Minister and Sonia Gandhi for their weak defence and foreign policies.

Rahul Gandhi, AICC General Secretary drove to Sirsa in support of the Congress candidate, Ashok Tanwar on May 1, 2009. He compensated the crowd for his late arrival by three hours, by going around the barricaded passage to shake hands with them. He even obliged about 20 girls to click his picture on their mobiles. On his way to air force station, he visited a family residing in Chatargarh Pati, a slum area. He got off his vehicle on seeing some children waving at him and went to their house and took a glass of water before leaving.

He also addressed the election rally at Nuh in support of Rao Inderjit on May 2, 2009. He counted the achievements of Man Mohan Singh government including implementation of NREGS. He admitted the problems of educational backwardness, water scarcity and unemployment of the Mewat area and promised to address them on priority basis.

Rao Inderjit Singh started his campaign in Gurgaon since the day the election was announced and he turned down the offer of Central Election Committee to contest from Bhiwani-Mahendergarh seat. He met the Congress President personally to brief her about his plan. Actually Bhupender Singh Hooda wanted to kill two birds with one stone. Fielding Inderjit Singh from Bhiwani-Mahendergarh seat would negate the claim of Bansi Lal clan. However, Kiran met Sonia Gandhi to explain her position in the constituency. Thus Hissar, Gurgaon, Sonepat and Bhiwani-Mahendergarh seats were held up and candidates were declared very late.

Selja invited the Congress in-charge, Moti Lal Vora for a party workers meeting at Ambala on January 19, 2009 to counter the claim of Phool Chand Mullana.

The BJP started its campaign from Ambala on October 8, 2008 under the leadership of L.K. Advani. He also addressed the senior leadership of the party. The BJP constituted 18 committees to campaign for the party candidates. These committees pertained election management, campaign, publicity and media. Experienced and dedicated leaders were put on these committees.

No political party came out with serious issues like higher educational reform, agriculture, health, defence and poverty alleviation programmes.

Actually, the INLD started to hold rallies after the return of O.P. Chautala from abroad in 2006. It held a series of rallies on October 5, November 3, 2006; September 25, 2007 and 2008 etc. to revive the vigour in its workers after the route in Assembly election, 2005. Addressing a rally at Pai, O.P. Chautala said 'the Congress is pro-industralist government who is much concerned about protecting the share market but not the farmers. The Central Govenment has failed to control the law and order and inflation.' He promised to increase old-age, widow and disabled pension to Rs. 700 per month.

The INLD organised a rally at Bhiwani on September 25, 2008 on Devl Lal's birth anniversary. The entire INLD hierarchy was deputed to mobilize support and crowds for the rally. Similarly the Congress held a Backward Classes Kranti Rally at Rohtak on October 5, 2008, the home town of the Chief Minister.

O.P. Chautala criticized the Hooda government for increasing unemployment. He promised to increase the rate of land to one crore per acre in NCR and 50 lakh in other areas, job reservation for women, co-operative loan at 5 per cent rate of interest, MSP enhancement, banning the acquisition of land for SEZs etc.

He also sought forgiveness for his past mistakes saying, '*Bhula Dena Meri Kamiyon Ko, Kyonki insan Kabhi khuda nahin hota*'. He also declared reservation for OBC in panchayats to Lok Sabha, abolitions CST 38 form, insurance for *safai karmachari*, commission of *Arahitya* be increased from 2½ per cent to 3½ per cent, wheat MSP be increased to Rs. 1400.

The Congress held a Backward Class rally at Rohtak on September 14, 2008 where the Chief Minister announced to allot 100 yard free plots and scholarship to students in schools and colleges.

Congress Brahmin Rally at Karnal : Again the Congress used the Saraswat Brahmin Sabha platform to woo Brahmins supports for the parliamentry election at Karnal on November 14, 2008. He counted the berth given to the Brahmins in the Cabinet, HPSC, SSC, University VCs, Boards and Corporations. The Congress Working President, Kuldeep Sharma also addressed the gathering of Brahmins.

The Congress organized another rally for backward classes which was addressed by the Chief Minister on September 14, 2008 at Rohtak. The party felicitated Hooda for his announcent for allotting 100 yard residental plots to backward classes as well as scholarships to the students of this category.

The NDA held Vijay Sanklap rally at Sonepat on November 1, 2008 and launched the election campaign for Lok Sabha polls, 2009. the party raised the issue of enhancing MSP for paddy and wheat, low rate interest loans to farmers. Lal Krishan Advani also addressed the rally who blamed the UPA government for flawed agri-policies leading the farmers to commit sucide in Punjab and Maharashtra.

The BJP, President, Rajnath Singh, Punjab Chief Minister, Prakash Singh Badal, BJP Vice-President, Mukhtar Abas Naqvi, Janata Dal President, Sharad Yadav, Biju Janata Dal leader, B.H. Mehtab, Kisan leader, Sharad Joshi also addressed the rally and blamed the UPA government for hobnobbing with Muslims, terrorists as well as bad law and order and forced land acquisition for SEZ etc.

The BJP workers did not participate in the NDA rally at Sonepat on November 3, 2008 and only green brigade dominated the scene. This was because of the party workers of BJP did not accept the alliance as they had faced humiliation at the time of previous alliance and developed a feeling that the INLD leadership had betrayed them and their party.

The Congress Party held Samajik Kranti rally at Panipat on October 2, 2008 which was addressed by Congress President Sonia Gandhi who distributed free plots to SCs & BCs. Similarly, the party organised an Aggarwal conference at Sirsa on October 5, 2008.

The INLD organized a rally at Pai on October 19, 2008. The party supremo O.P. Chautala criticized the Central Government for being anti-farmers, soft on terrorism and inflation etc.

The HJC (BL) supremo, Kuldeep Bishnoi announced to reduce the age from 65 to 58 years for pension and to increase the amount to

Rs. 700 per month, one women in each family to get Rs. 600 per month and interest free loan up to Rs. 3 lakh to farmers.

Janakrosh Yatra was started by the INLD on January 14, 2009 and the BJP leaders, Shah Nawaz Hussain, Mukhtar Abbas Nagavi, Trilochan Singh joined it.

While addressing a Prerna Rally at Rohtak on January 31, 2009, Sushma Swaraj raised the issues of inflation and terrorism.

The INLD Chief Om Parkash Chautala announced political reservation for backward classes in Lok Sabha and Vidhan Sabha ticket distribution on the line of job reserved at the backward classes unity rally held at Jind on March 1, 2009. He cirticized the government for poor law and order situation. The farmers would be given loan at 4 per cent rate of interest and home loan up to Rs. 50,000 would be written off.

While addressing the Vijay Sanklap rally of the alliance at Karnal, Om Prakash Chautala lashed out the UPA government for ignoring farmers, misusing government funds and perpetuating corruption. All corrupt people would be booked. He promised Rs. 1400 as MSP for wheat and implementation of 6th Pay Commission in total and an inquiry into large scale bungling in the allotment of free plots to BPL families would be conducted.

The INLD demanded a white paper on public debt and loans taken by Haryana government in the last five years and the use of its funds. It accused the government of weakening the economic and fiscal situation of the state and making it debt-ridden. Chautala said that the debt of the state was Rs. 23000 crore up to March 2005 which rose to Rs. 40000 crore in 2009 whereas the state budget involves 33000 crore. The state loans were Rs. 4700 crore in March 2008 rose to Rs. 11000 crore in 2009 and the state debt was likely to increase in the ensuing year.

Chautala said in Vijay Sanklap rally at Rewari in February 28, 2009 that Hooda government had indulged in a huge racket of Rs. 70000 crore in change of land use (CLU) of over 35000 acres of agriculture land over the past five years, big scandals in SSA, SEZ land requirements. He announced that if NDA was voted to power such recketeers would be behind the bars.

Sonia Gandhi laid foundation stone of Medical College for Women in Bhagat Phool Singh Mahila Vishwavidyalaya on March 1, 2009. She also inaugurated Rajiv Gandhi College at Jind on the invitation of Birender Singh, Finance Minister. She applauded the Finance Minister for setting up college which reminded her of the role of her late husband, Rajiv Gandhi in setting Jawahar Navodaya Vidyalaya for the children of rural areas. She also referred to the decision to set up National Defence University in Gurgaon and extension of AIIMS in Jhajjar.

Bhupender Singh Hooda counted his success in terms of setting up Rajiv Gandhi Education City at Sonepat, Rajiv Gandhi Scholarship to SC and BC students, free 100 yard plots to the poor.

Sonia hoped that the development work carried out by the UPA government in the last five years would reap rich dividends in the coming Lok Sabha election. She also addressed a rally at Mewat which fell under Faridabad Lok Sabha constituency.

The Kumhar community decided to support the Congress in a meeting at Chaubisi Chabutra on Febuary 10, 2009 and decided to hold a rally at Jhajjar and Kalanaur. They exist in a good number in Beri, Salahwas, Hassangarh, Jhajjar, Badli and Bahadurgarh Assembly segments. They also raised their demand to the Chief Minister for due representation in the state politics.

A faction of Haryana Sikh Guru Dawar Parbandhak Committee led by Didar Singh Nalwi decided to support the Congress candidates in Haryana in the Lok Sabha elections particularly in Sirsa, Kurukshetra, Ambala, Karnal having a large number of Sikh electors. Nalwi took this decision after meeting the Chief Minister, Bhupender Singh Hooda in Delhi on April 17, 2009. During the meeting he raised the issue of — of HSGPC, second language status to Punjabi constitution of State Minority Panel in Haryana etc.

Voting and Results

Voting in these elections was 67.94 per cent, i.e. 2.25 per cent more than 2004. This included 69.42 per cent by men and 66.17 per cent by women. The Kurukshetra parliamentary constituency recorded the highest turnout 75.29 per cent followed by Sirsa - 75.01 per cent, Bhiwani-Mahendergarh – 72.53 per cent, Hissar – 69.71 per cent, Sonepat – 65.15 per cent, Gurgaon – 61.12 per cent, Faridabad 56.81 per cent, Karnal – 66.86 per cent, Ambala – 68.95 per cent, Rohtak – 66.62 per cent. A view of elections and voters is shown in Table 13.5.

Table 13.5 : Electorate in Haryana: a Category-wise View

Constituency	*Seats*	*Electors*			*Voters*		
		Men	*Women*	*Total*	*Men*	*Women*	*Total*
General	8	5193165	4320131	9513296	3521661	2785851	6307512
SCs	2	1397789	1176625	2574414	1014161	833191	1847352
Total	10	6590954	5496756	12087710	4535822	3619042	8154864

The residents of Bairsal village of Karnal district asserted them 'not to cast' their votes to express their resentments against the politicians of all hues. The residents under the banner of Nishan, a voluntary organization reached the polling station to cast negative votes but were driven away by the police which maintained that it was not a legally valid option. However, the village revolutionary committee confronted the police and asserted that no voter could be forced to cast his or her vote. After consultations with senior officers, the voters were allowed to register their negative votes after identifying themselves and giving in writing to the presiding officer under section 49 of election rules that "they do not want to vote for the politicians who never visited or bothered about them".

Some villages like Kamaskhera, Ramraikhera and Thranj Kalan boycotted the voting for non-availability of drinking water and non-performance of local MLA and not even a single voter turned up despite the efforts made by the candidates of various political parties to persuade them to vote. Similarly, only a single vote was polled in Jhanikhurd and Baroda in Sonepat parliamentary constituency.

The villagers did not allow the local MLA to address the public meeting at Julana. Similarly, residents of Bhatla village boycotted the voting against the shortage of drinking and irrigation water in Hissar constituency. They also decided to socially boycott any person who would vote. The village women broke pitchers in front of SDM's office in protest against the non-availability of drinking water.

The BSP and the HJC complained of rigging in the Lok Sabha poll in Rohtak and Gurgaon. The HJC candidate from Rohtak, Krishan Murti Hooda filed a complaint of large scale booth capturing in Rohtak from where Deepender, the son of the Chief Minister, Hooda was the Congress candidate. Similarly, the BSP candidate, Zakir Hussain from Gurgaon reported that voters in Assembly segments of Nuh, Firozpur-Jhirka, Punhana were denied their right to vote.

The Election Commission ordered repoll at one booth in Narwana Assembly segment (Reserved) under Sirsa parliamentary constituency (Reserved) on May 13, 2009. The repoll was ordered under Section 58 of the Peoples Reprentation Act, 1951 after receiving complaints of some irregularities at the booth. The vote of a person living abroad was cast by someone. Similarly, the vote of a deceased was also polled.

For counting of votes, 90 stations at 24 different locations were arranged where 3837 officials were deputed with 5855 supporting staff. The counting was conducted at 1249 tables and each table had one supervisor and two counting assistants apart for a micro-observer for the centre. A duty magistrate was appointed at each counting station with DSP as in-charge of security there. A total of 8100 police personnel were deployed to repoll in Lok Sabha elections.

Results

A history of sorts was created in Haryana when the Congress retained its previous tally of 9 Lok Sabha seats as no ruling party had been able to achieve this feat in the state ever. In Haryana, the voters are known to be highly volatile. If in one election it would give all seats to one party in the next the same party would be reduced to nil.

The results proved all pre- and post-election surveys wrong when the Congress bagged 9 seats.

Deepender Singh Hooda recorded the highest wining margin in the state when he retained his Rohtak seat by a margin of 445736 votes. He created a national record of wining the seat successively with such a high margin. All his rivals including Nafe Singh Rathee of the INLD lost their security deposits. The second highest margin was in Sonepat where Jatinder Singh Malik of the Congress defeated the BJP MP, Kishan Singh Sangwan by 161284 votes. Naveen Jindal of the Congress defeated Ashok Arora of the INLD with a margin of 118729 votes in Kurukshetra. Rao Inderjit Singh of the Congress defeated Zakir Hussain of the BSP by 84863 votes in Gurgoan where Arvind Sharma of the Congress won by a margin of 76346 votes when he defeated Maratha Virender Verma of the BSP in Karnal. Avatar Singh Bhadana of the Congress defeated Ram Chander Bainda of the BJP by 68201 votes in Faridabad.

It is appropriate here to have a glance at the figures pertaining to electorate in the state as a whole as well as a constituency-wise break-up is given in Table 13.6.

Table 13.6 : Constituency-wise: Electors, voters

Constituencies	*Electors*			*Voters*		
	Men	*Women*	*Total*	*Men*	*Women*	*Total*
Ambala	691750 (54.68%)	573157 (45.32%)	1264907	481015 (55.51%)	385446 (44.49%)	866461
Kurukshetra	637997 (54.68%)	528687 (45.32%)	1166684	482025 (55.06%)	393397 (44.94%)	875404
Sirsa	706039 (53.91%)	603468 (46.09%)	1309507	533146 (54.35%)	447745 (45.65%)	980891
Hissar	653423 (54.68%)	541266 (45.32%)	1194689	457932 (55.29%)	370269 (44.71%)	828201
Karnal	670412 (55.08%)	546565 (44.92%)	1216977	460404 (56.77%)	350542 (43.23%)	810946
Sonepat	491762 (%)	408216 (%)	1099978	404276 (56.77%)	307784 (43.23%)	712060
Rohtak	695376 (54.54%)	569596 (45.46%)	1274972	468014 (56.01%)	367524 (43.99%)	835538
Bhiwani-Mahendergarh	646450 (53.31%)	566083 (46.69%)	1212513	460515 (53.25%)	403603 (46.75%)	864118
Gurgoan	664532 (53.40%)	579905 (46.60%)	1244437	419911 (55.51%)	336413 (44.49%)	756324
Faridabad	616759 (55.1%)	486287 (44.09%)	1103046	368584 (55.98%)	256337 (44.02%)	624921

Source : Lok Sabha Election Report, 2009.

Secretary General of the INLD, Ajay Chautala was humbled by Shruti Chaudhary by 55053 votes in Bhiwani-Mahendergarh. This was the second successive defeat of Chautala, he was defeated by Kuldeep Bishnoi in 2004. In Sirsa (Reserved), the native district of Chautalas, Ashok Tanwar, the President of All India Youth Congress defeated Sita Ram of the INLD by 35499 votes. In Ambala (Reserved), the sitting MP, Selja defeated Rattan Lal Kataria of the BJP by 14570 votes.

Despite several constraints like the BSP taking away a considerable chunk of the Congress vote, open sabotage by party MLAs/ministers in many constituencies, etc., the Congress won these seats.

The election saw a complete rout of the INLD-BJP alliance. It has happend for the first time that the alliance between these two parties had drawn a blank. Thus, the alliance which was not approved by the rank and file of the two parties had also been rejected by the electorate.

The humiliation of the INLD was further compounded by the fact that its vote percentage which was second to the Congress in 2004, fell to the third. The INLD share decreased from 22.43 per cent in 2004 to 15.68 per cent in 2009.

The BSP not only increased its share in the vote bank from 4.98 per cent to 15.73 per cent but managed to wrest the second position from the BJP in Gurgaon and Karnal. However, the vote percentage of the BJP decreased from 2004 to 12.09 per cent in 2009. The HJC (BL) got 9.89 per cent vote and the elecorate rejected the claim of Kuldeep Bishnoi that in 2004 and 2005 the people had voted for the Congress to make his father, Bhajan Lal as the Chief Minister of the state.

The results silenced the critics of Bhupender Singh Hooda who said that his influence was confined to the old Rohtak district only.

Deepender Singh Hooda led in all nine Assembly segments of Rohtak parliament constituency. The development factor mattered the most there. Similarly, Naveen Jindal from Kurukshetra seat led in all nine Assembly segments. The social work launched by him there paid off.

The Congress captured Sonepat seat after a period of 18 years. Last time it was Dharmpal Malik of the Congress who was elected in 1991. Shruti Chaudhary registered a nominal margin in three Assembly segments of Narnaul, Nangal Chaudhary and Ateli where Rao Narender Singh led all the way. She led in Bhiwani, Charki-Dadri, Loharu, Badhra and Tosham.

Sirsa defeat could be treated as a severe blow to the INLD whereas in the Assembly poll, 2005, the district returned three MLAs of the INLD. The party won one Assembly seat in Fetehabad also. Thus, out of 9 MLAs, 4 came from Sirsa parliamentary constituencies. Now, it lost in 6 out of 8 Assembly segments there.

Jai Prakash of Congress lost in all 9 assembly segments of Hisar parliamentary constituency. In Uchana, which was represented by Birender Singh, Jai Prakash got about a half votes in comparison to Sampat Singh of the INLD. The voters of Gihrai represented by Chhaterpal Singh, an adversary of Jai Prakash, also defeated him. The party workers from Hissar shifted to Kurukshetra in support of Naveen Jindal.

The stunned INLD and BJP introspected the debacle. For this, the INLD convened a meeting on May 18, 2009 to introspect the reasons for its failure at the hustings. At the same time, the BJP called a meeting of senior party leaders at Rohtak on the same day.

The BJP co-incharge of party offices in Haryana, H.S. Grewal said that people did not receive the alliance well because they were probably not sure about its workability, i.e. "we could not make them understand the alliance. It was there and then we fell out. Again we joined hand last year, it has not been consistent. We will look into all these issues."

The INLD and the BJP hoped to revive their formation in the Lok Sabha polls and agreed to old sharing formula of five seats each with which they had struck gold in 1999 Lok Sabha election making a clean sweep in the state. Together, they were always a force to reckon with. However, there was a big question mark about its effectiveness this time as most of the state unit leaders of the BJP vehemently opposed renewal of ties with Chautala and majority of them favoured the HJC (BL).

As the coalition failed to work on the ground, the vote share of the two parties plummated to 28.59 per cent from 39.64 per cent in 2004.

Though the BJP leaders were seen with the INLD candidates throughout the election campaign, there were hiccups in the transfer of votes. Gripped by despondency some members of the group which had opposed the tie up with Chautala, had already begun murmuring about the need to review the alliance and go with the HJC (BL).

The BSP polled 379574 votes in 18 assembly segments of Kurukshetra and Karnal Lok Sabha seats and led in Nilokheri, Indri and Gharada segments where it polled 800 votes less than the Congress in Asandh. The INLD-BJP polled 463912 votes in these two Lok Sabha constituencies.

A Party-wise performance is given in Table 13.7.

Table 13.7: Result: Lok Sabha Elections, 2009

Parties	*Votes Polled*	*Percentage*	*Seats Won*
Congress	4203765	41.77	9
INLD	1286573	15.77	–
BJP	986136	12.9	–
BSP	1284040	15.74	–
HJC(BL)	623650	9.80	1
NCP	12776	0.31	–
CPM	18999	0.23	–
CPI	14929	0.17	–
JKNPP	9376	0.11	–
LJP	17994	0.22	–
SP	8398	0.10	–
SHS	1031	0.01	–
JKNPP	9376	0.11	–
RASAP	7682	0.09	–
RPI	1211	0.01	–
BRPP	1527	0.01	–
NELU	585	0.01	–
RDMP	2159	0.02	–
JKM	1727	0.02	–
AIFB(S)	2758	0.03	–
JJJKMC	1100	0.01	–
RND	2583	0.03	–
JUP	595	0.01	–
AIRP	678	0.01	–
RWS	2322	0.03	–

(Contd..)

Table 13.7 : (Contd..)

RJAP	960	0.01	–
BHBP	2975	0.03	–
IJP	9861	0.12	–
SMBHP	14435	0.17	–
VAJP	1117	0.01	–
RASAP	913	0.01	–
BHC	1069	0.01	–
KKJHS	456	0.01	–
RDMP	578	0.01	–
UWF	2552	0.03	–
JCP	2987	0.03	–
NSSP	573	0.01	–
Independents	229466	28.14	–

Total electors : 12087710
Total voters : 8154864
Valid votes : 8154018

Source: Report, Lok Sabha Election, 2009.

The candidates of HJC (BL) from Ambala, Sirsa, Kurukshetra, Karnal, Sonepat, Gurgaon, Rohtak, Faridabad lost their security deposits.

Reasons of the INLD Defeat

The INLD rationalized the defeat of its candidates and those of the BJP because of national issues, said O.P. Chautala in party's executive meeting at Hissar. But Sampat Singh said that party was defeated because of its commercialization and opposed the statement given by Chautala. He said that (1) Isolation from the common masses particularly the poor. (2) No respect for the party workers and they were humiliated often. (3) Denial of party tickets to old and dedicated party men like Sushil Indora, Kailasho Saini and Balwan Singh Suhag.

The Haryana BJP decided to take action against 10 of its senior leaders who remained inactive during the Lok Sabha polls including the party MLA, Naresh Malik. The party at its state executive meeting at Panchkula found three reasons of its defeat, e.g. (1) A part of its vote bank was transferred to the BSP, (2) Some votes went to the HJC, and (3) Its failure to attract the youth towards party.

Performance of various Political Parties

The performance of the Congress is given in Table 13.8.

Table 13.8 : Performance of the Congress: Constituency-wise View

Constituencies	*Votes Polled*	*Percentage*
Ambala (Res.)	322258	39.52
Kurukshetra	397204	48.71
Karnal	304698	37.36
Sonepat	338795	41.54
Rohtak	585016	71.74
Faridabad	257864	31.62
Gurgaon	278516	34.55
Bhiwani-Mahendergarh	302293	37.07
Hissar	204539	25.08
Sirsa (Res.)	411624	50.48

The Congress got maximum votes in Rohtak constituency-71.74 per cent, followed by Sirsa-50.48 per cent, Kurukshetra-48-71 per cent, Sonepat-41.54 per cent and minimum in Faridabad-31.62 per cent as given in Table 13.8

The performance of the INLD is given in Table 13.9.

Table 13.9 : Performance of the INLD and the BJP : Constituency-wise View

Constituencies	*Votes Polled*	*Percentage*
Ambala (Res.)	307688(BJP)	37.73
Kurukshetra	278475(INLD)	34.15
Karnal	185437(BJP)	22.74
Sonepat	177511(BJP)	21.76
Rohtak	139280(INLD)	17.08
Faridabad	189663(BJP)	23.26
Gurgaon	125837(BJP)	15.43
Bhiwani-Mahendergarh	247240(INLD)	30.32
Hissar	241493(INLD)	29.61
Sirsa (Res.)	376499(INLD)	46.17

The performance of the INLD and the BJP was better in Sirsa and Ambala, both the reserved constituencies where they secured 46.17 and 37.73 per cent votes respectively. The INLD could not get more than 30 per cent votes except Kurukshetra-34.15 per cent. Similarly, the BJP could not get more than 23 per cent votes in Karnal, Sonepat and Gurgaon constituencies as depicted in Table 13.9.

The constituency-wise performance of the BSP is given in Table 13.10.

Table 13.10 : Performance of the BSP : Constituency-wise view

Constituencies	*Votes Polled*	*Percentage*
Ambala (Res.)	188596	23.12
Kurukshetra	151231	18.54
Karnal	228352	28.00
Sonepat	112907	13.84
Rohtak	68210	0.83
Faridabad	113463	13.91
Gurgaon	193653	23.74
Bhiwani-Mahendergarh	59078	0.72
Hissar	90277	1.10
Sirsa (Res.)	75267	0.92

The performance of the HJC is given in Table 13.11.

Table 13.11 : Performance of the HJC (BL) Lok Sabha Election, 2009

Constituencies	*Votes Polled*	*Percentage*
Ambala (Res.)	30688	0.37
Kurukshetra	16839	0.20
Karnal	49226	0.60
Sonepat	42400	0.51
Rohtak	20472	0.25
Faridabad	31163	0.38
Gurgaon	117260	14.38
Bhiwani-Mahendergarh	214141	26.26
Hissar	248476	30.47
Sirsa (Res.)	45229	0.55

The BSP secured maximum votes in Karnal constituency-28 per cent, followed by Gurgaon-23.7 per cent, Ambala-23.12 per cent. But it got less than one per cent votes in Rohtak, Bhiwani, Mahendergarh and the reserved constituency of Sirsa as shown in Table 13.10.

The HCJ performed better in Hissar-30.47 per cent, Bhiwani-Mahendergarh-26.26 per cent and Gurgaon-14.38 per cent. But in all the remaining 7 constituencies, it could not get even one per cent votes as given in Table 13.11

Conclusion

From the ongoing discussion, it may be concluded that the Congress regained 9 seats despite the element of dissidence and several other problems. However, the INLD-BJP combine could not make any dent in the voting pattern of any section of society facing the partisan development approach of the state government. Similarly, other political outfits also could not make any difference in the support-base of the Congress Party.

The next Lok Sabha elections are due in May 2014 and all political parties have started to hold parties have started to hold rallies and party workers meetings to be prepared for the poll. The ban on rallies on caste lines as well as a ban on criminals to contest the elections by the Allahabad High Court and Supreme Court respect Ely are to have greet impact on the coming elections.

14

Parliamentary Elections 2014

Fifteenth Lok Sabha was dissolved and a notification was made on March 5, 2014 for holding the 16th Lok Sabha elections in India. The elections were held in nine phases between April 7 and May 12, 2014. It was April 10 for Haryana, Chandigarh and Delhi people to cast their votes. In Punjab it was April 13 and Himachal May 7, 2014.

Further notification was made by Chief Election Officer, in Haryana on March 14, 2014 declaring schedule of elections: nominations -March 15 to 22, scrutiny -March 24, withdrawals-March 26 and voting- April 10, 2014.

The contestants were required to deposit Rs. 250000 as security in cash whereas the SC candidates Rs. 12500 in cash only.

Nominations : Almost all major political parties were preparing themselves for the poll for the last many months. The Congress High Command formed a 24 member Haryana Pradesh Election Committee[1] to short-list the candidates for the Lok Sabha elections. All factions in the divided state Congress unit were represented in the panel headed by the State Congress Chief, Phool Chand Mullana.

Four Congress MPs- Avtar Singh Bhadana – Faridabad, Ashok Tanwar- Sirsa, Rao Inderjit – Gurgaon, Selja – Ambala and Jitender Malik – Sonepat, refused to contest the Lok Sabha polls, 2014 in view of the poor position of the party.

Over 100 Congress leaders applied for Lok Sabha tickets in Haryana. These applications were received by the HPCC up to December 28, 2014. In Rohtak there was only one applicant – Deepender Singh Hooda, sitting MP and son of Bhupender Singh

Hooda, Chief Minister, whereas 22 applications were received from Sonepat but the sitting MP, Jitender Malik refused to contest the polls, Hisar-18, Ambala-15, Kurukshetra-13 and Sirsa-13, Karnal-3, Faridabad-2, Bhiwani-Mahendergarh-5, Gurgaon-10 from where the sitting MP – Rao Inderjit Singh has quit the party.

Both Hooda and Mullana met M.P. Joshi and Madhusudan Mistri, AICC General Secretaries and recommended that barring one or two candidates, all sitting MPs should be retained.

Former Union Minister and Haryana Legislator, Vinod Sharma quit the Election Committee as it was against the announcement made by Rahul Gandhi in January 2014.

He was also against the inclusion of the Bhupender Singh Hooda, Birender Singh and Sejla in the poll committee. He said that such committees did not serve any purpose as per announcement of Rahul Gandhi, the candidate should be directly selected by the party workers at the block level. These committees used to impose those candidates on the electorate which they did not want. He also favoured the idea of 'recall' the elected representatives in case of their non-performance.

A nine member Lok Sabla Election Committee of the INLD invited applications and visited all segments to consult party workers. The final decision was taken by the INLD Supremo, Om Prakash Chautala.

The INLD received 261 applications for 10 Lok Sabha seats in Haryana, the highest 62 from Karnal, 61 from Sirsa, 24 from Kurukshetra, 32 from Sonepat, 19 from Gurgaon, 29 from Faridabad and 23 from Rohtak and 11 from Ambala.

In the BJP as many as 100 candidates claimed the tickets for 10 Lok Sabha seats. The BJP and HJC have formed a 6 members committee for sharing the seats between them.[2] The BJP gave tickets to Congress rebels in five constituencies at the cost of dedicated and old guards of the party. Even outsiders were given tickets in many constituencies. Being a business community party, it did not nominate any Punjabi or Bania from any constituency. Ramesh Kaushik's nomination was unjustified in a Jat dominated constituency, Sonepat. Even in Rohtak an outsider was nominated at the cost of prominent local leaders.

So, a rift in Haryana BJP over ticket allocation surfaced and the

BJP State President was shown black flags at Rohtak, Bhiwani and Sonepat for nominating the wrong candidates. The supporters of Naresh Malik demonstrated at Rohtak BJP office, in Sonepat the supporter of Pradeep Sangwan threaten to leave the party and to contest as independent and the nomination of Dharambir who recently defected from the Congress for Bhiwani-Mahendergarh Lok Sabha seat, was also opposed.

The State BJP Secretary, Pradeep Sangwan threatened to resign if Ramesh Kaushik was not changed as party candidate from Sonepat by March 19, 2014. He alleged a big monetary deal has taken place before giving the ticket to Kaushik who defected from the Congress nearly 6 months back.

Sunita Duggal, wife of Superintendent of Police, Rohtak was nominated from Sirsa Lok Sabha seat by the BJP. Sunita resigned as Assistant Commissioner of Income Tax. Capt. Ajay Singh Yadav, who was nominated from Gurgaon by the BJP, refused to contest and requested that his son Charanjeev Yadav be given ticket who was President of Haryana Youth Congress. Actually Yadav had already started campaigning for his son two months back.

Similarly the AAP was also not free from wrong nominations. The supporters of AAP sat on dharna against the nomination of Balwinder Kaur from Kurukshetra Lok Sabha seat and after 17 days demonstration they fielded Gurmeet Singh as a rebel candidate from there who resigned from AAP on March 19, 2014 and formed Lok Sawaraj Manch. AAP got another setback when former Haryana IGP, Ranbir Sharma who joined it after taking VRS, criticized the party high command for its wrong decisions in giving the tickets. He also supported the nomination of Gurmeet Singh from Kurukshetra.

Charanjit Singh, MLA from Kalawanwali of SAD resigned from the membership of Haryana Vidhan Sabha on March 16, 2014. He was nominated from Sirsa Lok Sabha seat by the INLD.

The CPM and CPI nominated their candidates in 5 Lok Sabha seats. The CPM nominated three – Phool Singh Sheokand – Hisar, Ram Kumar Bahbalpuria – Sirsa and Master Sher Singh – Bhiwani. The CPI nominated two – Maman Chand Saini – Karnal and Arun Kumar – Ambala.

Nominations and Contestants : Lok Sabha Elections, 2014

Constituencies	*Nominations*	*Contestants*
Ambala	20	14
Kurukshetra	36	22
Sirsa	25	18
Hisar	47	41
Karnal	33	23
Sonepat	29	23
Rohtak	19	14
Bhiwani-M.Garh	32	26
Gurgaon	27	22
Faridabad	32	27
Total	**300**	**230**

Nominations & Contestants : Men-Women Ratio in Lok Sabha Elections, 2014

	Nominations		*Contestants*	
Constituency	*M*	*W*	*M*	*W*
Ambala	16	4	13	1
Kurukshetra	31	5	20	2
Sirsa	24	1	18	0
Hisar	43	4	40	1
Karnal	29	4	21	2
Sonepat	26	3	23	0
Rohtak	17	2	14	0
Biwani-M.Garh	30	2	25	1
Gurgaon	24	3	21	1
Faridabad	28	4	24	3
Total	**268**	**32**	**219**	**11**

Total Women Contestants, Winness in Lok Sabha Elections; 1967-2014

Party	*Contestants*	*Women*
CONGRESS	8	5
BJP	5	1
INLD	3	2
JP/SAMTA	5	1
HVP	1	–
BSP	1	–
INDEPENDENTS	30	–

Nominations : A Comparative Look of 2009 & 2014 Lok Sabha Elections

Constituencies	*2009*	*2014*
Ambala (Res.)	16	14
Kurkushetra	27	22
Karnal	29	23
Sonepat	27	23
Rohtak	23	14
Faridabad	30	27
Bhiwani-M. Garh	34	26
Hisar	50	41
Gurgaon	27	22
Sirsa (Res.)	21	18
Total	**285**	**300**

The Supreme Court debarred those behind the bars or in police custody from contesting the election and to disqualify the elected representatives – MPs and MLAs on being convicted. There is a provision in Section 62(5) of Representation of People Act that a person shall not vote if he is confined in jail or is in lawful custody of the police and the Supreme Court reminded that a person who has no right to vote is not an elector and therefore is not qualified to contest the election.

The Haryana Janshakti Party led by Didar Singh Nalwi could not field its candidate because it could not be registered well in time.

Dharmbir Singh, the CPS quit the Congress and joined the BJP when he was not nominated from Bhiwani-Mahendergarh seat. Earlier, he was directed to contest the Assembly elections 2009 from Sohna, whereas he contested from Bawal in 2004. He criticized the Party High Command for wrong distribution of tickets.

Lt. Gen. O.P. Kaushik and Gen. V.K. Singh also joined the BJP. Bahadur Singh, an Education Minister in the INLD government as well as a defector to the Congress joined the BJP on March 14, 2014.

Rameshwar Dayal an MLA of the INLD, resigned from the party for neglecting the senior leaders in nominations for Lok Sabha seat. Earlier the senior Vice-President, Rao Ajit Singh resigned from the party Such developments adversely affected the prospects of Babadur Singh, candidate from Bhiwani-Mahendergarh constituency.

Pradeep Sangwan after denial of BJP ticket fielded his nomination as an independent candidate and later joined the Congress. Congress leader and Gurgaon MP, Rao Inderjit Singh announced his resignation at Rewari saying that party has become Hooda's Private Ltd. on September 23, 2013 while speaking at Saheedi Samman Diwas to commemorate the birth anniversary of Rao Tula Ram.

Ending his 35 year old association with the Congress amid roaring applause, he told not to contest next Lok Sabha election from the Congress ticket. He challenged the Chief Minister to resign and contest election against him from Gurgaon. The Chief Minister has turned this state and party into corporate company that works according to his whims and wishes and this is against the ideology of the Congress party. Development is based on personal relationship, caste and constituency. I can't go along with this any more, Rao said. Earlier he demanded a thorough probe into the land deals of Robert Vadra. Capt. Abhimanu welcomed Rao Inderjit Singh's exit from the corruption-ridden Congress.

Rao Inderjit Singh's exit from the Congress was taken to change the political landscape in the Ahirwal reagon spread over three parliamentary constituencies – Gurgaon, Bhiwani-Mahindergarh and Rohtak and nearby 14 Assembly segments.

The BJP President, Rajnath Singh shared his willingness to get Rao in the party and so the INLD. The BJP wanted to open its account in Lok Sabha in Haryana and the INLD to fetch the state power again.

Vinod Sharma, a legislator from Ambala quit the Congress party on March 5, 2014 and tried to join HJC but not allowed by Sushma Swaraj, its ally leaders.

Attar Singh Saini, a former Irrigation and Power Minister defected to the INLD from the Congress on January 28, 2014. Earlier, Shamsher Singh Kharkara, Mange Ram Gupta, former Finance Minister, Hari Singh, Surender Madan, Rambir Mandola, Dr. Mala Singh all ministers, Zakir Hussain, Ex-MLA, Surender Dalal, Rajpal Yadav, Vijay Batra, Joginder Kohli, Chhotu Ram, Hawa Singh, Manoj Mitra etc. joined the INLD.

Four Congress leaders including three ministers joined the BJP on including Krishna Gahlawat, Bahadur Singh and Santosh Sharma and Ramesh Dalal. Former bureaucrat M.P. Bidhlan joined the BJP and opted to contest from Sirsa Lok Sabha seat. He was a member of HPSC.

A Punjabi Ekta Sammelan was held at Rohtak on September 29, 2013 under the banner of Punjabi Ekta Manch, when the Congress legislator B. B. Batra and ex-legislator Subhash Batra participated. The later criticized the Congress Government for ignoring the interests of Punjabi community. Punjabis and Sainis joined hands to form an alliance in the Punjabi – Saini Sadbhawana Manch on November 18, 2013 at Hisar. The Akhil Bhartiya Punjabi Jagriti Manch demanded 2 Lok Sabha seats for Punjabis in its meeting held at Rohtak on December 6, 2013. Shamsher Kharkara supported the demands of Subhash Batra, the convenor of the Manch.

The T.M.C. decided to field Punjabis on four Lok Sabha seats as disclosed by K.D. Singh while addressing a Punjabi convention at Rohṭak on December 15,2013. The convention was organized by Akhil Bhartiya Punjabi Jagriti Manch led by Subhash Batra, a former minister. Gen. V.K. Singh also spoke on the occasion.The Punjabi leaders within the BJP demanded three seats for their community – Karnal. Kurukshetra and Faridabad. So these seats should not be given to HJC. The Punjabi Manch decided to support the INLD as the party has given tickets to the community members from Faridabad, Sirsa and Karnal. No other political party nominated even a single member in the Lok Sabha elections. The Chief of the Manch, Subhash Batra who resigned from the Congress Party a few months back held some rallies to empower the community and demanded 25 Assembly seats.

The Baniya community claimed 16 Vidhan Sabha seats[3] in the elections to be held in October 2014.

Alliance : The BJP entered into an alliance with the HJC where as the INLD was much willing for it. The HJC held a rally at Hisar on December 1, 2013 which was attended by Arun Jaitly, who said that the alliance of BJP and HCJ should have come into existence in 2009. Had it been done, Bhupender Singh Hooda would not have become the Chief Minister of state. Sometimes, we make a mistake in public life and this was a mistake. Ram Bilas Sharma, Krishanpal Gujjar and Kuldeep Bishnoi also spoke on the occasion.

However, Parkash Singh Badal, the Chief Minister of Punjab made last minute efforts to persuade the BJP to form an alliance with the INLD. He met Narender Modi and some other BJP leaders. A formula for a maha-alliance was suggested where the BJP would contest 5 seats, giving 3 to the INLD and 2 to the HJC. Badal also demanded one seat for SAD-Sirsa.

But the BJP-HJC differences surfaced in Sonepat rally, addressed by the party President, Rajnath Singh on October 21, 2013. when, one group including leaders like Arun Jaitly was in favour of having alliance with the INLD. Rao Inderjit Singh after leaving the Congress party also tried to bring the INLD, BJP and HJC on one platform to make a strong alliance to defeat the Congress in Haryana. The indications were given that the BJP with 5 Lok Sabha seats, 3 to the INLD, one to the HJC and one to Inderjit.

Narender Modi called a meeting of Haryana BJP leaders at Delhi on December 24, 2013 to discuss the issue of seat sharing. The distribution of seats between the BJP and HJC could not be finalized because the BJP was willing to provide Sonepat or Karnal or Bhiwani to HJC apart from Hisar in view of its good support.

To begin with, Karnal seat was given to Chander Mohan, elder brother of Kuldeep Bishnoi. Thus both the brothers became candidates for Lok Sabha election as only two seats were given by the BJP under the alliance. However, it was not liked by the BJP and under pressure Chander Mohan declined to contest the election saying that his father wanted that some Balmiki should contest from Karnal. Lateron the BJP allotted the Sirsa seat to the HJC.

Parkash Singh Badal and Sukhbir Singh Badal campaigned for the INLD candidate Dushyant in Hisar. Kuldeep Bishnoi lodged a complaint to the BJP President, Rajnath Singh that SAD in alliance with the BJP in Punjab had violated coalition dharma by opposing his party in Haryana and urged him to rein in Badals. But Badals addressed the INLD rallies in Sirsa and Kurukshetra. Moreover, the SAD leaders made it clear that they prefer family alliance over political alliance.

The Haryana Janshakti Party decided to contest Kurukshetra and Sirsa seats and extended support to other party in Karnal and Ambala.

Campaigning

Generally, a party starts its campaign with the release of its manifesto. But no political party could declare its manifesto up to March 25, 2014 and they canvassed without it. To add the INLD, the BSP and the HJC could not release their manifestos up to April 7, 2014. Even the BJP released it on April 7, whereas the Congress and AAP released it earlier.

The Congress released its manifesto on March 26, 2014 with focus on 8% growth, reducing the fiscal deficit to 3%, passage of GST bills, 10 crore jobs in 5 years, 1 trillion investment in infrastructure, special envoy to track black money, universal health coverage, right to home, pension for all labour, widows, destitudes and disabled, quota in education and jobs for economically weaker sections of all communities, SC/ST reservation in private sector jobs, un-employment allowance of Rs. 10000 to young graduates, judicial appointment commission, women reservation bill would be passed, 25% of quota for women in police station, Shrestha Siksha Abhiyan etc.

The BJP released its manifesto on April 7, 2014 which focused on simplification of tax structure, task force for bringing black money from foreign banks, modernization of madarsas, 100 new cities to be developed, interlinking rivers, women IITs, drinking water and toilet in every house, AIIMS in every state, no FDI in retail, single window approval for industrial projects, control on inflation more employment, transparency and e-governance for reducing corruption, more public participation in decision-making, constitution of National Youth Advisory Council, 33% reservation for women in legislatures, transparent land acquisition policy, quality education, uniform civil code, abolition of Article 370, implementation of Swaminathan report on agriculture etc.

The CPM released its manifesto on April 1, 2014 with a stress on implementation of Swaminathan Committee report on agriculture, change in land acquisition policy, transparency and accountability in governance, no privatizaion in education and health, end of contract system, strong labour laws, 33% reservation for women in legislatures etc.

It was all rally time in Haryana when the Congress, the INLD and the BJP organized a series of public meetings to show their support base in the state.

Meanwhile, it would be pertinent to cite some decisions of the apex court whereby the political parties were guided not to offer freebies to the voters. Moreover, no public rally be held on caste lines. For this purpose the Supreme Court directed the Election Commission to frame guidelines for preventing political parties from offering freebies to voters in return for electing them to power as such practices shake the root of free and fair elections. In consultation with all recognized political parties the Election Commission should include these guidelines in model code of conduct. The Supreme Court gave this verdict in a case against political parties in Tamil Nadu winning elections on the plank of freebies at the cost of state exchequer.

The Allahabad High Court disallowed the public rallies on caste lines in Uttar Pradesh on July 11, 2013. The Court gave this decision on a PIL saying that such rallies were against the spirit of the Indian Constitution.

Bhupender Singh Hooda decided to launch the UPAs flagship food security scheme on August 20, 2013, the birth anniversary of former Prime Minister, Rajiv Gandhi, in order to scuttle Birender Singhs' show of strength rally at Jind on the same day and persuaded Sonia Gandhi successfully not to attend his rally.

After declaring Narender Modi as the Prime Minister candidate for the 2014 Lok Sabha elections, the BJP held an impressive ex-servicemen rally at Rewari. All its leaders except Advani participated in the rally on September 15, 2013. Modi stressed the need of strong regime at Delhi to ensure national security and a check on its neighbours. He pointed out the intrusions made by China, Pakistan into our territory due to weak Union government. He said, the problem is not at the border, it is in Delhi and the solution will also emerge from Delhi itself.

He launched a guarded attack on the Centre for weak foreign policy, poverty, inflation, illiteracy and terrorism. He demanded a white paper from the Central government on the status of action taken on longstanding demand of ex-servicemen of - one rank one pension.

A meeting of core group of Haryana BJP was held at Chandigarh under the leadership of the National President, Rajnath Singh on September 23, 2013. The workers sammelan were convened in all Lok Sabha constituencies from November 10 to December 10, 2013. Moreover, public rallies were organized and as many as 15672 booth level committees were constituted.

The UPA government declared the constitution of 7th Pay Commission much earlier only to attract the attention of voters on the eve of Assembly elections in five states and Lok Sabha elections in the beginning of 2014. Further, the Union Government declared to distribute mobile to 2.5 crore workers and their expenses for two year would be paid by the government. Those who have worked at least for 25 days under MNREGA programme will be given mobiles in phases. Total expenditure on the project was estimated to Rs. 4850 crores.

The HJC organized a rally at Sohna on September 29, 2013. Addressing the rally Kuldeep Bishnoi said he would never join the Congress. He blamed the Hooda government for biased approach of development.

Birender Singh, M.P. Rajya Sabha demanded again and again to change the President of the HPCC. He favoured the youth to join politics. The Congress organized a Jan Shakti rally at Sirsa on September 30, 2013 under the supervision of Ranjit Singh. It was addressed by the Chief Minister and Shakeel Ahmed, in charge of Haryana affairs, HPCC President etc. A resolution was moved for Modi to restore land to hundreds of farmers of Punjab and Haryana uprooted from the Bhuj area in Gujarat on the lines of Haryana where the Chief Minister has done for the Sikh families in Pehowa. Shakeel Ahmed used the rally to hit at Modi as well as detractors within the Congress. He laid foundation stones of various development projects costing to 90 crores in different parts of the state. The Haryana government declared that more than 3860 houses would be built under Rajiv Gandhi Aawas Yojna in three cities – Rohtak, Sirsa and Ambala for BPL families.

The BJP organized Vijay Sanklap rally at Palwal on October 2, 2013 which was addressed by the former President, Nitin Gadkari. He raised the issues of corruption, poverty, bad law and order, exploitation of farmers, regional bias in development, unemployment etc. Ram Bilas Sharma, President and Satpal Malik, Vice President, Jagdish Mukhi, Incharge of Haryana Affairs, Om Parkash Dhankhar, President of Farmer Morcha etc. spoke on the occasion.

The Congress general secretary, Shakeel Ahamed incharge of Haryana affairs advised to the state leaders not to air grouses in public while launching the party's official website and addressing the workshop on food security and land acquisition bills on October 6, 2013 at Chandigarh.

In a cautious attack on Hooda's detractors, he urged the leaders to sort out differences on the table. Any one going to media is very weak and incapable of fighting his own battle as well as it is also an insult to the party. The Congress is a big family where its members can have their own point of views but it does not mean that you are opposed to each other. If things remain unresolved at the state level, may be taken up at the higher level of the party in Delhi. He urged the leaders to bury their differences and present a united face. Birender, Selja, Ishwar Singh were present but Shruti Chaudhary, Ashok Tanwar and Naveen Jindal were absent.

In Haryana, the rate of VAT was reduced on textile products from 12% to 5% to please the business community. It would cost the state exchequer Rs. 450 crore per annum. Earlier property tax and tax on cotton were reduced. Form C was taken out from the purview of VAT. The milling charges from rice millers were reduced from Rs. 20 lakh to Rs. 5 lakh.

Deepender Hooda addressed a public meeting in the ancestral village of INLD supremo, Om Prakash Chautala on October 12, 2013. He told that his grand father Ranbir Singh Hooda was in jail along with Devi Lal before independence. He declared a grant of Rs. 1.11 crore for the development of the village. He also laid the foundation stone of a 33 KV power sub-station there. K.V. Singh, OSD and his son, Amit Singh organized the meeting. He criticized the BJP model of development in Gujarat where the amount of old age pension, wages of MNREGA were much less than Haryana.

Bhupender Singh Hooda, addressed a public meeting at Faridabad and told the public that more than Rs. 4000 crore were spent on the development of the city since 2005. The city is linked with metro.

Hooda, Selja came out in the open when they targeted each other over developmental issues during the foundation laying ceremony of Rs. 100 crore technology park being set up at Suha near Ambala on October 23, 2013. The event was attended by K.H. Muniyappa, Union Minister for Micro, Small and Medium enterprises. Selja voiced her concerns over the disparity in development in her constituency and accused the Hooda government for the neglect. She also blamed the government for atrocities on dalits.

All major political parties held public rallies to set the tone for the Lok Sabha election 2014. However, the bigger rallies were – state level rally by the INLD at Kurukshetra on November 1, 2013, the birth anniversary of Ch. Devi Lal, the Congress's rally at Gohana on November 10, 2013 and HJC rally at Hisar on December 2, 2013. The BJP organized such a rally at Rewari.

The issue of reservation of OBC including Jat was handled deftly, implemented the food security scheme on August 20, 1013, railway coach factory for Sonepat, operation of Rewari – Jhajjar-Rohtak rail line, establishment of more than 20universities including central university at Mahedergarh, defence university at Gurgaon etc, were some of the major achievements highlighted by the Chief Minister during his compaign.

At the same time, the opposition parties raised the issues of Robert Vadra land disputes, involvement of ministers in crimes and conviction to jail, Mirchpur case, increase in rape cases, failure of SEZ scheme, disputes in Maruti, defeat of Congress in Hisar bye-election, crisis of power etc, during their compaign.

A meeting of Sarpanches and representatives of PRIs was convened by the Chief Minister at Chandigarh on November 5, 2014 and told them to make the Gohana rally a grand success. At the same time he took some decisions to favour the members of his council of minister. The discretionary grant of the Chief Minister was increased to Rs. 22.50 crore per annum, Speaker and Deputy Speaker Rs. 3.25 crore and Rs. 2.50 crore, Cabinet Ministers Rs. 3.25 crore, State Minister Rs. 2.50 crore, Parliamentary Secretaries Rs.1.75 crore.

The INLD asked 20 questions to the Chief Minister just one day before the Gohana rally on November 10, 2013 like : what about deteriorating law and order situation, atrocities on women, involvement of ministers in crime, lack of power, sub-standard machinery in Yamunanagar plant, failure of electricity corporations, employment in foreign countries, abolition of V.A.T., construction of SYL, incomplete Kundli Maneshar express way, supply of 12 gas cylinders, favours to developers, land scandals, inquiry of corrupt ministers by Lokayukta, increase of Rs. 50 in old age pension every year, discrimination in employment etc. as the promises made by him are never taken up.

Bhupender Singh Hooda declared a number of schemes in Shakti Rally at Gohana on November 13, 2013, e.g. old age pension, widow pension, allowance for physically handicapped increased from Rs. 700 to Rs.1000 per month, minimum wages for labour enhanced from 5432 to Rs.8100 per month, interim relief of Rs. 2000 per month to class III and IV employees till the receipt of 7th Pay Commission, police persons were given risk allowance of Rs. 5000 per month, insurance plan of Rs. 5 lakh for a family of farmer/agri labour in case of death in the field, one time allotment scheme for long to a short-term loans with 50% rebate on total interest, filling backlog of 15041 reserved posts – 8781 for SCs and 6260 for BCs in a year, the right to service act for efficient delivery of services etc. The Chief Minister declared before the rally at Gohana that – Hanste aayoga, nachte jayoge etc. However, Birender Singh, Rajya Sabha MP, Selja, Union Minister, Rao Inderjit Singh, MP did not attend the rally.

The INLD held Samman rally at Kurukshetra on November 5, 2013 which was attended by Prafula Kumar Mahanto, President of Assam Gana Parishad, Nageshwar Rao, MP of TDP, Ram Das Athawale, President of RPI, Mukhtar Abbas Naqvi, Vice President of the BJP, Rao Inderjeet, Congress M P from Gurgaon.

The INLD organized a rally at Rohtak on December 3, 2013 to celebrate the golden jubilee of Ch. Devi Lal where a record number of workers donated their eyes. The opposition parties including the INLD sought a white paper on HCS selections in the state. They alleged that the selected candidates included – Rohit Yadav, son-in-law of Power Minister- Ajay Yadav, Ekta Chopra, daughter of OSD to CM, M.S. Chopra, Radhika – daughter of HPSC Chairman – Manbir Singh, Gagandeep, son of Sarban Singh, IAS, Meenakshi Goyal of S.K. Goyal, IAS, Gauri Middha niece of B.B. Batra, MLA, Rohtak, all CM's men and his house at Rohtak was gheraod by the workers on December 19, 2013.

On the other hand, the 129th Foundation Day of Congress Party was celebrated by the Haryana unit at Chandigarh on December 28, 2013. All block and district units heads were asked to propogate the government policies among the masses. However, Selja and Birender Singh did not attend the meeting and they attended such meeting at Delhi. Bhupender Hooda said that workers are the eyes and ears of the party and they should resolve the problem of general public.

Rahul Gandhi, Vice-President of the Congress addressed an election rallies at Sirsa and Panipat on April 6, 2014 and sought votes for the party candidates. He criticized the BJP for fielding the defectors and corrupt persons as Lok Sabha candidates in Karnataka and Haryana. Their balloon with a slogan- India shining-in 2004 and 2009 brusted both the times. This time the balloon with gas of Gujarat model would also burst. He praised the Haryana development model. He accused the BJP for blocking the passage of Women Reservation Bill in the parliament.

Sushma Swaraj addressed the election rally of the BJP candidate, Kishan Pal Gujjar at Faridabad on April 6, 2014 where she blamed the Congress government for spiraling price-rise, corruption and only Modi can deal with these problems in a better way. She praised the Vajpayee government for providing foodgrain to the people of India.

The Haryana Vidhan Sabha Speaker, Kuldeep Sharma and Karnal MP, Arvind Sharma used hot words against each other. Kuldeep Sharma said that Arvind was jailed in murder case at Rohtak and was an accused in a cheating case against Kurukshetra MP. He is maligning his image in Naib-Teshildar case unnecessarily. Moreover, Jindal with a delegation would apprise Rahul Gandhi about it.

Interestingly, the unmarried male voters formed an organization and demanded reservation in jobs for unmarried youth. They would vote for the party conforming to their demand. This is also important that the unmarried youth are being isolated from the main social stream. Therefore in case, they get employment, they would easily be married. So they said – get us married and get our votes.

The Supreme Court's declined to stay on Jat reservation notification issued by the Central Government on April 9, 2014 which worked as a booster for the Congress party workers in Haryana.

The Chief Minsiter declared some sops for agriculture sector like farmers and agriculture labour life protection scheme, enhancement in Nambardar – Chowkidar's honorarium, compensation of Rs. 10 thousand per acre for damage in crops due to natural calamities, compensation of Rs. 50,000 for casualties of milch cattles etc at Jhajjar on January 20, 2014.

At the same time a Dalit rally was organized in Rohtak by Kanta Alahria, President of Indian Bahujan Samajwadi Party on January 20, 2014 which was addressed by Udit Raj a leader of SC and ST Federation who later joined the BJP.

More than 3 lakh employees of Sarva Karmchari Sangh went on 3-day strike on January 20, 2014 demanding to remove contract and outsourcing of employees in government departments. Vacancies be filled up, regularization of employees with 2 years of service, cashless medical facilities, pay on Central Government lines etc.

Land was acquired for 101 SEZs but no one was started. The Ambani's acquired thousand of acres land in Gurgaon, Jhajjar, Sonepat, Rohtak, Faridabad on the name of SEZs and did not return the land to the farmers as per provision of SEZs Act, 2005. The Haryana government also did not undertake any efforts for this purpose and rather favoured Ambanis.

Rahul Gandhi's visit to Gannaur in Sonepat to address the farmers regarding the manifesto was deferred in view of protests over land acquisition and compensation. Farmers groups planned to show black flags to him on February 11, 2014. It was later organized on February 24, 2014 when some selected farmers/party workers were invited. Instead, the farmers organized their parallel panchayat at Pritampura near Rai and showed black flags as well burnt the effigy of Rahul. Earlier the panchayat was to be held near Gannaur but the police arrested the farmers and 13 of them were injured when they put a blockade at Uchana demanding the implementation of the Swaminathan report. As many as 25 persons were arrested.

The newly appointed President of the HPCC, Ashok Tanwar told that he would bring all factions of the Congress together in the state. He is the 19th President[4] of the HPCC as B.D. Sharma was the first President. Sumitra Chauhan was appointed as the President of Haryana Mahila Congress while replacing the Karnal MLA, Sumita Singh.

A public rally was held by AAP at Rohtak on February 23, 2014. Kejriwal accused the Chief Minister, Bhupender Singh Hooda of misusing the powers in the land acquisition process and favoured the colonizers and industrial houses like Ambani and DLF, and Robert Vadra son-in-law of Sonia Gandhi is given a huge chunk of land. He called Hooda, as the agent of Mukesh Ambani. He praised Ch. Devi Lal and told him an honest real farmer.

The entry of AAP in Haryana politics would not be easy as it has caste barrier, cadre based parties, deep rooted khaps and AAP having no grassroots level organizations, factionalism in AAP, poor performance in Delhi, overlooking the workers in distribution of ticket by landing the parashoot candidates, strong opposition parties like the INLD, the BJP out of power for the last 10 years etc. Kejriwal could not present any election agenda in his rally at Rohtak for Haryana public except criticising the present government and opposition parties for corruption.

The Haryana government declared a 50% bus fare rebate for senior citizens above 65 years. A sports university was declared at Bhiwani, a law university at Sonepat, upgradation of Jind regional centre to a full-fledged university, two regional centres of Khanpur Women university at Lula Ahir at Rewari and Kuaral in Jind, regional centre of Maulana Azad Urdu university of Hyderabad at Nuh in Mewat, medical colleges at Bhiwani. He also declared for one-time road tax and passenger tax for auto rikshaws, three wheelers and goods carriers up to weight of one tonne and an insurance cover was also declared for them. About 13000 safai karamchari's would be appointed soon. He also announced 50% rebate on property tax on apartment up to 2000 square feet, 100% rebate on building under lal dora included in muncipalities till March 31, 2014. VAT on scientific instruments was reduced from 12.5 to 5% and rebate on timely payment of property tax.

Jats withdrew their agitation on the quota when the Central Government declared and decided in the Cabinet to grant them reservation in central jobs on March 2, 2014. To begin with the demand was made in March 2008. They thanked the Chief Minister, Bhupender Singh Hooda and Ajit Singh for helping them.

We have several khaps of different gotras in Haryana e.g. – Gathwala, Malik, Dahiya, Dalal, Kandela, Sangwan and Sheoran etc. in Sonepat, Jind, Rohtak, Jhajjar. Almost all political parties have praised the role of khaps in dealing with important social issues to woo them for electoral purposes.

The INLD got a big jolt when the party supremo, Om Prakash Chautala was sentenced to jail in a teacher recruitment case along with his son, Ajay Singh Chautala in January 2013. But Ahay Singh Chautala showed his courage to manage the party affairs by holding its first successful meeting at Jind and declared it a Congress - CBI conspiracy. He along with party workers toured all the 21 districts and hold public rallies to restore the confidence of the party supporters. He was exemplary when he released CASH for CLU CDs against some ministers and MLAs of the Congress. He established a strong agent force of 3.5 lakh workers with the help of party chief, Ashok Arora. Moreover, the sons of Ajay Chautala – Digvijay and Dushyant came forward to assume a more active role in electoral politics of the state.

Kiran Chaudhary, Public Health Minister was injured when attacked by persons with stones in Koriyawas Village near Narnaul. She was referred to Medicity, Gurgaon in unconscious condition by the doctors of civil hospital, Narnaul on March 20, 2014.

Narender Modi addressed an election rally at Gohana on March 29, 2014 when he reminded the public of his two tenure as Incharge, Haryana BJP Affairs. He said Haryana is the trend setter of electoral politics in north India and it works like a catalyc of change in the country. He promised to solve the SYL water issue. He also told that he has eaten salt of Haryana and would be loyal to it. He raised the issue of corruption and black money deposited in foreign banks, housing facilities to all poor people.

The BSP Chief, Mayawati dubbed the BJP and the Congress pro-capitalist while addressing an election rally in Ambala city in support of the party candidates in Haryana on March 31, 2014. She asked the voters not to vote for communal forces and capitalists. She favoured reservation of higher castes on economic basis.

Sonia Gandhi addressed an election rally at Nuh on March 31, 2014 when she accused the BJP to divide the country on communal basis. But people were disappointed when she did not announce anything new for them in the rally.

The BJP Chief, Rajnath Singh termed the Congress as mother of corruption while addressing an election rally at Barwala on April 4, 2014. There is a nexus between Sonia Gandhi's son-in-law and Haryana Chief Minister, Bhupender Singh Hooda in land deals. When rulers turn into robbers the public gets dragged into heavy debt, he said. He also blamed the Central Government for inflation, rampant corruption, poverty, black money in foreign banks. He pointed out the miserable condition of farmers in Haryana as their land is sold at low prices to the developers. Our borders are unsafe as Pakistan dragged away our jawans from there, chopped their heads and celebrated to the utter silence of the Indian Government, while addressing an election rally at Gharaunda on April 4, 2014. He appealed the voters to wipe out the Congress from the country. He also addressed another rally at Bhiwani when Ajay Gupta, son of former Chief Minister, B.D. Gupta joined the BJP.

Land acquisition policy was a major issue in Haryana Lok Sabha election, as all major political parties put Bhupender Singh Hooda on the mat for snatching farmers land at low prices and to sell at higher prices and several cases of such sale were quashed by the courts. Moreover, the issue of SEZs surfaced as no such zones were started by the corporate houses even after acquiring several lakhs acre of land which is in violation of the SEZs Act, 2005. The land was acquired for public purposes but later on given to the developers at higher prices. All incentives declared for the affected parties still remained on papers only as alleged by the INLD leader, Abhay Singh Chautala.

Kumar Visvash of the AAP visited Rohtak and addressed an election rally at Chhotu Ram Dharamshala on April 6, 2014. He criticized the state government for forcible acquisition of farmers land and corruption.

The Congress General Secretary, Digvijay Singh addressed an election rally at Jathlana village of Yamunanagar district on April 6, 2014 to seek votes for Naveen Jindal. He racked up the Babri Masjid issue and termed Modi as chronic liar. He praised Haryana government for the developmental works carried out by it. He also visited Rajaund and sought votes for the Congress candidate. He talked of Food Security Act for the poor people.

Modi addressed an election rally at Gurgaon on April 6, 2014 and sought vote for Rao Inderjeet Singh. He said that Bhupender Singh Hooda has cheated helpless farmer by wresting their land and later lending over to the rich and powerful to further commercial interests. One middleman and high ups made hundred and thousands of crores of rupees due to distress sale by the farmers. Whereas the Sahazada lauded the acquisition policy as favoured his brother-in-law Robert Vadra who has made crores of rupees out of illegal sale of land in Haryana. Lashing out at the UPA dynastic rule where mother and his son are doing business and in Haryana father and son are obliging them in the process while addressing an election rally at Jhajjar on April 7, 2014. He criticized the Central and State governments for being corrupt and middle man in illegal land business. He said the business is being run by Maa-Beta at the Centre and Baap Beta in Haryana. The Haryana Chief Minister has mortgage the state interest with Robert Vadra by gifting him thousands of acres land freely. He raised the issue of unemployment, toll plazas in the state. He also condemned the Central Government for weak defence policy and partisan role of CBI.

Constituency-wise Compagning

Kurukshetra **:** The holy city Lok Sabha Constituency comprises 9 Vidhan Sabha segments – 4 in Kurukshetra district – Thanesar, Pehowa, Ladwa and Shahabad, 4 in Kaithal district – Pundri, Kalayat, Kaithan and Guhla and one in Yamunanagar district – Radaur. It has a total of 1692227 electors with 909708 : 782519 male-female ratio.

The contestants were Naveen Jindal, a sitting MP of the Congress, Raj Kumar Saini of the BJP, Balbir Singh Saini of the INLD and Balwinder Kaur of AAP and a few independent.

The constituency first election was held in 1977 when Ragbhir Singh Virk of the BLD won, in 1980 M.L. Soni of Janata Party captured the seat, Sardar Harpal Singh of the Congress got it in 1984 and Gurdial Singh of Janata Dal in 1989, Tara Singh of the Congress in 1991, O.P. Jindal of the HVP in 1996, Kailasho Saini of HLD (R) in 1998 and 1999 on the INLD ticket, Naveen Jindal of the Congress in 2004 and 2009.

Thus, the seat is captured by the Congress- 6times, the Janta/ INLD-5 times, the HVP-once, and Guljari Lal Nanda – twice, Kailash Saini–twice.

The caste composition of the electorate is – Jat – 241862, Brahmins – 123121, Ror – 56814, Rajputs – 35344, Saini – 82666, Kashyap – 65724, Kamboj – 48928, Bajigar – 39726, Sikh – 172487, Muslim – 2274- Christian – 2482, SC – 213673, BC – 124144, Others – 98439.

No new project could be started in the area as the revival of Saraswati river and opening of National Institute of Design are kept pending for many years. Moreover, direct rail link between Kurukshetra and Yamunanagar, overbridges, trauma centre etc. were also pending.

Three new parties – AAP, Jana Shakti Party, Indian Bahujan Sawdesh Party were in the fray apart from the Congress, BSP, BJP and INLD.

Sonepat **:** The constituency has 1417188 electorate with 777824 : 639364 male-female ratio. The main contestants are Jagbir Singh Mali of the Congress, Ramesh Kaushik – a defector from Congress – BJP, Padam Singh Dahiya of the INLD, Jai Singh of the AAP apart from some independents.

The electorate comprise 479553 Jats, 56632 Bania, 94379 Punjabi, 145213 Brahmins and others.

Rohtak : There are 1567504 electors with male – 850128 and female – 717376

The contestants are – Depender Hooda – a sitting MP of the Congress, Om Prakash Dhankhar of the BJP, Shamsher Singh Kharkara of the INLD, Naveen Jaihind alias Sharma of the AAP, Dhanjay Yadav of the BSP and some independents.

The Rohtak Lok Sabha has been captured by the Congress 8 times since 1952, thrice by the Janata Party, twice by the SJP and the INLD and once by the Jana Sangh.

The caste-wise composition is : Jats – 625406, Punjabi – 113711, Brahmin – 122986, Bania – 52708, Ahir – 150139 and others.

Ambala : It has 1685381 electors with 904990: 780391 male-female ratio. In the 1st Lok Sabha elections 1952, the seat was one of the four constituencies of Pepsu and covered Patiala to Shimla and Karnal areas. It was won by Tek Chard of the Congress, which was known as Ambala – Shimla seat. In 1957, it become Ambala seat but elected two MPs – Subhadra Joshi and Chuni Lal.

However, in 1962 it was won by Chuni Lal, as a reserved seat. At present it covers three districts of Ambala, Yamunanagar and Panchkula.

The seat is captured six times by the Congress, five times by the BJP, once by BSP. In other words Ram Prakash of the Congress – four times, Suraj Bhan of the BJP – four times. But no independent could win it so far.

Since Selja was nominated to Rajya Sabha, the Ambala constituency became a tough walk for the Congress, Moreover, the cold war between Selja and Bhupender Singh Hooda for biased developmental work influenced the voters. The exit of Vinod Sharma, MLA from Ambala city was an another factor against the party. Anti-incumbency factor amplified due to inflation and unemployment.

On the other hand, the BJP prospects were high because of Modi factor in urban area whereas, INLD's because of strong base in rural areas.

No major project could take off in the area apart from poor conditions of roads, protest from toll plazas, property tax etc.

The reserved seat is contested by Raj Kumar Balmiki of the

Congress, Kusum Sherwal of the INLD, Rattan Lal Kataria of the BJP, Surender Pal of AAP, Arun Kumar of CPI, Kapur Singh of BSP along with some independents.

A cast-wise composition of electorate is : Jat – 112712, Brahmin – 138105, Bania – 95968, Punjabi – 225694, Dalits – more than 700000 and others.

Bhiwani-Mahendergarh : The total electors are 1473912 with 792166: 681746 male-female ratio. The constituency has witnessed an exciting battle among three Lals sons of Haryana – Kuldeep Bishnoi, Ajay Chautala and Surender Singh in Lok Sabha polls 2004. The seat was won by Bansi Lal family 6 times so far.

In 2014, the contestants were Shruti Chaudhary, sitting Congress MP, Dharambir Singh who managed to get the BJP ticket within 24 hours of quitting the Congress, Rao Bahadur Singh- the INLD sitting MLA from Nangal Chaudhary, Lalit Aggarwal – AAP and some independents.

It comprised 9 Assembly constituencies – Loharu, Baroda, Dadri, Bhiwani, Tosham, Ateli, Mahendergarh, Narnaul and Nangal Chaudhary. One of the biggest constituencies in Haryana in terms of area, witnessed triangular contest among the Congress, INLD and BJP. It has 372670 Jat, 32416 Punjabi, 144695 Brahmin, 48229 Bania, 280237 Ahirs 42553 Gujjar and other.

Hisar : It comprises 1517606 electors with 825628: 691918 male-female voters. A Jat non-Jat battle is very common in Haryana elections. The caste issue has vitiated the social fabric in many constituencies. However, the Hisar district is taken as the nerve centre of caste politics in view of the Mirchpur, Dabra and Bhagana incidents as well as Jat quota agitation.

The non-Jat voters were in favour of Kuldeep Bishnoi and Jats – Dushyant Chautala of the INLD.

The issues were damaged roads, problem of potable water and unemployment. In 1967, Ram Kishan Gupta of the Congress, 1971 – Mani Ram Godara of the Congress, 1977 Inder Singh Sheokand of Janta Party, 1980 – Mani Ram Bagri of Janata Party, 1984 – Jai Prakash of Janata Dal, 1991 – Narain Singh of the Congress, 1996 – Jai Prakssh of the HVP, 1998 – Surender Barwala of Haryana Lok Dal, 1999 –

Surender Singh Barwal of the INLD, 2004 – Jai Prakash of the Congress, 2009 – Bhajan Lal – HJC, 2011 bye election – Kuldeep Bishnoi – HJC won the election.

Caste-wise voters include – Jat – 494000, SC – 251512, Punjabi – 72000, Brahmins – 97000, Kumhar – 68904, Vaish – 53755, Sami – 41000, Bishnoi – 43959, Rajput – 30000, Ahir – 20000, Nai – 18000 and others.

The opposition took the card of biased developmental and recruitment of jobs by the Chief Minister. The contestants were Kuldeep Bishnoi – HJC, Sampat Singh - Congress, Dushyant Singh Chautala – INLD, Yudhvir Khaylia – AAP, Mange Ram Sharma – BSP, Phool Singh Sheokand – CPM apart from some independents.

Since 1952, Jats have won the seat 10 times as 32% votes (475000) belonged to the community.

The division of Jat votes between the INLD and the Congress undermined the prospects of three parties the BSP, AAP and BJP ate into non-jat votes.

Karnal : A total of 1684321, electorate with 913321: 771000 male female ratio is there in the constituencies.

The contestants include Arvind Sharma of the Congress, Jasminder Singh Sindhu of the INLD, Virender Maratha of the BSP, Paramjit Singh of AAP, Mam Chand of the CPI and some independents.

The issue that the SOMA,- a construction company was given contract to build 71 flyovers, 5 viaducts, 44 underpasses, 58 pedestrian underpasses and 8 railway over-bridges. However, out of 71 flyovers, 40 are yet to be started, many are incomplete and the deadline expired on November 11, 2011 which was extended to March 12, 2012. The roads were in bad shape. The residents of the area questioned why they are made to pay toll charges and there was clear resentment among the voters against the government for siding with the construction company.

The caste-wise composition of electorate was – Jat – 196325, Ror – 106261, Rajput – 74027. Sikh – 83888, Brahmin – 139574, Bania – 61823, Kamboj – 26696, Arora – 169613, SC – 136011, Gadria – 25043, Gujjar – 56326, Kasshyap – 79156, Kumhar – 32853, Muslim – 37963, Odd – 24567, Saini – 41095 and others.

The seat is captured by the Congress 9 times since 1967, once by BLD, twice by the BJP. However, Chiranji Lal Sharma won it four times.

Arvind Sharma, sitting MP of Congress was pitted against Maratha

Virender Verma – BSP, BJP's Ashwani Chopra, INLD's Jaswinder Singh Sandhu, AAPs Paramjit Singh, CPI's Mam Chand Saini and others. The issues like registration of criminal case against of the former Transport Minister Om Prakash Jain and Chief Parliamentary Secretary, Zile Ram Sharma in a Sarpanch death case, rift between the MP and Vidhan Sabha Speaker, allegation of lopsided development by the Congress leaders, toll plazas were discussed this time. The seat is mostly won by a Brahmin candidate.

Faridabad : It composed of 16097034 electors with 8716854 : 730180 male female ratio.

The contestants were Avtar Singh Bhadana of the Congress, Krishanpal Gujjar of the BJP. R.K. Anand of the INLD, Rajender Sharma of the BSP, Purshotam Dagar of the AAP and a few independents.

There are 216662 Jats, 184141 Gujjar, 117520 Brahmins, 110749 Punjabi, 79825 Bania and others.

Sirsa : This constituency is surrounded by Punjab and Rajasthan and comprise the electorate of three districts – Jind, Fatehabad and Sirsa. It has 1660557 electors will 886303 : 774254 male female ratio.

The main contestants were Ashok Tanwar of the Congress, Charnjit Rori of the INLD, Sushil Indora of the BJP apart from others.

The seat is captured by Dalbir Singh four times and Selja twice, Sushil Indora – twice, Atma Singh – once, Het Ram – once, Ashok Tanwar – once and most of them were not resident of the district. However, 5 of the 9 seats of the Vidhan Sabha were in possession of the INLD at the time of Lok Sabha elections.

The Parliamentary seat, is represented by the State Congress Chief Ashok Tanwar. It has nine Assembly segments.

The INLD has won 8 times since 1969 and the BJP never. The Congress counted the railway link to Fatehabad and 23500 crore nuclear plant to Gorakhpur and an additional investment of Rs. 11500 crore in Sirsa constituency as claimed by Ashok Tanwar.

Despite his big claims he was unwilling to contest the election from this seat and preferred Ambala which was not accepted by the Party High Command.The AAP and the CPM nominated Poonam Chand Ratti and Ram Kumar Bahbalpuria.

HJC candidate, Sushil Indora had to face stiff opposition from his own Dhanak community in Fatehabad in a meeting on March 24, 2014. The community opposed him saying that he had done nothing for it and verbal alteration took place and be had to leave the meeting hastily. In the process some persons were injured. Indora joined HJC after leaving the Congress on March 20, 2014.

However, the people of the area opposed the nuclear plant and sat on *dharna* for months together.

The role of Dera Sacha Saudha is always crucial in the election.

Caste-wise number of voters in Sirsa is :– Jat – 3.50 lakh, SCs – 5.25 lakh, Sikh – 180 lakh, Bachwards – 2.75 lakh, Bishnoi – 80000 and others.

Unemployment, lack of industries, education and health were some of the main issues.

Gurgaon : The constituency has 1844908 with 984609: 860299 male female ratio. In Mewat area worth 4.8 lakh electorate but has poor infrastructure, unemployment, poverty, low literacy and high drop out rates in schools, rising crime, scarcity of potable water, no health facilities, poor transport facilities etc. The condition of women is bad to worse with high rate of teenage pregnancies, IMMR, mal-nutrition, exploitation and harassment etc. This area has been cheated in every election by every political party.

The contestants are : Dharma Pal of the Congress, Rao Inderjit Singh of the BJP, Jakir Hussain of the INLD, Dharambir Rathee of the BSP, Yogender Yadav of AAP apart from some independents.

It has 283802 Ahirs, 134667 Punjabis, 71407 Brahmin, 44395 Bania, 124924 Jats, 67753 Gujjar and others.

Voting Day

The state has 16097034 electorate on March 23, 2014 to decide the fate of 230 candidates in 10 Lok Sabha elections held on April 10, 2014. The male : female ratio was 8716854 : 7380180. For this purpose 16244 polling stations were set up and over 34000 poll officials were deployed apart from 1600 personnel to supervise the process. More than 65000 police with para military staff was put on duty to ensure peaceful polling.

In India, the total voters are 81.45 crore and 9.3 lakh polling stations. The increase in voters was by 10 crore in October Lok Sabha elections, 2014.

It may be noted that NOTA – (None of the above option) was introduced for the first time in Lok Sabha election where the voter can exercise it.

As many as 4000 members of Gadaria Lohar – nomadic community are deprived of their right to vote as they do not have any residential proof or birth certificate and keep on moving from one place to another. However, those living at one place more than 10 years are also not registered as voters.

All claims of the state government to enroll the children of the community in schools proved slogans only and no serious efforts are made to register them as voters so far.

A caste wise break up of voters is :- Jat – 29%, SCs – 16%, Muslim – 2%, Sikh – 3%, Rajput – 3%, Kamboj – 4%, Ahir – 5%, Bania 5%, Brahmin – 8%, others – 29%.

Repoll in Mewat

Just after the voting on April 10, 2014, the candidate of the AAP from Gurgaon demanded repoll because of rigging and booth capturing in over 110 polling stations. Later the candidates of the BJP and BSP also lodged similar complaints. However, Rao Inderjeet Singh pointed out that in 11% booths in Mewat the voting is over 90% which is a proof of rigging and booth capturing with the help of village heads there.

After considering the complaint of various political parties, the Election Commission ordered repoll in 8 Mewat polling booths[5] on May 15, 2014. However, the INLD candidate opposed the order terming the complaints false and fake.

Amid stringent security measures, the repoll at eight polling station[5] in Mewat was héld peacefully. A booth at Thek in Punhana registered 94.17% polling, in Banarasi in Ferozpur Jhirka 94.71%, Neemkhera 65.69 as against 97.17% on April 10, Shahpu 66.07% compared 95.24% earlier, said an official. earlier Rehana "Six out of eight centres witnessed high voter turnout," 96.46%, polling, Tapkan 97.31% and Sudaka 96.23%, and Bawala area in Sohna registered 89.93% turnout as against 97% earlier.

The INLD candidate Zakir Hussain and his wife came to cast their votes. The BSP candidate Dharampal Rathee also visited the polling booths. But Rao Inderjeet Singh of the BJP and AAP's Yogendra Yadav, who alleged of rigging in Mewat and demanded re-poll, did not visit the booths.

Psephologists claim the re-poll will not have a major effect on results sent a message that it will be fair elections in Mewat. It is the beginning here, said Yogendra Yadav.

A constituency-wise data of electorate with male-female ratio is given below :—

Haryana: Constituency-wise Electorates Lok Sabha Elections, 2014.

Constituency	*Male*	*Female*	*Total*
Gurgaon	984609	860299	1844908
Rohtak	850128	717376	1567504
Ambala (R)	909708	782519	169227
Sirsa (R)	886303	774254	1660557
Sonepat	777824	639364	1417188
Hisar	825688	691918	1517606
Karnal	913321	771000	1684321
Kurukshetra	807700	690759	1498459
Faridabad	8716854	7380180	16097034
Bhiwani-'M'/Garh	792166	687746	1473912

The maximum electorate Gurgaon – 1844908 and the minimum 1417188 in Sonepat.

In Haryana, we have males and females voters whereas their percentage is much higher 52 in Pondicherry. 51% in Kerala, and Manipur, 50.90% in Mizoram, 50.40% in Meghalya and 50.10% in Arunachal Pradesh.

Voters in the Young Age Group (18-40 years)

Gurgaon	923051
Faridabad	877077
Karnal	827687
Sirsa	820144
Ambala	784265
Kurukshetra	704037
Hisar	775247
Sonepat	679322
Rohtak	699062
Bhiwani/'M' Garh	670619
Total	7760511

Source : State Election Commission, Haryana

Voting in 2009 and 2014 Elections

Constituencies	*2009*	*2014*
Ambala	68.95	72.34
Kurkushetra	75.29	77.05
Karnal	66.86	71.07
Sonepat	65.16	69.87
Rohtak	67.71	66.62
Faridabad	65.18	56.81
Bhiwani-'M' Garh	72.53	71.03
Hisar	69.71	76.52
Gurgaon	61.12	72.14
Sirsa (Res.)	75.01	77.11
Average	67.94%	71.10%

The population of scheduled caste has increased from 19.4 to 20.2% as disclosed by centre for rural research and industrial development, Haryana. It is maximum 30.2% in Fetehabad but minimum 6.9% in Mewat. The maximum scheduled castes are in Ratia, Barwala, Kalanaur, Bawani Khera Assembly segments.

The delimitation of constituencies had disturbed the caste equations in many Lok Sabha constituencies when the Assembly segments having dominance of a particular caste were attached with other one and strongly those having maximum S.Cs population are kept general and those having majorly of higher caste voters are kept reserved.

Mewat women cast their vote but don't press the EVM button themselves as the males accompanied them do so and this is the practice as told by 459 women during the survey undertaken by the Centre for Haryana Studies, M.D. University, Rohtak. When confronted the government officials they also admitted this fact on anonymous bases. Yogender Yadav, AAP candidate from Gurgaon made a complaint to the Returning Officer in this regard.

The maximum voting was made in 1977 – 73.26%% followed by 1967 – 72.61% and 2014 – 71.86%. Women = 70% 66.17 in 2009.

The Sirsa constituency recorded the highest 77.11% followed by Hisar – 76.52%, Kurukshetra – 77.05%, Ambala – 72.34%. Gurgaon – 72.14%, Karnal – 71.07%, Bhiwani-Mahendergarh – 71.03%, Sonepat – 69.87%, Rohtak – 67.71% and Faridabad – 65.18%. In 2009 Lok Sabha elections, the voting percentage in Rohtak was 68.83%. However it was less than 50% in 75 booths. In Vidhan Sabha election it came down to 62.14%.

The computer teachers of the state decided to boycott the Lok Sabha elections in a meeting of its association at Rohtak on April 9, 2014.

The electorate of Sultanpura village in Sirsa and Ambala Nizampur, Shimla Maulana in Panipat district, Kosli village in Rewari district decided to boycott the election.

Voting Percentage in Lok Sabha Elections: 1967-2014

Year	Voting %
1967	76.51
1971	64.95
1977	76.01
1980	65.88
1984	69.23
1989	64.04
1991	68.11
1996	72.22
1998	70.85
1999	68.16
2004	66.95
2009	68.20
2014	71.10

There is no connection between literacy and the voting percentage in Haryana as the districts with lower levels of literacy recorded higher voting e.g. Mewat-76.16% voting with literacy rate of about 56%. On the other hand, Gurgaon with highest literacy of 84.4% recorded 70.4% voting. Similar is the situation in other districts.

Women voters broke the literacy barriers in all districts e.g. Mewat with 36% literacy recorded 73% voting of women, Palwal-65%, Kurukshetra-77%, Yamunanagar-77% etc.

Results

The BJP secured 34.7% votes in comparison to 12.9% in 2009. Whereas the base of the Congress declined from 41.29% in 2009 to 22.9% in 2014. However, the INLD fetched 24.4% in comparison to 15.78% in 2009. Whereas the percentage of the BSP declined steeply from 15.75% in 2009 to 4.06% in 2014 and so the HJC from 10.01% to 6%.

The BJP secured 7 seats out of 8 contested. However, its ally, the HJC lost both the seats from Sirsa and Hisar. The INLD won 2 seats despite its senior leaders Om Prakash Chautala an Ajay Chautala being in jail.

The Congress got -22.9% votes, AAP-4.2%, BSP-4.6%, HJC-6.1%, CPI-0.2%, CPM-0.2% and independents-1.7%.

The BJP contested the Lok Sabha elections for the first time in 1984 and got 7.54% votes only. In 1989 it rose to 8.31%, 1991-10.17% but 1996 to 19.70% with four MPs in alliance with HJP. The vote base declared to 18.89% in 1998 and could win one seat in 1999 it rose to 29.21% and won 5 seats in alliance with the INLD. But it declined to 17.21% in 2004 and 2009 when it contested alone.

Because of its bickering and Modi wave, the Congress could secure only one seat. However, in 1977 all the 10 seats were won by the BLD whereas the Congress captured all the 10 in 1984. The BLD secured 70.35% votes in 1977 and no party could have broken this record so far as the Congress could obtain 55% votes in 1984. No other party could have obtained 50 % votes so far. The Congress got 17% votes in 1977.

The hopes of AAP to gain some support base in Haryana after Delhi, dashed to ground and could not open its account even. The issues of corruption and dynastic politics raised by Kejriwal failed to influence the voters. The wrong choice of candidates and lack of organizational structure proved fatal to the party.

Rohtak candidate, Deepander Singh Hooda made a hat trick and saved the face of the Congress. The Congress remained third in four Assembly segments in the constituency. Krishan Pal Gujjar won with a margin of 4.34 lakh from Faridabad while defeating Avtar Singh Bhadana who polled 1.81 lakh votes.

Haryana Result

Status known for 10 out of 10 Constituencies

Party	*Won*	*Leading*	*Total*
Bharatiya Janata Party	7	0	7
Indian National Congress	1	0	1
Indian National Lok Dal	2	0	2
Total	**10**	**0**	**10**

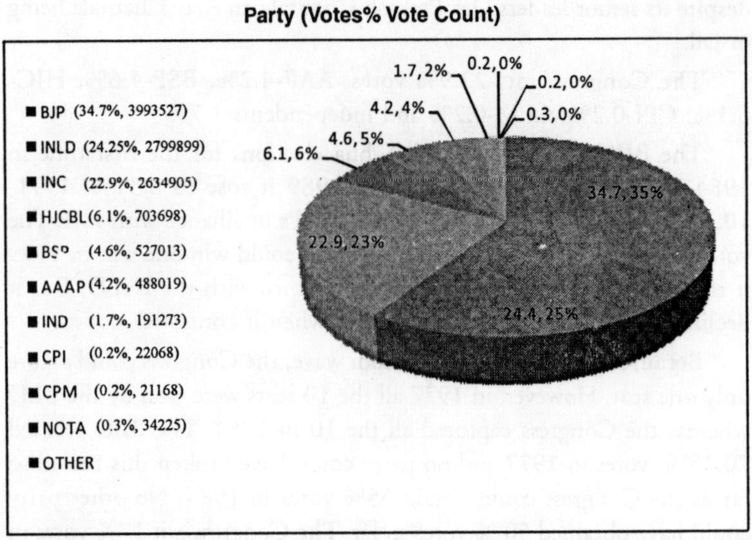

Ashiwani Kumar Chopra won with a margin of 3.60 lakh votes from Karnal defeating Arvind Sharma who polled 2.34 lakh votes. Rattan Lal Kataria won from Ambala (Res.) by 3.47 lakh votes and the defeated Congress candidate Raj Kumar Balmiki secured 2.72 lakh. Rao Inderjeet Singh won by 2.88 lakh votes while defeating the INLD candidate in Gurgaon. Dharambir Singh won from Bhiwani-Mahanderagarh by 1.28 lakh votes defeating the INLD's Bahadur Singh. Similarly Ramesh Kaushik defeated Jagbir Singh Malik of the Congress by 77000 votes in Sonepat. Dushyant of the INLD defeated Kuldeep Bishnoi of HJC by 31847 votes in Hisar. Raj Kumar Saini defeated the INLD's Balbir Singh by 1.29 lakh votes in Kurukshetra. The INLD candidate Charanjeet Singh Rori polled 5.06 lakh votes who defeated the HPCC President, Ashok Tanwar by 1.15 lakh votes in Sirsa.

A total of 34188 voters exercised the NOTA.

The only consolation for the Congress is retaining the Rohtak seat.

It is for the first time in the history of the state that the BJP has performed so well.

Dushyant Chautala of the INLD created history by winning Hisar seat by defeating HJP Chief, Kuldeep Bishnoi as well as became the youngest M.P. in the country.

Result : A Comparison of 2009 & 2014 Lok Sabha Elections

Parties	2009 *Votes Polled*	2009 *Percentage*	2009 *Seats Won*	2014 *Votes Polled*	2014 *Percentage*	2014 *Seats Won*
Congress	4203765	41.77%	9	2634905	22.9%	1
INLD	1286573	15.77%	–	2799899	24.4%	2
BJP	986136	12.9%	–	3993527	34.7%	7
BSP	1284040	15.74%	–	527013	4.6%	–
HJC (BL)	623650	9.80%	1	703698	6.1%	–
NCP	12776	0.31%	–	–	–	–
CPM	18999	0.23%	–	21168	0.02%	–
CPI	14929	0.17%	–	22068	0.2%	–
JKNPP	9376	0.11%	–	–	–	
LJP	17994	0.22%	–	–	–	–
SP	8398	0.10%	–	–	–	–
RASAP	7682	0.09%	–	–	–	–
RPI	1211	0.01%	–	–	–	–
BRPP	1527	0.01%	–	–	–	–
NELU	585	0.01%	–	–	–	–
RDMP	2159	0.02%	–	–	–	–
JKM	1727	0.02%	–	–	–	–
AIFB(S)	2758	0.03%	–	–	–	–
JJJKMC	1100	0.01%	–	–	–	–
RND	2583	0.03%	–	–	–	–
JUP	595	0.01%	–	–	–	–
AAP	–	–	–	488019	4.2%	–
AIRP	678	0.01%	–	–	–	–
Independents	229466	28.14%	–	191237	1.7%	–

A large number of Congress leaders quit the party before the election which adversely influenced the voting behaviour and many more declared to quit it after the declaration of results.

Many Congress candidates blamed the state leadership for not extending support to them in the elections.

The BJP led in 52 Assembly segments in compare to only 17 in 2009, whereas the Congress tally fell from 51 in 2009 to 17, the INLD improved its tally from 6 to 16. The HJC led in 7 segments in compare to 9 in 2009. The BSP which led in 8 segments in 2009 failed to lead in any one in 2014.

The BJP led in all the nine Assembly segments in Ambala, Karnal and Faridabad Lok Sabha seats. The Congress led in all in Rohtak. Moreover, the BJP led in 6 in Kurukshetra, Congress in two and INLD in one. In Sirsa, the INLD led in 7 and Congress & HJC one each. However, the HJC led in 6 in Hisar, the INLD in 3 segments.

In Sonepat, the BJP led in 5, Congress-3 and INLD-1. In Bhiwani, the BJP led in 6, Congress -2 and INLD-1. In Gurgaon the BJP got first place in 6 and the INLD in three.

The Modi wave and anti-incumbency proved fatal for the Congress who lost a seats.

The vote for change also cost the HJC Chief, Kuldeep Bishnoi his Hisar seat.

Even those Congress leaders like Dharambir Singh, Ramesh Kaushik, Rao Inderjeet Singh, who switched over to the BJP just before the polls, won the elections off hand.

Due to factionalism and anti-party activities, the Congress performed very poorly.

The concentration of powers in the hands of father, mother and son- Bhupander Singh Hooda, Asha Hooda and Deepander Hooda and neglect of party workers led to such a poor situation.

The Hisar result had given a big blow to Bishnoi's political prospects. His own poll strategy to make it a Jat v/s non -Jat contest seemed to have gone awry as it led to extreme polarisation of the Jats in favour of the INLD.

Better management and early election campaign helped the INLD in Sirsa and Hisar. Ashok Tanwar who was willing to shift to Ambala also affected the result adversely. The INLD had constituted committee to keep the booth level activists on their toes all the time proved helpful in getting two seats.

- Slipping of urban votes from the Congress hands also cost it very dearly.
- The Chief Minister and the HPCC Chief blamed the bureaucracy and inter party differences for the party's severe drubbing in Haryana.
- The poor delivery system and the apathetic attitude of those at the helm of the affairs towards party workers and the public also added the woes of the Congress.
- Ashok Tanwar alleged that certain leaders who amassed huge wealth through dubious means betrayed the party at the time of the election.
- Discrimination in job and development works also affected the results.
- AAP's fight against corruption apparently found no match for Modi's development model.
- The results have shattered caste- based politics in most of the constituencies, giving parties a reason to think for new principles and goals.
- Congress defeat from Sonepat seat can be seen as a personal set back to the Chief Minister as he had paid special attention to it after Rohtak.

Kuldeep Bishnoi's wife Renuka Bishnoi alleged that his husband was defeated due to rigging and booth capturing.

- The corruption in CLU and Vadra factor also affected the Congress adversely.

The BJP is to reconsider the alliance with the HJC after the later defeat in Lok Sabha poll.

Performance of main political parties Congress

The Congress's performance with vote percentage in different constituencies.

	2014		*2009*
Contituencies	*Votes*	*Percentage*	
Ambala	272047	22.3	39.52
Kurukshetra	288376	25.3	48.71
Karnal	234675	19.7	37.36
Sonepat	269789	27.4	41.54
Hisar	102508	8.8	25.05
Sirsa	390634	30.5	50.48
Bhiwani-'M' Garh	268115	26.0	37.07
Gurgaon	133713	10.2	34.55
Faridabad	185643	16.4	31.02
Rohtak	490063	46.9%	71.24

The BJP Performance of the BJP A constituency-wise breakup

	2014		*2009*
Ambala	612121	50.53	37.73 (BJP)
Kurukshetra	418112	36.80	—
Karnal	594817	49.96	22.74(BJP)
Sonepat	347203	35.31	21.76(BJP)
Hisar	462631	40.07	—
Sirsa	241067	18.90	—
Bhiwani-'M'Garh	404542	39.33	—
Gurgaon	644780	48.92	15.43(BJP)
Faridabad	652516	57.69	23.26(BJP)
Rohtak	319436	30.73	—

The INLD Performance of the INLD A constituency-wise breakup

	2014		*2009*
Ambala	129571	10.69	—
Kurukshetra	288376	23.38	34.15
Karnal	187902	15.78	—
Sonepat	264404	26.89	—
Hisar	494578	42.84	29.61
Sirsa	506370	39.71	46.17
Bhiwani-'M' Garh	275148	26.75	30.32
Gurgaon	370058	28.07	—
Faridabad	132472	11.71	—
Rohtak	151120	14.53	17.08

Proformance of the Congress : Constituency-wise view in 2009 and 2014

Consituences	*2009*	*2014*
Ambala (Res.)	39.52%	22.3%
Kurukshetra	48.71%	25.3%
Karnal	37.36%	19.7%
Sonepat	41.54%	27.4%
Rohtak	71.74%	46.9%
Faridabad	31.62%	16.4%
Gurgaon	34.55%	10.2%
Bhiwani-Mahindergarh	37.07%	26.0%
Hisar	25.08%	8.8%
Sirsa (Res.)	50.48%	30.5%
Average	41.77%	22.9%

Proformance of the INLD and the BJP Constituency-wise view in 2009 and 2014

Consituences	*2009*	*2014*	
		INLD	*BJP*
Ambala (Res.)	37.73% (BJP)	10.69%	50.53%
Kurukshetra	34.15% (INLD)	23.38%	36.80%
Karnal	22.74%(BJP)	15.78%	49.96%
Sonepat	21.76% (BJP)	26.89%	35.31%
Rohtak	17.08% (INLD)	14.53%	30.73%
Faridabad	23.26% (BJP)	11.71%	57.69%
Gurgaon	15.43% (BJP)	28.07%	48.92%
Bhiwani-Mahindergarh	30.32% (INLD)	26.75%	39.33%
Hisar	29.61%(INLD)	42.84%	40.07%
Sirsa (Res.)	41.17%(INLD)	39.71%	18.90%
Average- INLD	15.77%	24.4%	34.07%
BJP	12.9%		

Winning Candidates

Constituency	*Winner*	*Runners up*	*Margin*
Ambala	Rattan Lal Kataria (BJP)	Raj Kumar Balmiki (Cong)	340074
Bhiwani-M'garh	Dharambir Singh (BJP)	Bahadur Singh (INLD)	129394
Faridabad	Krishan Pal Gurjjar (BJP)	Avtar Singh Bhadana (Cong)	466873
Gurgaon	Rao Inderjit Singh (BJP)	Zakir Hussain (INLD)	274722
Hisar	Dushyant Chautala (INLD)	Kuldeep Bishnoi (HJC)	31847
Karnal	Ashwini Kumar Chopra (BJP)	Arvind Sharma (Cong)	360147

Table (Contd...)

Kurubshetra	Raj Kumar Saini (BJP)	Balbir Singh Saini (INLD)	129736
Rohtak	Deepender Singh Hooda (Cong)	Om Prakash Dhankar (BJP)	170627
Sirsa	Charanjeet Singh Rori (INLD)	Ashok Tanwar (Cong)	115736
Sonepat	Ramesh Kaushik (BJP)	Jagbir Singh Malik (Cong)	77414

Women and Lok Sabha Elcection, 2014

Nominations : Women

As many as 32 women filed their nominations out of a total of 300. 48 were rejected and 22 wilhdrew from the field leaving 230 in the fray. The number of women contestant was 11. No woman contested from Sirsa, Rohtak and Sonepat constituencies.

Figures releting to nominations and contestants are given below:

Women Nominations and Contestants : Lok Sabha Elections, 2014

Constituencies	*Nominations*	*Conestants*
Ambala	4	1
Kurukshetra	5	2
Sirsa	1	–
Hisar	4	1
Karnal	4	2
Sonepat	3	–
Rohtak	2	–
Bhiwani-M.Garh	2	1
Gurgoan	3	1
Faridabad	4	3
Total	**32**	**11**

The INLD and AAP fielded one candidate each whereas the BJP, BSP, HJC, CPM and CPI did not nominate any women candidate.

Constituencies	*Contestants*	*Women*
Faridabad	= 27	= 3
Bhiwani-M.Garh	= 26	= 1
Karnal	= 23	= 2
Sonepat	= 23	= 0

Table (Contd...)

Kurukshetra	= 22	= 2
Gurgaon	= 22	= 1
Sirsa	= 18	= 0
Rohtak	= 14	= 0
Ambala	= 14	= 1
Hisar	= 41	= 1
Total	**= 230**	**= 11**
Male	= 219	
Female	= 11	

Total Women Contestants, winners in Lok Sabha Elections 1967-2014

Party	*Contestants*	*Women*
Congress	8	5
BJP	5	1
INLD	3	2
JP/Samta	5	1
HVP	1	–
BSP	1	–
Independents	30	–

In Haryana, since 1967 - 9 women are sent to the Lok Sabha.

The voting percentage in Lok Sabha elections was 71.86% against 70% by the women. The Karnal constituency has a record of never electing a woman as MP since 1967 and so the Rohtak.

The support base of women candidates since 1967 Lok Sabha elections has been given below :

Percentage of Candidates	*Support base*
Above 50%	3 to 5.5%
41 to 49%	4.7%
30 to 40%	3.5%
20 to 29%	5.9%
10 to 19%	3.0%
5 to 9%	1.8%
1 to 4%	13.0%
Less than1%	55%

REFERENCES

1. The panel included – Chief Minister, Leaders of dissident camp – Selja,

Birender Singh, Kiran Chaudhary, two MPs- Ashok Tanwar and Avtar Singh Bhadana, Capt. Ajay Yadav, Randeep Singh Surjewala, Geeta Bhukkal, Savitri Jindal and Aftab Ahmad apart from Vinod Sharma, H.S. Chitha, Ram Prakash, Suresh Gupta, Raj Kumar Balmiki, Shadi Lal Batra, Balbir Pal Shah, Jagdish Mohan etc.

2. Its members comprised Krishan Pal Gujjar, Capt. Abhimanu, Dharampal Malim, Chiranji Lal and Hemant Batra. It would also prepare the panel of candidates for each constituency.
3. Panchkula, Ambala Cantt, City, Jagadhari, Kaithal, Karnal, Sonepat, Jind, Sirsa, Tohana, Hisar, Bhiwani, Rohtak, Ballabhgarh, Faridabad, Gurgaon whereas the Banias demanded the Karnal Lok Sabha seats. Karnal and Kurukshetra as well as 16 Assembly segments.
4. 1966 B.D. Sharma was the first President of HPCC, thereafter Ram Kishan Gupta, Ramacharan Chand Mittal, Rao Nehal Singh, Ranbir Singh, Sultan Singh, Dalbir Singh, Harpal Singh, Sultan Singh, Birender Singh, Harpal Singh, Balbir Pal Shah, S.S. Surjewala, Birender Singh, Dharam Pal Malik, Bhupender Singh Hooda, Bhajan Lal, Phool Chand Mullana.
5. These include on booth each in Sohna and Punhana, 3 in Nuh and Firozpur-Jhirka each namely Thek, Banarasi, NeemKhera, Shapur, Rehana, Barwala, Tapkan & Sudaka.

15

Conclusion

The political process in Haryana region started in 1921 when it was a part of composite Punjab. The Congress could not muster any substantial support in elections of Central Legislature from 1923 to 1937 and the Unionist Party secured the maximum seats. However, after the death of Sir Chhotu Ram, the Congress got 51 seats out of 175 in 1946 elections.

After independence, the Congress captured all the seats falling in Haryana region like Ambala, Karnal, Rohtak, Jhajjar-Rewari, Gurgaon, Hissar and Sirsa in the successive parliamentary elections held in 1952, 1957 and 1962.

1967 Elections

After coming into existence as a separate state on November 1, 1966, the parliamentary elections were held in 1967 when as many as 86 candidates filed their nominations and finally, 67 contested the poll. 329601 of the 459451 electors exercised their franchise, i.e. 70 per cent. The ratio of men-women voters was 1756757 : 1428538. The Congress fetched 7 (with 44% votes) of 9 seats leaving one to BJS and Independent each with 19.9 per cent and 19.8 per cent votes respectively. More than 94 per cent Independents lost their security deposits.

1971 Elections

The 1971 elections were pre-poned by one year because of split in the

Congress in 1969. A total 109 candidates filed their nominations including one female but only 63 males contested after rejections and withdrawals. It was the Congress Party which contested all the 9 seats. 3068699 (64.35 per cent) of the 4768740 electorate exercised their voting right including 55.86 per cent males and 44.13 per cent females. The Congress again got 7 seats with 55.25 per cent in comparison to 44 per cent in 1967. The BJS got one seat with 10.9 per cent in comparison to 19.8 per cent in 1967 and one seat went in the account of VHP with 8.93 per cent.

1977 Elections

In 1977, the number of Lok Sabha seats was increased to 10 and that of the Assembly to 90. A total of 106 nominations including 2 from women were received but less than half, i.e. 50 contested the elections. Out of 5766654 electors 4224405 (73.26 per cent) cast their votes including 2310566 men and 1913839 women.

It was a watershed in the history of parliamentary election in India where the Congress was dethroned at the Centre and the BLD captured all the 10 seats in Haryana making other parties to lick the dust. It obtained about 70 per cent votes. The Congress which dominated the electoral scene since 1952 could get 17.62 per cent votes with no seat and 4 of its candidates lost their deposits. The impact of excesses of the emergency in particular and that of Bansi Lal was clear in Haryana when people were sterilised forcibly. He was defeated by a huge margin of 161242 votes.

1980 Elections

The Janata rule at the Centre could not last long and the government fell under its own pressure after 30 months when mid-term elections were declared in 1980. As many as 224 candidates filed their nominations and after withdrawal about 137 contested.

The Congress got 5 seats with 32.29 per cent votes followed by Janata (S) 4 with 33.75 per cent votes. The Janata Party secured 28.11 per cent votes with one seat only. The Lok Dal candidates led in 44 of the 90 Assembly segments of the 10 Lok Sabha constituencies in

Haryana, whereas the Congress led in 29 segments and the Janata Party in 17. The Congress fared badly in rural areas whereas Lok Dal in urban areas. At the Centre the Congress led by Indira Gandhi staged a come back and Bhajan Lal who was sworn in as the Chief Minister of the State in 1979 after the fall of Devi Lal government, defected to the Congress along with 40 MLA in 1980.

1984 Elections

In 1984 parliamentary elections, as many as 383 nominations were received and 200 candidates including 167 Independents and 16 women contested the election after the scrutiny of papers. 5163799 – 66.85 per cent electors including 2245719 women exercised their franchise. The issues influencing the voting behaviour were Blue-star operation and consequent assassination of Indira Gandhi leading to sympathy wave in favour of Rajiv Gandhi. As a result the Congress won all the 10 seats in Haryana securing 53.98 per cent votes. The Lok Dal got 19.10 per cent votes but no seat. The Congress (J) and the BJP obtained 10.49 per cent and 7.54 per cent voters respectively but could not open their accounts in the Lok Sabha. Almost all the Independents lost their deposits. As compared to 1980 elections, the Congress gained a swing of 22.6 per cent votes whereas the DMKP, earlier Lok Dal came down from 33.74 per cent to 19.10 per cent and Janata Party fell steep to 1.44 per cent votes in comparison to 28.11 per cent in 1980. No women candidate out of 10 including the party ones could save their deposits.

1989 Elections

The parliamentary elections were held in 1989 after the fall of National Front Government., when Lok Sabha was dissolved one month earlier than its full term of five years. Devi Lal was the Deputy Prime Minister and during this period, the Chief Minister of Haryana was changed four times at the stance of the Party High Command. The elections witnessed a steep increase in the nominations to 480 including 10 women in comparison to earlier elections. Finally, as many as 324 candidates contested the election. The number of electorate grew from 7725946 in 1984 Elections to 9636688 in 1989, i.e. by 19.82 per cent and 64.41 per cent people including 2628944 women exercised their franchise. The Congress got 46.15 per cent with 4, the Janata Dal 38.90 per cent with 6 seats, the BJP 9.37 per cent with no seat.

1991 Elections

1991 parliamentary elections were held under the President rule in Haryana when the State government was dismissed. The V.P. Singh government could last less than two years and Parliament was dissolved. A total of 344 nominations including 10 women were received in comparison to 480 in 1989. The number of contestants also came down to 198 from 324 in 1989. 6403796 of the 9725297 electorate including 2794927 women cast their votes. The Congress got 37.22 per cent with 9 seats and the HVP got 5.35 per cent with one seat. The Janata Dal with 12.49 per cent and the BJP with 10.17 per cent votes, Janata Party with 25.41 per cent votes but could not get any seat in the election.

1996 Electons

In Parliamentary election, 1996, a total of 459 nominations including 15 women were received and finally 294 contested the polls including 9 women candidates. 7860683 (70.48 per cent) of the 11152856 electorate cast their votes including 3539125 women.

The BJP-HVP alliance fetched 7 seats leaving 2 for the Congress and one for Independents. The alliance won the 20 Assembly segments falling in urban areas, which are considered as the stronghold of the Congress. Moreover, it got negative votes against the Congress. Bansi Lal was successful in getting the major share of Jat votes at the cost of Devi Lal. The Samata Party finished second in Sonepat, Kurukshetra, Rohtak, Hissar and Sirsa. The analysis proved that in case of an alliance with the BJP, the party could have won a majority of seats. In terms of support base, the Congress got 22.04 per cent votes while leading in 9 Assembly segments of Ambala, Kurukshetra, Karnal, Rohtak, Faridabad, Mahendergarh, Hissar while the HVP-BJP combine obtained 35.93 per cent (HVP-16.19% & BJP-19.74%) votes. The Samata Party (earlier as S.J.P.) got 19.04 per cent votes and could not open its account in the Lok Sabha.

1998 Elections

The number of nominations fell drastically from 494 in 1996 to 197 in 1998 Lok Sabha election. Likewise, the number of contestants came down to 140 in comparison to 294 in 1996. However, 11 women filed nominations and 6 contested the elections. 7649117(68.99%) of the 11086895 electors cast their votes including 3319042 women.

1999 Elections

In 1999 elections, a total of 142 nominations were filed including 4 women. After scrutiny of papers 114 candidates were in the fray. Out of 11038955 electors 7029964 (63.68%) exercised their franchise including 2927158 women. The INLD-BJP combine swept the election getting all the 10 seats perhaps due to the abnormal behaviour of the Congress of first supporting the HVP government and then withdrawing it suddenly.

Thus, instead of gaining from the anti-incumbency factor, Congress even lost the 3 seats it had, 2 to the BJP and one to the INLD. This was despite a near 9 per cent swing that raised its vote share from 26.02 to 34.93 per cent, 23 point lower than the BJP-INLD combine's total of 57.93 per cent.

Bansi Lal's Haryana Vikas Party, which had run a coalition with BJP for over two years before the saffron party switched sides in return for Chautala's backing at the Centre after the HVP lost its clout in the 1998 Lok Sabha poll, yielded its lone seat to the INLD. Its vote share dropped 8.89 points from 11.6 to 2.71 per cent.

The HVP ally BSP too lost its only seat to BJP as its support fell 5.75 points from 7.68 to 1.93 per cent. Two candidates of the CPM and the JDS polled a minuscule 0.15 and 0.02 per cent, while 13 'others' and 74 Independents shared 2.33 per cent. Winning 5 seats with 29.21 per cent, over 10 points higher than the 18.89 it got last time, the BJP gained 4 seats, 2 from Congress and one each from the BSP and Chautala's party then going under the name of Haryana Lok Dal

(Rashtriya). The INLD too won 5 seats for 28.72 per cent, one more than what his earlier party won for 25.90 per cent in 1998. It wrested a seat each from the Congress and the HVP, while retaining 3 the HLDR seats. Two SC seats were shared by the BJP and the INLD, with the first snatching Ambala from the BSP, and the second taking the Sirsa seat it had won last time as HLDR.

Former Congress Chief Minister, Bhajan Lal, who went out of power in the simultaneous Assembly poll in 1996, lost Karnal by 147854 votes to the BJP's I.D. Swami, whom he had defeated by 52601 votes in 1998. Haryana Congress Chief, Bhupinder Singh Hooda, who had thrice in a row, defeated Chautala's father, '*Tau*' Devi Lal, 85, a former Deputy Prime Minister in his home turf of Rohtak since 1991, lost to little known Inder Singh of the INLD by 144693 votes.

Bansi Lal's son Surender Singh who had defeated his own brother and Chautala's son Ajay Chautala last time finished a distant third in Bhiwani with the junior Chautala trouncing Dharamvir of the Congress by over two lakh votes.

The BJP's Sudha Yadav, widow of a Kargil martyr, unseated Inderjit Singh of Congress in Mahendergarh and Kailasho Devi retained Kurukshetra for the INLD. A third woman candidate contesting on the SP ticket lost her deposit in Rohtak.

The INLD

The relatively small swing in favour of the INLD may be explained, in the first instance, by the fact that it contested a lesser number of seats in the 1999 elections, five seats to be precise instead of the six that it had contested in the 1998 elections. It had to surrender Sonepat parliamentary constituency, which it had won in the 1998 elections by a huge margin, to its alliance partner, the BJP. It also appears that the BJP too could not get its votes fully transferred to the INLD. A segment of the non-agriculturist high castes and the Punjabi supporters of the BJP did not vote for the candidates of the INLD because they continued to perceive it as an anti-urban, anti-trader, anti-non-agriculturist high castes and anti-Punjabi party. The alliance with the BJP, a party which represents these sections, did not change their perception.

Even the all out efforts of O.P. Chautala led INLD government to woo them by making all types of promises to remove the grievances of the BJP supporters could not remove their apprehensions which were bassed on the wide publicity of the rowdy activities of the Jai Parkash led, Green-Brigade, the youth wing of its earlier incarnation, the Lok Dal. The fact that Jai Parkash had left that party in 1995 and joined Bansi Lal's HVP, and then jumped to the Congress (I) in 1998 along with his followers failed to change the image of the INLD in their eyes.

Chautala's organizational skill proved very useful in mobilizing their support. The formation of the INLD government by him before these elections helped in galvanizing the workers of the party. This helped in mobilizing a high turnout of its voters in the elections. The populist promises of free supply of electricity and water to the agriculturists also played some part in increasing the electoral support of the party. The INLD also once again encashed anti-Bansi Lal feelings in the peasantry which it had exploited in the 1998 parliamentary elections. Chautala also made a very careful choice of the candidates and gave priority to their winning capacity over other factors.

The BJP

There was, however, a large scale swing in the percentage of votes polled by the BJP in the 1999 parliamentary elections despite the fact that it contested five seats instead of seven. The projection of Atal Bihari Vajpayee as the National Democratic Alliance (NDA) candidate for the office of the Prime Minister proved useful to the BJP because of the positive appeal of his personality and satisfaction of most of the voters with the overall performance of his administration. The sympathy for Vajpayee due to the overthrow of his government in April 1999 by one vote and with little justification also benefited the party.

The politicization of the Kargil issue by the BJP proved very effective in Haryana because of the martyrdom of a large number of army personnel and parliamentary forces belonging to Haryana.

But the most important factor that accounted for the large scale gain in electoral support for the BJP was its alliance with the INLD. Despite the fact that the BJP could not get its votes fully transferred to the INLD, the later ensured *en bloc* transfer of its voters to the BJP. It is evident from the fact it secured 29.21 per cent votes in these elections while it had obtailed 19.74 and 18.59 per cent votes in respectively in the 1996 and the 1998 parliamentary elections that it had contested as an alliance partner of the HVP.

The Congress (I)

Despite intense factionalism in the state unit of the party, the Congress (I) was able to make large gains in electoral support in the 1999 elections in comparison with the earlier ones. A primary factor is that the party was more united. In the earlier elections, the Bhupinder Singh Hooda Congress (I) faction is reported to have had a secret understanding with the HVP of Bansi Lal, while the Bhajan Lal Congress (I) faction is alleged to be have allied with the O.P. Chautala's 'Party'. Moreover, the Congress (I) put up very strong candidates in the 1999 elections in almost all the parliamentary constituencies, whereas it had fielded weaker candidates in the earlier elections. Since leaders of all three Congrerss factions, Bhajan Lal, Bhupinder Singh Hooda and Birender Singh, were in the electoral fray this time, they had little time for sabotaging the elections of their competitors.

The Sonia factor also appears to have helped the Congress (I) in Haryana because the issue of her foreign origin did not become salient in rural Haryana where the caste of a woman is determined by the caste of her husband and not by her own caste. This is evident from the popular saying : '*Jat Ke Ghar Ai To Jatani*' (If a woman of any caste is married to a Jat, she becomes a Jat).

However, the party could not take advantage of the anti-Bansi Lal feelings among the voters because its leadership failed to launch any movement against the unpopular decisions of the Bansi Lal government. It could not do so because of the weakness of the party organization owing to factionalism at all levels. The allegation of the existence of a secret understanding between the president of the Haryana Pradesh Congress Committee, Bhupinder Singh Hooda, and Bansi Lal also proved damaging to the party in this context. The decision of the Congress (I) to extend support to Bansi Lal government in the hope that he would merge the HVP with the Congress (I) only gave credence to the collusion charges. The subsequent withdrawal of Congress (I) support to Bansi Lal's HVP government could not counter the damage done by its earlier decision. Instead, the fall of Bansi Lal's government and the formation of Chautala's INLD state government had a demoralizing effect of the workers of the Congress (I). But for these negative steps, the Congress (I) would have been able to further increase its electoral support.

The HVP

The large scale decline in support for the HVP could be attributed in the first instance to the unpopularity of Bansi Lal owing to the persistence of his authoritarian governing style. He could not retain his earlier image of a development oriented leader as he failed to bring about the economic development in the state during his three years as Chief Minister. His obsession with the introduction of total prohibition in Haryana deprived the state of a significant part of its revenue. Besides, he diverted the energy of his administration to imposing and enforcing prohibition instead of development. Moreover, he had to levy heavy taxes on various sections of society for compensating the loss of the excise duty on liquor. These taxes made his government unpopular. Although he scrapped prohibition after the defeat of his party in the 1998 parliamentary elections, he did not change his style of leadership and had failed to take steps for checking the erosion in his support base.

Stubbornly, Bansi Lal refused to learn any lesson from the defects of his party in the 1998 parliamentary elections. Since he did not share power with his ministers, it remained centralized in his hands as Chief Minister, members of his family and the Chief Minister's Secretariat. This led to frequent revolts by his ministers who made consistent efforts to topple his government. Instead of accommodating the dissident ministers by sharing power with them, he decided to stay in power through manipulation of support from the BJP leadership of the Congress (I) at the national and state levels. These tactics made an adverse impact upon his support base as his credibility and integrity now become questionable.

The BSP

The almost total evaporation of the BSP electoral support in the 1999 elections has to be ascribed to the ineffective and unpopular leadership of the party at the state level on the one hand and the lack of party organization on the other. The breaking of its alliance with the INLD deprived the BSP of support from the agriculturist castes and the Sikhs who constitute its most reliable vote bank. This is evident from the comparison of its performance in the 1998 and the 1999 parliamentary elections. It also failed to get votes from Gujjars this time because it did not field a candidate from the caste in Faridabad constituency which it had left for its alliance partner, the HVP. Its support base among the Ahirs also almost totally eroded due to the decline in the popularity of its candidate from the Mahendergarh parliamentary constituency. Moreover, it fielded a very weak candidate from Karnal constituency in 1999. The alliance with the HVP also proved very costly to the BSP.

2004 Elections

In 2004 elections, as many as 232 nominations were filed including 20 women. After the withdrawls and rejections, 160 contested the elections including 8 women. The number of electorate increased from 11034955 to 12320557 in 2004. the men-women ratio was 6660631: 5659926. 65.67 per cent electorates cast their votes including 3554361 women. The Congress swept the poll while getting 9 seats with 42.13 per cent votes and BJP got 17.21 per cent votes with 1 seat. The INLD got 22.43 per cent votes with no seat.

The Congress nominee, Selja-Ambala, Jai Parkash-Hissar, both got a higher percentage of votes. At the same time Bhupender Singh Hooda also got more than 48 per cent votes followed by Naveen Jindal-42.55 per cent, Avtar Singh Bhadana-42.30 per cent, Rao Inderjit Singh-42.24 per cent and the least Kishan Singh Sangwan-31.67 per cent.

It was realized that the INLD and the BJP should have contested together. Had they contested in tandem, the combined could have won about two seats and given close contest in 34 Assembly segements.

The anger of the voter was so severe that the ruling INLD candidates lost even in Jat hinterland and candidates in four constituencies lost their deposits. It all happened despite a lot of developmental works were undertaken in the state because people were annoyed with the rude behaviours as well as total centralization of power in the hands of Chief Minister's sons.

The annoyance with BKU also cost the party dear and so the Sikh community. The business community was unhappy with Chautala for implementing the VAT in the state.

In these elections, parties like HVP, Ekta Shakti etc. witnessed a virtual elimination as their votes shifted to the Congress to ensure its victory.

The INLD and the BJP blamed each other for their defeat but they never tried to realize the mood and sentiments of party workers before entering into alliance which led to poor show of both parties.

The neglect of the party leaders at grass roots level as well as those of dedicated workers also led to the defeat of the INLD. The arbitrary allocation of tickets to the nearer and dearer also lost the party heavily.

Some pertinent questions are to be answered like:

First, it is essential to answer the questions why there is a large discrepancy between the votes polled and the seats won by the major political parties that contested the 1999 parliamentary elections. It can be explained partly by the fact that the alliance between the INLD and BJP resulted in effectively combining the votes of their supporters in many constituencies. Since their combined votes were higher than that of the Congress (I) or the HVP, the INLD-BJP alliance won all the seats. Congress (I) which polled 8.91 per cent more votes in the 1999 elections than secured by it in the 1998 parliamentary elections nonetheless failed to retain the three seats won by it in 1998. Secondly, the virtual conversion of the electoral contest into a direct one between it and the Congress (I) helped the INLD-BJP alliance in sweeping the elections. This happened due to the almost total decimation of the HVP-BSP alliance. Consequently, the anti-Congress (I) votes became polarized in favour of the candidates of the INLD-BJP alliance in all the 10 parliamentary constituencies.

As regards the changes in the support bases of various parties that took place in Haryana in the 1999 parliamentary elections, these have to be understood by taking into account the pattern of social cleavages and political alignments on the one hand and the role of the national and state level factors on the other. While the national level factors included the pattern of the performances, promises and images of the leaders of the BJP and the Congress (I), the state level factors included the nature of the alliances between the political parties and factions as well as the performances, promises and images of their leaders. The political situation at the national and state level has also to be kept in view as it had a significant bearing on the electoral performance of various contenders.

2009 Elections

The Lok Sabha elections, 2009 were held after delimitation of the constituencies where some new one's were created and old one's were abolished. A total of 285 candidates filed their nomination and finally, 210 contested the election including 14 women. Of the total 12087710 electors men-women ratio was 6590954 : 5496756.

A history of sorts was created in Haryana when the Congress retuned its previous tally of 9 Lok Sabha seats as no ruling party had been able to achieve this feat in the state ever. In Haryana the voters are known to be highly volatile. If in one election it would give all seats to one party in the next the same party would be reduced to nil.

The results proved all pre- and post-election surveys wrong when the Congress bagged 9 seats.

Deepender Singh Hooda recorded the highest winning margin in the state when he retained his Rohtak seat by a margin of 445736 votes. He created a notional record of winning the seat successively with such a high margin. All his rivals including Nafe Singh Rathee of the INLD lost their security deposits. The second highest margin was in Sonepat where Jatinder Singh Malik of the Congress defeated the BJP, MP, Kishan Singh Sangwan by 161284 votes. Naveen Jindal of the Congress defeated Ashok Arora of the INLD with a margin of 118729 votes. Rao Inderjit Singh of the Congress defeated Zakir Hussain of the BSP by 84863 votes where Arvind Sharma of the Congress won by a margin of 76346 when he defeated Maratha Virender Verma of the BSP. Avatar Singh Bhadana of the Congress defeated Ram Chander Bainda of the BJP by 68201 votes.

Secretary General of the INLD, Ajay Chautala was humbled by Shruti Chaudhary by 55053 votes. This was the second successive defeat of Chautala for this seat as he was defeated by Kuldeep Bishnoi in 2004. In Sirsa (Reserved), the native district of Chautalas, Ashok Tanwar, the President of All India Youth Congress defeated Sita Ram of the INLD by 35499 votes. In Ambala (Reserved), the sitting MP, Selja defeated Rattan Lal Kataria of the BJP by 14570 votes.

Despite several constraints like – the BSP taking away a considerable chunk of the Congress vote, open sabotage by party MLAs/ministers in many constituencies, etc., the Congress won these seats.

The election saw a complete rout of the INLD-BJP alliance. It has happend for the first time that the alliance between these two parties had drawn a blank. Thus, the alliance which was not approved by the rank and file of the two parties had also been rejected by the electorate.

The humiliation of the INLD was further compounded by the fact that its vote percentage which was second to the Congress in 2004, fell to the third. The INLD share decreased from 22.43 per cent in 2004 to 15.68 per cent in 2009.

The BSP not only increased its share in the vote bank from 4.98 per cent to 15.73 per cent but managed to wrest the second position from the BJP in Gurgaon and Karnal but the vote percentage of the BJP decreased from in 2004 to 12.09 per cent in 2009. The HJC (BL) got 9.89 per cent vote and the elecorate rejected the claim of Kuldeep Bishnoi that in 2004 and 2005 the people had voted for the Congress to make his father, Bhajan Lal as the Chief Minister of the state.

The results silenced the critics of Bhupender Singh Hooda who said that his influence was confirmed to the old Rohtak district only.

Deepender Singh Hooda led in all nine Assembly segments of Rohtak parliamentary constituency. The development factor mattered the most there. Similarly, Naveen Jindal from Kuruksetra seat led in all nine Assembly segments. The social work launched by him there paid off.

The Congress captured Sonepat seat after a period of 18 years. Last time it was Dharmpal Malik of the Congress who was elected in 1991. Shruti Chaudhary registered a nominal margin in three Assembly segments of Narnaul, Nangal Chaudhary and Ateli where Rao Narender Singh led all the way. She led in Bhiwani, Charki-Dadri, Loharu, Badhra and Tosham.

Sirsa defeat could be treated as a severe blow to the INLD in these elections whereas in the Assembly poll, 2005, the district returned three MLAs of the INLD. The party won one Assembly seat in Fetehabad also. Thus, out of 9 MLAs, 4 came from Sirsa parliamentary constituency. Now it lost in 6 out of 8 Assembly segments there.

Jai Prakash of Congress lost in all 9 assembly segments of Hissar parliamentary constituency. In Uchana, which was represented by Birender Singh, Jai Prakash got about a half votes in comparison to Sampat Singh of the INLD. The voters of Gihria represented by

Chhaterpal Singh an adversary of Jai Prakash, also defeated him. The party workers from Hissar shifted to Kurukshetra in support of Naveen Jindal.

The stunned INLD-BJP introspected the debacle. For this, the INLD convened a meeting on May 18, 2009 to introspect the reasons for its failure at the hustings. At the same time, the BJP called a meeting of senior party leaders at Rohtak on the same day.

The BJP co-incharge of party offices in Haryana, H.S. Grewal said that people did not receive the alliance well because they were probably not sure about its workability, i.e. "we could not make them understand the alliance. It was there and then we fell out. Again we joined hand last year, it has not been consistent. We will look into all these issues."

The INLD and the BJP hoped to revive their formation in the Lok Sabha polls and agreed to old sharing formula of five seats each with which they had struck gold in 1999 Lok Sabha election making a clean sweep in the state. Together, they were always a force to reckon with. However, there was a big question mark about its effectiveness this time as most of the state unit leaders of the BJP vehemently opposed renewal of ties with Chautala and majority of them favoured the HJC (BL).

As the coalition failed to work on the ground, the vote share of the two parties plummated to 28.59 per cent from 39.64 per cent in 2004.

Though the BJP leaders were seen with the INLD candidates throughout the election campaign, there were hiccups in the transfer of votes. Gripped by despondency some members of the group which had opposed the tie up with Chautala, had already begun murmuring about the need to review the alliance and go with the HJC (BL).

The BSP polled 379574 votes in 18 assembly segments of Kurukshetra and Karnal Lok Sabha seats and led in Nilokheri, Indri and Gharada segments where it polled 800 votes less than the Congress in Asandh. The INLD-BJP polled 463912 votes in these two Lok Sabha constituencies.

Reasons of the INLD Defeat

The INLD tried to ratioalise the defeat of its candidates and those of the BJP because of some national issues, said O.P. Chautala in party's executive meeting at Hissar. But Sampat Singh said that party was defeated because of neglect of party workers and opposed the statement given by Chautala. Moveover, Isolation from the common masses particularly the poor and humilation of seniorand dedicated party leaders.

Denial of party ticket to old and loyal party men like Sushil Indora, Kailasho Saini, B.S. Suhag etc.

The Haryana BJP decided to take action against 10 of its senior leaders who remained inactive during the Lok Sabha polls including the party MLA, Naresh Malik. The party at its state executive meeting at Panchkula found three reasons of its defeat, e.g, a part of its vote bank was transferred to the BSP, some votes went to the HJC and its failure to attract the youth towards party.

2014 Election

The BJP led in 52 Assembly segments in compare to only 17 in 2009, whereas the Congress tally fell from 51 in 2009 to 17, the INLD improved its tally from 6 to 16. The HJC led in 7 segments in compare to 9 in 2009. The BSP which led in 8 segments in 2009 failed to lead in any one in 2014.

The BJP led in all the nine Assembly segments in Ambala, Karnal and Faridabad Lok Sabha seats. The Congress led in all in Rohtak. Moreover, the BJP led in 6 in Kurukshetra, Congress in two and INLD in one. In Sirsa, the INLD led in 7 and Congress & HJC one each. However, the HJC led in 6 in Hisar, the INLD in 3 segments.

In Sonepat, the BJP led in 5, Congress-3 and INLD-1. In Bhiwani, the BJP led in 6, Congress -2 and INLD-1. In Gurgaon the BJP got first place in 6 and the INLD in three.

The Modi wave and anti-incumbency proved fatal for the Congress who lost a seats.

The vote for change also cost the HJC Chief, Kuldeep Bishnoi his Hisar seat.

Even those Congress leaders like Dharambir Singh, Ramesh Kaushik, Rao Inderjeet Singh, who switched over to the BJP just before the polls, won the elections off hand.

Due to factionalism and anti-party activities, the Congress performed very poorly.

The concentration of powers in the hands of father, mother and son- Bhupander Singh Hooda, Asha Hooda and Deepander Hooda and neglect of party workers led to such a poor situation.

The Hisar result had given a big blow to Bishnoi's political prospects. His own poll strategy to make it a Jat v/s non -Jat contest seemed to have gone awry as it led to extreme polarisation of the Jats in favour of the INLD.

Better management and early election campaign helped the INLD in Sirsa and Hisar. Ashok Tanwar who was willing to shift to Ambala also affected the result adversely. The INLD had constituted committee to keep the booth level activists on their toes all the time proved helpful in getting two seats.

- Slipping of urban votes from the Congress hands also cost it very dearly.
- The Chief Minister and the HPCC Chief blamed the bureaucracy and inter party differences for the party's severe drubbing in Haryana.
- The poor delivery system and the apathetic attitude of those at the helm of the affairs towards party workers and the public also added the woes of the Congress.
- Ashok Tanwar alleged that certain leaders who amassed huge wealth through dubious means betrayed the party at the time of the election.
- Discrimination in job and development works also affected the results.
- AAP's "fight against corruption apparently found no match for Modi's development model.
- The results have shattered caste- based politics in most of the constituencies, giving parties a reason to think for new principles and goals.
- Congress defeat from Sonepat seat can be seen as a personal set back to the Chief Minister as he had paid special attention to it after Rohtak.

Kuldeep Bishnoi's wife Renuka Bishnoi alleged that his husband was defeated due to rigging and booth capturing.

- The corruption in CLU and Vadra factor also affected the Congress adversely.

The BJP is to reconsider the alliance with the HJC after the later defeat in Lok Sabha poll.

Women's Participation in Lok Sabha Elections

Haryana has participated in 11 Lok Sabha elections since its formation. The state witnessed its first Lok Sabha elections in 1967 when 67 candidates had entered the fray. These included one woman candidate but in the 1971 Lok Sabha elections, not even a single woman candidate contested the poll. However, the 1984 Lok Sabha elections proved the best for women candidates when of the 200 contenders, the ever highest number of 10 women participated in the elections. In the 1989 Lok Sabha elections, about 324 candidates entered the fray which included only three women. In the 1996 Lok Sabha elections, only nine women entered the race whereas in 2004, eight women candidates entered the fray.

But the 2009 Lok Sabha elections have set a record with the participation of 14 women candidates. Of the 10 Lok Sabha constituencies, the maximum of three women candidates are in the race for the Bhiwani-Mahendergarh constitutency while not even a single woman contestant has entered the fray from Rohtak. On the last day of withdrawal of nominations, four of the 18 women candidates had withdrawn their names.

In 2014, as many as 11 women contested out of 230 total candidates. No women contested from Sirsa, Rohtak and Sonepat Constituecies. The INLD and AAP only fielded one women each. However, only one women could win by election.

Annexure-1

Elections During Composite Punjab

General Election, 1920

Constituencies		
Name of Constituency	*Extent*	*Seats*
Non-Muhammadan	Ambala Division	1
Muhammadan	Ambala Division	1
Sikh	Ambala Division	1

Election Returns

Non-Muhammadan

Ambala Division, Votes 46.31 (35%) and Pt. Jawahar Lal Bhargava won. The other contestants were Baljit Nath, Atma Ram, Faqir Chand.

Muhammadan

East Punjab, Votes - 2080 (35%) and N. Mohd. Ibrahim Ali Khan won with 595 votes whereas Mir Mohd. Khan got 107 votes.

Sikh

East Punjab, Votes 2505 (52%) and Bhai Man Singh won with 385 votes whereas S. Jasjit Singh got 312, Rajender Singh 306, and Sajjan Singh 254.

General Election, 1923

Constituencies

Name of Constituency	*Extent*	*Seats*
Non-Muhammadan	Ambala Division	1
Muhammadan	Ambala Division	1
Sikh	Ambala Division	1

Election Returns

Non-Muhammadan

The Ambala Division, votes 5058 (65.5%) and Duni Chand won with 1756 votes followed by Pt. Thakur Das Bhargava with 947 and RS Ch. Daryao Singh 580 votes.

Muhammadan

East Punjab, votes 2485 (71.8%) and M.N. Abdul Haye won with 1111 votes and Mohd. Liaqat Ali Khan got 386 and Rasul Ahmed Khan 2.

Sikh

East Punjab, votes 2711 (58.4%) and W. S. Kartar Singh won with 1287 votes and S. Man Singh got 255, Sodhi Lal Singh 94.

General Election, 1923

Constituencies

Name of Constituency	*Extent*	*Seats*
Non-Muhammadan	Ambala Division	1
Muhammadan	Ambala Division	1
Sikh	Ambala Division	1

Election Returns

Non-Muhammadan

Ambala Division, votes 6731 (63.38%) and Pt. Thakur Das Bhagrava (H) won the seat defeating Sham Lal (SW).

Muhammadan

East Panjab, votes 3098 (59.21%) and M.N. Abdul Haye (EU) won the election.

Sikh

East Punjab, votes 3219 (52.16%) and S. Kartar Singh won while defeating S. Kapur Singh.

General Election 1926

Constituencies

Name of Constituency	*Extent*	*Seats*
Non-Muhammadan	Ambala Division	1
Muhammadan	Ambala Division	1
Sikh	Ambala Division	1

Election Returns

Non-Muhammadan

Ambala Division, votes 7102 and R.S. Hari Das (EU) won the election.

Muhammadan

East Punjab, votes 3361 (64.21%) and Hon. Lt. Mohd. Ibrahim Ali Khan won with 1987 while defeating M.N. Abdul Haye with 1071 votes.

Sikh

East Punjab, votes 3227 (49.89%) and S. Harbans Singh 927 votes while defeating S. Kartar Singh who got 683 votes.

Bye-Election

Ambala Division (NM)

Bye Election caused by the resignation of Hari Das in February 1931 and Bhai Parmanand won the election.

General Election, 1934

Constituencies

Name of Constituency	*Extent*	*Seats*
Non-Muhammadan	Ambala Division	1
Muhammadan	Ambala Division	1
Sikh	Ambala Division	1

Election Returns

Non-Muhammadan

Ambala Division, votes 7577 (76.7%) and Sham Lal (C) won with 2982 votes and Pt. Thakur Das Bhargava got 2779 and was defeated.

Muhammadan

East Punjab, votes 3695 and Ghulam Bhik Nairang (EU) won the election.

Sikh

In East Punjab, votes 3122 (75.8%) and Mangal Singh (CN) won with 864 votes whereas Fateh Singh got 807, Harnam Singh 624 and Rajender Singh 69.

Bye-Election

Ambala Division (C)

Bye-election caused by the demise of Sham Lal, when Thakur Das Bhargava won the election.

General Election, 1934

Constituencies

Name of Constituency	*Extent*	*Seats*
Non-Muhammadan	Ambala Division	1
Muhammadan	Ambala Division	1
Sikh	Ambala Division	1

Election Returns

Non-Muhammadan

Ambala Division, 9525 (62.48%) when Pt. Thakur Das Bhargava (C) won with 5352 votes and Bhai Parmanand (H) got 569 votes, Manohar Lal (I) - 2 and Makhan Lal (I) only one.

Muhammadan

East Punjab, votes 5109 when Ghulam Bhik Nairang (ML) (EU) won the election.

Sikh

East Punjab, votes 3899 (70.01%) and Mangal Singh (AK) won with 1659 votes and Kapur Singh (C) got 1042 votes.

THE COUNCIL OF STATE, 1920-1947

General Election, 1920

Constituencies

Name of Constituency	*Extent*	*Seats*
Non-Muhammadan	Punjab Entire Punjab	1
Muhammadan	East Punjab Ambala, Jullundur Divs.	1
Sikh	Punjab Entire Punjab	1

Election Returns

Non-Muhammadan

Punjab, votes 858 (47%) and Ram Saran Das won with 176 votes and Pindi Das got 65, Moti Sagar 60, Dewan Sant Ram 30, Dr. Hira Lal 29, Hari Chand, 22, L. Harkishan Lal 15 and Nand Lal 2.

Muhammadan

East Punjab, votes 262 (66%) and Zulfiqar Ali Khan won with 124 votes whereas Ahad Shah got 43, Ma. Imam Ali 4 and Ch. Sher Mohd. Khan 2.

Sikh

Punjab, votes 365 and Jogendar Singh (EU) won the election.

Genaral Election, 1925

Constituencies

Name of Constituency	*Extent*	*Seats*
Non-Muhammadan	Punjab Entire Punjab	1
Muhammadan	East Punjab Ambala, Jullundur Divisions	1
Sikh	Punjab Entire Punjab	1

Election Returns

Non-Muhammadan

Punjab, 1038 votes and Ram Saran Das (EU) won the election.

Muhammadan

East Punjab, votes 1082 (66%) and Mohd. Mehr Shah Gilani won with 502 votes and Ghulam Yasin got 212 votes.

Sikh

Punjab, 519 (73%) when Jogendar Singh won with 263 votes and Baba Kartar Singh Bedi got 116 votes.

Bye-Election

Punjab (S)

Bye-election caused by the resignation of Joginder Singh. Polling was held in March 1926 and Shiv Dev Singh Uberoi won it while defeating Dalip Singh and Gulab Singh.

General Election, 1930

Constituencies

Name of Constituency	*Extent*	*Seats*
Non-Muhammadan	Punjab Entire Punjab	1
Muhammadan	East Punjab Ambala, Jullundur Divs.	1
Sikh	Punjab Entire Punjab	1

Election Returns

Non-Muhammadan

In Punjab, votes 1016 and Ram Saran Das (EU) won the election.

Muhammadan

East Punjab, votes 479 (84.79%) when Ch. Mohd. Din won with 233 votes and Nisar Ali Khan was defeated with 171 votes.

Sikh

Punjab, votes 573 and Shiv Dev Singh Uberoi (EU) won the election.

Bye-Election

Punjab (S)

Bye-election caused by the resignation of Shiv Dev Singh Uberoi. Polling was held in June 1932 and Buta Singh won it.

General Election, 1936

Constituencies

Name of Constituency	*Extent*	*Seats*
Non-Muhammadan	Punjab Entire Punjab	1
Muhammadan	East Punjab Ambala, Jullundur Divs.	1
Sikh	Punjab Entire Punjab	1

Election Returns

Non-Muhammadan

In Punjab, Ram Saran Das (EU) won the election.

Muhammadan

In East Punjab Ch. Mohd. Din (EU) won it.

Sikh

In Punjab Buta Singh (EU) secured the seat.

Bye-Election in October 1946

Punjab (NM)

Bye-election caused by the death of Ram Saran Das when Rup Chand won it.

The Constituent Assembly of India : Members from Punjab, 1946

Muhammadans

Muzaffar Ali Khan Qizilbash, Muhammed Ali Jinnah, Abdul Rab

Nishtar, Iftikhar Hussain Khan, Mumtaz Mohd. Khan Daultana, Mohd. Feroz Khan Noon, Raja Ghazannfar Ali Khan, Prof. Abu Maber Ahmad Haleem, Mohd. Iftikhar-ud-din, Mohd. Hassan, Sheikh Karamt Ali, Begum Jhanara Shah Nawaz, Mir Ghulam Bhik Nairang, Nazir Ahmad Khan, Omar Hayat, Amjad Ali.

Hindus include

Rao Suraj Mal, Dr. Gopi Chand Bhargava, Pt. Shri Ram Sharma, Tek Chand, Prithvi Singh Azad, Dewan Chaman Lal, Mehar Chand Khanna, Harbhaj Ram.

Sikhs include

Harnam Singh, Kartar Singh, Partap Singh, Ujjal Singh.

THE PUNJAB LEGISLATIVE COUNCIL (1919-1936)/ASSEMBLY (1937-1947)

General Election, 1920

Constituencies

Name	*Extent*	*Seat*
Non-Muhammadan-Urban Lahore City	Mun. and Cantt. of Lahore	1
Amritsar City	Mun. and Cantt. of Amritsar	1
South-East Towns	Muns. of Bhiwani, Hissar, Sirsa, Hansi, Rohtak, Jhajjar, Rewari, Panipat, Karnal, Kaithal, Shahbad, n. as of Karnal (civil sta.), Kaithal, Hidayatpur Chhaoni (Gurgaon)	1
North-East Towns	Muns. of Ambala, Jagadhari, Simla, Ludhiana, Jagraon, Hoshiarpur, Jullundur, Cantts. of Ambala, Kasauli, Dagbhai, Sabathu, Jutogh, Jullundur.	1
East-West Central Towns	Muns. of Easur, Farozpur, Fazilka, Gurdaspur, Batala, Dalhousie, Sialkot, Dharamsala, cants. of Ferozepur, Balun, Bakloh, Sialkot, Dharamsala	1

(Contd.)

Table *(Contd...)*

North-West Towns	Muns. of Gujarat, Jalalpur, Jattan, Bhera, Khushab, Jhelum, Pind Dadan Khan, Rawalpindi, Muree, Mianwali, Gujranwala, Wazirabad, Cantts. of Jhelum, Rawalpindi, Muree, Campbellpur, Attock, n. as. of Sargodha, Compbelipur, Sheikhupura.	1
West Punjab Towns	Muns. of Montgomery, Chiniot, Multan, Lyallpur, Muzaffargarh, Jhang-Maghians, Dera Ghazi Khan, Cantt. of Multan	1
Non-Muhammadan-Rural Hisar	Hissar Div.	1
South-East Rohtak	Jhajjar, Sonepat, Gohana tehs. of Rohtak district.	1

Chronology of Political Parties in Punjab, 1877-1947*

1877 Lahore Indian Association founded by Surendra Nath Banerjee.

1885 Indian National Congress founded at Bombay, Branch opened in Punjab.

1902 Chief Khalsa Dewan founded.

1906 Muslim League founded in Punjab by Sir Fazl-i-Husain (February).

1907 Muslim Association founded after some months by Mian Mohd. Safi.

1907 All-India Muslim League branch founded, Fazil and Shafi merged their Parties.

1907 Punjab Hindu Sabha founded, All-India Hindu Muhasabha born out of it in December 1913.

1920 Central Sikh League founded.

1920 Akali Dal founded, Split after 1925 into Shrimoni Akali Dal and Central Akali Dal.

1921 Rural Block (subsequently Rural Party) formed by Sir Fazl-i-Husain.

1921-22 Communist Party Organizational Work began.

1922	Swarajya Party founded.
1923	Rural Party became the Unionist Party.
1924	National Progressive Party formed by Raja Narender Nath.
1926	Naujwan Bharat Sabha founded by Dr. Satyapal.
1926	Independent Congress Party founded by L. Lajpat Rai.
1929	Majlis-i-Ahrar founded at Lahore.
1930	Khaksar Party founded by Allama Inayatullah Khan Mashriqi of Lahore.
1934	Congress Nationalists Party formed by Hindu, Congressites against Communal Award.
1934	Socialist Party founded as an offshoot of Congress.
1936	Khalsa National Party founded.
1936	All-Indian Kisan Sabha Wing organized.
1936	Itihad-i-Millat formed.
1941	Jamat-i-Islami founded by Abdullah Maududi.

* Elections in Punjab were not fought on party lines before 1923.

Annexure-2

Voting Details of Individual Candidates Since 1952

Lok Sabha Election, 1952 : Haryana Region of Composite Punjab

Ambala Simla : Number of Seats 1

Tek Chand INC	98249	49.12%
Sohan Lal BJS	53866	26.93%
Krishan SP	19340	9.67%
Dalip Singh IND	13466	6.73%
Gurbaksh Singh IND	7259	3.63%
Bachan Singh IND	4983	2.49%
R. L. Kohli IND	2865	1.43%

Electors : 365025 Voters : 200028
Poll Percentage : 54.80% Valid Votes 200028

Karnal : Number of Seats 1

13.	Subhadra Joshi INC	203588	24.15%
14.	Virendra Kumar INC	151802	18.01%
10.	Madhav Acharya RRP	89475	10.61%
2.	Jugal Kishore BJS	66877	7.93%
5.	Ram Dhan ZP	47907	5.68%
4.	Chaman Lal IND	44855	5.32%
7.	Risala IND	42310	5.02%
3.	Jairam Sarup IND	41795	4.96%
1.	Arjan Singh IND	32878	3.90%
8.	Shanti Prashad IND	30092	3.57%
11.	Muni Lal Mehra IND	29788	3.53%
12.	Yodh Raj BJS	28932	3.43%
6.	Ram Sarup IND	20830	2.47%
9.	Krishna Azad DCL	11789	1.40%

Electors : 765032 Voters : 842918
Poll Percentage : 55.09% Valid Votes 842918

Rohtak : Number of Seats 1

4.	Ranbir Singh INC	108148	42.71%
3.	Hari Ram ZP	81776	32.30%
1.	Suresh Chandra IND	43229	17.07%
2.	Fateh Singh IND	20035	7.91%

Electors : 363546 Voters : 253188
Poll Percentage : 69.64% Valid Votes 253188

Jhajjar Rewari : Number of Seats 1

5.	Ghamandi Lal INC	102435	41.60%
1.	Partap Singh ZP	98503	40.01%
2.	Shamsher Singh SP	28596	11.61%
4.	Nihal Chand IND	11048	4.49%
3.	Lal Singh IND	5642	2.29%

Electors : 382413 Voters : 246224
Poll Percentage : 64.39% Valid Votes 246224

Gurgaon : Number of Seats 1

6.	Thakar Das INC	113269	44.96%
1.	Jiwan Khan IND	36615	14.53%
3.	Kishan Chand ZP	32518	12.91%
4.	Manphul Singh IND	30391	12.06%
2.	Khubi Ram IND	26285	10.43%
5.	Hari Har Lal IND	12868	5.11%

Electors : 381963 Voters : 251946
Poll Percentage : 65.96% Valid Votes 251946

Hissar : Number of Seats 1

8.	Achint Ram INC	66266	35.18%
7.	Hardev Sahai IND	36295	19.27%
5.	Man Singh ZP	30596	16.24%
2.	Udebir Singh CPI	14116	7.49%
3.	Chitra Devi RRP	12948	6.87%
4.	Sham Lal BJS	12453	6.61%
6.	Hardwari Lal IND	8002	4.25%
1.	Amokal Singh IND	7713	4.09%

Electors : 370693 Voters : 188389
Poll Percentage : 50.82% Valid Votes 188389

Fazilka Sirsa Number of Seats 1

6.	Atma Singh INC	75412	35.17%
4.	Gur Raj Singh SAD	55245	25.77%
1.	Balwant Singh IND	47592	22.20%
5.	Hari Chand IND	13313	6.21%
3.	Chuni Lal BJS	12672	5.91%
2.	Prithi Singh IND	10179	4.75%

Electors : 360933 Voters : 214413
Poll Percentage : 59.41% Valid Votes 214413

1957 Lok Sabha Elections

Ambala : Number of Seats 1

2.	Subhdra Joshi INC	317926	34.54%
1.	Chuni Lal INC	269991	29.33%
4.	Tek Chand Chitkara BJS	190889	20.74%
3.	Telu Ram BJS	141640	15.39%
5.	Bansi Lal PSP	0	0.00%

Electors : 788454 Voters : 920446 Poll
Percentage : 58.37% Valid Votes 920446

Kaithal : Number of Seats 1

2.	Mool Chand INC	119388	46.61%
1.	Birbal Dass BJS	50787	19.83%
3.	Ranpat Singh IND	47203	18.43%
4.	Sohan Lal SCF	38742	15.13%
5.	Vijai Singh IND	0	0.00%

Electors : 402728 Voters : 256120
Poll Percentage : 63.60% Valid Votes 256120

Rohtak : Number of Seats 1

3.	Ranbir Singh INC	104690	38.25%
1.	Dhaja Ram IND	78075	28.53%
4.	Ram Chand BJS	46144	16.86%
5.	Hari Ram SCF	29203	10.67%
2.	Piare Lal IND	15586	5.69%

Electors : 394077 Voters : 273698
Poll Percentage : 69.45% Valid Votes 273698

Jhajjar : Number of Seats 1

1.	Partap Singh CPI	148979	55.05%
2.	Ghamandi Lal Bansal INC	121658	44.95%

Electors : 422351 Voters : 270637
Poll Percentage : 64.08% Valid Votes 270637

Gurgaon : Number of Seats 1

1.	Maulana Abdul Kalam Azad INC	191221	66.68%
2.	Mool Chand BJS	95553	33.32%
3.	Taj Mohammad IND	0	0.00%

Electors : 434621 Voters : 286774
Poll Percentage : 65.98% Valid Votes 286774

Mahendergarh : Number of Seats 1

4.	Ram Krishan INC	82930	34.72%
3.	Ratan Singh IND	70615	29.57%
2.	Bikram Singh Yadva CPI	45759	19.16%
1.	Ganpat Rai BJS	39529	16.55%
5.	Manohar Lal IND	0	0.00%

Electors : 452591 Voters : 238833
Poll Percentage : 52.77% Valid Votes 238833

Hissar : Number of Seats 1

5.	Thakar Dass Bhargava INC	127059	54.16%
4.	Net Ram IND	41815	17.82%
2.	Nanak Chand IND	37968	16.18%
3.	Ram Swarup PSP	20818	8.87%
1.	Sham Lal IND	6939	2.96%

Electors : 419250 Voters : 234599
Poll Percentage : 55.96% Valid Votes 234599

Ferozepur : Number of Seats 1

1.	Iqbal Singh INC	120548	43.18%
6.	Wadhawas Ram CPI	73109	26.18%
2.	Sat Pal BJS	41702	14.94%
4.	Mast Ram PSP	20467	7.33%
3.	Fateh Singh IND	18569	6.65%
5.	Labh Singh IND	4809	1.72%

Electors : 428416 Voters : 279204
Poll Percentage : 65.17% Valid Votes 279204

1962 Lok Sabha Elections

Ambala (SC)

1.	Chuni Lal M INC	121943	46.66%
2.	Jugal Kishore M JS	86109	32.95%
3.	Telu Ram S/o Punnu Ram M REP	26852	10.27%
4.	Atma Ram M IND	19058	7.29%
5.	Telu Ram S/o Waru Ram M IND	7389	2.83%

Electors : 439952 Voters : 271449
Poll Percentage : 61.70% Valid Votes : 261351

Karnal

1.	Rameshwaranand M JS	134458	42.54%
2.	Virender M INC	121748	38.52%
3.	Prem Nath M SWA	31091	9.84%
4.	Banwari Ram M REP	22853	7.23%
5.	Lal Chand M IND	5916	1.87%

Electors : 477020 Voters : 327861
Poll Percentage : 68.73% Valid Votes : 316066

Kaithal

1.	Dev Dutt M INC	150127	43.40%
2.	Inder Singh M SWA	130524	37.73%
3.	Birbal Dass M JS	38651	11.17%
4.	Ser Singh M IND	11361	3.28%
5.	Ram Chander Singh M RRP	8023	2.32%
6.	Om Dutt M IND	7243	2.09%

Electors : 518275 Voters : 360791
Poll Percentage : 69.61% Valid Votes : 345929

Rohtak

1.	Lehri Singh M JS	155618	46.10%
2.	Randhir Singh M INC	135511	40.14%
3.	Lachhmi Narayan M IND	27881	8.26%
4.	Phul Singh M IND	18573	5.50%

Electors : 477391 Voters : 348401
Poll Percentage : 72.98% Valid Votes : 337583

Jhajjar

1.	Jagdev Singh M HLS	118667	34.11%
2.	Partap Singh Daulata M INC	111005	31.90%
3.	Sheodan Singh M IND	34032	9.78%
4.	Rampat Village Ismaila M REP	20655	5.94%
5.	Jagan Nath M IND	20433	5.87%
6.	Duli Chand M JS	17115	4.92%
7.	Taqdir Singh M IND	11342	3.26%
8.	Ram Pat Village Kapriwas M IND	7748	2.23%
9.	V. N. Kaushik M IND	6929	1.99%

Electors : 505869 Voters : 360204
Poll Percentage : 71.20% Valid Votes : 347926

Gurgaon

1.	Gajraj Singh M INC	112342	37.15%
2.	Devi Singh M IND	93924	31.06%
3.	Hardayal Devgun M JS	39305	13.00%
4.	Rahmat Khan M IND	27068	8.95%
5.	Abdul Ghani M REP	21446	7.09%
6.	Same Singh M IND	8318	2.75%

Electors : 500008 Voters : 319542
Poll Percentage : 63.91% Valid Votes : 302403

Mahendergarh

1.	Yudhvir Singh M JS	105027	33.87%
2.	Ram Kishan M INC	93768	30.24%
3.	Devi Prashan M IND	32039	10.33%
4.	Kulda Ram M IND	21189	6.83%
5.	Parmjit Kumar M SWA	16676	5.38%
6.	Rattan Singh M IND	15902	5.13%
7.	Bhartu Ram M IND	10120	3.26%
8.	Sudhan M IND	8114	2.62%
9.	Manohar Lal M IND	7269	2.34%

Electors : 527828 Voters : 321990
Poll Percentage : 61.00% Valid Votes : 310104

Hissar

1.	Mani Ram M SOC	152369	44.35%
2.	Ghamandi Lal M INC	125136	36.42%
3.	Rattan Singh M JS	24397	7.10%
4.	Dwarka Prashad M IND	16964	4.94%
5.	Bhagu M IND	14152	4.12%
6.	Balkar Singh M IND	10533	3.07%

Electors : 567814 Voters : 356615
Poll Percentage : 62.80% Valid Votes : 343551

General Electionns, 1967

Ambala (SC)

1.	S. Bhan M BJS	128003	40.47%
2.	P. Wati F INC	119303	37.72%
3.	G. Singh M IND	26928	8.51%
4.	I. Dass M IND	21117	6.68%
5.	N. Ram M IND	20918	6.61%

Electors : 459451 Voters : 329601
Poll Percentage : 71.74% Valid Votes : 316269

2. Karnal

1.	M. Ram M INC	168204	50.03%
2.	R. Nand M BJS	168001	49.97%

Electors : 463594 Voters : 350081
Poll Percentage : 75.51% Valid Votes : 336205

3. Kaithal

1.	G.L. Nanda M INC	180770	50.54%
2.	I. Singh M SWA	153760	42.99%
3.	T. Nath M IND	17345	4.85%
4.	T. Singh M IND	5816	1.63%

Electors : 484420 Voters : 372708
Poll Percentage : 76.94% Valid Votes : 357691

4. Rohtak

1.	R. Singh M INC	176258	50.26%
2.	R. Sarup M BJS	120662	34.41%
3.	B. Dass M IND	23496	6.70%
4.	S.R. Sharma M IND	8722	2.49%
5.	B. Singh M IND	7026	2.00%
6.	P. Chand M SSP	6803	1.94%
7.	M. Ram M IND	6255	1.78%
8.	J. Ram M IND	1478	0.42%

Electors : 477706 Voters : 362943
Poll Percentage : 75.98% Valid Votes : 350700

5. Jhajjar

1.	S. Singh M INC	209492	58.80%
2.	M. Parshad M IND	67401	18.92%
3.	R. Pat M CPI	27467	7.71%
4.	L. Narain M BJS	17206	4.83%
5.	D. Singh M IND	11806	3.31%
6.	M. Chand M SSP	9038	2.54%
7.	M. Ram M CPM	8899	2.50%
8.	B. Singh M IND	4978	1.40%

Electors : 501785 Voters : 367852
Poll Percentage : 73.31% Valid Votes : 356287

6. Gurgaon

1.	A. Gani M IND	88326	25.28%
2.	G. Singh M INC	87018	24.91%
3.	D.P. Shastri M BJS	70166	20.08%
4.	S. Rai M RPI	41213	11.80%
5.	G. Singh M CPM	16580	4.75%
6.	J. Rai M IND	14959	4.28%
7.	D.C. Jallan M IND	13974	4.00%
8.	J. Khan M CPI	12276	3.51%
9.	S. Kumar M IND	4882	1.40%

Electors : 527625 Voters : 369196
Poll Percentage : 69.97% Valid Votes : 349394

7. Mahendergarh

1.	G. Singh M INC	93903	29.91%
2.	M. Chand M BJS	47165	15.02%
3.	G. Dhar M RPI	29707	9.46%
4.	H. Krishna M IND	25376	8.08%
5.	M.S.A.S.M. Lal M IND	21063	6.71%
6.	K. Singh M SSP	19695	6.27%
7.	D. Karan M IND	19142	6.10%
8.	S. Singh M IND	18686	5.95%
9.	R. Singh M IND	16271	5.18%
10.	K. Ram M IND	12655	4.03%
11.	B. Dass M IND	5745	1.83%
12.	B. Dev M IND	4590	1.46%

Electors : 491115 Voters : 332233
Poll Percentage : 67.65% Valid Votes : 313998

8. Hissar

1.	R. Kishan M INC	115963	36.09%
2.	M. Ram M SSP	108784	33.86%
3.	Y. Singh M BJS	54635	17.01%
4.	K. Ram M IND	16025	4.99%
5.	M. Lal M IND	11076	3.45%
6.	R. Singh M IND	7477	2.33%
7.	R. Chander M IND	7320	2.28%

Electors : 473354 Voters : 335463
Poll Percentage : 70.87 % Valid Votes : 321280

9. Sirsa (SC)

1.	D. Singh M INC	193919	55.34%
2.	T. Singh M IND	34638	9.89%
3.	A. Singh M IND	27877	7.96%
4.	F. Chand M SSP	23653	6.75%
5.	R. Sarup M SWA	17191	4.91%
6.	D. Ram M CPI	12015	3.43%
7.	S. Ram M PSP	10905	3.11%
8.	P. Ram M IND	9151	2.61%
9.	S. Singh M IND	6859	1.96%
10.	S. Ram M IND	5153	1.47%
11.	S.Ram M IND	5127	1.46%
12.	H. Singh M IND	3907	1.12%

Electors : 507661 Voters : 365218
Poll Percentage : 71.94 % Valid Votes : 350395

General Elections, 1971

1. Ambala (SC)

1.	Ram Prakash M INC	196709	68.37%
2.	Suraj Bhan M BJS	74433	25.87%
3.	Gurbachan Singh M SAD	9413	3.27%
4.	Sohel Singh M IND	7164	2.49%

Electors : 490572 Voters : 295410
Poll Percentage : 60.22 per cent Valid Votes : 287719

2. Karnal

1.	Madho Ram M INC	152249	48.06%
2.	Rameshwara Nand M BJS	116988	36.93%
3.	R. P. Kapoor M NCO	22558	7.12%
4.	Jaikrishan Sharma M IND	7653	2.42%
5.	Iqbal Krishna M IND	7069	2.23%
6.	Jogi Ram M RPK	6449	2.04%
7.	Kashmira Singh M IND	3814	1.20%

Electors : 504480 Voters : 327638
Poll Percentage : 64.95 per cent Valid Votes : 316780

3. Kaithal

1.	Gulzari Lal Nanda M INC	155000	45.23%
2.	Inder Singh M NCO	129462	37.78%
3.	Nanu Mal M IND	18952	5.53%
4.	Bishan Singh M IND	13077	3.82%
5.	Jagjit Singh Rohloo M BKD	10995	3.21%
6.	Krishn Kumar M FBL	6604	1.93%
7.	Surta M CPM	3817	1.11%
8.	Madan Gopal Mittal M PSP	3300	0.96%
9.	Sukhwant Singh M IND	1491	0.44%

Electors : 519031 Voters : 351635
Poll Percentage : 67.75 per cent Valid Votes : 342698

4. Rohtak

1.	Mukhtiar Singh M BJS	143409	44.46%
2.	Randhir Singh M INC	138738	43.01%
3.	Bharat Singh M IND	16550	5.13%
4.	Munshi Ram M IND	11315	3.51%
5.	Bhim Singh M IND	5771	1.79%
6.	Balwan M IND	3692	1.14%
7.	Ran Singh M SUC	1592	0.49%
8.	Panna M IND	1470	0.46%

Electors : 514278 Voters : 329327
Poll Percentage : 64.04per cent Valid Votes : 322537

5. Jhajjar

1.	Sher Singh M INC	189860	52.35%
2.	Rizaq Ram M NCO	143245	39.50%
3.	Jai Ram M SUC	15985	4.41%
4.	Ram Saroop M RPK	13564	3.74%

Electors : 551818 Voters : 370363
Poll Percentage : 67.12% Valid Votes : 362654

6. Gurgaon

1.	Tayyab Hussain M INC	199333	51.48%
2.	K. Narendra M IND	131391	33.93%
3.	Mohmad Hansur Ali Khan M VHP	22979	5.93%
4.	Har Prasad Nanda M IND	13609	3.51%
5.	Sopat Rai M RPK	6781	1.75%
6.	Rama Nand M IND	2909	0.75%
7.	Roop Chand M IND	2505	0.65%
8.	Ramesh Chander M IND	2089	0.54%
9.	Mohan Lal M IND	1939	0.50%
10.	Bhajan Lal M IND	1499	0.39%
11.	Abdul Gani M IND	1196	0.31%
12.	S. P. Sharma M IND	976	0.25%

Electors : 584957 Voters : 398638
Poll Percentage : 68.15% Valid Votes : 387206

7. Mahendergarh

1.	Birender Singh M VHP	159125	46.80%
2.	Nihal Singh M INC	157226	46.24%
3.	Ramchander M IND	12098	3.56%
4.	Raj Singh M IND	6083	1.79%
5.	Ladli Prashad M PBI	3108	0.91%
6.	Santos M IND	2391	0.70%

Electors : 527551 Voters : 349098
Poll Percentage : 66.17% Valid Votes : 340031

8. Hissar

1.	Mani Ram Godara M INC	170204	53.98%
2.	Mani Ram Bagri M SSP	86510	27.44%
3.	Ram Kishan M NCO	43948	13.94%
4.	Sheo Bux Jangra M IND	6056	1.92%
5.	Mandal Singh M IND	2646	0.84%
6.	Bakhtawar Singh M IND	2398	0.76%
7.	Chhote Ram M IND	2113	0.67%
8.	Ram Singh Bedharak M RPK	1436	0.46%

Electors : 514678 Voters : 321994
Poll Percentage : 62.56% Valid Votes : 315311

9. Sirsa

1.	Dalbir Singh M INC	213610	67.26%
2.	Jagan Nath M VHP	91987	28.96%
3.	Bhagirath Dukhi M RPK	4878	1.54%
4.	Chanda Ram M IND	4485	1.41%
5.	Om Prakash M PSP	2642	0.83%

Electors : 561375 Voters : 324596
Poll Percentage : 57.82% Valid Votes : 317602

General Elections - India, 1977

1. Ambala (SC)

1.	Suraj Bhan M BLD	264590	68.34%
2.	Ram Prakash M INC	99096	25.59%
3.	Des Raj M CPI	14021	3.62%
4.	Sumer Chand M IND	9482	2.45%

Electors : 521047 Voters : 396269
Poll Percentage : 76.05% Valid Votes : 387189

2. Kurukshetra

1.	Raghbir Singh M BLD	322164	76.92%
2.	Devdutt Puri M INC	71322	17.03%
3.	Harnam Singh M CPI	11268	2.69%
4.	Bhim M IND	4875	1.16%
5.	Sardarilal M IND	3240	0.77%
6.	Nannumal M IND	2822	0.67%
7.	K. K. Toofan M IND	2656	0.63%
8.	Kartar Singh M IND	510	0.12%

Electors : 538852 Voters : 425945
Poll Percentage : 79.05% Valid Votes : 418857

3. Karnal

1.	Bhagwat Dayal M BLD	340961	81.99%
2.	Jagdish Prasad M INC	64125	15.42%
3.	Dalpat Singh M IND	6712	1.61%
4.	Surajbhan M IND	2535	0.61%
5.	Amilal Alias Prithvi Lal M IND	1504	0.36%

Electors : 556203 Voters : 422745
Poll Percentage : 76.01% Valid Votes : 415837

4. Sonepat

1.	Mukhtiar Singh M BLD	346900	80.95%
2.	Subhashni F INC	66677	15.56%
3.	Dilbag Singh M IND	7341	1.71%
4.	Sarup Singh M IND	5301	1.24%
5.	Hari Singh M IND	2305	0.54%

Electors : 597668 Voters : 434643
Poll Percentage : 72.72% Valid Votes : 428524

5. Rohtak

1.	Sher Singh M BLD	320550	81.59%
2.	Munphool Singh M INC	60905	15.50%
3.	Attar Singh M IND	5440	1.38%
4.	Balwant M SUC	3497	0.89%
5.	Chander Bhan M IND	2479	0.63%

Electors : 577990 Voters : 398627
Poll Percentage : 68.97% Valid Votes : 392871

6. Faridabad

1.	Dharam Vir Vasisht M BLD	184948	44.30%
2.	Khurshid Ahmad M IND	157615	37.75%
3.	Tayyab Hussain M INC	58079	13.91%
4.	T. B. Kamle Bhola Ji Kamle M IND	7674	1.84%
5.	Karan Singh M IND	7096	1.70%
6.	Islam Alias Islamuddin M CPM	1118	0.27%
7.	Vir Singh Dagar M IND	955	0.23%

Electors : 601224 Voters : 425700
Poll Percentage : 70.81% Valid Votes : 417485

7. Mahendergarh

1.	Manoharlal M BLD	255881	55.28%
2.	Birender Singh M VHP	192867	41.67%
3.	Agni Vesh M IND	4291	0.93%
4.	T. B. Kamle M IND	3185	0.69%
5.	Ramchander M IND	2860	0.62%
6.	K. K. Toofan M FBL	2444	0.53%
7.	Satyawan M SUC	1353	0.29%

Electors : 652913 Voters : 472459
Poll Percentage : 72.36% Valid Votes : 462881

8. Bhiwani

1.	Chandrawati F BLD	289135	67.62%
2.	Bansi Lal M INC	127893	29.91%
3.	Chhotu M IND	10556	2.47%

Electors : 590889 Voters : 435502
Poll Percentage : 73.70% Valid Votes : 427584

9. Hissar

1.	Inder Singh M BLD	322456	80.31%
2.	Jaswant Singh M INC	79072	19.69%

Electors : 553756 Voters : 409400
Poll Percentage : 73.93% Valid Votes : 401528

10. Sirsa (SC)

1.	Chandram M BLD	270861	68.44%
2.	Dalbir Singh M INC	117693	29.74%
3.	Gurnam Singh M IND	5489	1.39%
4.	Ajmer Singh M IND	1745	0.44%

Electors : 576112 Voters : 403115
Poll Percentage : 69.97% Valid Votes : 395788

General Elections - India, 1980

1. Ambala (SC)

1.	Suraj Bhan M JNP	145293	35.23%
2.	Som Nath M INC(I)	142998	34.67%
3.	Ram Prasad M JNP(S)	100931	24.47%
4.	Ramji Dass M IND	11520	2.79%
5.	Sumer Chand M IND	7160	1.74%
6.	Ranjit Singh M IND	2816	0.68%
7.	Bimla Devi F IND	1690	0.41%

Electors : 615475 Voters : 420934
Poll Percentage : 68.39% Valid Votes : 412408

2. Kurukshetra

1.	Manohar Lal M JNP(S)	159196	37.37%
2.	Bishan Singh M JNP	131267	30.82%
3.	Jagjit Singh Marwaha M INC(I)	109573	25.72%
4.	Milkhi Ram Aggarwal M IND	5484	1.29%
5.	Jagdish M IND	3801	0.89%
6.	Pratap Singh Pawaria M IND	3446	0.81%
7.	Vinod Kumar M IND	2465	0.58%
8.	Phula Ram M IND	1837	0.43%
9.	Kapoora M IND	1654	0.39%
10.	Nand Kishore Bhardwaj M FBL	1650	0.39%
11.	Ved Prakash M IND	1575	0.37%
12.	Harbial Singh Chitranjana M IND	1287	0.30%
13.	Makhan Lal M IND	1178	0.28%
14.	Raghunandan Lal Vaid M IND	900	0.21%
15.	Ishwar Chand Latka M IND	663	0.16%

Electors : 650213 Voters : 434978
Poll Percentage : 66.90% Valid Votes : 425976

3. Karnal

1.	Chiranji Lal M INC(I)	151786	35.25%
2.	Sushma Swaraj F JNP	129458	30.06%
3.	Raghbir Singh M JNP(S)	117861	27.37%
4.	Jai Singh M IND	9349	2.17%
5.	Kalawati F IND	2619	0.61%
6.	Dharam Pal S/O Surjan M IND	2420	0.56%
7.	Ram Singh M IND	2011	0.47%
8.	Surender Urf Surender Kumar M IND	1693	0.39%

9.	Nihal Chand M RRP	1480	0.34%
10.	Hukum Singh M RPK	1424	0.33%
11.	Ram Diya M IND	1221	0.28%
12.	Susheel Kumar M IND	1212	0.28%
13.	Amolak Raj M IND	1180	0.27%
14.	Laxmi Chand Chechi M IND(U)	1041	0.24%
15.	Suraj Bhan M IND	889	0.21%
16.	Jasbir Singh M IND	747	0.17%
17.	Kharaiti Lal M IND	717	0.17%
18.	Raj Roop M IND	692	0.16%
19.	Ami Lal M IND	611	0.14%
20.	Kashmir Singh M IND	544	0.13%
21.	Manphoola Urf Manphool Singh M IND	526	0.12%
22.	Dharma Pal S/O Teka Ram M IND	420	0.10%
23.	Gian Chand M IND	404	0.09%
24.	Bala Ram Urf Balak Ram M IND	330	0.08%

Electors : 667048 Voters : 439470
Poll Percentage : 65.88% Valid Votes : 430635

4. Sonepat

1.	Devi Lal M JNP(S)	255363	54.89%
2.	Randhir Singh M INC(I)	97572	20.97%
3.	Mukhtiar Singh M JNP	87344	18.77%
4.	Ishwar Singh M IND	7089	1.52%
5.	Sardar Singh M IND	3899	0.84%
6.	Feru Ram M IND	3754	0.81%
7.	Shri Ram M IND	2501	0.54%
8.	Satish Mohan M IND	2360	0.51%
9.	Ram Kishan M INC(U)	2141	0.46%
10.	Puran Mal M IND	1785	0.38%
11.	Kanwal Singh M IND	1461	0.31%

Electors : 708973 Voters : 475413
Poll Percentage : 67.06% Valid Votes : 465269

5. Rohtak

1.	Inder Vesh M JNP(S)	219004	52.13%
2.	Sher Singh M JNP	97564	23.22%
3.	Chand Ram M INC(I)	78396	18.66%
4.	Kesho Ram M IND	7425	1.77%
5.	Bharat Singh M IND	3541	0.84%
6.	Kapoor Singh M IND	3342	0.80%
7.	Shamsher Singh M IND	1726	0.41%
8.	Shiv Lal M IND	1701	0.40%
9.	Jot Ram M IND	1413	0.34%
10.	Ishwar Dass M IND	1252	0.30%
11.	Krishan Kumar M IND	1078	0.26%

12.	Ram Lal M IND	997	0.24%
13.	Satish Chand M IND	756	0.18%
14.	Nand Lal M IND	675	0.16%
15.	Ramesh Chander Gupt M IND	534	0.13%
16.	Zile Singh M IND	411	0.10%
17.	Radha Krishan Hooda M IND	325	0.08%

Electors : 690015 Voters : 430889
Poll Percentage : 62.45% Valid Votes : 420140

6. Faridabad

1.	Tayyab Hussain M INC(I)	151665	34.40%
2.	Khurshed Ahmed M JNP	151507	34.37%
3.	Dharamvir Vashist M JNP(S)	119043	27.00%
4.	Parma Nand Verma M IND	7463	1.69%
5.	Kadam Singh Sardana M IND	2881	0.65%
6.	Phool Chand Aggarwal M IND	2789	0.63%
7.	Sopat Raj Bodh M RPK	1895	0.43%
8.	Suresh Chand M IND	1686	0.38%
9.	Maulana Din Mohamed Ali M IND	1216	0.28%
10.	Ali Sher Khan Chhirklot M IND	708	0.16%

Electors : 740832 Voters : 449927
Poll Percentage : 60.73% Valid Votes : 440853

7. Mahendergarh

1.	Birender Singh M INC(I)	247238	50.71%
2.	Ram Bilas M JNP	155891	31.97%
3.	Nihal Singh M JNP(S)	73931	15.16%
4.	Chiranji Lal M IND	5443	1.12%
5.	Satyawan M SUC	1982	0.41%
6.	Manohar Shyam M IND	1973	0.40%
7.	Ganpat Ram M IND	1108	0.23%

Electors : 779222 Voters : 498745
Poll Percentage : 64.01% Valid Votes : 487566

8. Bhiwani

1.	Bansi Lal M INC(I)	194437	41.81%
2.	Balwant Rai Tayal M JNP	144366	31.05%
3.	Chandrawati F JNP(S)	99578	21.41%
4.	Bhale Ram M IND	9544	2.05%
5.	Bakhtawar Singh M IND	3045	0.65%
6.	Shiv Baksh Jangra M RPK	2850	0.61%
7.	Jagdish Chander Manju M IND	2633	0.57%
8.	Duni Chand M RRP	1494	0.32%
9.	Puran Mal M IND	1268	0.27%
10.	Ramesh M IND	1135	0.24%
11.	Ishwar Singh Yadav Sihore M IND	809	0.17%
12.	Rajender Prasad M IND	722	0.16%

13.	Balbirsingh M IND	571	0.12%
14.	Hoshiar Singh M IND	565	0.12%
15.	Manohar Lal M IND	564	0.12%
16.	Hawa Singh M IND	546	0.12%
17.	Gajraj Singh M IND	417	0.09%
18.	Ishwar Singh Devsar M IND	245	0.05%
19.	Bajrang M IND	231	0.05%

Electors : 709065 Voters : 474103
Poll Percentage : 66.86% Valid Votes : 465020

9. Hissar

1.	Mani Ram S/o Harji Ram M JNP(S)	192074	45.76%
2.	Mani Ram S/o Ramjas M INC(I)	99363	23.67%
3.	Inder Singh M JNP	93228	22.21%
4.	Parma Nand S/O Moti Ram M IND	13857	3.30%
5.	Hawa Singh M IND	5053	1.20%
6.	Munshi Ram Alias Munshi M IND	3474	0.83%
7.	Jagdish M IND	2386	0.57%
8.	Mool Shanker M IND	2156	0.51%
9.	Tek Chand M IND	1867	0.44%
10.	Henry Waldhein Sunray M IND	1503	0.36%
11.	Panna Lal M IND	1468	0.35%
12.	Banwari Lal M IND	1341	0.32%
13.	Chhatar Singh M IND	822	0.20%
14.	Randhir Singh M IND	592	0.14%
15.	Parma Nand S/O Kali Ram M IND	521	0.12%

Electors : 659166 Voters : 428928
Poll Percentage : 65.07% Valid Votes : 419705

10. Sirsa (SC)

1.	Dalbir Singh M INC(I)	153233	37.04%
2.	Phool Chand M JNP(S)	131732	31.84%
3.	Kesra Ram M JNP	96996	23.45%
4.	Phool Nath M IND	7754	1.87%
5.	Tulsi Devi F IND	7751	1.87%
6.	Tansukh Ram M IND	6451	1.56%
7.	Sham Lal M IND	2325	0.56%
8.	Baldev Singh M IND	1980	0.48%
9.	Lahore M IND	1833	0.44%
10.	Bhani Ram M RRP	1802	0.44%
11.	Buta Singh M IND	971	0.23%
12.	Hari Ram M IND	885	0.21%

Electors : 692956 Voters : 423139
Poll Percentage : 61.06% Valid Votes : 413713

General Elections - India, 1984

1. Ambala (SC)

1.	Ram Prakash M INC	283062	59.52%
2.	Suraj Bhan M BJP	105710	22.23%
3.	Desh Raj M CPI	44475	9.35%
4.	Khem Chand M LKD	15370	3.23%
5.	Amna Kumar M IND	6311	1.33%
6.	Nar Singh S/O Kalaneri M IND	3990	0.84%
7.	Nar Singh S/O Net Ram M JNP	3709	0.78%
8.	Ram Saran M IND	2557	0.54%
9.	Ram Lal M IND	2062	0.43%
10.	Gurnam M IND	1981	0.42%
11.	Dharam Paul M IND	1841	0.39%
12.	Dharam Raj M IND	1142	0.24%
13.	Sumer Chand M IND	1005	0.21%
14.	Paramjit M IND	805	0.17%
15.	Ranjeet Singh M IND	775	0.16%
16.	Shashi Bhooshan M IND	758	0.16%

Electors : 694840 Voters : 485364
Poll Percentage : 69.85% Valid Votes : 475553

2. Kurukshetra

1.	Harpal Singh M INC	275112	54.08%
2.	Manohar Lal M LKD	131836	25.92%
3.	Bishan Singh M JNP	40410	7.94%
4.	Kamla F BJP	37432	7.36%
5.	Surjeet Singh Kayshap M IND	4675	0.92%
6.	Faquiria M IND	2675	0.53%
7.	Kala F IND	1941	0.38%
8.	Babu Ram Saini M IND	1788	0.35%
9.	Ramesh Kumar M IND	1684	0.33%
10.	K.K. Toofan M IND	1496	0.29%
11.	Ram Lal Garg M IND	1479	0.29%
12.	Gurdial Singh Saini M IND	1435	0.28%
13.	Vichitra Nand M IND	1044	0.21%
14.	Sunil Kumar M IND	974	0.19%
15.	Partap Singh M IND	910	0.18%
16.	Balbir Singh M IND	894	0.18%
17.	Hukum Singh Saini M IND	889	0.17%
18.	Rakesh Kumar M IND	826	0.16%
19.	Ramji Lal M IND	798	0.16%
20.	Gian Singh Maniani M IND	414	0.08%

Electors : 727716 Voters : 516555.
Poll Percentage : 70.98% Valid Votes : 508712

3. Karnal

1.	Chiranji Lal M INC	247063	48.67%
2.	Devi Singh M ICJ	148111	29.18%
3.	Sushma Swaraj F BJP	77870	15.34%
4.	Ved Parkash M IND	9549	1.88%
5.	Darshan Singh M IND	2482	0.49%
6.	Kashmira Singh M IND	2458	0.48%
7.	Ajit Singh M JNP	2279	0.45%
8.	Reet Mohan M IND	1984	0.39%
9.	Gaje Singh M IND	1372	0.27%
10.	Bhim Raj M IND	1322	0.26%
11.	Gurnam Singh M IND	1100	0.22%
12.	Rameshwar M IND	761	0.15%
13.	Harbhagwan M IND	757	0.15%
14.	Sheetal Singh Rawal M IND	744	0.15%
15.	Sher Singh M IND	736	0.15%
16.	Kalawati F IND	718	0.14%
17.	Ram Diya M IND	675	0.13%
18.	Om Prakash M IND	653	0.13%
19.	Gurucharan M IND	625	0.12%
20.	Dalbir Singh M IND	620	0.12%
21.	Dalip Singh M IND	618	0.12%
22.	Ram Singh M IND	579	0.11%
23.	Ram Bhaj M IND	546	0.11%
24.	Mahabir Singh M IND	511	0.10%
25.	Prem Chand M IND	480	0.09%
26.	Jasbir Kaur F IND	477	0.09%
27.	Zile Singh M IND	449	0.09%
28.	Amar Singh M IND	419	0.08%
29.	Parbati F IND	384	0.08%
30.	Bhim Sain Batra M IND	373	0.07%
31.	Jeeta M IND	356	0.07%
32.	Sushil Kumar Aggarwal M IND	328	0.06%
33.	Prithvi Singh M IND	187	0.04%

Electors : 746675 Voters : 516886
Poll Percentage : 69.23% Valid Votes : 507586

4. Sonepat

1.	Dharam Pal Singh M INC	243491	48.54%
2.	Devi Lal M LKD	240550	47.95%
3.	Nafe Singh M JNP	3920	0.78%
4.	Rajender Kumar Mittal M IND	1780	0.35%
5.	Hamid M IND	1528	0.30%
6.	Chattar Singh M IND	1398	0.28%
7.	Raghbir Singh M IND	1182	0.24%

8.	Omparkash Shorewala M IND	1155	0.23%
9.	Omparkash Kagra M IND	1080	0.22%
10.	Raghubir Nath M IND	909	0.18%
11.	Bhupan M IND	895	0.18%
12.	Kanwal Singh Bedharak M IND	830	0.17%
13.	Omparkash M IND	817	0.16%
14.	Suraj Bhan M IND	793	0.16%
15.	Jai Lal M IND	613	0.12%
16.	Narender Singh M IND	383	0.08%
17.	Bhale Ram Chhilar M IND	334	0.07%

Electors : 782505 Voters : 509262
Poll Percentage : 65.08% Valid Votes : 501658

5. Rohtak

1.	Hardwari Lal M INC	216294	49.27%
2.	Sarup Singh M LKD	185363	42.22%
3.	Hukum Chand Goel M BJP	22207	5.06%
4.	Nand Lal Bansal M IND	2618	0.60%
5.	Sumer Singh M IND	2456	0.56%
6.	Dharam Vir M IND	1702	0.39%
7.	Dharam Pal Jindal M IND	1410	0.32%
8.	Jai Pal M IND	1083	0.25%
9.	Richhpal M IND	997	0.23%
10.	Jai Bhagwan M IND	709	0.16%
11.	Ram Kunwar M IND	666	0.15%
12.	Nirmal Kumar Jain M IND	640	0.15%
13.	Duli Chand M IND	618	0.14%
14.	Hawa Singh Malik M IND	571	0.13%
15.	Umed M IND	447	0.10%
16.	Ram Narain M IND	421	0.10%
17.	Chittar Sain M IND	336	0.08%
18.	Ram Singh M IND	272	0.06%
19.	Mohan Lal M IND	227	0.05%

Electors : 742030 Voters : 446881
Poll Percentage : 60.22% Valid Votes : 439037

6. Faridabad

1.	Rahim Khan M INC	285214	54.01%
2.	Tayyab Hussain M ICJ	150843	28.57%
3.	Swami Inder Vesh M IND	32761	6.20%
4.	Cheti Lal Verma M IND	32228	6.10%
5.	Krishan Kumar Gupta M IND	9707	1.84%
6.	Keshav Prashad Sharma M IND	2038	0.39%
7.	Prem Pal Anand M IND	1627	0.31%

8. Satish Sharma M IND	1485	0.28%
9. Vijay Kumar M IND	1417	0.27%
10. Fatte M IND	1406	0.27%
11. Ashok Kumar Bansal M IND	1386	0.26%
12. Ishwar Parsad M IND	1121	0.21%
13. Sanjay M IND	1103	0.21%
14. Chandgi Ram M IND	995	0.19%
15. Umrao Singh M IND	956	0.18%
16. Phool Chand Aggarwal M IND	890	0.17%
17. Bihari Lal M IND	798	0.15%
18. Jitender Kumar M IND	784	0.15%
19. Banwari Lal M IND	532	0.10%
20. Dharam Pal M IND	413	0.08%
21. Parma Nand Verma M IND	346	0.07%

Electors : 869828 Voters : 537552
Poll Percentage : 61.80% Valid Votes : 528050

7. Mahendergarh

1. Birender Singh M INC	360971	60.68%
2. Ram Bilas M BJP	130757	21.98%
3. Nihal Singh M ICJ	73223	12.31%
4. Raghu Yadav M JNP	5458	0.92%
5. Bimla Devi F IND	4967	0.83%
6. Budh Ram M IND	3633	0.61%
7. Om Wati F IND	3280	0.55%
8. Chander Singh M IND	2166	0.36%
9. Mohan Lal Josh M IND	1826	0.31%
10. Rajinder M IND	1813	0.30%
11. Megh Singh M IND	1274	0.21%
12. Jeewan Ram M IND	1202	0.20%
13. Mam Chand M IND	1072	0.18%
14. Har Lal M IND	849	0.14%
15. Budhi Ram M IND	636	0.11%
16. Kuldeep Singh Rao M IND	625	0.11%
17. Uttam Singh M IND	584	0.10%
18. Narvir Singh M IND	556	0.09%

Electors : 855878 Voters : 606971
Poll Percentage : 70.92% Valid Votes : 594892

8. Bhiwani

1. Bansi Lal M INC	347226	66.00%
2. Jai Narain M ICJ	160149	30.44%
3. Puran Mal M IND	3670	0.70%
4. Pardeep Kumar M IND	2395	0.46%
5. Bishan Lal M IND	2330	0.44%

6. Bakhtawar M IND	1453	0.28%
7. Dhyan Chand M IND	1252	0.24%
8. Man Singh M IND	1190	0.23%
9. Jaimal Singh M IND	1111	0.21%
10. Manohar Lal M IND	1037	0.20%
11. Jagdish M IND	722	0.14%
12. Krishan Kumar M IND	705	0.13%
13. Chaman Lal M IND	689	0.13%
14. Dharma M IND	610	0.12%
15. Subhash Chander M IND	590	0.11%
16. Sat Narain M IND	523	0.10%
17. Mohar Singh A/O Kohar M IND	411	0.08%

Electors : 782290 Voters : 535634
Poll Percentage : 68.47% Valid Votes : 526063

9. Hissar

1. Birender Singh M INC	251367	51.98%
2. Om Parkash M LKD	200161	41.39%
3. Balwant Rai Tayal M JNP	11217	2.32%
4. Sumitra Devi F IND	3248	0.67%
5. Trilok Saini M IND	2862	0.59%
6. Bahadur Singh Fauji M IND	2648	0.55%
7. Ram Kishan M IND	2437	0.50%
8. Dharam Vir Mandan M IND	2088	0.43%
9. Narain Dass Dhamija M IND	1829	0.38%
10. Jawahar Lal M IND	1299	0.27%
11. Rajinder Kumar Gupta M IND	1013	0.21%
12. Harbans Kaur F IND	775	0.16%
13. Kanahia Lal Verma M IND	702	0.15%
14. Mahinder Singh Pannu M IND	630	0.13%
15. Atam Parkash Kukreja M IND	511	0.11%
16. Mool Shankar Bhayana M IND	436	0.09%
17. Bimal Rai M IND	334	0.07%

Electors : 737467 Voters : 491750
Poll Percentage : 66.68% Valid Votes : 483557

10. Sirsa (SC)

1. Dalbir Singh M INC	277855	54.66%
2. Mani Ram M LKD	195923	38.54%
3. Jaswant Singh M BJP	8471	1.67%
4. Ram Sarup M JNP	6115	1.20%
5. Jogi Ram M IND	3844	0.76%
6. Sahab Ram M IND	2829	0.56%
7. Ram Kumar M IND	2003	0.39%
8. Boota Singh M IND	1269	0.25%

9.	Jagdish M IND	1168	0.23%
10.	Mohinder M IND	1163	0.23%
11.	Dhana Ram M IND	963	0.19%
12.	Raid Chand M IND	905	0.18%
13.	Lal Singh M IND	853	0.17%
14.	Ram Singh M IND	718	0.14%
15.	Anil Kumar M IND	657	0.13%
16.	Darbara Singh M IND	652	0.13%
17.	Sawarn Singh M IND	634	0.12%
18.	Gurdev Singh M IND	536	0.11%
19.	Dalip Singh M IND	468	0.09%
20.	Phool Singh M IND	436	0.09%
21.	Gurdial Singh M IND	434	0.09%
22.	Tara Chand M IND	403	0.08%

Electors : 786717 Voters : 516944
Poll Percentage : 65.71% Valid Votes : 508299

General Elections - India, 1989

1. Ambala (SC)

1.	Ram Parkash M INC	264074	46.24%
2.	Suraj Bhan M BJP	241425	42.27%
3.	Aman Kumar M BSP	45389	7.95%
4.	Nar Singh S/O Neta Ram M IND	7036	1.23%
5.	Nar Singh S/O Kaldori M Ddp	5056	0.89%
6.	Mukh Ram M IND	2280	0.40%
7.	Sumer Chand Yatri M LKD (B)	2088	0.37%
8.	Kartar Chand M IND	2014	0.35%
9.	Nathi Ram M IND	1767	0.31%

Electors : 899299 Voters : 581089
Poll Percentage : 64.62% Valid Votes : 571129

2. Kurukshetra

1.	Gurdial Singh Saini M JD	301640	49.72%
2.	Harpal Singh M INC	263452	43.43%
3.	Gian Singh M JNP (Jp)	12281	2.02%
4.	Harbans Singh M BSP	8912	1.47%
5.	Fazuir Chand M IND	2868	0.47%
6.	Ramji Lal M IND	2819	0.46%
7.	Ram Lal M IND	2276	0.38%
8.	Rampal M IND	1506	0.25%
9.	Gurdev Singh Saini M IND	1405	0.23%
10.	Lachman Dass M DDP	1233	0.20%
11.	Raghubir M IND	858	0.14%
12.	Jitender M IND	703	0.12%
13.	Lal Singh Saini M LKD (B)	663	0.11%
14.	Devidayal M IND	616	0.10%
15.	Surinder Kumar M IND	578	0.10%
16.	Jagdish Parsad M IND	534	0.09%
17.	Ramesh Gupta M IND	512	0.08%
18.	Partap Singh M IND	505	0.08%
19.	Ram Singh M IND	460	0.08%
20.	Karam Chand M IND	436	0.07%
21.	Angrej M IND	370	0.06%
22.	Mamchand M IND	345	0.06%
23.	Sumer Chand Yatri M IND	330	0.05%
24.	Amar Nath M IND	321	0.05%
25.	Durga Parsad M IND	289	0.05%
26.	Gulu Ram M IND	278	0.05%
27.	Manjit Singh M IND	247	0.04%
28.	Mahender Singh M IND	220	0.04%

Electors : 915880 Voters : 615902
Poll Percentage : 67.25% Valid Votes : 606657

3. Karnal

1.	Chiranjit Lal M INC	274465	46.11%
2.	Sushma Swaraj F BJP	265792	44.65%
3.	Raghbir Singh M CPI	15161	2.55%
4.	Mai Lal M BSP	7631	1.28%
5.	Bir Singh M IND	5876	0.99%
6.	Bhim Ram Singla M DDP	5064	0.85%
7.	Tejbir M IND	2433	0.41%
8.	M.C.Sharma M IND	2081	0.35%
9.	Raghbir M IND	1689	0.28%
10.	Lal Chand M IND	1468	0.25%
11.	Kausal Pal M JNP (Jp)	1444	0.24%
12.	Chand Ram M RPI	1382	0.23%
13.	Raj Pal M IND	1245	0.21%
14.	Jai Bhagwan Prajapat M IND	984	0.17%
15.	Samsher Singh M IND	746	0.13%
16.	Raj Bala F IND	717	0.12%
17.	Man Singh Saini M IND	714	0.12%
18.	Jani Bhagwan M IND	702	0.12%
19.	Ram Sharma M IND	607	0.10%
21.	Jogi Ram M IND	598	0.10%
20.	Isham Singh M IND	593	0.10%
22.	Dalipe M IND	573	0.10%
23.	Mohammed Yamin M IND	476	0.08%
24.	Surinder Kumar M IND	471	0.08%
25.	Naresh Kumar Gupta M IND	464	0.08%
26.	Devi Dayal M IND	385	0.06%
27.	Amar Singh Johri M IND	338	0.06%
28.	Parkash Man Parmodi M IND	273	0.05%
29.	Amar Jeet Manocha M IND	248	0.04%
30.	Sumer Chand M IND	208	0.03%
31.	Madan Mohan M IND	198	0.03%
32.	Kulwant Singh M IND	159	0.03%
33.	Satwant Singh M IND	113	0.02%

Electors : 946620 Voters : 606237
Poll Percentage : 64.04% Valid Votes : 595298

4. Sonepat

1.	Kapil Dev M JD	308291	50.95%
2.	Dharampal Singh M INC	237287	39.21%
3.	Kitab Singh M IND	29251	4.83%
4.	Jagdish S/o Tek Ram M IND	6610	1.09%
5.	Jagdish S/o Hukam M IND	3631	0.60%
6.	Rohtash Singh M IND	3236	0.53%
7.	Shyaml Chand M IND	3163	0.52%

8.	Yogesh Kumar M BSP	2190	0.36%
9.	Rajender Singh S/Oh. Singh M DDP	1446	0.24%
10.	Om Rani F IND	1406	0.23%
11.	Anang Pal M IND	1363	0.23%
12.	Om Parkash M LKD (B)	880	0.15%
13.	Ranbir M IND	854	0.14%
14.	Bhim Singh M IND	746	0.12%
15.	Hira Lal M IND	661	0.11%
16.	Kanwal Singh M IND	652	0.11%
17.	Rajender Singh S/o Amar M IND	556	0.09%
18.	Kunwar Kanwal Singh M IND	502	0.08%
19.	Ranvir Singh M IND	480	0.08%
20.	Ram Kishan S/o L.Chand M IND	461	0.08%
21.	Jai Singh M IND	434	0.07%
22.	Anil Ankush M IND	389	0.06%
23.	Chand Ram M IND	331	0.05%
24.	Ram Kishan S/o Mauji M IND	302	0.05%

Electors : 943188 Voters : 615411
Poll Percentage : 65.25% Valid Votes : 605122

5. Rohtak

1.	Devi Lal M JD	390243	64.21%
2.	Hardwari Lal M INC	201238	33.11%
3.	Krishan M IND	2426	0.40%
4.	Mohinder Singh M JNP (Jp)	2047	0.34%
5.	Zile Singh M BSP	1998	0.33%
6.	Krishan M IND	1835	0.30%
7.	Bhale Ram M IND	1137	0.19%
8.	Kartar M IND	778	0.13%
9.	Balbir Singh S/o Prithi M DDP	692	0.11%
10.	Subhash Chand M IND	683	0.11%
11.	Dharam Chand M IND	644	0.11%
12.	Tarif Singh M IND	514	0.08%
13.	Surender Dutt M IND	470	0.08%
14.	Satpal M IND	466	0.08%
15.	Jaipal M IND	462	0.08%
16.	Roshan Lal M IND	368	0.06%
17.	Balbir Singh S/o Molar M IND	337	0.06%
18.	Hawa Singh M IND	272	0.04%
19.	Suresh Chand M IND	249	0.04%
20.	Prem Kumar M IND	231	0.04%
21.	Subhash Chander M IND	224	0.04%
22.	Ved Parkash Vats M IND	173	0.03%
23.	Kuldeep M IND	145	0.02%
24.	Laxmi Narain M IND	131	0.02%

Electors : 908794 Voters : 619262
Poll Percentage : 68.14% Valid Votes : 607763

6. Faridabad

1.	Bhajan Lal M INC	404646	57.81%
2.	Khursid Ahmad Chaudhry M JD	273419	39.06%
3.	Shiv Narian M BSP	6723	0.96%
4.	Raj Singh M IND	4301	0.61%
5.	Phool Singh M IND	2472	0.35%
6.	Mani Ram Sharma M IND	1059	0.15%
7.	Ram Iqbal Parsad M DDP	1045	0.15%
8.	Jai Pal Singh M IND	1001	0.14%
9.	Kanwal Singh M PDL	918	0.13%
10.	Phool Chand Aggarwal M IND	700	0.10%
11.	Mir Singh M IND	665	0.10%
12.	Nihal M LKD (B)	654	0.09%
13.	Aditya Vesh M IND	623	0.09%
14.	Dayala M IND	419	0.06%
15.	Anil Kumar Gupta M IND	416	0.06%
16.	V.J.Dayal M IND	323	0.05%
17.	Prehlad Singh M IND	308	0.04%
18.	Ramji Lal M IND	240	0.03%

Electors : 1131257 Voters : 710487
Poll Percentage : 62.81% Valid Votes : 699932

7. Mahendergarh

1.	Birender Singh M JD	304805	47.83%
2.	Ram Singh M INC	301295	47.28%
3.	Raender Singh M JNP (Jp)	7159	1.12%
4.	Ghanshyam M IND	4798	0.75%
5.	Daya Ram M DDP	3875	0.61%
6.	Shiv Kumar M IND	2655	0.42%
7.	Kishan Lal M IND	2350	0.37%
8.	Ratan Lal M SUC	2232	0.35%
9.	Rati Ram M IND	1192	0.19%
10.	Ram Kishore M IND	1079	0.17%
11.	Budh Ram M IND	1034	0.16%
12.	Mahavir M IND	910	0.14%
13.	Chiranji M IND	844	0.13%
14.	Jaswant M IND	798	0.13%
15.	Mahabir M LKD (B)	646	0.10%
16.	Bhoop Singh M IND	617	0.10%
17.	Chaturbhuj Dixit M IND	594	0.09%
18.	Sudarshan Kumar M IND	320	0.05%

Electors : 1057536 Voters : 650168
Poll Percentage : 61.48% Valid Votes : 637203

8. Bhiwani

1.	Bansi Lal M INC	357625	60.13%
2.	Dharambir M JD	200295	33.67%
3.	Rajender M BSP	14609	2.46%
4.	Mahesh M IND	3606	0.61%
5.	Karambir Singh M IND	1218	0.20%
6.	Bajrang Lal M IND	926	0.16%
7.	Ram Mehar M IND	909	0.15%
8.	Risal Singh M IND	636	0.11%
9.	Balbir M IND	608	0.10%
10.	Satya Narain M IND	573	0.10%
11.	Bhalle Ram Paria M IND	554	0.09%
12.	Chhabila Ram M IND	509	0.09%
13.	Prem Singh M IND	491	0.08%
14.	Ishwar Singh M IND	431	0.07%
15.	Ram Singh M IND	430	0.07%
16.	Diwan Singh M IND	423	0.07%
17.	Makhan M IND	385	0.06%
18.	Ranbir Singh M IND	355	0.06%
19.	Ramnij Dass M IND	323	0.05%
20.	Bijender Singh M IND	318	0.05%
21.	Gokal Chand M IND	311	0.05%
22.	Dharma Pal M IND	299	0.05%
23.	Raj Kumar M IND	294	0.05%
24.	Surender Kumar M IND	288	0.05%
25.	Brij Pal M IND	279	0.05%
26.	Atma Ram M IND	267	0.04%
27.	Ranbir M IND	263	0.04%
28.	Jagdish M IND	231	0.04%
29.	Man Singh M IND	229	0.04%
30.	Ram Avtar M IND	208	0.03%
31.	Ranjit Singh M IND	195	0.03%
32.	Jagparvesh M IND	185	0.03%
33.	Shamsher Singh M IND	180	0.03%
34.	Chander Bhan M IND	179	0.03%
35.	Dharamvir M IND	179	0.03%
36.	Dharamender M IND	179	0.03%
37.	Phool Singh M IND	163	0.03%
38.	Man Singh M DDP	143	0.02%
39.	Ramswarup M IND	136	0.02%
40.	Surender Singh M IND	128	0.02%
41.	Om Parkash M IND	126	0.02%
42.	Assa Nand M IND	124	0.02%
43.	Uda Singh M IND	119	0.02%
44.	Ram Kumar M IND	115	0.02%
45.	Mohar Singh M IND	110	0.02%
46.	Tara Chand M IND	108	0.02%
47.	Jalle M IND	107	0.02%

48.	Rajender M IND	105	0.02%
49.	Ram Bhagat M IND	104	0.02%
50.	Azad M IND	99	0.02%
51.	Pawan Kumar M IND	98	0.02%
52.	Sudhan Singh M IND	98	0.02%
53.	Ram Niwas M IND	96	0.02%
54.	Bhoop M IND	95	0.02%
55.	Jaivir M IND	95	0.02%
56.	Dilbagh M IND	93	0.02%
57.	Suresh Kumar M IND	92	0.02%
58.	Roshan Lal M IND	87	0.01%
59.	Mange Ram M IND	86	0.01%
60.	Ram Partap M IND	86	0.01%
61.	Om Parkash M IND	83	0.01%
62.	Nihal Singh M IND	83	0.01%
63.	Puran Lal M IND	78	0.01%
64.	Dalbir M IND	76	0.01%
65.	Laxman M IND	76	0.01%
66.	Suraj Bhan M IND	73	0.01%
67.	Parkash M IND	70	0.01%
68.	Phool Kumar M IND	70	0.01%
69.	Diwan Singh M IND	69	0.01%
70.	Ramphal M IND	68	0.01%
71.	Prithvi Singh M IND	68	0.01%
72.	Ram Mehar M IND	66	0.01%
73.	Jagwant M IND	65	0.01%
74.	Lajpat M IND	64	0.01%
75.	Shishpal M IND	64	0.01%
76.	Satbir Bhardwaj M IND	63	0.01%
77.	Gurjagat Singh M IND	61	0.01%
78.	Deep Chand M IND	60	0.01%
79.	Vijender M IND	60	0.01%
80.	Surender M IND	60	0.01%
81.	Jaikaran M IND	59	0.01%
82.	Bhoop Singh M IND	58	0.01%
83.	Madan Singh M IND	58	0.01%
84.	Ishwar M IND	57	0.01%
85.	Devender M IND	57	0.01%
86.	Ishwar M IND	57	0.01%
87.	Om Parkash M IND	56	0.01%
88.	Dhoop Singh M IND	56	0.01%
89.	Hawa Singh M IND	55	0.01%
90.	Nihal Singh M IND	54	0.01%
91.	Mukhtayar Singh M IND	54	0.01%
92.	Ramphal M IND	54	0.01%
93.	Krishan M IND	53	0.01%
94.	Rajbir M IND	53	0.01%
95.	Mahender Singh M IND	51	0.01%
96.	Ram Niwas M IND	48	0.01%

97. Harchand M IND	48	0.01%
99. Hawa Singh M IND	48	0.01%
96. Umed Singh M IND	48	0.01%
100. Sudershanpal M IND	47	0.01%
101. Om Parkash M IND	45	0.01%
102. Hawa Singh M IND	45	0.01%
103. Puran M IND	44	0.01%
104. Rajbir M IND	42	0.01%
105. Sumer M IND	42	0.01%
106. Jaivir M IND	40	0.01%
107. Jaivir M IND	38	0.01%
108. Krishan M IND	37	0.01%
109. Rajbir M IND	37	0.01%
110. Krishan Kumar M IND	36	0.01%
111. Mahinder Singh M IND	36	0.01%
112. Sajjan Singh M IND	36	0.01%
113. Ram Singh M IND	35	0.01%
114. Ved Parkash M IND	35	0.01%
115. Sumer M IND	34	0.01%
116. Mahedner M IND	31	0.01%
117. Swaraj Singh M IND	30	0.01%
118. Dalbir M IND	28	0.00%
119. Rajbir M IND	26	0.00%
120. Om Parkash M IND	22	0.00%
121. Suraj Bhan M IND	19	0.00%
122. Dalbir M IND	11	0.00%

Electors : 944629 Voters : 604350
Poll Percentage : 63.98% Valid Votes : 594800

9. Hissar

1. Jai Parkash M JD	291073	50.72%
2. Virender Singh M INC	246394	42.94%
3. Ram Kumar M IND	11059	1.93%
4. Jagan Nath M BSP	3074	0.54%
5. Partap M IND	2732	0.48%
6. Bala Singh M IND	2623	0.46%
7. Satbir Singh M IND	1987	0.35%
8. Babu Lal M IND	1797	0.31%
9. Ajmer Singh M IND	1403	0.24%
10. Zile Singh M IND	1169	0.20%
11. Trilok Singh M IND	1160	0.20%
12. Jogi Ram M IND	1075	0.19%
13. Abhe Ram M IND	865	0.15%
14. Virender M IND	842	0.15%
15. Mahender M DDP	830	0.14%
16. Anil Kumar M IND	820	0.14%
17. Nafe Singh M IND	567	0.10%

18.	Ram Niwas M IND	545	0.09%
19.	Dharam Pal M IND	532	0.09%
20.	Balwant M IND	502	0.09%
21.	Raj Kumar M IND	377	0.07%
22.	Ram Phal S/o Gokal M IND	310	0.05%
23.	Parkash Chand M IND	309	0.05%
24.	Ram Phalko Devilal M IND	245	0.04%
25.	Bhale Ram M IND	240	0.04%
26.	Raghubir Singh M IND	238	0.04%
27.	Munshi M IND	215	0.04%
28.	Shivbaksh Jangra M IND	201	0.04%
29.	Jagdev M IND	192	0.03%
30.	Ved Parkash M IND	179	0.03%
31.	Sher Singh M IND	154	0.03%
32.	Sat Parkash M IND	136	0.02%

Electors : 912985 Voters : 583150
Poll Percentage : 63.87% Valid Votes : 573845

10. Sirsa (SC)

1.	Het Ram M JD	304768	49.80%
2.	Mani Ram M INC	266355	43.52%
3.	Gopi Ram M JNP (Jp)	18048	2.95%
4.	Surjan Ram M BSP	8638	1.41%
5.	Gokal M IND	6037	0.99%
6.	Joginder Singh M DDP	1619	0.26%
7.	Milkh Raj M IND	901	0.15%
8.	Phali Ram M IND	860	0.14%
9.	Jogi Ram M IND	817	0.13%
10.	Devi Lal M IND	715	0.12%
11.	Ranjit M IND	683	0.11%
12.	Thakar Ram M IND	610	0.10%
13.	Upas Kumar M IND	588	0.10%
14.	Sham Lal M IND	492	0.08%
15.	Kartar M IND	470	0.08%
16.	Amar Singh M IND	422	0.07%

Electors : 976500 Voters : 621055
Poll Percentage : 63.60% Valid Votes : 612023

General Elections - India, 1991

1. Ambala (SC)

1.	Ram Prakash M INC	196406	31.03%
2.	Suraj Bhan M BJP	124464	19.66%
3.	Chand Ram M JP	112028	17.70%
4.	Aman Kumar M BSP	111353	17.59%
5.	Shyam Chand M JD	56138	8.87%
6.	Shakuntala (W) F IND	11309	1.79%
7.	Sadhu Ram M IND	10872	1.72%
8.	Kaka Ram Samplay M IND	4483	0.71%
9.	Nar Singh M DDP	3516	0.56%
10.	Sumer Chand Yatri M RPK	1325	0.21%
11.	Lal Singh M IND	1132	0.18%

Electors : 912390 Voters : 653526
Poll Percentage : 71.63% Valid Votes : 633026

2. Kurukshetra

1.	Tara Singh M INC	212783	33.44%
2.	Shyam Singh M JP	182758	28.72%
3.	Gurdial Singh M JD	135117	21.24%
4.	Shiv Partap Bajaj M BJP	79653	12.52%
5.	Vishav Nath M IND	5976	0.94%
6.	Lachhman Dass M DDP	4520	0.71%
7.	Chanda M IND	4062	0.64%
8.	Partap Singh M IND	3150	0.50%
9.	Jasbir Singh M IND	2410	0.38%
10.	Krishna Dutt M IND	1705	0.27%
11.	Roshan Lal M IND	1364	0.21%
12.	Prem Nath M IND	1203	0.19%
13.	Harish Gargi M IND	1039	0.16%
14.	Ram Pal M IND	553	0.09%

Electors : 927976 Voters : 656693
Poll Percentage : 70.77% Valid Votes : 636293

3. Karnal

1.	Chiranji Lal Sharma M INC	200770	32.17%
2.	Chasham Pal Singh M JD	145598	23.33%
3.	Ranjit M JP	132444	21.22%
4.	Fateh Chand Vij M BJP	81780	13.10%
5.	M.C. Kaushik M IND	13482	2.16%
6.	Kanwal Singh Bedharak M IND	9104	1.46%

7.	Krishan Chand Rajput M IND	8294	1.33%
8.	Phool Singh Kambooj M IND	5565	0.89%
9.	Devinder Singh Mann M LKD	4527	0.73%
10.	Sunhera Ram M IND	4468	0.72%
11.	Zila Singh M IND	3754	0.60%
12.	Param Vir Chauhan M IND	3072	0.49%
13.	Dalel Singh M JKMP	1993	0.32%
14.	Mahabir M IND	1451	0.23%
15.	Harish Kumar M IND	1171	0.19%
16.	Bhim Raj M DDP	1162	0.19%
17.	Kalawati (W) F IND	1122	0.18%
18.	Raj Kumar M IND	1037	0.17%
19.	Jogi Ram M IND	936	0.15%
20.	Pawan Kumar M IND	895	0.14%
21.	Shamsher Singh M IND	754	0.12%
22.	Ravinder Kumar Sharma M IND	680	0.11%

Electors : 950987 Voters : 647701
Poll Percentage : 68.11% Valid Votes : 624059

4. Sonepat

1.	Dharampal Singh M INC	247572	42.08%
2.	Kapil Dev M JP	202770	34.46%
3.	Rajender M JD	74011	12.58%
4.	Dharamvir M BJP	29773	5.06%
5.	Mahender Kaur (W) F JKMP	15870	2.70%
6.	Jai Singh M IND	6036	1.03%
7.	Pushpa (W) F IND	2858	0.49%
8.	Inderjeet M IND	2689	0.46%
9.	Ranbir Singh M IND	2286	0.39%
10.	Dalel M DDP	2264	0.38%
11.	Kanwal Singh Bedharak M PDL	2213	0.38%

Electors : 949007 Voters : 604686
Poll Percentage : 63.72% Valid Votes : 588342

5. Rohtak

1.	Bhupender Singh M INC	241235	44.00%
2.	Devi Lal M JP	210662	38.43%
3.	Inder Singh M HVP	43804	7.99%
4.	Raj Kumar M BJP	23802	4.34%
5.	Jai Pal M IND	13348	2.43%
6.	Jai Parkash M IND	1929	0.35%
7.	Yash Aggarwal M IND	1628	0.30%
8.	Balbir M DDP	1382	0.25%
9.	Narender Singh M IND	1185	0.22%

10.	Rohtas M IND	1152	0.21%
11.	Krishan M RKD	1125	0.21%
12.	Joginder S. Alias Dharti Pakar M IND	900	0.16%
13.	Birbal M IND	874	0.16%
14.	Ram Kanwar M IND	554	0.10%
15.	Bhajan Lal M IND	539	0.10%
16.	Karamvir M IND	532	0.10%
17.	Lalit Kumar M IND	465	0.08%
18.	Ramesh Kumar M IND	463	0.08%
19.	Sita Ram M IND	414	0.08%
20.	Bhale Ram M IND	406	0.07%
21.	Hawa Singh M IND	399	0.07%
22.	Prem Kumar M IND	367	0.07%
23.	Satbir M IND	298	0.05%
24.	Hari Singh M IND	296	0.05%
25.	Raghubir Singh M IND	256	0.05%
26.	Ram Bhoola M IND	208	0.04%

Electors : 919868 Voters : 564886
Poll Percentage : 61.41% Valid Votes : 548223

6. Faridabad

1.	Avtar Singh Bhadana M INC	268965	38.84%
2.	Khurshid Ahmed M JD	217443	31.40%
3.	Brahma Singh Tanwar M BJP	103403	14.93%
4.	Cheti Lal Verma M JP	70972	10.25%
5.	Ved Narayan Tripathi M IND	10278	1.48%
6.	Banwari Lal M LKD	4297	0.62%
7.	Jagdish M IND	3224	0.47%
8.	Ayub Khan Peer Jada M IND	1896	0.27%
9.	Om Parkash M IND	1745	0.25%
10.	Majid M IND	1487	0.21%
11.	Maulana Sher Mohammed M IND	1356	0.20%
12.	M.S. Rakesh M DDP	1226	0.18%
13.	Giyan Chand Bhadana M IND	1136	0.16%
14.	Vijender M HMS	1053	0.15%
15.	Hakimuddin M IND	840	0.12%
16.	Arjun M IND	784	0.11%
17.	Phool Chand Aggarwal M IND	711	0.10%
18.	Jhangi Ram M IND	509	0.07%
19.	Nawal Dagar M IND	371	0.05%
20.	Prem Chand Arya M IND	317	0.05%
21.	Prem Chand Premi M IND	183	0.03%
22.	Shree Chand Gupta M IND	153	0.02%
23.	Dhansi Ram Garg M IND	118	0.02%

Electors : 1141760 Voters : 715602
Poll Percentage : 62.68% Valid Votes : 692467

7. Mahendergarh

1.	Ram Singh M INC	241808	38.58%
2.	Birender Singh M JP	169820	27.09%
3.	Raghu Yadav M SJJP	70368	11.23%
4.	M.L. Yadav M BJP	60342	9.63%
5.	Naresh M HVP	46134	7.36%
6.	Suresh (W) F IND	7492	1.20%
7.	Data Ram M IND	6418	1.02%
8.	Jaswant Singh M IND	4920	0.78%
9.	Jagat Singh M IND	4253	0.68%
10.	Daya Ram M DDP	3674	0.59%
11.	Raghubir Singh M IND	2138	0.34%
12.	Naval Singh M IND	2131	0.34%
13.	Bhagat Singh M JKMP	1488	0.24%
14.	Mam Chand M IND	1135	0.18%
15.	Gugan Singh M IND	1118	0.18%
16.	Ram Chander M FBL	987	0.16%
17.	Ved Krishan M IND	920	0.15%
18.	Madhu Sudan M IND	827	0.13%
19.	Mahavir M IND	826	0.13%

Electors : 1063934 Voters : 647021
Poll Percentage : 60.81% Valid Votes : 626799

8. Bhiwani

1.	Jangbir Singh M HVP	210090	36.25%
2.	Jai Narain M INC	179525	30.98%
3.	Hukum Singh M JP	100288	17.31%
4.	Ramesh Chander M BJP	48570	8.38%
5.	Budh Ram M DDP	4305	0.74%
6.	Ghan Shyam M IND	4179	0.72%
7.	Nathu Ram M IND	4042	0.70%
8.	Harpal Singh M IND	3328	0.57%
9.	Tara Chand M IND	1936	0.33%
10.	Vijender M IND	1926	0.33%
11.	Kirpal Singh M IND	1878	0.32%
12.	Jagdev M IND	1258	0.22%
13.	Prabhu M IND	1248	0.22%
14.	Dalip Singh M IND	1186	0.20%
15.	Ramji Dass M IND	1119	0.19%
16.	Banwari Lal M IND	1070	0.18%
17.	Prem Kumar Anand M IND	992	0.17%
18.	Anand Kumar M IND	960	0.17%
19.	Ram Bhagat M IND	943	0.16%
20.	Balwan M IND	922	0.16%
21.	Rajender M IND	864	0.15%

22.	Prem Singh M IND	791	0.14%
23.	Joginder S. Urf Dharti Pakad M IND	785	0.14%
24.	Shiv Kumar M IND	732	0.13%
25.	Ramesh Ram M IND	614	0.11%
26.	Kiran Singh M IND	596	0.10%
27.	Vijay Kumar M IND	593	0.10%
28.	Ishwar Singh M IND	561	0.10%
29.	Sudershan Pal M IND	466	0.08%
30.	Bir Singh M IND	458	0.08%
31.	Rati Ram M IND	452	0.08%
32.	Ram Bir M IND	435	0.08%
33.	Bhanwar Singh M IND	431	0.07%
34.	Suraj Bhan M IND	386	0.07%
35.	Sultan M IND	307	0.05%
36.	Sumer M IND	285	0.05%
37.	Puran Mal M IND	279	0.05%
38.	Baljit M IND	249	0.04%
39.	Satyanarayan M IND	234	0.04%
40.	Rajender Prashad M IND	234	0.04%

Electors : 949440 Voters : 596369
Poll Percentage : 62.81% Valid Votes : 579517

9. Hissar

1.	Narain Singh M INC	233012	38.37%
2.	Jai Parkash M JP	206818	34.06%
3.	Parma Nand M JD	85241	14.04%
4.	Siri Niwas Goel M BJP	35486	5.84%
5.	Daulat Ram M IND	22946	3.78%
6.	Ram Niwas M IND	11235	1.85%
7.	Dilbagh M IND	2156	0.36%
8.	Rangi Ram M IND	2142	0.35%
9.	Nape Singh M IND	1513	0.25%
10.	Panna Lal M IND	1340	0.22%
11.	Mahender M DDP	1303	0.21%
12.	Mahipat M IND	971	0.16%
13.	Ved Parkash M IND	938	0.15%
14.	Krishan M IND	714	0.12%
15.	Pawan Kumar M IND	642	0.11%
16.	Bhag Chand M IND	394	0.06%
17.	Ram Kishan M IND	389	0.06%

Electors : 919440 Voters : 627037
Poll Percentage : 68.20% Valid Votes : 607240

10. Sirsa (SC)

1.	Shailja (W) F INC	287927	42.92%
2.	Het Ram M JP	188829	28.15%
3.	Sakhi Ram M JD	61665	9.19%
4.	Payare Lal Fauji M BJP	43873	6.54%
5.	Ram Sharan M HVP	31766	4.74%
6.	Jameet Singh M IND	27648	4.12%
7.	Prem Chand M IND	8299	1.24%
8.	Chanan Dass M IND	7609	1.13%
9.	Gokal M IND	3951	0.59%
10.	Rajneet M IND	3004	0.45%
11.	Amar Singh Rahi M IND	1861	0.28%
12.	Dharam Paul M IND	1274	0.19%
13.	Phali Ram M IND	1184	0.18%
14.	Bhagwana M DDP	1144	0.17%
15.	Daryav Singh M IND	793	0.12%

Electors : 991095 Voters : 690275
Poll Percentage : 69.65% Valid Votes : 670827

General Elections - India, 1996

1. Ambala (SC)

1.	Suraj Bhan M BJP	253555	31.77%
2.	Sher Singh M INC	166408	20.85%
3.	Aman Kumar Nagra M BSP	164288	20.58%
4.	Balwant Singh M SAP	135702	17.00%
5.	S.C.Dhosiwal M AIIC(T)	11780	1.48%
6.	Ishwar Dass M IND	9624	1.21%
7.	Dev Dutt Kashyap M JD	8836	1.11%
8.	Gurnam M IND	7998	1.00%
9.	Sheo Ram M IND	6967	0.87%
10.	Jaswant Rai M IND	6592	0.83%
11.	Karam Chand M IND	5858	0.73%
12.	Vinod Kumari F IND	5127	0.64%
13.	Ram Kumar M IND	2596	0.33%
14.	Ronak Singh M IND	2419	0.30%
15.	Bhag Mal M IND	2334	0.29%
16.	Puran Lal M IND	2071	0.26%
17.	Anil Kumar M IND	1828	0.23%
18.	Purshotam Kumar M IND	1726	0.22%
19.	Rajshree F IND	1276	0.16%
20.	Lal Singh M IND	1175	0.15%

Electors : 1098767 Voters : 824298
Poll Percentage : 75.02% Valid Votes : 798160

2. Kurukshetra

1.	Om Parkash Jindal M HVP	292172	36.45%
2.	Kailasho Devi F SAP	240395	29.99%
3.	Tara Singh M INC	142302	17.76%
4.	Singh Ram M BSP	52670	6.57%
5.	Jagdeep Singh Cheema M AIIC(T)	25641	3.20%
6.	S.M.Ashri M JSTP	9305	1.16%
7.	Amir Singh M JD	7032	0.88%
8.	Narender Nath M IND	4185	0.52%
9.	Sarjit Singh M IND	3388	0.42%
10.	Vinod Kumar M IND	3282	0.41%
11.	Ramji Lal M IND	3195	0.40%
12.	Om Parkash M IND	2525	0.32%
13.	Ram Dular Tiwari M BLP	1900	0.24%
14.	Chintaman M IND	1838	0.23%
15.	Rajender M IND	1614	0.20%
16.	Ram Charan M IND	1449	0.18%
17.	Kishori Lal M IND	1444	0.18%
18.	Krishan Dutt M IND	1243	0.16%
19.	Shamsher Singh M BKD(J)	882	0.11%

20.	Hari Kishan M IND	806	0.10%
21.	Ram Pal M IND	783	0.10%
22.	Yash Aggarwal M IND	759	0.09%
23.	Dharam Pal M IND	722	0.09%
24.	Kuldeep Kumar M IND	713	0.09%
25.	Ratan Singh M IND	691	0.09%
26.	Yogender Singh M IND	539	0.07%

Electors : 1100534 Voters : 829029
Poll Percentage : 75.33% Valid Votes : 801475

3. Karnal

1.	Ishwar Dayal Swami M BJP	338013	42.20%
2.	Chiranji Lal Sharma M INC	146148	18.25%
3.	Shyam Singh Rana M SAP	126604	15.81%
4.	Raghuveer Singh M BSP	55484	6.93%
5.	Chasham Pal Nain M JD	45797	5.72%
6.	Shamsher Singh Gogi M AIIC(T)	27932	3.49%
7.	Daryao Singh Malik M IND	13465	1.68%
8.	Mai Lal M IND	6797	0.85%
9.	Amarjit Singh Rana M IND	6537	0.82%
10.	Madan Gopal Gupta M IND	5936	0.74%
11.	Raj Kumar Kashyap M IND	4775	0.60%
12.	Chhakan Lal Khurana M IND	4684	0.58%
13.	Harkesh Sharma M SHS	4395	0.55%
14.	Mahabir Singh Panwar M ICS	2268	0.28%
15.	Gurdial Singh M IND	1931	0.24%
16.	Sunehra M IND	1660	0.21%
17.	Randhir Singh Saini M IND	1582	0.20%
18.	Santosh F FBL	1548	0.19%
19.	Ved Parkash M IND	1490	0.19%
20.	Jogi Ram M IND	1335	0.17%
21.	Raj Kumar M IND	1276	0.16%
22.	Ram Phal M IND	1250	0.16%

Electors : 1149141 Voters : 829916
Poll Percentage : 72.22% Valid Votes : 800907

4. Sonepat

1.	Arvind Kumar M IND	231552	33.07%
2.	Rijaq Ram M SAP	182012	26.00%
3.	Abhey Ram Dahiya M HVP	151294	21.61%
4.	Dharam Pal Singh Malik M INC	57615	8.23%
5.	Ram Kumar M JPS	15112	2.16%
6.	Bimla Mor F AIIC(T)	8638	1.23%
7.	Shanker Lal M SP	7247	1.04%
8.	Naresh Kashyap M IND	6686	0.95%

9. Jai Kishan M IND	6273	0.90%
10. Daryao Singh M IND	5727	0.82%
11. Hoshiyar Singh S/o Charan Singh M JD	5159	0.74%
12. Suraj Mal M JP	3204	0.46%
13. Nafe Singh M IND	1921	0.27%
14. Ramesh Kumar M IND	1833	0.26%
15. Dharambir M IND	1756	0.25%
16. Ram Das M SHS	1727	0.25%
17. Ramesh M IND	1478	0.21%
18. Kanwal Singh Bedharak M IND	1470	0.21%
19. Hoshyar Singh S/o Hira Singh M IND	1408	0.20%
20. Jora Singh M IND	1310	0.19%
21. Satbir Singh M ICS	1150	0.16%
22. Sanjay Kumar M IND	1098	0.16%
23. Ashok M IND	1065	0.15%
24. Ramphal Sharma M IND	967	0.14%
25. Karnail M IND	903	0.13%
26. Sat Pal M IND	672	0.10%
27. Subhash M IND	544	0.08%
28. Satguru Das M IND	314	0.04%

Electors : 1058964 Voters : 725975
Poll Percentage : 68.56% Valid Votes : 700135

5. Rohtak

1. Bhupender M INC	198154	31.71%
2. Devi Lal M SAP	195490	31.28%
3. Pardeep Kumar M BJP	158376	25.34%
4. Ramesh Dalal M IND	11439	1.83%
5. Nafe M IND	8272	1.32%
6. Ajit Singh M ARS	6367	1.02%
7. Ranbir Singh M IND	6164	0.99%
8. Hari Narain M IND	4973	0.80%
9. Joginder Singh Hooda M IND	3645	0.58%
10. Mangat Ram M JHM	3450	0.55%
11. Jasbir M IND	2805	0.45%
12. Raj Singh M JP	2751	0.44%
13. Ashok Kumar M IND	2452	0.39%
14. Ram Phal M IND	2129	0.34%
15. Narinder Singh M SHS	2079	0.33%
16. Narinder M IND	1786	0.29%
17. Bhalle Ram M IND	1618	0.26%
18. Dharam Pal M IND	1563	0.25%
19. Laxman Singh M JD	1505	0.24%
20. Harish Chander Ahlawat M IND	1249	0.20%
21. Ravinder Pal Singh M IND	1142	0.18%
22. Om Parkash M IND	1113	0.18%

23.	Daya Nand M IND	905	0.14%
24.	Santosh Singh F JSTP	829	0.13%
25.	Ranbir Singh M IND	708	0.11%
26.	Raj Bir Singh M IND	550	0.09%
27.	Krishan Singh M RKD	520	0.08%
28.	Ishwar Singh M IND	488	0.08%
29.	Satbir M IND	484	0.08%
30.	Jai Bhagwan Joon M IND	444	0.07%
31.	Jagbir M IND	394	0.06%
32.	Hari Singh M IND	389	0.06%
33.	Vinod Tanwar M IND	340	0.05%
34.	Satyawan M IND	337	0.05%

Electors : 949760 Voters : 644480
Poll Percentage : 67.86% Valid Votes : 624910

6. Faridabad

1.	Ram Chander M BJP	292294	35.76%
2.	Avtar Singh Bhadana M INC	230778	28.23%
3.	Hidayat Khan M SP	65005	7.95%
4.	Shiv Narain M BSP	56733	6.94%
5.	Shantvir Vashist M SAP	35372	4.33%
6.	Rati Ram S/O.Ammi M AIIC(T)	32676	4.00%
7.	Swaraj Lamba M JD	32633	3.99%
8.	Vali Mohammed M IND	8611	1.05%
9.	Devi Singh Tewatia M IND	6858	0.84%
10.	Aas Mohamad Khan M IND	6367	0.78%
11.	Daya Ram Seini M IND	5595	0.68%
12.	Usman Khan M IND	4959	0.61%
13.	Pandit Nathin Ram Kaushik M IND	4330	0.53%
14.	Ram Dutt Aheriya M IND	4272	0.52%
15.	Tayub Hussain M IND	2460	0.30%
16.	Prem Chand Premi M IND	2399	0.29%
17.	Banwari Lal M JP	2316	0.28%
18.	Ajmat Khan M IND	2098	0.26%
19.	Jakir Hussain M IND	2044	0.25%
20.	Shibbu M IND	1865	0.23%
21.	Mamender Kumar M IND	1581	0.19%
22.	Khem Chand M IND	1527	0.19%
23.	Abdul Hamid M IND	1303	0.16%
24.	Satbir Rawat M IND	1111	0.14%
25.	Kamal Singh M IND	1107	0.14%
26.	Jhangi Ram M IND	969	0.12%
27.	Mukhi Bhim Sain M IND	882	0.11%
28.	Rajesh Khurana M IND	874	0.11%
29.	Mohammed Ajaz Khan M IND	808	0.10%

30.	Kasham M IND	799	0.10%
31.	Braham Pal Bhadana M IND	796	0.10%
32.	Rishi Pal M IND	794	0.10%
33.	Ashwani M IND	691	0.08%
34.	Rati Ram S/o Siya M IND	668	0.08%
35.	Santosh F IND	645	0.08%
36.	Iqbal M IND	639	0.08%
37.	Umar Mohammed M IND	604	0.07%
38.	Kabir Ahmed M IND	554	0.07%
39.	N.M.Lal M IND	476	0.06%
40.	Iqbal Jeet Singh M IND	466	0.06%
41.	Zan Mohammed M IND	457	0.06%

Electors : 1394387 Voters : 844989
Poll Percentage : 60.60% Valid Votes : 817416

7. Mahendergarh

1.	Ram Singh M BJP	265034	33.45%
2.	Rao Birender Singh M INC	216999	27.39%
3.	Raghu Yadav M BSP	136475	17.23%
4.	Kanwar Singh Kalwari M SAP	66049	8.34%
5.	Raj Dahiya M AIIC(T)	27583	3.48%
6.	Prabhu Lal Batra M ABJS	14292	1.80%
7.	Jai Narain Singh Yadav M SP	13920	1.76%
8.	Ved Parkash Vidrohi M JD	7774	0.98%
9.	Gobind Singh Rao M IND	4628	0.58%
10.	Mool Chand M IND	4133	0.52%
11.	Aphria Ram Singh M IND	4112	0.52%
12.	Surjeet Singh M IND	3977	0.50%
13.	Birju Singh M JP	3804	0.48%
14.	Bharat Lal M RKP	3635	0.46%
15.	Santosh Kumar Sain M IND	3441	0.43%
16.	Mohan Lal Joshi M IND	2939	0.37%
17.	Braham Parkash M IND	2735	0.35%
18.	Deshraj Yadav M IND	2287	0.29%
19.	Dharamvir M IND	1867	0.24%
20.	Daulat Ram M IND	1833	0.23%
21.	Ranjeet M IND	1204	0.15%
22.	Randhir M IND	1198	0.15%
23.	Dhansi M IND	942	0.12%
24.	Ravinder Pal Singh M IND	726	0.09%
25.	Radhe Shyam Mudgil M IND	633	0.08%

Electors : 1237989 Voters : 819455
Poll Percentage : 66.19% Valid Votes : 792220

8. Bhiwani

	Candidate	Votes	%
1.	Surender Singh M HVP	406454	55.66%
2.	Jangbir Singh M INC	181271	24.82%
3.	Gopi Ram Vashistha M SAP	73654	10.09%
4.	Bhola Ram M AIIC(T)	8516	1.17%
5.	Ram Swaroop Verma M JD	8109	1.11%
6.	Dharmender M IND	6351	0.87%
7.	Ran Singh S/o. Jiwan Singh M JHM	5954	0.82%
8.	Puran Mal Sharma M IND	4742	0.65%
9.	Sushil Kumar M IND	4236	0.58%
10.	Subhash Saini M IND	2336	0.32%
11.	Kundan Kumar M RPI	2332	0.32%
12.	Ranbir M ABDUP	1996	0.27%
13.	Devi Lal M IND	1937	0.27%
14.	Karamvir M JP	1803	0.25%
15.	Satpal M IND	1768	0.24%
16.	Partap M IND	1452	0.20%
17.	Ran Singh S/o Patram M IND	1335	0.18%
18.	Daya Ram M IND	1283	0.18%
19.	Sher Singh M IND	1244	0.17%
20.	Om Parkash M IND	1131	0.15%
21.	Vinod Kumar M SHS	1022	0.14%
22.	Sube Singh M IND	963	0.13%
23.	Sultan Singh M FBL	884	0.12%
24.	Ranbir Singh M IND	873	0.12%
25.	Chhotu Ram M IND	869	0.12%
26.	Puran M IND	815	0.11%
27.	Sewadhari M IND	760	0.10%
28.	Hanuman M IND	720	0.10%
29.	Jogender M IND	706	0.10%
30.	Rajbir Singh M IND	558	0.08%
31.	Chhallu Ram M IND	468	0.06%
32.	Inder Singh M IND	404	0.06%
33.	Suraj Bhan M IND	402	0.06%
34.	Satbir M IND	388	0.05%
35.	Raj Kumar M IND	382	0.05%
36.	Jagdish Prasad M IND	360	0.05%
37.	Balwan M IND	356	0.05%
38.	Satya Narayan M IND	321	0.04%
39.	Laxman Das M IND	287	0.04%
40.	Bharat Bhushan M IND	246	0.03%
41.	Ram Mehar M IND	238	0.03%
42.	Jaivir M IND	172	0.02%
43.	Rajiv M IND	167	0.02%

Electors : 1060563 Voters : 749299
Poll Percentage : 70.65% Valid Votes : 730265

9. Hissar

1.	Jai Parkash S/o Harikesh M HVP	306402	42.32%
2.	Gauri Shanker M SAP	131750	18.20%
3.	Surjeet Singh M INC	107953	14.91%
4.	Phool Singh Sheokand M IND	56307	7.78%
5.	Sukh Dev M BSP	36308	5.01%
6.	Vijay Kumar M AIIC(T)	28239	3.90%
7.	Rajiv Kumar M IND	10162	1.40%
8.	Sher Singh M IND	8289	1.14%
9.	Suraj Bhan M IND	6250	0.86%
10.	Ved Parkash Sharma M IND	2740	0.38%
11.	Sat Pal M IND	2522	0.35%
12.	Ram Niwas M IND	2329	0.32%
13.	Sajjan Singh M IND	2226	0.31%
14.	Chander Bhan M IND	2103	0.29%
15.	Chander Shekhar M JP	2082	0.29%
16.	Dharam Vir S/o Kesho Ram M IND	1782	0.25%
17.	Anil M IND	1515	0.21%
18.	Sunder Singh M IND	1311	0.18%
19.	Lalit Kumar M IND	1242	0.17%
20.	Vidya Devi F IND	1102	0.15%
21.	Ramesh M IND	1067	0.15%
22.	Ram Gopal M IND	1059	0.15%
23.	Sham Lal M IND	979	0.14%
24.	Jai Parkash S/o Nathu Ram M IND	922	0.13%
26.	Narinder Kumar M IND	891	0.12%
25.	Ajay Kumar M PPNMS	889	0.12%
27.	Rattan Lal M IND	826	0.11%
28.	Dharam Vir S/o Arjun M IND	822	0.11%
29.	Moti Lal M IND	789	0.11%
30.	Bharthu M IND	781	0.11%
31.	Raj Kumar M IND	770	0.11%
32.	Babu Ram M IND	543	0.08%
33.	Jagat Singh M IND	536	0.07%
34.	Gulshan M IND	279	0.04%
35.	Anand M IND	232	0.03%

Electors : 1030467 Voters : 746249
Poll Percentage : 72.42% Valid Votes : 723999

10. Sirsa (SC)

1.	Selja F INC	275459	33.50%
2.	Sushil Kumar M SAP	260312	31.66%
3.	Hans Raj M BJP	195451	23.77%
4.	Parkash Singh M CPI	27573	3.35%

5.	Baldev Singh Badal M IND	15130	1.84%
6.	Gian Parkash M IND	8832	1.07%
7.	Phool Singh M IND	5700	0.69%
8.	Devi Lal M IND	5251	0.64%
9.	Ram Swroop M IND	5119	0.62%
10.	Pyare Lal M IND	4191	0.51%
11.	Dharam Singh M IND	3025	0.37%
12.	Ranjit M IND	2531	0.31%
13.	Makhan Lal Alias Madan Lal M IND	2234	0.27%
14.	Didar Singh M IND	2196	0.27%
15.	Om Parkash M IND	1997	0.24%
16.	Raj Kumar M IND	1754	0.21%
17.	Radhe Shyam M IND	1620	0.20%
18.	Khazan Singh M IND	1539	0.19%
19.	Kartara Ram M IND	1153	0.14%
20.	Mahabir Singh M IND	1089	0.13%

Electors : 1072284 Voters : 847173
Poll Percentage : 79.01% Valid Votes : 822156

General Elections - India, 1998

1. Ambala (SC)

1.	Aman Kumar Nagra M BSP	273792	36.97%
2.	Suraj Bhan M BJP	270928	36.58%
3.	Raj Kumar M INC	174171	23.52%
4.	Amar Dass M JD	6258	0.85%
5.	Maya Ram M BSP(A)	5819	0.79%
6.	Man Phool Singh M SJP(R)	5421	0.73%
7.	Sunder Lal M IND	2414	0.33%
8.	Kehar Singh M IND	1257	0.17%
9.	Jagdish Lal M IND	486	0.07%

Electors : 1092422 Voters : 748313
Poll Percentage ; 68.50% Valid Votes 740546

2. Kurukshetra

1.	Kailasho Devi F HLD(R)	333387	43.57%
2.	Kuldip Sharma M INC	191867	25.07%
3.	Jatinder Singh Kaka M HVP	181791	23.76%
4.	Shyam Singh Rana M SJP(R)	42105	5.50%
5.	Hawa Singh M AIIC(S)	6559	0.86%
6.	Balbir M IND	2368	0.31%
7.	Mahinder Singh M SP	2285	0.30%
8.	Bali Ram M IND	2274	0.30%
9.	Amar Sharma M SHS	1264	0.17%
10.	Gurnam Singh M IND	705	0.09%
11.	Raj Kumar M IND	629	0.08%

Electors : 1089508 Voters : 773841
Poll Percentage: 71.03% Valid Votes 765234

3. Karnal

1.	Bhajan Lal M INC	327750	41.14%
2.	I.D. Swami M BJP	275689	34.60%
3.	Umed Singh Kashyap M HLD(R)	156565	19.65%
4.	Chasam Pal Singh Nain M JD	15900	2.00%
5.	Rajender Singh Verma M SJP(R)	9837	1.23%
6.	Bijender M IND	4114	0.52%
7.	Ishwar Chand Aggarwal M SP	2827	0.35%
8.	Naresh M IND	1016	0.13%
9.	Mittar Pal M AJBP	996	0.13%
10.	Mohan Rao Saheb M IND	644	0.08%

11.	Manphool Singh M IND	484	0.06%
12.	Laj Pat Rai M IND	423	0.05%
13.	Chhakan Lal M IND	264	0.03%
14.	Som Parkash Kashyap M IND	229	0.03%

Electors : 1137817 Voters : 806138
Poll Percentage : 70.85% Valid Votes 796738

4. Sonepat

1.	Kishan Singh M HLD(R)	290299	41.94%
2.	Abhey Ram Dahiya M HVP	152975	22.10%
3.	Arvind Kumar M SHS	143911	20.79%
4.	Balbir M INC	82292	11.89%
5.	Sanjay M SP	3774	0.55%
6.	Harsarup Singh M IND	3362	0.49%
7.	Ramehar M IND	3152	0.46%
8.	Kitab Singh M IND	2747	0.40%
9.	Raj Singh Tehlan M JP	1865	0.27%
10.	Raj Pal M IND	1676	0.24%
11.	Basant M IND	1643	0.24%
12.	Hari Parkash M IND	1461	0.21%
13.	Rajesh Kumar M IND	1376	0.20%
14.	Rohtas M IND	870	0.13%
15.	Sat Guru Dass M IND	282	0.04%
16.	Dharamvir M IND	279	0.04%
17.	Kelawati F IND	243	0.04%

Electors : 1059823 Voters : 699624
Poll Percentage : 66.01% Valid Votes 692207

5. Rohtak

1.	Bhupinder Singh M INC	254951	38.66%
2.	Devi Lal S/o Lekh Ram M HLD(R)	254568	38.61%
3.	Swami Indervesh M BJP	130895	19.85%
4.	Ram Chander Jangra M IND	4628	0.70%
5.	Anoop Singh M IND	3776	0.57%
6.	Kaptan Singh Rathee M SP	2717	0.41%
7.	Omkar M IND	1623	0.25%
8.	Mukesh Kumar M IND	1093	0.17%
9.	Umed Singh M JP	1071	0.16%
10.	Vijay Kumar M IND	906	0.14%
11.	Mukhtare M IND	805	0.12%
12.	Radhey Shyam M IND	775	0.12%
13.	Nafe M IND	461	0.07%

14.	Ramdhari Attkan M IND	366	0.06%
15.	Devi Lal S/O Gurdayal M IND	270	0.04%
16.	Lt.Col.Hari Narayan M IND	191	0.03%
17.	Mukhtiar Singh M IND	164	0.02%
18.	Harish Chander M IND	154	0.02%

Electors : 939007 Voters : 667639
Poll Percentage : 71.10% Valid Votes 659414

6. Faridabad

1.	Ramchander Bainda M BJP	304022	33.81%
2.	Khurshid Ahmad M INC	288679	32.10%
3.	Avtar Singh Bhadana M SJP(R)	173890	19.34%
4.	Dharmbir Bhadana M BSP	118009	13.12%
5.	Mohd. Azaz Khan M SP	4180	0.46%
6.	Mahadev Sharma M JD	3194	0.36%
7.	Farook M IND	2303	0.26%
8.	Krishan Kumar M IND	1036	0.12%
9.	Mange Ram M MSP	968	0.11%
10.	Sumitra F IND	800	0.09%
11.	Poonam Singh F AJBP	673	0.07%
12.	Rattan Singh M IND	528	0.06%
13.	Prempal Singh M ABHS	441	0.05%
14.	Satyavir M IND	314	0.03%
15.	Dhyan Singh M IND	250	0.03%

Electors : 1390542 Voters : 913821
Poll Percentage : 65.72% Valid Votes. 899287

7. Mahendergarh

1.	Inderjit Singh M INC	329126	41.50%
2.	Col.Ram Singh M BJP	260990	32.91%
3.	Raghu Yadav M BSP	188351	23.75%
4.	Tek Chand M IND	4936	0.62%
5.	Mahender Singh S/O Lal Singh M IND	3330	0.42%
6.	Professor Surjit Singh M IND	2143	0.27%
7.	Comrade Rajender M IND	2040	0.26%
8.	Major Parbhu Batra M ABJS	1677	0.21%
9.	Satendra Prasad M IND	546	0.07%

Electors : 1225797 Voters : 803923
Poll Percentage : 65.58% Valid Votes. 793139

8. Bhiwani

1.	Surender S/o Bansi Lal M HVP	361257	48.17%
2.	Ajay Singh M HLD(R)	351546	46.87%
3.	Ranbir Singh Mahender M INC	27789	3.71%
4.	Chhaju Ram M JD	3161	0.42%
5.	Bir Singh Fauji M IND	886	0.12%
6.	Mahender S/o V. Parkash M IND	792	0.11%
7.	Dr. Ram Singh Pachar M IND	781	0.10%
8.	Mahender S/o Gig Raj M IND	726	0.10%
9.	Raj Pal M IND	491	0.07%
10.	Laxmi F ABHM	426	0.06%
11.	Sukhchen M IND	358	0.05%
12.	Surender S/o Dhoop M IND	322	0.04%
13.	Vinod Kumar M SHS	277	0.04%
14.	Paramjit Singh M IND	204	0.03%
15.	Surender M IND	188	0.03%
16.	Satvir Singh M IND	171	0.02%
17.	Surender Kumar M IND	150	0.02%
18.	Ram Mehar M IND	145	0.02%
19.	Tara Chand M IND	135	0.02%
20.	Sat Pal M IND	122	0.02%
21.	Hawa Singh M IND	63	0.01%

Electors : 1052297 Voters : 759887
Poll Percentage : 72.21% Valid Votes. 749990

9. Hissar

1.	Surender Barwala M HLD(R)	260271	35.89%
2.	Om Parkash Jindal M HVP	179780	24.79%
3.	Jai Parkash Alias J.P. M SJP(R)	171129	23.60%
4.	Ranjit Singh M INC	73251	10.10%
5.	Phool Singh Sheokand M CPM	25366	3.50%
6.	Ashwani Kumar M LS	2992	0.41%
7.	Ram Kumar M IND	2867	0.40%
8.	Prem Singh M IND	2396	0.33%
9.	Ajay M IND	1957	0.27%
10.	Bahadur Singh M BKKGP	1819	0.25%
11.	Jai Parkash S/o Jai Lal M IND	1154	0.16%
12.	S. B. Bhushan M NPAP	919	0.13%
13.	Kartar Singh M IND	648	0.09%
14.	Surender Singh M IND	573	0.08%

Electors : 1026332 Voters : 733865
Poll Percentage : 71.50% Valid Votes. 725122

10. Sirsa (SC)

1.	Sushil Kumar Indora M HLD(R)	309451	42.33%
2.	Selja F INC	215521	29.48%
3.	Hans Raj M BJP	184562	25.24%
4.	Joginder Singh M CPI	11270	1.54%
5.	Darshan Lal M IND	2397	0.33%
6.	Sushil Kumar M IND	1598	0.22%
7.	Chhota Singh M IND	1371	0.19%
8.	Phool Singh M IND	1137	0.16%
9.	Partap M IND	1034	0.14%
10.	Om Parkash M IND	1008	0.14%
11.	Raj Kumar M IND	899	0.12%
12.	Baljeet Singh M IND	879	0.12%

Electors : 1073350 Voters : 742037
Poll Percentage : 69.13% Valid Votes. 731127

General Elections - India, 1999

Ambala (SC)

1.	Rattan Lal Kataria M BJP	357460	51.63%
2.	Phool Chand Mullana M INC	232982	33.65%
3.	Aman Kumar Nagra M BSP	83644	12.08%
4.	Maya Ram M BSP(A)	6630	0.96%
5.	Krishan Chand M RPI	5176	0.75%
6.	Sushil M IND	3743	0.54%
7.	Ajay M IND	1578	0.23%
8.	Baljeet Singh Mandebar M JD(S)	1124	0.16%

Electors : 1091846 Voters : 698854
Poll Percentage : 64.01% Valid Votes : 692337

Kurukshetra

1.	Prof Kailasho Devi F INLD	438701	60.61%
2.	Om Parkash Jindal M INC	275091	38.01%
3.	Om Parkash M IND	3177	0.44%
4.	Balbir Singh M IND	2814	0.39%
5.	Dharm Singh M IND	1567	0.22%
6.	Rajender Parshad M IND	1097	0.15%
7.	Tilak Raj M IND	791	0.11%
8.	Ramji Lal M IND	519	0.07%

Electors : 1073147 Voters : 730566
Poll Percentage : 68.08% Valid Votes : 723757

Karnal

1.	I.D. Swami M BJP	433733	56.25%
2.	Bhajan Lal M INC	285879	37.07%
3.	Pardeep Kumar M BSP	26860	3.48%
4.	Ramphal Sharma M IND	7405	0.96%
5.	Sukhvinder Singh M IND	6150	0.80%
6.	Bajinder Singh M IND	3479	0.45%
7.	Nar Singh Dass Gupta M SP	3045	0.39%
8.	Dwarka Parsad M IND	1258	0.16%
9.	Anoop Singh M IND	816	0.11%
10.	Devi Lal M IND	755	0.10%
11.	Ugar Sain M IND	553	0.07%
12.	Ami Lal M IND	472	0.06%
13.	Om Parkash M IND	354	0.05%
14.	Tapesh Bagati M IND	342	0.04%

Electors : 1131448 Voters : 771194
Poll Percentage : 68.16% Valid Votes : 771101

Sonepat

1.	Kishan Singh Sangwan M BJP	457056	69.83%
2.	Chiranji Lal M INC	190918	29.17%
3.	Sanjay M SP	1999	0.31%
4.	Kawal Singh M NCP	1844	0.28%
5.	Sant Ram M IND	1373	0.21%
6.	Hariparkash M IND	1319	0.20%

Electors : 1057175 Voters : 659535
Poll Percentage : 62.39% Valid Votes : 654509

Rohtak

1.	Inder Singh M INLD	366926	57.93%
2.	Bhupinder Singh M INC	222233	35.09%
3.	Arvind Kumar Sharma M IND	27265	4.30%
4.	Kanta F SP	5295	0.84%
5.	Suraj Mal Hooda M IND	4956	0.78%
6.	Satender M IND	2387	0.38%
7.	Anoop Singh M IND	921	0.15%
8.	Devender Kumar M IND	753	0.12%
9.	Risal Singh M IND	554	0.09%
10.	Nafe M IND	540	0.09%
11.	Sajjan Singh M IND	497	0.08%
12.	Col. Rampal Singh M IND	418	0.07%
13.	Mukhtiar Singh M IND	338	0.05%
14.	Ram Phal M IND	290	0.05%

Electors : 938878 Voters : 634235
Poll Percentage : 67.55% Valid Votes : 633373

Faridabad

1.	Ram Chander Bainda M BJP	367842	49.34%
2.	Zakir Hussain M INC	333594	44.75%
3.	Shyam Sunder Kapoor M HVP	37045	4.97%
4.	Daulat Singh Khatana M SP	1980	0.27%
5.	Rattan Singh M IND	1169	0.16%
6.	Tej Pal M IND	940	0.13%
7.	Baldev Singh M IND	738	0.10%
8.	Madan Lal Sharma M IND	734	0.10%
9.	Tek Chand M IND	500	0.07%
10.	Shiv Kumar M IND	421	0.06%
11.	Ram Kishan Beniwal M IND	354	0.05%
12.	Harsh Mani M IND	167	0.02%

Electors : 1330157 Voters : 755003
Poll Percentage : 56.76% Valid Votes : 745484

Mahendergarh

1.	Dr. Sudha Yadav F BJP	420706	56.49%
2.	Inderjit Singh M INC	281566	37.81%
3.	Raghu M BSP	25826	3.47%
4.	Braham Dutt M IND	3793	0.51%
5.	Lal Singh M IND	3485	0.47%
6.	Manohar Lal M SP	3114	0.42%
7.	Ajit Singh M IND	2890	0.39%
8.	Ravinder Yadav M NCP	2096	0.28%
9.	Major Prabhu Lal Batra M ABJS	1230	0.17%

Electors : 1236918 Voters : 752654
Poll Percentage : 60.85% Valid Votes : 744706

Bhiwani

1.	Ajay Singh Chautala M INLD	381255	52.01%
2.	Dharambir M INC	177849	24.26%
3.	Surender Singh M HVP	151686	20.69%
4.	Comrade Parbhat Singh M CPM	10511	1.43%
5.	Ramesh M SP	3171	0.43%
6.	Ashok Kumar M IND	955	0.13%
7.	Diwan Chand M IND	667	0.09%
8.	Karan Singh M IND	624	0.09%
9.	Krishan Kumar M IND	583	0.08%
10.	Mahender Singh M IND	528	0.07%
11.	Darshan M IND	495	0.07%
12.	Ramesh Kumar M IND	489	0.07%
13.	Dharam Pal Singh M IND	472	0.06%
14.	Mahipal M IND	471	0.06%
15.	Ved Prakash M IND	447	0.06%
16.	Bhim Sen Chhabra M IND	371	0.05%
17.	Om M IND	363	0.05%
18.	Raj Kumar M IND	287	0.04%
19.	Ravinder M IND	253	0.03%
20.	Rajender Singh M IND	232	0.03%
21.	Umed Singh S/O Udai Singh M IND	208	0.03%
22.	Tajvir Singh M IND	188	0.03%
23.	Surender M IND	165	0.02%
24.	Kartar M IND	165	0.02%
25.	Ramehar M IND	164	0.02%
26.	Umed Singh S/o Bairishal Singh M IND	154	0.02%
27.	Sukhchen M IND	109	0.01%
28.	Mahavir Prasad M IND	100	0.01%
29.	Rajbir M IND	80	0.01%

Electors : 1053603 Voters : 740347
Poll Percentage : 70.27% Valid Votes : 733042

Hissar

1.	Surender Singh Barwala M INLD	396540	62.03%
2.	Birender Singh M INC	236088	36.93%
3.	Roopender Singh M AJBP	2204	0.34%
4.	Surender M IND	1648	0.26%
5.	Neeraj M IND	1260	0.20%
6.	Bhajja Ram M IND	576	0.09%
7.	Rattan Lal M IND	510	0.08%
8.	Subhash Chand M IND	476	0.07%

Electors : 1025344 Voters : 646513
Poll Percentage : 63.05% Valid Votes : 639302

Sirsa (SC)

1.	Dr. Sushil Kumar Indora M INLD	419278	65.98%
2.	Om Parkash M INC	199552	31.40%
3.	Babu Lal M SP	10789	1.70%
4.	Brij Lal M IND	2689	0.42%
5.	Dr Sudarshan Kumar M IND	2372	0.37%
6.	Raj Kumar Nagar M IND	748	0.12%

Electors : 1100439 Voters : 641063
Poll Percentage : 58.26% Valid Votes : 635428

General Elections - India, 2004

1. Ambala (SC)

4. Selja F 41 SC INC	415264	48.98%
3. Rattan Lal Kataria M 52 SC BJP	180329	21.27%
2. Balwant Singh M 54 SC INLD	130972	15.44%
1. Chander Pal M 56 SC BSP	57028	6.72%
5. Aman Kumar Nagra M 49 SC HVP	22039	2.59%
7. Ranbir Singh M 36 SC ES	13292	1.56%
13. Sunil Kumar M 30 SC IND	9574	1.29%
12. Raunaq Singh M 68 SC IND	7324	0.86%
10. Jaswinder Singh M 45 SC IND	3477	0.41%
9. Hem Raj M 41 SC LJNSP	2262	0.26%
6. Arvind Sonkar M 31 SC ABHM	2224	0.26%
11. Ram Sarup M 52 SC IND	2098	0.24%
8. Sanjeev Gharu M 29 SC SAP	1842	0.21%
Total:	847725	

2. Kurukshetra

3. Naveen Jindal M 34 Gen INC	362054	42.55%
1. Abhay Chautala M 41 Gen INLD	201864	23.72%
2. Gurdayal Saini M 57 Gen BJP	126910	14.91%
6. Jatinder (Kakka) M 51 Gen HVP	77136	9.6%
5. Sardar Jagmeet Saini M 59 Gen ES	31202	3.66%
4. Mona Ram M 41 Gen BSP	23057	2.70%
13. Raghubir Chand M 43 SC IND	8667	1.01%
15. Sunil Gupta M 44 Gen IND	7381	0.86%
14. Roop Chand M 70 Gen IND	3470	0.40%
7. Vishal Jolly M 35 Gen SP	2310	0.27%
12. Bhupender Singh M 39 Gen IND	2169	0.25%
10. Jagir Singh M 38 Gen IND	1623	0.19%
11. Jai Singh M 40 Gen IND	1346	0.15%
9. Jagmohan M 50 Gen IND	964	0.11%
8. Atam Prakash M 47 Gen IND	705	0.08%
Total:	850858	

3. Karnal

1. Arvind Sharma M 42 Gen INC	318948	38.94%
4. I. D. Swami M 74 Gen BJP	154186	18.82%
2. Ashok Arora M 44 Gen INLD	113510	13.86%
9. Raj Kumar M 35 Gen ES	82430	10.06%

3.	Ashok Kashyap M 37 Gen BSP	67392	8.22%
14.	Kuldip Sharma M 47 Gen IND	27223	3.32%
10.	Ram Chander Jangra M 53 Gen HVP	21371	2.60%
16.	Naresh Sachdeva M 41 Gen IND	6282	0.76%
17.	Mahinder Rana M 47 SC IND	4807	0.59%
8.	Raghumal Bhatt M 36 SC SP	3696	0.45%
20.	Ram Mehar Singh M 46 Gen IND	2490	0.30%
7.	Mahinder M 48 Gen CPI(Ml)(L)	2487	0.30%
13.	Rishi Ram Gupta M 47 Gen IND	2364	0.28%
19.	Rajbir Chauhan M 56 Gen IND	2088	0.25%
5.	Angrej Singh Joon M 30 Gen RGD	1977	0.24%
15.	Duli Chand Malik M 66 Gen IND	1888	0.23%
12.	Surinder Hooda M 34 Gen LJNSP	1729	0.21%
18.	Raj Kashyap M 41 Gen IND	1707	0.20%
11.	Roshan Lal Bindal M 53 Gen SHS	1315	0.16%
6.	Premo A. P. Kashyap F 35 Gen FCI	1037	0.12%
Total:		818927	

4. Sonepat

1.	Kishan Sangwan M 54 Gen BJP	233477	31.67%
3.	Dharam Pal Malik M 60 Gen INC	225908	30.64%
2.	Krishna Malik F 51 Gen INLD	198866	26.97%
4.	Sugan Gupta M 50 Gen BSP	37185	5.04%
11.	Jagbir Malik M 50 Gen IND	21126	2.86%
16.	Shamsher M 35 Gen IND	2926	0.39%
17.	Sant Ram M 39 SC IND	2889	0.39%
19.	Sityender M 26 Gen IND	2055	0.27%
14.	Basant M 35 Gen IND	1787	0.24%
18.	Satbir M 46 Gen IND	1662	0.22%
20.	Hari Parkash M 50 Gen IND	1640	0.22%
5.	Kirpal Singh M 41 Gen JD(S)	1346	0.18%
15.	Braham Singh M 52 Gen IND	1184	0.16%
6.	Balbir Singh M 48 SC RSBP	999	0.13%
10.	Jagdish Aggarwal M 63 Gen IND	949	0.12%
9.	Krishan M 30 Gen IND	747	0.10%
8.	Sube Singh M 56 Gen JCP	671	0.09%
13.	Naveen Kumar M 28 Gen IND	597	0.08%
12.	Jai Kishan M 35 Gen IND	574	0.07%
7.	Satya Pal M 43 Gen LJNSP	531	0.07%
Total:		737119	

5. Rohtak

4.	Bhupinder M 54 Gen INC	324235	48.97%
1.	Abhimanyu M 36 Gen BJP	173800	26.25%
3.	Bhim Singh M 62 Gen INLD	105640	15.95%
2.	Geeta F 28 Gen BSP	24228	3.95%
7.	Usha F 56 Gen HVP	10334	1.56%
5.	Ajay Singh M 34 Gen AIFB	2637	0.39%
16.	Jaipal M 59 Gen IND	2575	0.38%
20.	Radhe Shyam M 49 Gen IND	2095	0.31%
17.	Nafe M 65 Gen IND	2033	0.30%
13.	Anoop Matanhail M 59 Gen IND	1984	0.29%
19.	Ranvir Singh M 58 Gen IND	1956	0.29%
10.	Bharpur M 39 Gen RLD	1849	0.27%
11.	Shishpal M 50 Gen SAP	1291	0.19%
21.	Ramphal M 56 Gen IND	976	0.14%
14.	Karan Singh M 58 Gen IND	959	0.14%
12.	Ajay Kumar M 33 Gen IND	949	0.14%
24.	Hari Singh M 83 Gen IND	938	0.14%
15.	Kuldeep Singh M 34 Gen IND	857	0.12%
9.	Bimla F 28 Gen BRPP	585	0.08%
23.	Satender M 38 Gen IND	466	0.07%
6.	Anoop Singh M 49 SC RVP	460	0.07%
18.	Mukhtiar Singh M 51 Gen IND	419	0.06%
22.	Sajjan Singh M 55 Gen IND	404	0.06%
8.	Jaimal M 40 Gen RSKP	379	0.05%
Total:		662049	

6. Faridabad

2.	Avtar Bhadana M 48 Gen INC	357284	42.29%
3.	Mohd. Ilyas M 49 Gen INLD	205355	24.31%
4.	Ramchander Bainda M 53 Gen BJP	171714	20.32%
1.	Haji Abdul Malik M 45 Gen BSP	71459	8045%
6.	Devender Bhadana M 36 Gen HVP	13042	1.54%
14.	Dr. K. P. Singh M 46 SC IND	4956	0.58%
5.	Chaudhary Akhtar M 46 Gen SP	4407	0.52%
9.	Subhash Baghel M 36 Gen LP(S)	4172	0.49%
8.	Lokendra Singh M 37 Gen SHS	3920	0.46%
12.	Chander Bhan M 33 Gen IND	3769	0.44%
13.	Baldev Singh M 48 Gen IND	2063	0.24%
7.	Ramniwas Rathi M 40 Gen LJNSP	1097	0.12%
11.	Kamal Godara M 37 Gen IND	856	0.10%
10.	Akhtar Husain M 35 Gen IND	624	0.07%
	Total:	844718	

7. Mahendragarh

1. Inderjit Singh M 54 Gen INC	358714	42.23%
4. Dr. Sudha Yadav F 39 Gen BJP	148373	17.46%
7. Raghu Yadav M 48 Gen SP	121062	14.25%
2. Swami Dharam Dev M 42 Gen INLD	115154	13.55%
3. Rohtash M 41 Gen BSP	56181	6.61%
6. Anil Rao M 45 Gen HVP	30134	3.54%
14. Satbir Kundu M 45 Gen IND	7207	0.84%
13. Rajender Singh M 46 Gen IND	3286	0.38%
5. Ajay Kumar M 28 Gen RVP	2939	0.34%
8. Ram Kishan M 41 Gen BRPP	1683	0.19%
11. Naresh M 33 Gen IND	1495	0.17%
12. B. B. Kishan Saini M 56 Gen IND	1439	0.16%
10. Alakh M. Mathur M 49 Gen IND	908	0.10%
9. Ved Prakash M 49 Gen NSSP	730	0.08%
Total:	849305	

8. Bhiwani

2. Kuldeep Bishnoi M 35 Gen INC	290936	33.39%
7. Surender Singh M 57 Gen HVP	266532	30.59%
1. Ajay Chautala M 43 Gen INLD	241958	27.77%
3. Ram Bilas M 56 Gen BJP	24467	2.80%
4. Ramanand M 60 Gen BSP	17216	1.97%
13. Mange Ram M 35 Gen IND	5638	0.64%
16. Surender M 34 Gen IND	4855	0.55%
15. Sanjeev M 26 Gen IND	4513	0.51%
8. Kuldeep M 33 Gen IND	4450	0.51%
6. Mahender Singh M 31 Gen SP	2977	0.34%
14. Raj Devi Jangra F 39 Gen IND	1950	0.22%
11. Bhal Singh M 48 Gen IND	1826	0.20%
10. Devi Lal M 38 Gen IND	1474	0.16%
5. Kaptan M 34 Gen LJNSP	891	0.10%
9. Tapesh Bagati M 31 Gen IND	846	0.09%
12. Mangal Singh M 43 Gen IND	615	0.07%
Total:	871144	

9. Hissar

1. Jai Parkash M 51 Gen INC	407210	52.89%
4. Surender Barwala M 52 Gen INLD	224442	29.15%
2. Swami Raghvanand M 51 Gen BJP	64722	8.40%
3. Sant Ram Prakash M 47 Sc BSP	25060	3.25%
5. Kanwal Singh M 66 Gen HVP	19475	2.52%

16.	Sunil Kumar M 35 Gen IND	9686	1.25%
13.	Ramji Lal M 46 Gen IND	4917	0.63%
15.	Satpal M 48 Gen IND	3115	0.40%
14.	Shamsher M 35 Gen IND	2933	0.38%
6.	Ramniwas M 50 Gen SP	2598	0.33%
12.	Randhir Singh M 56 Gen IND	2105	0.27%
11.	Balwan Arya M 32 Gen IND	1386	0.18%
9.	Parmeshwar Das M 56 Gen IND	666	0.08%
10.	Pritam Kumar M 44 Gen IND	575	0.07%
8.	Niraj M 34 Gen IND	535	0.06%
7.	Atam Prakash M 47 Gen IND	426	0.05%
	Total:	769851	

10. Sirsa (SC)

1.	Atma Singh Gill M 66 Sc INC	349397	41.51%
4.	Dr. Sushil Indora M 41 Sc INLD	277922	33.01%
2.	Mahavir Parshad M 50 Sc BJP	115128	13.67%
6.	Rair Chand M 51 SC HVP	46059	5.47%
3.	Dr. Ramesh Bhukal M 47 Sc BSP	24448	2.90%
8.	Vikaramjit M 31 SC IND	13132	1.56%
5.	Ami Lal M 36 SC RVP	10823	1.28%
7.	Desraj M 49 SC IND	4773	0.56%
	Total:	841682'	

General Elections - India, 2009

1. Ambala (Total Electors 1264907)

1.	Chander Pal M 63 SC BSP	188608	21.76%
2.	Rattan Kataria M 57 SC BJP	307688	35.50%
3.	Selja F 46 SC INC	322258	37.19%
4.	Dalbir Singh M 42 SC HJCBL	30689	3.54%
5.	Hem Raj M 46 SC LJP	4597	0.53%
6.	Amar Singh M 53 SC IND	3815	0.44%
7.	Narinder Kumar M 37 SC IND	8967	1.03%
Total:		866622	

2. Kurukshetra (Total Electors 1166684)

1.	Ashok Arora M 49 Gen INLD	278475	31.81%
2.	Gurdyal Saini M 62 Gen BSP	151231	17.27%
3.	Naveen Jindal M 39 Gen INC	397204	45.37%
4.	Jaswant Cheema M 61 Gen HJCBL	16839	1.92%
5.	Pardhan Chauhan M 47 SC SP	2443	0.28%
6.	Ashwini Hrittwal M 46 Gen IND	1156	0.13%
7.	Atam Parkash M 52 Gen IND	926	0.11%
8.	Tarsem Lal M 47 Gen IND	639	0.07%
9.	Yash Pal M 51 Gen IND	631	0.07%
10.	Ran Singh M 27 SC IND	1460	0.17%
11.	Virender Singh M 29 Gen IND	2132	0.24%
12.	Vishnu Aggarwal M 61 Gen IND	7053	0.81%
13.	Suneeta Dhariwal F 40 Gen IND	7139	0.82%
14.	Subhash Mahendra M 47 Gen IND	8126	0.93%
	Total:	875454	

3. Sirsa (Total Electors 1309507)

1.	Ashok Tanwar M 33 Sc INC	415584	2.35%
2.	Rajesh Kumar M 35 Sc BSP	76010	7.75%
3.	Comrade Ram M 41 Sc CPM	18999	1.94%
4.	Dr. Sita Ram M 41 Sc INLD	380085	8.74%
5.	Raj Kumar Nagar M 38 Sc JKNPP	8436	0.86%
6.	Rajendra Prasad M 43 Sc HJCBL	45709	4.66%
7.	Swarn Singh M 37 Sc RASJP	3594	0.37%
8.	Hans Raj M 37 Sc RPI	1211	0.12%
9.	Jaibir Singh M 26 Sc IND	1077	0.11%
10.	Desraj M 53 Sc IND	4407	0.45%
11.	Narender Pal M 41 Sc IND	1699	0.17%
12.	Pawan Kumar M 39 Sc IND	3436	0.35%

13. Pushpa Rani F 39 Sc IND	3069	0.31%
14. Vazir Singh M 41 Sc IND	3293	0.34%
15. Shanker Lal M 54 Sc IND	14630	1.49%
Total:	981239	

4. Hissar (Total Electors : 1194689)

1. Jai Parkash M 56 Gen INC	204539	24.69%
2. Ram Dayal Goyal M 63 Gen BSP	90277	10.90%
3. Sampat Singh M 62 Gen INLD	241493	29.15%
4. Karan Singh M 36 Gen BRPP	1527	0.18%
5. Krishan S/O Hariram M 43 Gen SJP	1228	0.15%
6. Gulab Singh M 47 Gen NELU	585	0.07%
7. Jang Bahadur M 35 SC BHBP	2029	0.24%
8. Bhajan Lal M 77 GEN HJCBL	248476	29.99%
9. Roshan Lal M 51 SC IJP	6310	0.76%
10. Satpal M 27 Gen SMBHP	4603	0.56%
11. Satpal Singh M 43 Gen LJP	970	0.12%
12. Anup M 32 Gen IND	896	0.11%
13. Mehta Anoop M 44 Gen IND	621	0.07%
14. Azad Singh M 39 Gen IND	1311	0.16%
15. Umrav Singh M 37 Gen IND	952	0.11%
16. Kuldeep Singh M 27 Gen IND	3227	0.39%
17. Kulwant Singh M 41 Gen IND	2550	0.31%
18. Arya Krishan M 40 Gen IND	1377	0.17%
19. Krishan S/O Gopi Ram M 37 Gen IND	767	0.09%
20. Chhotu Ram M 41 Gen IND	408	0.05%
21. Chhotu Ram S/O Ladhum 44 Gen IND	333	0.04%
22. Jagdish Chander Asija M 35 Gen IND	525	0.06%
23. Jag Ram M 41 Gen IND	749	0.09%
24. Jogender Kumar M 38 Gen IND	798	0.10%
25. Devi Lal M 29 Gen IND	1168	0.14%
26. Devender M 26 SC IND	380	0.05%
27. Nand Kishor M 54 Gen IND	639	0.08%
28. Parvesh M 31 Gen IND	706	0.09%
29. Bhajan Lal M 27 SC IND	1149	0.14%
30. Bhateri F 39 Gen IND	1157	0.14%
31. Manu Digvijay Singh M 33 Gen IND	1958	0.24%
32. Raj Kumar M 42 Gen IND	1931	0.23%
33. Rajender M 45 Gen IND	1216	0.15%
34. Rohtas M 37 Gen IND	305	0.04%
35. Shamsher M 36 SC IND	259	0.03%
36. Sharvan Kumar M 28 Gen IND	191	0.02%
37. Sanjay Kumar M 25 Gen IND	267	0.03%
38. Sandeep M 25 Gen IND	584	0.07%
Total:	828461	

5. Karnal (Total Electors 1216977)

1.	Arvind Sharma M 46 Gen INC	304698	37.57%
2.	Mam Chand M 66 Gen CPI	13587	1.68%
3.	Virender Verma M 58 Gen BSP	228352	28.16%
4.	I.D.Swami M 79 Gen BJP	185437	22.86%
5.	Kalpana Singh F 34 Gen RPI(A)	1536	0.19%
6.	Prem Kumar M 38 Gen SHS	1031	0.13%
7.	Manoj Kashyap M 36 Gen VAJP	1117	0.14%
8.	Ramesh Chhabra M 57 Gen HJCBL	49226	6.07%
9.	Rajiv Ahuja M 43 Gen SP	985	0.12%
10.	Ram Pal M 44 Gen RASAP	913	0.11%
11.	Hawa Singh M 41 Gen RASJP	1019	0.13%
12.	Anoop Singh M 28 Gen IND	3494	0.43%
13.	Ashok Kumar M 36 Gen IND	1428	0.18%
14.	Dushyant Kumar M 30 Gen IND	1375	0.17%
15.	Narender Saroha M 34 Gen IND	1080	0.13%
16.	Balwan Ruhal M 43 Gen IND	3248	0.40%
17.	Mukesh Kumari F 33 Gen IND	3379	0.42%
18.	Ramesh Singla M 40 Gen IND	1567	0.19%
19.	Lal Singh Kashyap M 59 Gen IND	2071	0.26%
20.	Shiv Parsad M 56 Gen IND	1659	0.20%
21.	Sanjeev M 44 Gen IND	506	0.06%
22.	Arya Sushil Garg M 42 Gen IND	2031	0.25%
23.	Sushil Gurjar Sirsi M 28 Gen IND	1290	0.16%
	Total:	811029	

6. Sonepat (Total Electors : 1099978)

1.	Kishan Sangwan M 59 Gen BJP	177511	24.92%
2.	Jitender Singh M 40 Gen INC	338795	47.57%
3.	Devraj Diwan M 66 Gen BSP	112837	15.84%
4.	Sukhbir Singh M 53 Gen NCP	12776	1.79%
5.	Pt. Umesh Sharma M 41 Gen HJCBL	42400	5.95%
6.	Om Parkash Mehta M 45 Gen BHC	1069	0.15%
7.	Krishan Kumar M 42 SC LJP	589	0.08%
8.	Gejender M 39 Gen KKJHS	456	0.06%
9.	Jyoti Parkash M 28 Gen SP	1046	0.15%
10.	Madangopal M 35 Gen RDMP	578	0.08%
11.	Raj Pal M 37 Gen CPI(MI)(L)	1332	0.19%
12.	Rajender Singh M 48 Gen UWF	2552	0.36%
13.	Rohtash Redhu M 33 Gen SMBHP	1359	0.19%
14.	Sushila F 42 Gen JCP	2987	0.42%
15.	Dalbir Singh M 39 Gen IND	2086	0.29%
16.	Dharamvirchotiwala M 37 Gen IND	2533	0.36%
17.	Balwan Kashyap M 50 Gen IND	2500	0.35%
18.	Bijender Kumar M 31 SC IND	1976	0.28%

19.	Rajesh Khan Machhri M 28 Gen IND	1405	0.20%
20.	Veerender Aryavrat M 36 Gen IND	2138	0.30%
21.	Shiv Narayan M 45 Gen IND	3333	0.47%
	Total:	712258	

7. Rohtak (Total Electors : 1274972)

1.	Deepender Singh M 31 Gen INC	585016	69.98%
2.	Nafe Singh Rathee M 51 Gen INLD	139280	16.66%
3.	Raj Kumar M 58 Gen BSP	68210	8.16%
4.	Krishan Murti M 60 Gen HJCBL	20472	2.45%
5.	Rajbir M 33 Gen IJP	710	0.08%
6.	Sudesh M 36 Gen RPI(A)	678	0.08%
7.	Sudesh Aggarwal M 56 Gen SMBHP	2150	0.26%
8.	Anup Matanhel M 64 Gen IND	1532	0.18%
9.	Ashok M 42 Gen IND	1097	0.13%
10.	Asha Nand M 38 Gen IND	2194	0.26%
11.	Karan Singh M 60 Gen IND	345	0.04%
12.	Gorav M 31 Gen IND	394	0.05%
13.	Jasmer M 38 Gen IND	857	0.10%
14.	Jasvir Arya M 43 Gen IND	3728	0.45%
15.	Rishal Singh M 52 Gen IND	2386	0.29%
16.	Satyawan Ranga M 33 SC IND	6876	0.82%
	Total:	835925	

8. Bhiwani-Mahendergarh (Total Electors : 1212513)

1.	Ajay Chautala M 44 Gen INLD	247240	28.60%
2.	Anil Kaushik M 45 Gen NCP	9731	1.13%
3.	Vikram Singh M 54 Gen BSP	61437	7.11%
4.	Shruti Choudhry F 33 Gen INC	302817	35.03%
5.	Jai Singh M 39 SC IJP	2841	0.33%
6.	Narender Singh M 46 Gen HJCBL	214161	24.78%
7.	Neelkanwal Aggarwal F 53 Gen SMBHP	3226	0.37%
8.	Mahender Singh M 30 SC BHBP	846	0.10%
9.	Ved Prakash M 54 Gen NSSP	573	0.07%
10.	Saroj Yadav F 48 Gen SP	1855	0.21%
11.	Hansraj M 37 SC RPI(A)	804	0.09%
12.	Ajay Singh M 43 Gen IND	648	0.07%
13.	Abhey Singh M 51 Gen IND	953	0.11%
14.	Jaimal Singh M 65 Gen IND	658	0.08%
15.	Dharmender Singh M 47 Gen IND	826	0.10%
16.	Puran Mal Sharma M 73 Gen IND	2772	0.32%
17.	Pyarelal M 42 SC IND	3414	0.39%

18.	Birender Singh M 27 Gen IND	536	0.06%
19.	Manmohan Singh M 32 SC IND	576	0.07%
20.	Mahabir Yadav M 50 Gen IND	1191	0.14%
21.	Raj Kumar M 32 Gen IND	609	0.07%
22.	Rajesh S/O Brijlal M 36 Gen IND	968	0.11%
23.	Rajesh S/O Hawa Singh M 33 Gen IND	350	0.04%
24.	Laxmi Narayan Asija M 40 Gen IND	1441	0.17%
25.	Vinod Kumar M 38 Gen IND	528	0.06%
26.	Shrichand M 60 SC IND	518	0.06%
27.	Surender M 30 Gen IND	512	0.06%
28.	Suresh Kumar M 43 Gen IND	1296	0.15%
29.	Harish Kumar M 35 SC IND	1065	0.12%
Total:		864392	

9. Gurgaon (Total Electors : 1244437)

1.	Inderjit Singh M 59 Gen INC	278516	36.83%
2.	Zakir Hussain M 47 Gen BSP	193652	25.61%
3.	Dinesh C. Yadav M 48 Gen NCP	2462	0.33%
4.	Sudha F 44 Gen BJP	125837	16.64%
5.	Ishpal Tomer M 62 Gen RDMP	2159	0.29%
6.	Narvir Singh M 48 Gen HJCBL	117260	15.51%
7.	Prabhu Lal Batra M 71 Gen RASAP	1841	0.24%
8.	Budh Ram M 46 Gen JKM	1727	0.23%
9.	Yashpal M 33 Gen LJP	11838	1.57%
10.	Ramesh Kumar M 36 Gen JKNPP	940	0.12%
11.	Sateesh M 38 Gen SMBHP	2175	0.29%
12.	Sunil Yadav M 26 Gen SP	1097	0.15%
13.	Amar Mohmmad M 33 Gen IND	699	0.09%
14.	Kusheshwar Bhagat M 38 Gen IND	1044	0.14%
15.	Jagan M 34 Gen IND	1152	0.15%
16.	Nazir Ahmed M 36 Gen IND	2520	0.33%
17.	Naresh Yadav M 27 Gen IND	2794	0.37%
18.	Naveen M 37 Gen IND	926	0.12%
19.	Balwant Aggarwal M 59 Gen IND	358	0.05%
20.	Bimla Devi F 53 Gen IND	1824	0.24%
21.	Manbir Singh M 30 Gen IND	1431	0.19%
22.	Rakesh M 38 Gen IND	663	0.09%
23.	Satbeer Kundu M 50 Gen IND	1991	0.26%
24.	Satinder Thakran M 25 Gen IND	1330	0.18%
	Total:	756236	

10. Faridabad (Total Electors : 1103046)

	Candidate	Votes	%
1.	Avtar Bhadana M 53 Gen INC	257864	41.26%
2.	Chetan Sharma M 43 Gen BSP	113453	18.15%
3.	R. Bainda M 58 Gen BJP	189663	30.35%
4.	Gajender Bhadana M 46 Gen AIFB(S)	2758	0.44%
5.	Chander Bhatia M 46 Gen HJCBL	31163	4.99%
6.	Devinder M 41 Gen JJJKMC	1100	0.18%
7.	Nisar Ahmed M 46 Gen RND	2583	0.41%
8.	Babu Lal M 58 Gen JUP	595	0.10%
9.	Mukesh Joshi M 42 Gen AIRP	678	0.11%
10.	Rekha Singh F 42 Gen SMBHP	922	0.15%
11.	Lata Rani F 31 SC SP	972	0.16%
12.	Subhash M 40 Gen RWS	2322	0.37%
13.	Suraj Bhan M 63 Gen RJAP	960	0.15%
14.	Avtar Singh M 33 Gen IND	1159	0.19%
15.	Teeka Ram Hooda M 33 Gen IND	1315	0.21%
16.	Brij Bhushan M 36 Gen IND	2417	0.39%
17.	Yash Pal Nagar M 49 Gen IND	8555	1.37%
18.	Samsuddin M 44 Gen IND	1385	0.22%
19.	Sahi Ram Rawat M 40 Gen IND	2425	0.39%
20.	Dr K P Singh M 50 Gen IND	468	0.07%
21.	Sukhbir Singh M 46 Gen IND	474	0.08%
22.	Sunder Singh M 50 Gen IND	499	0.08%
23.	Harsh Bhatia M 48 Gen IND	1207	0.19%
	Total:	624937	

Parliamentary Constituency Wise Election Information 2014

Name of State : HARYANA

No. & Name of Parliamentary/Assembly Constituencies	General Electors			Service Electors			Total Electors			Polling Stations		
	Male	Female	Total	Male	Female	Total	Male	Female	Total	Regular	Auxiliary	Total
1	2	3	4	5	6	7	8	9	10	11	12	13
1. AMBALA (SC) PC												
1. Kalka	83656	72522	156178	105	45	150	83761	72567	156328	195	0	195
2. Panchkula	103457	90623	194080	197	115	312	103654	90738	194392	180	0	180
3. Nariangarh	89487	77510	166997	945	411	1356	90432	77921	168353	182	0	182
4. Ambala Cantt	90584	79695	170279	470	242	712	91054	79937	170991	177	0	177
5. Ambala City	118884	106001	224885	253	61	314	119137	106062	225199	226	0	226
6. Mullana (SC)	103536	86944	190480	1064	521	1585	104600	87465	192065	216	0	216
7. Sadhaura (SC)	103910	88461	192371	1125	490	1615	105035	88951	193986	206	0	206
8. Jagadhari	104521	88366	192887	289	110	399	104810	88476	193286	190	2	192
9. Yamunanagar	106955	90269	197224	270	133	403	107225	90402	197627	187	1	188
PC Total	**904990**	**780391**	**1685381**	**4718**	**2128**	**6846**	**909708**	**782519**	**1692227**	**1759**	**3**	**762**
2. KURUKSHETRA PC												
10. Radaur	95808	81949	177757	403	161	564	96211	82110	178321	187	0	187
11. Ladwa	87282	76363	163645	499	221	720	87781	76584	164365	185	0	185
12. Shahbad (SC)	77576	67676	145252	538	234	772	78114	67910	146024	159	0	159
13. Thanesar	86828	75498	162326	238	122	360	87066	75620	162686	161	0	161
14. Pehowa	83992	74579	158571	582	268	850	84574	74847	159421	174	0	174
15. Guhla (SC)	85824	75265	161089	314	125	439	86138	75390	161528	169	0	169
16. Kalayat	101039	81202	182241	465	194	659	101504	81396	182900	180	0	180
17. Kaithal	96172	82199	178371	186	85	271	96358	82284	178642	158	8	166
18. Pundri	89585	74446	164031	369	172	541	89954	74618	164572	161	0	161
PC Total	**804106**	**689177**	**1493283**	**3594**	**1582**	**5176**	**807700**	**690759**	**1498459**	**1534**	**8**	**1542**

(Contd...)

3.	**SIRSA (SC) PC**												
38.	Narwana (SC)	102505	85063	187568	226	86	312	102731	85149	187880	188	0	188
39.	Tohana	107782	95689	203471	181	48	229	107963	95737	203700	195	2	197
40.	Fatehabad	117385	101712	219097	297	108	405	117682	101820	219502	206	0	206
41.	Ratia (SC)	102604	92146	194750	208	71	279	102812	92217	195029	191	1	192
42.	Kalanwali (SC)	85586	74844	160430	217	57	274	85803	74901	160704	171	2	173
43.	Dabwali	96953	84857	181810	99	34	133	97052	84891	181943	192	0	192
44.	Rania	86475	76547	163022	74	23	97	86549	76570	163119	172	0	172
45.	Sirsa	96551	85271	181822	84	32	116	96635	85303	181938	187	0	187
46.	Ellenabad	88977	77628	166605	99	38	137	89076	77666	166742	171	0	171
	PC Total	**884818**	**773757**	**1658575**	**1485**	**497**	**1982**	**886303**	**774254**	**1660557**	**1673**	**5**	**1678**
4.	**HISAR PC**												
37.	Uchana Kalan	105125	84945	190070	511	231	742	105636	85176	190812	200	0	200
47.	Adampur	82327	70249	152576	195	102	297	82522	70351	152873	159	0	159
48.	Uklana (SC)	97717	80705	178422	348	158	506	98065	80863	178928	169	0	169
49.	Narnaund	102384	82649	185033	754	333	1087	103138	82982	186120	188	0	188
50.	Hansi	89257	75312	164569	752	347	1099	90009	75659	165668	176	0	176
51.	Barwala	84067	71941	156008	315	170	485	84382	72111	156493	140	1	141
52.	Hisar	82641	72284	154925	151	81	232	82792	72365	155157	132	1	133
53.	Nalwa	80619	69619	150238	258	138	396	80877	69757	150634	137	2	139
59.	Bawani Khera (SC)	96515	81737	178252	1752	917	2669	98267	82654	180921	208	0	208
	PC Total	**820652**	**689441**	**1510093**	**5036**	**2477**	**7513**	**825688**	**691918**	**1517606**	**1509**	**4**	**1513**
5.	**KARNAL PC**												
19.	Nilokheri (SC)	99758	85227	184985	703	212	915	10046	85439	185900	172	0	172
20.	Indri	93081	79447	172528	413	112	525	93494	79559	173053	176	0	176

(Contd...)

21.	Karnal	106711	95437	202148	214	98	312	106925	95535	202460	170	1	171
22.	Gharaunda	101556	84841	186397	666	119	785	102222	84960	187182	176	1	177
23.	Assandh	107929	90060	197989	629	210	839	108558	90270	198828	181	0	181
24.	Panipat Rural	108163	88217	196380	172	66	238	108335	88283	196618	164	8	172
25.	Panipat City	107529	91744	199273	52	32	84	107581	91776	199357	168	1	169
26.	Israna (SC)	86281	72860	159141	444	215	659	86725	73075	159800	166	0	166
27.	Samalkha	98640	81889	180529	380	214	594	99020	82103	181123	175	0	175
	PC Total	**909648**	**769722**	**1679370**	**3673**	**1278**	**4951**	**913321**	**771000**	**1684321**	**1548**	**11**	**1559**
6. SONIPAT PC													
28.	Ganaur	82973	67615	150588	509	291	800	83482	67906	151388	176	0	176
29.	Rai	83580	65839	149419	255	153	408	83835	65992	149827	156	0	156
30.	Kharkhoda (SC)	77558	62472	140030	599	320	919	78157	62792	140949	151	0	151
31.	Sonipat	92294	82155	174449	246	151	397	92540	82306	174846	144	0	144
32.	Gohana	83267	68870	152137	555	292	847	83822	69162	152984	173	0	173
33.	Baroda	89417	70119	159536	1139	627	1766	90556	70746	161302	184	0	184
34.	Julana	88352	71826	160178	775	349	1124	89127	72175	161302	170	0	170
35.	Safidon	89675	73671	163346	399	176	575	90074	73847	163921	168	0	168
36.	Jind	85853	74251	160104	378	187	565	86231	74438	160669	153	0	153
	PC Total	**772969**	**636818**	**1409787**	**4855**	**2546**	**7401**	**777824**	**639364**	**1417188**	**1475**	**0**	**1475**
7. ROHTAK PC													
60.	Mehem	90499	73487	163986	1675	890	2565	92174	74377	166551	205	0	205
61.	Garhi Sampla-Kiloi	101536	83521	185057	1696	903	2599	103232	84424	187656	194	1	195
62.	Rohtak	89308	81213	170521	334	188	522	89642	81401	171043	144	1	145
63.	Kalanaur (SC)	93870	78881	172751	1550	807	2357	95420	79688	175108	185	0	185
64.	Bahadurgarh	98513	80556	179069	536	205	741	99049	80761	179810	155	7	162
65.	Badli	83999	71258	155257	2065	800	2865	86064	72058	158122	167	0	167
66.	Jhajjar (SC)	81839	71807	153646	3254	1080	4334	85093	72887	157980	164	0	164

(Contd...)

67.	Beri	83866	70071	153937	2647	667	3314	86513	70738	157251	162	0	162
73.	Kosli	108909	98641	207550	4032	2401	6433	112941	101042	213983	236	0	236
	PC Total	**832339**	**709435**	**1541774**	**17789**	**7941**	**25730**	**850128**	**717376**	**1567504**	**1612**	**9**	**1621**
8. BHIWANI-MAHENDRAGARH PC													
54.	Loharu	89299	76733	166032	949	533	1482	90248	77266	167514	205	1	206
55.	Badhra	86606	75823	162429	3389	1741	5130	89995	77564	167559	198	1	199
56.	Dadri	91581	79639	171220	3302	1687	4989	94883	81326	176209	181	4	185
57.	Bhiwani	94714	82085	176799	1229	617	1846	95943	82702	178645	172	9	181
58.	Tosham	97878	83846	181724	1428	723	2151	99306	84569	183875	201	0	201
68.	Ateli	88030	77779	165809	1941	995	2936	89971	78774	168745	185	0	185
69.	Mahendragarh	89755	78768	168523	1972	787	2759	91727	79555	171282	190	0	190
70.	Narnaul	66874	58422	125296	920	439	1359	67794	58861	126655	130	0	130
71	Nangal Chaudhry	71224	60567	131791	1075	562	1637	72299	61129	133428	156	0	156
	PC Total	**775961**	**673662**	**1449623**	**16205**	**8084**	**24289**	**792166**	**681746**	**1473912**	**1618**	**15**	**1633**
9. GURGAON PC													
72.	Bawal (SC)	96299	86310	182609	2922	1685	4607	99221	87995	187216	214	0	214
74.	Rewari	106827	94326	201153	1424	738	2162	108251	95064	203315	210	0	210
75.	Pataudi (SC)	100580	89499	190079	2320	600	2920	102900	90099	192999	180	0	180
76.	Badshahpur	162638	144897	307535	735	485	1220	163373	145382	308755	292	5	297
77.	Gurgaon	150410	137163	287573	325	208	533	150735	137371	288106	268	4	272
78.	Sohna	100267	86523	186790	1260	686	1946	101527	87209	188736	171	0	171
79.	Nuh	79669	67120	146789	302	178	480	79971	67298	147269	148	3	151
80.	Ferozepur Jhirka	96983	81497	178480	54	30	84	97037	81527	178564	177	3	180
81.	Punhana	81497	68298	149795	97	56	153	81594	68354	149948	133	8	141
	PC Total	**975170**	**855633**	**1830803**	**9439**	**4666**	**14105**	**984609**	**860299**	**1844908**	**1793**	**23**	**1816**

(Contd...)

10. FARIDABAD PC													
82.	Hathin	101726	83791	185517	549	249	798	102275	84040	186315	174	0	174
83	Hodal (SC)	88397	72508	160905	550	310	860	88947	72818	161765	163	7	170
84	Palwal	108090	89179	197269	451	256	707	108541	89435	197976	193	0	193
85	Prithla	89644	73918	163562	519	222	741	90163	74140	164303	158	0	158
86	Faridabad NIT	119015	89365	208380	167	76	243	119182	89441	208623	178	15	193
87	Badhkal	118786	95811	214597	50	32	82	118836	95843	214679	198	0	198
88	Ballabgarh	111376	83776	195152	106	56	162	111482	83832	195314	175	3	178
89	Faridabad	105225	85871	191096	94	56	150	105319	85927	191246	180	5	185
90	Tigaon	124484	95361	219845	178	108	286	124662	95469	220131	189	7	196
	PC Total	**966743**	**769580**	**1736323**	**2664**	**1365**	**4029**	**969407**	**770945**	**1740352**	**1608**	**37**	**1645**
	STATE TOTALS	**8647396**	**7347616**	**15995012**	**69458**	**32564**	**102022**	**8716854**	**7380180**	**16097034**	**16129**	**115**	**16244**

Form No. 20 Part-II
(To be used for Parliamentary Election only)
Result Sheet of 01-Ambala (SC) Parliamentary Constituency

No. & Name of Assembly	No. of Valid Votes cast in favour of									
	Arun Kumar	Dr. Kapoor Singh	Dr. Kusum Sherwal	Rattan Lal Kataria	Raj Kumar Balmiki	Rajender Kumar Bhatauli	Ram Jawari	Surinder Pal Singh	Ishwar Singh	Gurnam Singh
	1	2	3	4	`5	6	7	8	9	10
1. Kalka	1402	3589	14496	58032	23873	278	145	7476	169	113
2. Panchkula	1119	3423	10597	71750	23458	232	162	15800	113	78
3. Naraingarh	1077	12570	15609	62781	29024	330	124	2272	156	98
4. Ambala Cantt.	800	3228	4619	61501	32803	259	124	8524	193	69
5. Ambala City	1016	6856	14515	74416	36957	318	147	9157	126	110
6. Mullana	1203	18544	20589	58622	36715	365	143	2554	162	110
7. Sadhaura	1649	26804	20028	65771	28942	715	149	3785	228	134
8. Lagadhri	1572	19347	13066	76674	34141	562	154	5337	160	133
9. Yamuna Nagar	1285	8258	16046	82355	26113	373	142	8703	139	88
Grand Total	11123	102619	129565	611902	272026	3432	1290	63608	1446	933
No. of Votes Recorded on Postal Ballot Papers	0	8	6	219	21	0	0	18	0	0
Total of Votes Polled	11123	102627	129571	612121	272047	3432	1290	63626	1446	933

(Contd...)

(Contd...)

No. & Name of Assembly	No. of Valid Votes cast in favour of				Total of Valid votes	No. of rejected votes	Nota	Total	No. of Tendered votes
	hool Chand	Bhupinder Kumar	Bhura Ram Rattuwala	Ramesh Chand					
	11	12	13	14	15	16	17	18	20
1. Kalka	264	377	355	187	110756	0	618	111374	0
2. Panchkula	184	261	276	144	127597	0	1191	128788	0
3. Naraingarh	391	480	365	306	125583	0	615	126198	2
4. Ambala Cantt.	185	233	260	149	112947	0	976	113923	1
5. Ambala City	269	401	362	236	144886	0	1084	145970	4
6. Mullana	434	498	466	419	140824	0	681	141505	4
7. Sadhaura	702	590	509	570	150576	0	901	151477	0
8. Lagadhri	429	550	438	457	153020	0	971	153991	1
9. Yamuna Nagar	237	375	257	247	144718	0	779	145497	1
Grand Total	3095	3765	3388	2715	1210907	0	7816	1218723	13
No. of Votes Recorded on Postal Ballot Papers	0	0	0	0	272	259	0	531	0
Total of Votes Polled	3095	3765	3388	2715	1211179	259	7816	1219254	13

Form 20
(See rule 56C(2)(c)
General Election to the House of People (Lok Sabha), 2014

Part II

Sr. No. of Polling Stataion		No. of valid votes cast in favour of												
		Chattar Singh	Naveen Jindal	Balbir Singh Saini	Raj Kumar Saini	Ashwani Malhotra	Onkar Singh	Kanta Allaria	Kiran Pal	Kuldeep Singh Mallhi	Curmeet Singh	Balwinder Kaur	Ram Kishan	Rameshwar Kumar Saini
		1	2	3	4	5	6	7	8	9	10	11	12	13
10.	Radaur	14752	32018	16823	67782	446	143	153	73	393	131	5538	148	601
11.	Ladwa	3992	33786	30237	54650	355	123	362	58	124	117	2992	203	513
12.	Shahbad	4940	31305	29083	41064	286	116	326	55	109	103	4727	166	188
13.	Thanesar	2725	26694	24337	57794	350	71	178	41	57	99	3913	161	153
14.	Pehowa	2939	45491	45044	23495	232	137	136	72	150	79	2313	192	145
15.	Guhla (SC)	6772	37775	29902	34428	393	503	102	111	500	283	5724	215	204
16.	Kalayat	13235	23730	52911	35930	425	124	115	75	99	109	2719	171	177
17.	Kaithal	9562	35859	30952	49190	424	144	91	75	97	101	2627	195	175
18.	Pundri	10004	21037	29045	63628	340	122	71	202	136	70	1985	184	188
	Total General Votes	68921	287695	288334	417961	3251	1483	1534	762	1665	1092	32538	1635	2344
	Postal Ballot	5	27	42	151	0	0	0	0	0	0	16	0	0
	G.Total	68926	287722	288376	418112	3251	1483	1534	762	1665	1092	32554	1635	2344

(Contd...)

(Contd...)

Sr. No. of Polling Stataion	Anil Kumar Kumar	Chuni Manoj Bhukri	Jasvinder Jasht Dhiman	Davinder Kumar	Master Dharampal Saini Braharnan	Ranbir	Raj Kumar Aggarwal	Vishnu Bhagwan Singal	C.A. Satish	Nota Votes	Total Valid Votes	Total Rejected	Grand Total	No. of Tender Votes
	14	15	16	17	18	19	20	21	22	23	24	25	26	27
10. Radaur	158	338	502	288	232	323	781	196	81	291	142191	0	142191	0
11. Ladwa	218	331	365	176	246	189	714	188	89	234	130262	0	130262	2
12. Shahbad	181	289	405	180	217	215	692	275	77	209	115208	0	115208	2
13. Thanesar	147	192	287	114	144	205	637	219	43	431	118992	0	118992	5
14. Pehowa	202	359	282	141	273	254	451	273	107	262	123129	0	123129	1
15. Guhla (SC)	261	407	588	305	303	470	666	301	122	303	120638	0	120638	0
16. Kalayat	146	304	503	346	179	497	653	191	74	245	132958	0	132958	1
17. Kaithal	181	316	478	274	252	384	767	256	97	340	132837	0	132837	0
18. Pundri	99	234	377	217	148	228	700	184	70	167	119436	0	119436	0
Total General Votes	1593	2770	3887	2041	1994	2765	6061	2083	760	2482	1135651	0	1135651	11
Postal Ballot	0	0	0	0	0	0	0	0	0	0	241	281	522	0
G.Total	1593	2770	3887	2041	1994	2765	6061	2083	760	2482	1135892	281	1136173	11

Form 20
Final Result Sheet
See Rule 56 C (2) (C)

ELECTION TO THE HOUSE OF THE PEOPLE FROM THE 03- SIRSA (SC) PARLIAMENTARY CONSTITUENCY
PART -II
(To be used for Parliamentary Election only)

Name of Assembly Segment	Ashok Tanwar	Charanjeet Singh Kori	Mangeram	Comrade Ram Kumar	Dr. Sushil Indora	Poonam Chand Rati	Balwant Singh	Raj Kumar Nagar	Sanjiv Bhojraj	Hansraj Hansa	Jagdish	Jaipal Bhatti
	1	2	3	4	5	6	7	8	9	10	11	12
38. Narwana (SC)	31012	74773	2836	736	23284	6848	182	308	110	243	206	101
39. Tohana	56637	47863	3761	1744	34375	6128	284	433	375	412	325	216
40. FatoLabad	34303	55425	3381	1815	55950	5807	404	568	332	604	311	231
41. Ratia (SC)	50853	52772	1164	3049	27359	10029	349	525	797	372	342	251
42. Kalenwali (SC)	43004	57765	1563	1322	13174	8831	184	476	161	190	136	123
43. Dabwali	56447	58432	2207	777	15092	7511	186	445	110	201	191	122
44. Rania	46675	55423	2119	702	15036	7914	158	371	116	187	172	70
45. Sirsa	30456	42920	1595	674	36554	8055	250	362	167	421	222	139
46. Ellenabad	41228	60840	2120	369	20204	5711	199	720	182	271	240	112
No. of votes recorded on postal	19	157	4	6	39	10	5	0	0	0	0	0
Total	390634	506370	20750	11194	241067	66844	2201	4208	2350	2901	2145	1365

Charanjeet Singh Rori Lead by 115736 Votes

(Contd...)

(Contd...)

Name of Assembly Segment	No. of valid votes cast in favour of										
	Fakir Chand.	Manjeet Singh	Mewa Singh	Ranvir Khobra	Rajbir Palna	Surender Kumar (Urf) Menpal Phoola	Total Valid Votes	No. of Rejected Votes	Nota	Total	No. of Tendered Votes
	13	14	15	16	17	18	19	21	22	23	24
38. Narwana (SC)	105	145	455	697	371	422	142834	0	233	143067	0
39. Tohana	181	202	601	1591	768	443	156339	0	425	156764	0
40. FatoLabad	168	199	1153	774	589	361	162375	0	528	162903	8
41. Ratia (SC)	256	262	619	1282	623	414	151318	0	339	151657	21
42. Kalanwali (SC)	105	117	304	670	723	449	129297	0	457	129754	0
43. Dabwali	121	138	324	794	741	406	144245	0	533	144778	0
44. Rania	78	79	266	525	628	335	130854	0	404	131258	0
45. Sirsa	88	101	189	459	547	266	123465	0	653	124118	0
46. Ellenabad	95	91	225	516	646	336	134105	0	459	134564	0
No. of votes recorded on postal	0	0	0	0	0	0	240	166	2	408	0
Total	1197	1334	4136	7308	5636	3432	1275072	166	4033	1279271	29

From 20
Part -II
(To be uæd for a parliamentary election only)

4 Hisar Parliamentary Constituency

Name of Assembly Segment	No. of valid votes cast in favour of														
	Kuldeep Bishnoi	Dushyant Chautala	Phul Singh	Mange Ram	Sampat Singh	Om Parkash	Kuldeep Singh S/o Shishpal	Mamta Rani	Dr. Yudhbir Singh Khyalia	Arun Kumar	Atam Parkash	Umed Singh	Kartar Singh	Kuldeep S/o Ishwar Singh	Kuldeep S/o Karan Singh
	HIC(BL)	INLD	CPI(M)	BSP	INC	BSMP	BMP	RPP (LB)	AAP	IND	IND	IND	IND	IND	IND
	1	2	3	4	5	6	7	8	9	10	11	12	13	14	15
37. Uchana Kalan	36254	87243	1469	5964	13070	151	40	53	3163	36	39	50	161	211	251
47. Adampur	59479	43286	557	1731	9289	264	53	76	2240	41	36	35	143	159	238
48. Uklana (SC)	40916	73563	750	5098	13002	203	266	267	3179	34	48	45	173	175	242
49. Namaund	39303	81681	631	2956	13351	150	55	100	3588	29	35	33	144	127	204
50. Barwala	55441	45876	605	3303	12093	149	46	94	4148	39	27	42	119	106	224
51. Barwala	56576	43462	725	4016	9352	167	60	392	2282	34	34	40	106	156	234
52. Hisar	67452	24238	417	1196	5035	107	43	83	4730	33	23	25	53	89	154
53. Nalwa	49494	44096	709	2567	11697	137	44	58	2319	27	36	33	127	110	147
59. Bawani Khera (SC)	57304	50762	668	3606	15602	136	98	72	2813	34	22	39	117	109	192
Total No. of Votes recorded at Polling stations	462219	494213	6531	30437	102491	1464	705	1195	28462	307	300	342	1143	1242	1886
No of votes recorded on Postal ballot papers	412	265	2	9	18	7	0	0	28	0	0	0	0	0	0
Total Votes polled	462631	194478	6533	30446	102509	1471	705	1195	28490	307	300	342	1143	1242	1886

(Contd...)

(Contd...)

	Kuldeep S/o Narayan Singh	Kuldeep S/o Parduman	Kuldeep S/o Madan Lal	Kuldeep S/o Sajan	Narinder Kumar	Narender	Naresh Batra	Baljeet	Balwan Singh	Yudhvir	Rakesh Kumar (Rinku Bhai)	Raj Kumar	Raj Singh	Dr. Rajesh Mehendia	Ram Phal
	IND	IND	IND	IND	IND	IND	IND	IND	IND	IND	IND	IND	IND	IND	IND
	16	17	18	19	20	21	22	23	24	25	26	27	28	29	30
37. Uchana Kalan	638	190	119	39	30	52	79	27	27	15	21	35	80	209	56
47. Adampur	526	280	117	58	27	50	81	33	27	30	36	38	67	158	60
48. Uklana (SC)	566	221	126	54	32	59	88	26	31	19	22	25	84	207	63
49. Narnaund	527	183	79	36	136	41	53	21	25	21	12	32	63	175	62
50. Barwala	678	412	124	48	46	45	58	20	15	22	14	22	69	189	56
51. Barwala	793	273	106	31	24	38	58	26	46	17	13	32	72	256	66
52. Hisar	481	467	89	55	20	45	53	16	16	37	20	29	61	266	28
53. Nalwa	467	274	102	49	34	35	55	19	17	20	21	25	54	107	40
59. Bawani Khera (SC)	575	287	97	25	39	43	62	20	9	16	17	17	50	156	32
Total No. of Votes recorded at Polling stations	5251	2587	959	395	388	408	587	208	213	197	176	255	600	1723	463
No of votes recorded on Postal ballot papers	0	0	0	0	0	0	0	0	0	0	0	0	0	0	0
Total Votes polled	5251	2587	959	395	388	408	587	208	213	197	176	255	600	1723	463

(Contd...)

(Contd...)

	Vijay	Kumar Sharma	Vishnu Kumar	Shiv Kumar	Shravan Kumar Ashija	Sarbir	Sita Ram	Sunder	Sushik Kaushik	Sushi Nidhi	Hansraj	Total of valid votes	No. of rejected votes (Test votes)	Votes for NOTA potion	Total	Total no. of tendered Votes
	IND	IND	IND	IND	IND	IND	IND	IND	IND	IND						
	31	32	33	34	35	36	37	38	39	40	41					
37. Uchana Kalan	99	201	89	63	34	40	10	14	100	79	36	150537	0	122	150659	0
47. Adampur	85	222	120	50	47	140	22	25	95	25	29	120075	0	131	120206	0
48. Uklana (SC)	88	193	95	54	54	32	20	18	95	82	24	140289	0	145	140434	0
49. Namaund	76	234	73	41	27	13	11	18	66	27	28	144473	0	161	144634	0
50. Barwala	73	224	166	50	46	39	14	10	69	29	29	124879	0	167	125046	0
51. Barwala	94	234	152	41	40	18	17	21	106	21	27	120258	0	161	120419	0
52. Hisar	58	181	122	54	80	25	11	12	46	23	25	105998	0	461	106459	9
53. Nalwa	51	133	103	53	22	23	12	10	62	22	26	113437	0	177	113614	0
59. Bawani Khera (SC)	60	166	128	40	21	33	10	6	61	15	21	133580	0	118	133698	0
Total No. of Votes recorded at Polling stations	684	1788	1048	446	371	363	127	134	700	273	245	1153526	0	1643	1155169	9
No of votes recorded on Postal ballot papers	0	0	0	1	0	0	1	0	0	0	0	743	563	2	1308	0
Total Votes polled	684	1788	1048	147	371	363	128	134	700	273	245	1154269	563	1645	1156477	9

Conduct of Elections Rules, 1961

(Statutory Rules and order)

Part II

Election to the House of the People from the 05-Karnal Parliamentrary Constituency

Name of Assembly Segment	*No. of valled votes cast in favour of*												
	Arvind Kumar Sharma	*Ashwini Kumar*	*Jaswinder Singh Sandhu*	*Mam Chand*	*Maratha Virende Verma*	*Ashish*	*Khatab Singh Mor*	*Duli Chand*	*Devender Jaglan*	*Davinder Sharma*	*Paramjit Singh*	*Pale Ram Kashyap*	*Puran Singh Panwar*
	1	2	3	4	5	6	7	8	9	10	11	12	13
19-Nilokheri (SC)	28293	55914	25699	1197	18764	182	62	127	104	159	1983	337	114
20-Indri	23773	69084	18944	1571	9571	151	363	109	82	92	2859	250	110
21-Karnal	24223	78825	14130	816	5901	190	86	70	81	111	9900	260	76
22-Gharaunda	26166	65824	22112	1425	16576	143	96	132	121	95	2418	317	166
23-Assandh	24526	43706	39039	1240	24632	247	92	140	100	106	3540	349	101
24-Panipat (Rural)	24006	77083	20046	1296	6659	129	58	117	107	97	2899	389	126
25-Panipat City	21959	92794	6533	1004	2241	78	56	52	60	65	4835	207	63
26-Israna (SC)	30480	45737	22816	894	11790	109	26	84	48	34	1790	267	42
27-Samalkha	31231	65737	18574	1502	6490	85	46	313	56	47	1833	278	67
Total 234657	594704	187893	10945	102624	1314	885	1144	759	806	32057	2654	865	
No. of votes recorded on postal ballot papers	13	113	9	0	4	0	0	0	0	0	3	0	0
Grand Total Place : Karnal	234670	594817	187902	10945	102628	1314	885	1144	759	806	32060	2654	865

(Contd...)

(Contd..)

Name of Assembly Segment	No. of valled votes cast in favour of													
	Arvind Tiwari	Kishmat Sharma	Jagdish	Jagbir Singh Rana	Mahmood Hassan	Mahinder pal	Rajesh Kumar	Ramphal Sharma	Shashi Salni	Savitri	Total of Valid votes	No. of rejected votes	NOTA	Total No. of tendered votes
	14	15	16	17	18	19	20	21	22	23	24	25	26	27
19. Nilokheri (SC)	190	233	540	237	257	200	165	106	111	144	135118	0	256	1
20. Indri	160	260	447	273	374	174	177	84	235	150	129293	0	218	0
21. Karnal	145	147	345	196	247	79	104	54	249	70	136305	0	607	6
22. Gharaunda	206	270	605	277	330	153	175	103	298	152	138160	0	303	1
23. Assandh	184	291	444	235	218	157	441	191	165	161	140305	0	225	11
24. Panipat (Rural)	127	198	393	425	334	199	321	127	168	219	135523	0	355	0
25. Panipat City	87	140	203	348	452	124	186	91	105	185	131868	0	452	11
26. Israna (SC)	38	75	132	373	173	77	202	90	99	178	115554	0	257	2
27. Samalkha	123	143	333	411	338	113	166	94	114	209	128303	0	256	2
Total	1260	1857	3442	2775	2723	1276	1937	940	1544	1468	1190429	0	2929	33
No. of votes recorded on postal ballot papers	0	0	0	0	0	0	0	0	0	0	142	197	0	0
Grand Total	1260	1757	3442	2775	2723	1276	1937	940	1544	1468	1190571	197	2929	33

Place : Karnal

Conduct of Elections Rules, 1961 (Statutory Rules and others)
Form 20
Final Result Sheet
(See Rule 56C(52)(C)
Election to the House of the People from the - 07 Rohtak Parliamentary Constituency
Part - II

Name of Assembly Segment	No. of Valid cast in Favour of									
	Om Parkash Dhankar	Deepender Singh Hooda	Manoj Kumar	Samsher Singh Kharkara	Anil	Jaklkaran Mandauthi	Naveen Jaihind	Raninder Kumar	Sunil Kumar	Karan Singh
	BJP	INC	BSP	INLD	RBHP	SUCI (Communist)	AAP	IBSP (Kashiram	AITC	IND
1	2	3	4	5	6	7	8	9	10	11
60 Meham	11384	61982	3852	38709	161	239	3411	41	81	48
61 Garhi Sampla-Kiloi	18671	82564	1663	19559	90	359	6208	42	71	36
62 Rohtak	41932	49379	1314	5530	63	204	9914	51	152	35
63 Kalanaur (S.C.)	25823	59151	3117	18997	143	344	6873	59	128	54
64 Bahadurgarh	46311	42783	2299	14106	78	306	8774	68	100	66
65 Badli	38629	49637	1811	10614	42	131	2696	36	87	33
66 Jhajjar (S.C)	29526	51740	1451	15881	77	211	2638	29	61	28
67 Beri	26950	55444	1689	14422	85	188	3451	41	75	23
73 Kosli	79758	37220	1486	13267	89	515	2774	51	192	71
Grand Total	318984	489900	18682	151085	828	2497	46739	418	947	394
No. of votes recorded on postal ballot papers	452	163	8	35	1	0	20	0	0	0
Total Votes Polled	319436	490063	18690	151120	829	2497	46759	418	947	394

(Contd...)

Name of Assembly Segment	No. of Valid cast in Favour of				Total of Valid Votes	Total No. of Rejected Votes	Total Votes for NOTA option	Total Votes	Total No. of Tendered Votes
	Jai Singh	Vishnu Dutt	Sajjan Singh	Satpal					
	IND	IND	IND	IND					
	12	13	14	15	16	17	18	19	20
60. Meham	99	234	291	290	120822	0	378	121200	0
61. Garhi Sampla-Kiloi	63	136	238	317	130017	0	459	130476	0
62. Rohtak	48	55	153	172	109002	0	660	109662	2
63. Kalanaur (S.C.)	17	2239	295	324	117664	0	502	118166	1
64. Bahadurgarh	65	103	192	225	115476	0	631	116107	0
65. Badli	44	69	198	277	104304	0	490	104794	0
66. Jhajjar (S.C)	49	127	188	230	102236	0	464	102700	0
67. Beri	43	93	167	283	102954	0	436	103390	1
73. Kosli	86	95	310	331	136245	0	911	137156	0
Grand Total	614	3151	2032	3449	1038720	0	4931	1043651	4
No. of votes recorded on postal ballot papers	0	0	0	0	679	1065	1	1745	0
Total Votes Polled	614	3151	2032	2449	1039399	1065	4932	1045396	4

Form 20
Part-II
(To be used for Parliamentary Election only)

Final Result Sheet of 9-Gurgaon Parliamentary Constituency

Number & Name of Assembly Segment	No. of Valid voes cast in favour of												
	Inderjit Singh Rao	Zakir Hussain	Dharampal	Rao Dharam Pal	Akbar Kasmi	Ashok Bhardwaj	Umed Singh	Yogendra Yadav	Hemant Kumar Saini	Abdul Latif	Ahshan Ali	Usha Rani Verma	Ombir Sharma
1	2	3	4	5	6	7	8	9	10	11	12	13	14
72. Bawal (SC)	84828	20387	11318	9612	94	103	35	5008	194	81	38	43	50
74. Rewari	95353	11298	6296	13093	109	79	74	11265	186	81	53	52	55
75. Pataudi (SC)	92020	18449	8193	12599	119	85	483	4448	134	90	113	52	70
76. Badshahpur	130918	18876	11665	22193	167	128	111	21670	171	127	71	85	104
77. Gurgaon	125164	11317	5147	17687	122	99	111	27601	254	97	57	92	78
78. Sohna	64165	46849	15816	8712	101	98	31	3650	83	112	49	55	74
79. Nuh	21121	69175	2591	17968	275	43	40	1884	36	37	28	48	57
80. Ferozepur	18172	92536	2101	18945	290	51	20	2065	75	36	32	38	41
81. Punhana	12745	81165	1880	12888	152	27	22	1847	20	38	14	24	37
Total	644486	370052	65007	133697	1429	713	927	79438	1153	699	455	489	566
No. of Votes recorded on Postal Ballot Papers	294	6	2	16	0	0	0	14	0	0	0	0	0
Grand Total Palce : Gurgaon	644780	3700	65009	133713	1429	713	927	79452	1153	699	455	489	566

(Contd...)

(Contd...)

Number & Name of Assembly Segment	No. of Valid voes cast in favour of									Total of Valid Votes	No. of rejected Votes	NOTA	Total	No. of tendered Votes
	Karan Singh Journalist	Kusheshwar Bhagat	Fauji Jai Kawar Tyagi Dixit	Manoj Yadav	Mahender Jat	Mulchand	Rajeev Yadav	Rajesh	Surinder Kumar Khullar					
	15	16	17	18	19	20	21	22	23	24	25	26	27	28
72 Bawal (SC)	119	628	384	422	103	92	50	46	28	133663	0	172	133835	0
74 Rewari	148	1136	352	565	85	95	96	63	54	140588	0	334	140922	4
75 Pataudi (SC)	138	662	420	399	99	78	47	286	23	139007	0	164	139171	0
76 Badshahpur	139	1870	709	556	129	138	87	44	103	210061	0	756	210817	0
77 Gurgaon	129	2222	364	443	87	72	93	48	409	191693	0	895	192588	1
78 Sohna	100	526	357	315	112	164	40	40	36	141485	0	196	141681	0
79 Nuh	65	314	193	112	97	55	26	12	12	114189	0	48	114237	0
80 Ferozepur	56	266	222	145	182	73	35	14	15	135410	0	57	135467	0
81 Punhana	44	197	146	86	127	37	19	12	6	111533	0	36	111569	0
Total	938	7821	3147	3043	1021	804	493	565	686	1317629	0	2658	1320287	5
No. of Votes recorded on Postal Ballot Papers	0	0	0	0	0	0	0	1	0	333	27	0	360	0
Grand Total	938	7821	3147	3043	1021	804	493	566	686	1317962	27	2658	1320647	5

Part - II

(To be used for Parliamentary Election only)

Final Result Sheet of 10-Fariadabad Parliamentary Constituency

Number & Name of Assembly Segment	No. of valid votes cast in favour of														
	Avtar Singh Bhadana	*R.K. Anand*	*Krishan Pal*	*Pt. Rajender Sharma*	*Advocate Kamal Chand*	*A Kusum Kumari*	*Khush Dil Sehgal (Kapoor)*	*Kheme Thakur*	*Chaudhary Daya Chand*	*Deepak Gaur*	*Nirmala*	*Purshotam Dagar*	*Mohd. Mukim*	*Ravinder Bhati*	*Sukhveer*
1	2	3	4	5	6	7	8	9	10	11	12	13	14	15	16
82-Hathin	37090	36760	45544	5242	81	59	56	161	35	11	40	2243	945	136	68
83-Hodal (SC)	20950	22829	55614	6951	98	44	52	161	31	33	41	1521	85	164	89
84-Palwal	8608	19301	86159	14191	158	89	87	264	74	43	53	3510	104	245	89
85-Prithla	20143	23330	56400	11487	138	77	61	190	46	59	51	2693	94	207	201
86-Faridabad NTT	18228	8443	84920	5188	105	70	79	236	129	60	203	9819	118	250	158
87-Badkhal	24170	4218	79598	4573	121	89	88	133	133	57	171	15158	102	173	121
88-Ballabgarh	14943	5047	78816	4164	82	62	105	172	89	98	98	9605	109	191	102
89-Faridabad	18306	5968	76450	6171	87	53	71	199	73	62	176	10241	65	102	114
90-Tigaon	23204	6569	88971	8033	97	77	86	424	101	56	143	12563	113	221	142
Total Votes	185642	132465	652472	66000	967	620	685	1940	711	479	967	67353	1735	1689	1084
No. of Votes recorded on postal ballot papers	1	7	44	0	0	0	0	0	0	0	0	2	0	0	0
Grand Total	185643	132472	652516	66000	967	620	685	1940	711	479	976	67355	1735	1689	1084

(Contd...)

(Contd...)

Number & Name of Assembly Segment	No. of valid votes cast in favour of												Total of valid vote (Test Votes)	No. of rejected Nota	Votes for option	Total	No. of tendered votes
	Hamid Khan	Dr. Kshetra Pal Singh	Aherwan Dharmender Raj	Nanak Chand	Mandheer Singh Maan	Mukesh Kumar Singh	Rajender	Laxman	Lalit Mittal	Vijay Raj	Sushila	Sanjay Maurya votes					
	17	18	19	20	21	22	23	24	25	26	27	28	29	30	31	32	
82-Hathin	237	223	77	148	57	31	24	49	28	31	35	81	129492	0	121	129613	0
83-Hodal (SC)	242	198	76	518	81	33	37	49	30	33	52	71	110083	0	128	110211	0
84-Palwal	255	171	83	272	101	58	45	74	99	42	72	117	134364	0	229	134593	2
85-Prithla	231	187	72	195	71	37	43	73	55	40	53	92	116326	0	151	116477	0
86-Faridabad NTT	434	237	75	361	91	71	65	102	58	64	83	189	129836	0	434	130270	7
87-Badkhal	387	270	79	310	57	43	63	103	36	48	57	139	130497	0	752	131249	0
88-Ballabgarh	339	184	75	264	65	49	49	57	46	57	72	169	115109	0	424	115533	12
89-Faridabad	274	223	62	205	48	44	37	72	33	52	43	132	119363	0	593	119956	0
90-Tigaon	362	249	66	277	73	76	47	77	35	40	57	114	142273	0	496	142769	0
Total Votes	2761	1942	665	2550	644	442	410	656	420	407	524	1104	1127343	0	3328	1130671	21
No. of Votes recorded on postal ballotpapers	0	0	0	0	0	0	0	0	0	0	0	0	54	207	0	261	0
Grand Total	2761	1942	665	2550	644	442	410	656	420	407	524	1104	1127397	207	3328	1130932	21

Bibliography

Primary Sources

(a) Government Documents:

India : Government, The Indian Franchise Committee, 1931, Calcutta: Government of India, 1932

India : Indian Delimitation Committee 1936, Delhi: Government of India, 1936, Vol. I.

India: Constituent Assembly Debates:

1948, Vol. VII; 1949, Vol. VII, VIII, X; 1950, Vol. IV, XI-XII.

India : Draft Constitution, Constituent Assembly, New Delhi.

India : Constitution, New Delhi: Ministry of Law, Government of India, 1966.

India : Parliament: Lok Sabha Debates, New Delhi: Lok Sabha Secretariat, Part II.

Census of India, 1921, Lahore, Civil and Military, Gazette Press, 1923, Part-2.

Census of India, 1921, Lahore, Civil and Military, Gazette Press, 2001, Directorate of Census Operations, Haryana, Chandigarh, Series 7, pp. X-XI.

The Punjab Administration Report, 1911-12, Lahore: 1912, p. 75.

For details see GOI No. 14 of November 15, 1909, Especially PGG of 22 November, 1912 which in a big way supersedes the former.

Who's Who, Lok Sabha, 1967, 1971, 1977, 1980, 1989, 1991, 1998, 1999, Census 2001, (Haryana) Series-7.

Economic Survey: Haryana, Publication No.; 1968 to 2011.

Election Manual, New Delhi: Lok Sabha Secretariat, 1951.

Manual of Election Law, New Delhi : Ministry of Law, Government of India:

1st ed. 1952

2nd ed. 1956

3rd ed. 1959

4th ed. 1961

5th ed. 1966

Representation of the People (Preparation of Electoral Rolls) Rules, 1950, New Delhi: Ministry of Law, Government of India, 1950.

Representation of the People (Preparation of Electoral Rolls) Rules, 1951, New Delhi: Ministry of Law, Government of India, 1951.

Representation of the People (Preparation of Electoral Rolls) Rules, 1956, New Delhi: Ministry of Law, Government of India, 1957.

Representation of the People (Preparation of Electoral Rolls) Rules, 1956, New Delhi: Ministry of Law, Government of India, 1956.

The Delhi Electoral College (Election of Members), Rules, 1958, New Delhi: Ministry of Law, Government of India.

Registration of Electors Rules, 1960, New Delhi: Ministry of Law, Government of India, 1961.

The Delimitation of Delhi, Electoral College (Election of Members) Rules, 1958, New Delhi: Ministry of Law, Government of India, 1958.

Conduct of Election Rules, 1961, New Delhi: Ministry of Law, Government of India, 1961.

Central Services (Classification, Control and Appeal), Rules, 1957, New Delhi: Ministry of Home Affairs, Government of India, 1957.

The Gazette of India Extraordinary:

Pt. II, Sec. III, 1950

Pt. II, Sec. III, 1951

Pt. II, Sec. III, 1953

(b) Election Commission's Publications

India: Election Commission: Report on the First General Elections in India 1951-1952, Vol. I, New Delhi: 1955.

——, Report on the First General Elections in India 1951-52, Vol. II, New Delhi, 1955.

——, Report on the Second General Elections in India 1957, Vol. I, New Delhi, 1958.

——, Report on the Second General Elections in India 1957, Vol. II, New Delhi, 1959.

——, Report on the Third General Elections in India 1962, Vol. I, New Delhi, 1965.

——, Report on the Third General Elections in India 1962, Vol. II, New Delhi, 1965.

——, Report on the Fourth General Elections in India 1967, Vol. I, New Delhi, 1967.

——, Report on the Fourth General Elections in India 1967, Vol. II, New Delhi, 1967.

——, Report on General Elections to the PEPSU 1951-52, Patiala: Chief Electoral Officer, 1952.

——, Report on the Second General Elections to the PEPSU and Travancore, Cochin Legislative Assemblies 1954, New Delhi: 1955.

——, Report on the General Elections to the Andhra Legislative Assembly 1955, New Delhi: 1956.

——, Report on the General Elections to the Kerala Legislative Assembly 1960, New Delhi: 1961.

——, Report on the Third General Elections to the Orissa Legislative Assembly 1961, New Delhi: 1962.

——, Report on the General Elections to the Kerala Legislative Assembly 1965, New Delhi: 1966.

——, Results of Bye-elections held between 31st July, 1955 and 31st October, 1956, New Delhi: 1957.

——, Results of Bye-elections held between April, 1957 and March, 1959, New Delhi: 1959.

——, Results of Bye-elections held between April, 1959 and May, 1960, New Delhi: 1960.

——, Results of Bye-elections held between June, 1960 and July, 1961, New Delhi: 1961.

——, Results of Bye-elections held between August, 1961 and June, 1963, New Delhi: 1963.

——, Results of Bye-elections held between July, 1963 and December, 1964, New Delhi: 1965.

——, Results of Bye-elections held between January, 1965 and December, 1966, New Delhi: 1966.

——, Delimitation of Parliamentary and Assembly Constituencies Order, 1951, New Delhi: 1951.

——, Delimitation of Parliamentary and Assembly Constituencies Order, 1956, New Delhi: 1957.

——, Delimitation of Parliamentary and Assembly Constituencies Order, 1961, New Delhi: 1961.

——, Delimitation of Parliamentary and Assembly Constituencies Order, 1966, New Delhi: 1966.

——, Election Law Reports, New Delhi:

1951-52, Vol. I
1952-53, Vol. II
1953, Vol. III-VIII
1953-54, Vol. IX
1954-55, Vol. X
1955-56, Vol. XI
1956, Vol. XII-XIII
1958, Vol. XIV-XVII
1959, Vol. XVIII-XX
1960, Vol. XXI, XXII
1962, Vol. XXIII
1963, Vol. XXIV
1964 Vol. XXV

——, Hand Book for Candidates, 1957, New Delhi: 1957.

——, Hand Book for Candidates, 1962, New Delhi: 1962.

——, Hand Book for Candidates, 1968, (in Hindi also). New Delhi: 1968.

——, Hand Book for Returning Officers (Part-I-II) 1957, New Delhi: 1957.

——, Hand Book for Returning Officers, 1962, New Delhi: 1961.
——, Hand Book for Returning Officers, 1967, New Delhi: 1967.
——, Hand Book for Returning Officers, 1968, New Delhi: 1968.
——, Hand Book for Presiding Officers, 1957, New Delhi: 1957.
——, Hand Book for Presiding Officers, 1962, New Delhi: 1957.
——, Hand Book for Presiding Officers, in Jammu and Kashmir, 1962, New Delhi: 1962.
——, Hand Book for Presiding Officers, 1967, New Delhi: 1967.
——, Instructions for Polling Agents, 1957, New Delhi: 1957.
——, Instructions for Polling Agents, 1962, New Delhi: 1962.

(c) Election Commission's Selected Unpublished Documents

Election Commission File No. 91/1/51
82/18/54
97/1/55
91/4/56
91/7/56
91/1/57
17/1/57
82/13/61
287/5/62
287/16/62

Election Commission Office Order No. 226/7/62.

Report Lok Sabha elections 1967, 1971, 1977, 1980, 1984, 1989, 1991, 1996, 1999, 2004, 2009 and 2014.

Secondary Sources

A.B. Moore, *Social Origins of Dictatorship and Democracy*, Boston: Beacon Press, 1969, p. 386.

A.B. Lal (ed.), *Indian Parliament*, Allahabad: Chaitanya Publishing House, 1956.

Acharya, N.C.N., *Indian Elections and Franchise*, Madras: The Alliance Co., 1937.

Advani, L.K., Dandavate, Madhu, Trivedi, R.K. & Trikha, N.K., *Electoral Systems in India*, Panchnad Research Institute, Chandigarh, 1987.

Aggarwal, S.P., and Aggarwal J.C., *Lok Sabha and Vidhan Sabha Elections in India*, 1989-90. Concept Publishing Company, New Delhi, 1990.

Ahmed, Bashiruddin, "Political Stratification of the Electorate", in D.L. Seth (ed.), *Citizens and Parties: Aspects of Competitive Politics in India*, New Delhi : Allied Publishers, 1975.

Aiyar, S.P, and Srinivasan, R. *Studies in Indian Democracy*, Bombay: Allied Publishers, 1965.

Akula Satyanarayan Rao, *Lok Sabha Election and M.Ps 1952-1996*, Hyedrabad, (A.P.), Rakesh Publications.

Ali, Sadiq, *A Survey of the General Elections 1957*, New Delhi: All India Congress Committee, 1959.

Almond, Gabriel A., and Verba, Sidney, *The Civic Culture: Political Attitudes and Democracy in Five Nations*, Princeton, N.J.: Princeton University Press, 1972.

Augus, Campbell, *Elections and the Political Order*, New York: John Wiley & Sons, 1966.

Apter, David E., *Introduction to Political Analysis*, New Delhi: Prentice Hall of India, 1978.

Arun Kumar, Battle Zones : *The Press Trust of India*, Delhi, Konark Publishers.

Ashford, E., Bright, *Ward's Parliamentary Elections*, London: Butterworth & Co., 1935.

Ayyear, R.V., Krishna and others (Ed.) *All India Election Guide*, Madras: Oriental Publishers, 1956.

B.B. Sinha, *The Fourth General Election in Haryana*, New Delhi, Orient Longman.

Bean, Louis, *How to Predict Elections*, New York: Mc-Graw Hill Book Company, 1948.

Bhalla, A.H., *Elections in India (1950-72)*, New Delhi: S. Chand & Co. (Pvt.) Ltd., 1973.

Bhambhri, C.P., *Elections 1991 – An Analysis*, B.R. Publishing Corporation, 1991.

Bhartiya Janata Party, Election Manifesto 1993.

Bhawani Singh, *Council of States: Organization and Working*, University of Rajasthan, Ph.D. Thesis, 1971.

Bhawani Singh, *Council of States in India*, Meerut: Meenakshi Prakashan, 1973, pp. 50-74.

Bimla Nagia, *Rajya Sabha At Work Since 1950*, Delhi University Ph.D. Thesis, 1971.

Birke, Wolfgang, *European Elections by Direct Suffrage*, Netherlands A.W. Sythoff. Leyden, 1961.

Blondal, J., *Voters, Parties and Leaders: The Social Fabric of British Politics* Harmondsworth: Penguin Books, 1969.

Butler, David E., *The British General Election of 1951*, London: Macmillan, 1952.

Butler David, Lahiri Ashok & Roy Prannoy, I*ndia Decides, Elections 1952-91*, Living Media Ltd., New Delhi, 1991.

Butler, D.E., *The British General Elections 1951*, London: Macmillan & Co., 1952.

Butler, D.E., *The British General Elections 1955*, London: Macmillan & Co., 1955.

Butler, D.E. and Anthony King, *The British General Elections of 1964*, London: Macmillan & Co., 1965.

Butler, D.E. and Others (Ed.), *Elections Abroad*, London: Macmillan & Co., 1959.

Butler, D.E. and Richard Rose, *The British General Elections of 1959*, London: Macmillan & Co., 1960.

Campbell, A., Gurin, G., and Miller, Warren E., *The Voter Decicdes*, Evanston: Row, Peterson and Co., 1954.

Campbell, Peter, *French Electoral Systems and Elections 1789-1957*, London: Faber and Faber, 1958.

Carson, G.B., *Electoral Practices in U.S.S.R.* London: Atlantic Press, 1955.

Chahar, S.S, *Dynamics of Electoral Politics in Haryana*, 2 Vols, New Delhi, Sanjay Parkashan, 2005.

Chahar, S.S. & Rani, Neera, *Social Structure and Political Recruitment in India*, New Delhi, Abhijeet Publications, 2010.

Chopra J.K., *Politics of Election Reforms in India*, Mittal Publications, Delhi, 1989.

Chowdhury, N.K. & Aggarwal J.C., *Election in India – Analysis* and *Overview*, Shipra Publications, New Delhi, 1992.

Congress and the Second General Elections 1957, New Delhi: All India Congress Committee, 1957.

Congress Party, Election Manifesto, 1993.

C.P. Bhambhari, *Elections 1991*, Delhi, B.R. Publishing Corporation.

Dahl, Robert A., *Modern Political Analysis,* New Delhi: Prentice Hall of India, 1965.

Dastur, Aloo, "The Bombay Voter (1967)", in ICSSR (ed.), *Studies in the Fourth General Elections*, New Delhi: Allied Publishers, 1972.

D. Butler, A. Lahiri, P. Roy, *India Decides Election 1952-1995*, Delhi, Books & Things.

D.D. Basu, *Constitution of India, An Introduction*, 7th Edition, New Delhi, Wadhwa and Co.

D.N. Dixit, *Council of States: Its Organization, Powers and Functions and its Role as Second Chamber from 1950 to the Present Day*, Agra University Ph.D. Thesis, 1971.

Denis Austin, *Democracy and Violence in India and Sri Lanka*, The Royal Institute of International Affairs, London, U.K. Printer Publishers.

Darmvir, *Political Science*, Jaipur, Hindi Granth Academy.

Ganguly, Bangendu and Ganguly, Mira, *Voting Behaviour in a Changing Society*, New Delhi: Sterling Publishers, 1975.

General Elections 1962: Facts and Figures, New Delhi: Indian Press Information Bureau, Election Unit, 1962.

Government of India, Ministry of Information and Broadcasting, *General Elections 1991, Reference Handbook, Vol. 1*, New Delhi, 1991.

G.V.L.N. Rao, K.B. Krishan, *Indian Election, The Nineties*, Delhi, Har-Anand Publications.

Gurhar Pal Singh, *Ethnic Concept in India : A Case Study of Punjab*, New York, St. Martins Press, Inc.

Hedge Ram Krishna, *Electoral Reforms*, Karnataka State Janata Party, Banglore.

India: Electoral Behaviour 1987-88, Election Archives, New Delhi, 1988.

Janata Dal, Election Manifesto, 1993.

Jagdish Chandra, *Freedom Struggle in Haryana, 1919-47*, Kurukshetra: Vishal, 1982, pp. 51-52.

J.C. Aggarwal, N.K. Chawdhary, *Election in India 1952-96*, Delhi, Shipra Publications.

J.C. and C.P. Aggarwal, *Lok Sabha and Vidhan Sabha Election 1989-1990 : Process and Result with Comparative Study of Manifestoes*, Delhi, Concept Publishing Company.

Jean Blondel, *Voters, Parties and Leaders*, Penguin, 1964, 10.

K.C. Yadav, *Modern Haryana : History and Culture*, New Delhi, Manohar, 2002, p. 204.

K.K. Bhardwaj, *Towards a Bi-Polar Polity and Election, 1999*, Independent Publishing Company.

Key, V.O. Jr., *The Responsible Electorate*, Cambridge, Mass: The Belknap Press of Harvard University Press, 1966.

Khanna, B.S. and Deva, Satya, "The Campaign and Voters, Behaviour in the Fourth General Election to the State Assemblies in the Punjab and Haryana in ICSSR" (ed.), *Studies in the Fourth General Elections*, New Delhi: Allied Publishers, 1972.

Kinn, N.G.S., *The City Voter in India: A Study of 1967 General Elections in Nagpur*, New Delhi, Allied Publishers, 1974.

Kini, "The Limits of Janata Wave: The Case of Maharashtra in 1977 Lok Sabha Elections", *Political Science Review*, Vol. 18(1), January-March, 1979.

Kitzinger, U.W., *German Electoral Politics*, Oxford: The Clarendon Press, 1960.

Kogekar, S.V. and Richard, L. Park, *Reports on the Indian General Elections, 1951-52*, Bombay: Popular Book Depot, 1956.

Krishna Mani, P.N., *Elections, Conditions and Voters*, New Delhi: New India Press, 1967.

Kulkarni, A.R., *The Second General Elections in Sholapur*, Sholapur: Institute of Public Administration, 1957.

Lakeman, Enid and James D., Mambert, *Voting in Democracies*, London: Faber and Faber, 1954.

Lal Shiv, *Elections to India's State Legislatures Since 1952*, The Election Archives, New Delhi.

Laxmi Mall Singhavi, *Lok Sabha Nirvachana 1980 : Survey and Analysis*, New Delhi, Rajpal and Sons.

Leuthold, David A., *Electioneering in a Democracy*, New York: John Wiley & Sons, 1967.

Mackenzie, W.J.M., *Free Election*, London, George Allen & Unwin Ltd., 1858.

Mackenzie, W.J.M., and Keneth Robinson (Eds.), *Five Elections in Africa*, Oxford: Clarendon Press, 1960.

Mackenzie, W.J.M., *Free Election*, London, George Allen & Unwin Ltd., 1967.

Masodkar, B.A., *Law Relating to Electoral Disqualification*, Bombay: N.M. Tripathi Pvt. Ltd., 1986.

Mehta, Ashoka, *The Political Mind of India: An Analysis of the General Elections*, Bombay: Socialist Party Control Office, 1952.

Mehta, Prayag, *Election Campaign: Anatomy of Mass Influence*, Delhi: National, 1975.

Meena Rao, *The Battle of Ballot*, Jaipur, Classic Publishing House.

Milbrath, Laster N., *Political Participation*, Chicago: Road McNally, 1965.

Mirchandani, G.G., *Assembly Elections 1980.*

Mitra, Subrata K, Chiriyankandath, James, *Electoral Politics in India*, Segment Books, New Delhi, 1992.

M. Pattabhiram, *General Election in India 1967*, New Delhi, Allied Publishers.

M.L. Ahuja, *Electoral Politics and General Election in India 1952-1998*, New Delhi, Mittal Publications.

M.S. Rana, *India Votes, Lok Sabha and Vidhan Sabha Election, 1998*, Delhi, B.R. Publishing Corp.

M.P. Singh, *Lok Sabha Election 1989, Indian Politics in 1990s*, Delhi, Kalinga Publication.

Myron Weiner & John Osgood Field, *Electoral Politics in the Indian State*, Delhi: Manohar Book Service, 1975.

Narain, Pande, K.C. and Sharma, Mohan Lal, *Linkage Elite and Elections : A Study of the Role of P.R. Functionaries in the Context of Electoral Politics of Rajasthan*, Meerut: Meenakshi Prakashan, 1978.

Narain, Paande, K.C. and Sharma, Mohan Lal, *Rural Elite and Elections in an Indian State*, New Delhi: National Publishing House, 1976.

N.D. Arora, *The Lok Sabha Election in India*, New Delhi, Pragati Prakashan.

N.K. Choudhary, *Assembly Election 1994-95*, Delhi, Sipra Publications.

N.N. Mallya, *Indian Parliament*, New Delhi, National, 1970.

N.S. Gehlot, *Election and Electoral Administration in India*, Delhi, Deep and Deep Publication.

Narayan Iqbal, *Election Politics in Indian States*, Agra, Shiv Lal Aggarwal Co.

Narayan, Iqbal and Sharma, Mohan Lal, *Election Studies in India: An Evaluation*, New Delhi: Allied Publishers, 1978.

O'Connor, Edward Robert, *India and Democracy : An Analysis of 1951-52 Elections and Political Impact 1954*, University of Norte Dame, Thesis, 1954, Microfilm.

P.N. Malhotra, *Provisional Parliament in India*, Agra University, Ph.D. Thesis, 1960.

Padam Nath Sharma, *7th Lok Sabha Election in Haryana : An Analytical Study*, Delhi, Rajpal and Sons.

Palkihivala, N.A., *We, the People–India–The Largest Democracy*, Seventh Impression, Bombay: Strand Book Stall, 1987.

Palmer, Norman D., *Elections and Political Development: The South Asian Experience*, New Delhi: Vikas, 1976.

Parliaments and Electoral Systems, London: Institute of Electoral Research, 1962.

Pathak, D.N., "Political Behaviour in Gujarat with Reference to the Fourth General Elections in ICSSR" (ed.), *Studies in the Fourth General Elections*, New Delhi: Allied Publishers, 1972.

Paul, Sharda, *General Elections in India-1989*, Associated Publishing House, New Delhi, 1990.

Penniman, Howard R. Saits, *American Parties and Elections*, New York: Appleton-Century Crofts Inc., 1952.

Pitkin, Hanna Fenichel, *The Concept of Representation*, Berkeley, Calif, University of California Press, 1967, p. 4.

Poplai, *1962 General Elections in India*, Delhi: Metropolitan Book Co., 1962.

Prabha Bhargav, *Election Manifestoes : A Pilot Study*, Delhi, Uppal Publishing House.

Purohig, B.R., "Voters and Voting Behaviour in the Fourth General Elections in Madhya Pradesh in ICSSR" (ed.), *Studies in the Fourth General Elections*, New Delhi: Allied Publishers, 1972.

Raghavan, G.S., Balachandran, G., *Forty Years of World's Largest Democracy*, Gian Publishing House, New Delhi, 1990.

Raisa Ali, *Representative Democracy and Concept of Free & Fair Elections*, Delhi, Deep & Deep Publishers.

Rajni Kothari, *Congress System in India : The Uncurtain Verdict*, New Delhi, Orient Longman.

Ranbir Singh, *The Contest in the Hindi Belt : A Study of Haryana, Electoral Politics in India*, Delhi, Segment Books.

Rao V., Bhaskar, *General Elections in India*, Uppal Publishing House, New Delhi, 1987.

R.B. Jain and P.N. Chaudhary, *Bureaucratic Values in Development*, Delhi: Centre for Policy Research Unpublished Report 1982, pp. 55-66.

Rose, Richard, *Influencing Voters: A Study of Campaign Rationality*, London: Faber and Faber, 1967.

Santosh Sharma, *Lok Sabha Mid-Term Election and House of Political Elite*, Delhi, Swati Publication.

Sharda Paul, *General Election in India 1977*, New Delhi, Associated Publishing House.

Sharda Paul, *General Election in India 1980*, Delhi, Associated Publishing House.

Shiv Lal, *Indian Election Since Independence 1972*, New Delhi, The Election Archives.

Sinah, B.B., "The Fourth General Election in Haryana", in S.P. Verma and Iqbal Narain (eds.), *Fourth General Elections in India*, New Delhi: Orient Longman, 1968.

Singh, Mahendra Prasad, *Lok Sabha Elections 1989*, Kalinga Publications, Delhi, 1992.

Singh, Nihal, *Count Down to Elections*, Allied Publishers Ltd., New Delhi, 1989.

Singh, S.C. and Chaudhary, D.S., *Fifth Lok Sabha Elections in Haryana: A Study of Voting Behaviour* (Unpublished Report, Department of Political Science, Kurukshetra University, Kurukshetra, 1973.

Siwach, J.R., "Elections and Caste Politics of Haryana", *Journal of the Society for the Study of State Government*, Vol. 7(2), April-June, 1974.

Siwach, J.R., *Government and Politics in Haryana, 1967-70*, Unpublished Paper, Kuru Department of Political Science, Kurukshetra University, Kurukshetra.

S.K. Mitra, J.C., Kandath, *Election Politics in India*, New Delhi, Segment Books.

Smith, T.E., *Elections in Developing Countries*, New York: Macmillan & Co., 1960.

Suri, Surinder, *1962 Elections: A Political Analysis*, New Delhi: Sudha Publications, 1962.

The Provisional Parliament of India: A Case Study in the Development of Parliamentary Democracy, a Ph.D. Dissertation submitted to Rajasthan University, 1971 (Mimeographed).

V. Bhaskara Rao, *General Election in India*, New Delhi, Uppal Publishing House.

V.B. Singh, Shankar Bose, *Election in India : Data Handbook on Lok Sabha*, New Delhi, Sage Publication, India.

V.B. Singh, *Election in India, Data Handbook on Lok Sabha Election, 1986-1991*, New Delhi, Sage Publication.

V.B. Singh, *Profile of Political Elites in India*, New Delhi, Ritu Publishers.

V.A. Pai Panadikar, A. Sud, *Changing Political Representative in India*, Delhi, Uppal Publishing House.

Venketarangaiya, M., *Fair and Free Elections*, Bombay: Hind Kitab, 1950.

Venketarangaiya, M., *Free and Fair Elections*, New Delhi: Ministry of Information and Broadcasting, Government of India, 1966.

Venkatarangaiya, *The General Election in Bombay City*, Bombay, 1953.

W.H. Morris Jones, *Parliament in India*, London: Longmans Green, 1957.

W.H. Morris, Jones, *Parliament in India*, Longmans, 1957, pp. 115-128.

Weiner, Myron and Kothari, Rajni (eds.) *Indian Voting Behaviour: Studies of the 1962 General Elections*, Calcutta : Firma, N.J. Mukhopadhyay, 1965.

Women and the Elections, New Delhi: Indian National Congress, 1956.

Articles

"Abstracts of Papers on the General Elections in India", *The Indian Journal of Political Science*, Lucknow: (13) 3-4, 1952, 1-35.

Alexander, Horace, "India's First General Elections", *Socialist Commentary*, London: May 1952, 133-35.

Ali, Sadiq, "Election Results: Assessment", *United Asia*, Bombay: (14) 5, 1962, p. 6.

Bhargava, G.S., "The Second General Elections in India", *Indian Affairs Record*, New Delhi, (3),k 1957, p. 29.

Chahar, S.S., Political Empowerment of Women : A Study of the Haryana Legislature, Vidhanmala, H.P. VI jan Sabha sect, Shimla, 2001.

Chahar, S.S., Women's Participation in Electoral Politics is Haryana : An Analytical Study (1966-2004), *Journal of Dynamics of Public Administration*, Lucknow University, January-December, 2002.

Chahar, S.S., Haryana Assembly Elections 2000 : An Analysis, *Indian Journal of Politics*, Aligarh Muslem University, Ktober, December, 2003.

Chahar, S.S., Parliamentary Elections in Haryana, 2004 : An Analysis, *Journal of Constitutional and Parliamentary Studies*, New Delhi, 2006.

Chahar, S.S., Haryana Assembly Elections, 2005 : An Analysis, Journal of Punjab Politics, GND. University, Amritsar, 2007.

Chahar, S.S., Why Haryana Women keep of Politics, The Tribune, October 15, 2009

Chandidas, R., "Changing Geography of Representation in India: Parliamentary Constituencies from 1951-66", *Economic and Political Weekly*, Bombay: (3), 41, 1968, pp. 181-90.

Chandidas, R., "Electoral Adjudication in India", *Economic and Political Weekly*: (3), 24, 1968, pp. 901-11.

Dolene, Marjan, "Elections in India", *Review of International Affairs*, Belgrade: (8) 166, 1957, 5-7.

Ghosh, Ajoy, "General Elections in India", *Labour Monthly*, London: (34), 5, 1952, pp. 226-34.

Ghosh, Ajoy, "The General Elections in India", *Political Affairs*, New York: (31), 3, 1952, pp. 34-44.

Ghosh, Ajoy, "The General Elections in India", *Political Affairs*, New York: (36), 5, 1957, pp. 52-64.

Gray, Hugh, "The 1962 General Elections is Murshidabad, Andhra Pradesh", *Journal of Local Administration*, Overseas, London: (2), 4, 1963, pp. 195-205.

Haqqi, S.A.H., "Adult Franchise and Democracy in India;" *The Indian Journal of Political Science*, Delhi; (23), 4, 1962, pp. 347-60.

Harris, Moinuddin, "In the interest of Free and Fair Elections", *Janata*; (11), 29, 1956, pp. 3-4.

Harrison, Martin, "Britain", *The Journal of Politics*: (25), 4, 1963, pp. 664-86.

Jha, Nagesh, "Delimitation of Constituencies: A Plea for More Effective Criteria", *The Indian Journal of Political Science*; (24) 2, 1983.

Kamal, "The Mandate of the 62 Elections", *Organizer*: (15), 34, 1962, p. 13.

Kasliwal, N.V. "My Election Experiences", *AICC, Economic Review*, New Delhi: (9), 2, 1957, 11-12.

Khanna, B.S., "Third General Elections in Punjab 1962". *The Indian Journal of Political Science*: (24), 1, 1963, pp. 51-64.

More, S.S., "Reform of the Indian Electoral System: General Principles of Reform", *AICC, Economic Review*: (9), 5-6, 1957, pp. 16-18, 8-11.

Narayan, Iqbal and Mohan Lal, "Election Politics in India: Notes Toward an Imperial Theory", *Asian Survey*, Berkeley: (9), 3, 1969, p. 220.

Peplai, S.L., "India's Third General Elections", *Indian Affairs Record*: (8) 3, 1962 (Whole Issue).

"The Elections and After", *Eastern Economist*, New Delhi: (28) 3, 1057, 469-70.

"The Indian General Elections", *World Today*, London: (8), 5, 1952.

Index